The Christology of the Fourth Gospel
Structure and Issues

Beiträge zur biblischen Exegese und Theologie
BET

Herausgegeben von
Jürgen Becker und Henning Graf Reventlow

BAND 23

PETER LANG

Frankfurt am Main · Berlin · Bern · New York · Paris · Wien

William Loader

THE CHRISTOLOGY OF THE FOURTH GOSPEL

STRUCTURE AND ISSUES

2nd, revised edition

PETER LANG

Frankfurt am Main · Berlin · Bern · New York · Paris · Wien

Die Deutsche Bibliothek - CIP-Einheitsaufnahme

Loader, William R. G.:

The christology of the fourth gospel : structure and issues
William Loader. - 2., überarb. Aufl. - Frankfurt am Main ; Berlin ;
Bern ; New York ; Paris ; Wien : Lang, 1992
    (Beiträge zur biblischen Exegese und Theologie ; Bd. 23)
    ISBN 3-631-44943-7

NE: GT

BT
198
.L57
1992

ISSN 0170-8716
ISBN 3-631-44943-7

© Verlag Peter Lang GmbH, Frankfurt am Main 1992
All rights reserved.

Printed in Germany 1   3 4 5 6 7

PREFACE TO THE FIRST EDITION

The present study is the fruit of research carried out on and off over a period of fifteen years, and made possible more latterly through six months sabbatical leave spent in Munich at the Institut für Neutestamentliche Theologie, 1982/82, as guest of Professor Ferdinand Hahn, and through study leave spent at home in the first six months of 1988, when a ruptured achilles tendon left no alternative to confinement, reading, writing, and so directly facilitated the final completion of this work!

The literature on the fourth gospel is almost despairingly immense. The limits of time and of living in the isolation of Perth, Western Australia, have contributed to the long process of the work's coming into being. In it I have sought to be as comprehensive as possible in taking into account the work of other scholars. I have appreciated and have benefitted from their work much more than the concise notes within this work can express. I have also found it an advantage to have grappled with the theme over a long period of time and the present publication represents only a pause along a continuing journey.

My initial concern had been to embark on a traditio-historiical study of the fourth gospel's christology, having completed such a study of Hebrews in the monograph, 'Sohn und Hoherpriester'. The more I pursued this, the more I became aware of the need first to analyse the transmitted text as a whole, before, and as a basis for, proceeding on this quest. In the present work, therefore, I have sought to offer an integrative study of Johannine christology which identifies an overall structure and examines the individual themes of ongoing research in its light. I hope it will prove useful, therefore, for both scholar and student.

The work is based as far as possible on secondary literature in its original language, where this has been available. I have translated scripture passages throughout the book directly into English.

I acknowledge the generosity of the Western Australian Synod of the Uniting Church in Australia which has made it possible for me to take periods of study leave and travel overseas. I should also like to express my appreciation to students and teaching colleagues at Murdoch University, the Perth College of Divinity and the Perth Theological Hall, and to my fellow Australian from the other side of the continent, Professor Eric Osborn, who read an earlier draft of the manuscript and made encouraging suggestions. I am also grateful to Professor Ferdinand Hahn for his continuing support and to Professor Jürgen Becker who, as editor, has welcomed the book into the present series.

Finally I want to thank my family who teach me that living out the insights of the fourth gospel is something far more than understanding ideas. To my wife, Gisela, whose challenging support over the years has encouraged me to go on, to my daughter, Stef, and my son, Chris, who also helped compile the indices, much more than thanks!

Perth, Western Australia, New Year's Day, 1989

PREFACE TO THE SECOND EDITION

The major change in the second edition of this work is its new printing format, which should make the book more 'user friendly'. In addition I have made some minor changes to form (eg. indentation of some detailed discussions of secondary literature) and to formulation (including corrections). The change in format has resulted in some minor variations from the pagination of the first edition, but never affecting more than one or two pages.

In substance the work remains the same, with the addition of references to my more recently published work on John.[1] The pace of Johannine publications has not slackened since the book first appeared,[2] but I have refrained from more extensive revision at this point, because reviews are still appearing. I have been encouraged by the very positive reception the book has found.[3] The changed printing format is a direct response to widespread feedback on the first edition.

Perth, Western Australia, February, 1992

---

1. 'John 1:50-51 and the "Greater Things" of Johannine Christology' in: Anfänge der Christologie. Für Ferdinand Hahn. Edited by C. Breytenbach and H. Paulsen (Göttingen: V & R, 1991) pp. 255-274; Review of M. Hengel, The Johannine Question (London: SCM, Philadelphia: TPI, 1989) in: Kings Theological Review XIII (1990) 50-52; The Johannine Epistles (London: Epworth, to appear 1992).

2. These include: J.H. Neyrey, An Ideology of Revolt. John's Christology in Social-Science Perspective (Philadelphia: Fortress, 1988); M.M. Thompson, The Humanity of Jesus in the Fourth Gospel (Philadelphia: Fortress, 1988); John Ashton, Understanding the Fourth Gospel (Oxford: Clarendon, 1991); D. Burkett, The Son of Man in the Gospel of John, JSNTSS 56 (Sheffield: JSOT Press, 1991): D.A. Carson, The Gospel according to John (Leicester: IVP, Grand Rapids: Eerdmans, 1991).

3. For instance, R. Schnackenburg in BZ 35 (1991) 135-137; X. Léon-Dufour in RSR 79 (1991) 300-303.

TABLE OF CONTENTS

Contents

PART I

INTRODUCTION

In his major review of Johannine research Kysar describes christology as 'the heartbeat of the theology of the Fourth Gospel.'[1] The investigation which follows seeks to listen for that 'heartbeat', to detect its rhythm and feel its strength. In the introduction I shall begin by examining one of the most sensitive and influential expositions of Johannine christology, that of Rudolf Bultmann. I shall then follow the way in which research has developed since Bultmann, partly in response to the issues which his synthesis raised.

In Part II I shall turn directly to the transmitted text of the gospel in order to listen for the patterns and themes and so identify the underlying structure or structures of the author's christology. On the basis of this reading of the text I shall return in Part III to major issues of interpretation which have emerged in current Johannine christological research reviewed in Part I or which have arisen through the analysis in Part II.

Johannine christology, one could say, is the gospel. Its scope is very wide and the issues of Johannine christology have been given attention in an ever increasing volume of literature. Many of its individual motifs and images have, themselves, demanded monograph treatment. The present volume will not aim at comprehensive detailed treatment of every feature, but will seek an overview, a 'map' of its contours, within which motifs and images are seen in perspective. This research has been undertaken in the confidence that a clarification of the overall structure of the gospel's christology will also facilitate a clearer understanding of its major themes and of the disputed issues which have arisen in its exposition.

The investigation works with the present form of the gospel as it has been passed down to us, but the issues of tradition and of the history of the gospel's composition and its community are not ignored. I believe that a careful analysis of the christology of the transmitted text necessarily raises such issues. I have adopted the method of first dealing primarily with the transmitted text as it stands. But in the final chapters I shall draw together questions and issues raised by the analysis concerning the history of Johannine christology, of its community, and of the composition of the gospel.

I have been mindful that the fourth gospel's christology developed in the context of a community of faith and its preaching, and that this remains the primary place of its use today. Accordingly I conclude with brief observations relating to this context. Sensitivity to the 'heartbeat' of Johannine theology was surely a mark, above all, of Bultmann's work on John's gospel. Accordingly I begin with a presentation of his exposition.

Bultmann on Johannine christology

The importance of Bultmann's description of Johannine christology is that he asked the question: what is at its centre?[2] His answer was at first sight simple: the sending of the Son. Expanded, the central story of Johannine christology tells how the Father sent the Son into the world to tell what he had seen and heard, to be the revealer. The Son came in fulfilment of the Father's will, manifested the divine glory in human flesh and, having completed his task, returned in exaltation to the glory of the Father.[3] The basic pattern is that of the Redeemer-Revealer sent by God.

For Bultmann this pattern is drawn from the gnostic redeemer myth.[4] Bultmann believed that this myth was reflected in the various gnostic systems from the second century onwards, but existed already in the world of the fourth gospel. It told the following story. Human beings are captive in the material world. Their spirits were once part of the heavenly world and there they belong. The heavenly Redeemer-Revealer comes to make known to them their true nature and origin. As the heavenly man he calls his brothers and sisters out of this world to their true home. Those who accept this 'gnosis' (knowledge), the 'gnostics', rejoice in their identity and await their final departure from the shackles of the material at death, when they follow the path forged for them by the Redeemer-Revealer.

Bultmann could point not only to the similar pattern of the coming of a Redeemer-Revealer from heaven, but also to numerous motifs which occur both in the fourth gospel and in gnostic literature, particularly in the Mandean writings, which in his view reflected first century gnostic traditions influential in the background of the Johannine church.[5]

But there are also differences. Bultmann points to the absence in John of the idea of souls once pre-existing in heaven, of the absolute dualism between spirit and material, and of the view that the Redeemer could not be a real human being as presupposed in the story of Jesus' incarnation and death.[6] While following the same basic pattern, the christological story in the fourth gospel could not be gnostic, but had developed under the influence of gnosticism and in reaction against it.[7]

More significant still is Bultmann's view of how the author of the fourth gospel understood the christological story. He observes inconsistencies in the author's statements about the Redeemer-Revealer. One is that the gospel repeatedly, and in numerous variations, speaks of the Son making known in the world what he had seen and heard in the heavenly world, but it never has the Son pass on such information.[8] The Son consistently presents himself as the Revealer, but, while using the formulations of revelation, never discloses revelation of heavenly words or events. Another is that sometimes John has Jesus speak in the present tense of telling what he sees and hears (as in 5:19f), whereas usually Jesus refers to pre-existent seeing and hearing (as in 3:31f).[9] Similarly sometimes the gospel portrays life as the gift of the incarnate one and of his earthly ministry (as in 6:35), while at other times it speaks of it as the fruit of his exaltation and return to the Father (as in 7:38f).[10] These discrepancies lead Bultmann to conclude that the author does not mean us to take the pattern of the story literally. The prologue, and, indeed, the gospel, remain an enigma until this is seen.[11]

Accordingly, unlike gnosticism, Johannine religion is not primarily about a Revealer who gives information, brings words, coming down as an emissary of the heavenly world and then returning. It is rather about one who presents himself and in presenting himself presents the Father. He is the divine Word.[12] The story or myth serves the evangelist as a vehicle for expressing the significance of the breaking through of God's word in Jesus of Nazareth. Jesus was not a pre-existent heavenly being.[13] He was not sent from above in that sense. These elements give expression to the fact that in him it is God, the 'other', who encounters us. That the Word, active at creation, became flesh is a way of saying that in Jesus we meet the possibility of finding our way to authentic existence, to becoming what we were created to be.[14]

The claim to present God, to offer the true bread, to be the giver of life, to be life and light, challenges human self-sufficiency, revealing human beings' inadequacy and confronting them with it. This 'negative' revelation which takes place within the situation of being encountered with the word of Jesus is at the same time a call to authentic human existence in relationship with the Son and therefore with the Father. It restores us to our true humanity, to what we were meant to be. In encounter the Son's claim to be one with the Father is a revelation of God, not in the sense of conveying information about him, but in the sense of an epiphany. The self-presentation of the Son as Revealer effects thus a double sided revelation, negative and positive. This absolute claim at the same time evokes crisis, for it divides the world of humanity into those who believe and those who do not believe. In this way it constitutes darkness as what rejects the Son and light as what comes to him and so belongs to him. This is dualism based on decision ('Entscheidungsdualismus').[15]

Bultmann is not thereby denying incarnation in the author's scheme. But incarnation is not, for the author, the entry into human flesh, according to Bultmann's analysis. Rather it means that the event of the revelation of the Father by the Son takes place in the fully human person Jesus of Nazareth.[16] In 1:14 the author sets himself clearly apart from gnostic redeemer myths, just as he does not espouse a notion of revelation like theirs.[17] For Bultmann, the Johannine christology holds fast to the paradox that the 'glory' is manifest in the humanity. That is the meaning of incarnation. It does not refer to an event at the commencement of Jesus' earthly life; the incarnation is not the means of revelation, but is another way of talking of revelation itself. Accordingly 1:51, which sees Jesus as the revelatory ladder, exegetes 1:14a. Incarnation refers to the human being of Jesus as the place where the divine human encounter takes place.[18]

The centering of Johannine christology on the event of Jesus of Nazareth leads Bultmann to the claim that elements of Jesus' earthly life receive a new evaluation in the gospel. The author, he suggests, probably did not intend that the miracles, such as the turning water into wine, should be taken literally.[19] In his hands they are no longer miracles. They have been transformed into 'signs' which proclaim that Jesus is the sent one. They are a 'redender Hinweis' (verbal pointer), they are 'verba visibilia', and response to them is the first step of faith.[20] The historical details of Jesus' earthly life are not of importance to the author. They belong to the past and of themselves are of no salvific significance. Central is the fact that in Jesus revelation has taken place, in him God has spoken. The meeting with the Word in the event of proclamation, not knowledge of the details of Jesus' earthly life, is the central concern. The earthly Jesus, therefore, belongs to the past. The meeting with the Word is not with the historical Jesus or with his teaching; it is an encounter made possible through the Paraclete.[21]

The paradox of the 'glory' made manifest in the flesh leads Bultmann to claim that in John it is the thoroughly human Jesus, about whom there was nothing extraordinary except his claim to be one with the Father, who is the place of the divine epiphany. This ordinariness reaches its climax in the passion and crucifixion. Jesus is presented as a pathetic figure ('Jämmergestalt') before Pilate.[22] Above all in the crucified one we meet the glory of the divine Word. In this way Bultmann attributes to the author a remarkable transformation of the conclusion of the Redeemer-Revealer story pattern. Where the story told of exaltation and return to glory, glorification in the presence of the Father in heaven, the author has transposed the reference of exaltation so that now the crucifixion is paradoxically portrayed as the moment of exaltation and glorification.[23] Accordingly the allusion to ascension in 6:62 is taken by Bultmann to refer to a greater offence to come: the crucifixion.[24] But even the glorification is no addition of glory; it is, rather, the completion and climax of the paradox of the divine glory in human flesh.[25] The glorification continues when the disciples believe and so are gathered into the community of faith.[26] Instead of following the pattern of the story as set out in the gnostic myth, the author achieves a challenging reinterpretation which redirects the focus to the encounter with the crucified, the incarnate one, as the place of revelation.

Similarly elements of the story which spoke of an actual return to the heavenly world and to the Father are reinterpreted as indicating the divine authority and source of Jesus' words. The fact that sometimes the gospel relates the promise of the gift of life to Jesus' coming and sometimes to his going, indicates, according to Bultmann, that these elements are not to be understood literally. Both coming and going bear the same basic import for the gospel: they serve to underline that in Jesus we meet God.[27]

Jesus' death is not only the climax of his earthly life as the event of revelation and therefore the climax of the crisis, the judgement which that revelation brings;[28] it is also the departure of Jesus which enables his true meaning to be comprehended.[29] Resurrection adds in itself nothing new to the revelation, at least, not as an inner worldly event.[30] It is only the encounter with the Word that matters and this continues in the event of proclamation. Here Bultmann picks up the notion of the Paraclete, which makes the writing of the gospel possible. The completion of Jesus' life opens the possibility of encountering the significance of that life, a significance obscured during the earthly ministry. By emphasising that distance from an event facilitates insight, Bultmann demythologises both Jesus' return and the coming of the paraclete.[31] Here we must distinguish between Bultmann's own demythologising and that attributed by him to the evangelist. But Bultmann can appeal to the fact that already the author displays a similar radical hermeneutic in merging the parousia of Jesus with the coming of the Spirit.

In discussing the post Easter perspective and the significance of the Paraclete for the gospel, Bultmann also draws a parallel with the Markan 'messianic secret'.[32] Mark, or his tradition, had sought to bridge the gap between what faith affirmed of Jesus after Easter and what Jesus said during his ministry by attributing to the disciples a high degree of misunderstanding during Jesus' earthly ministry. This led to their not being able to affirm for themselves what Jesus claimed of himself, that is, what faith had come to affirm that Jesus affirmed of himself. In John the Paraclete, the Spirit, while not guiding the pen of the evangelist in writing down exactly what the historical Jesus said, nevertheless brings into the present the word, the event, the encounter which then broke into the world in the person of Jesus. The Paraclete guarantees the continuity and its integrity. It is to this end that the gospel is written. It so tells the story that the encounter may take place. That retelling involves the use of traditions, but they serve now neither to narrate what actually may have happened nor to reproduce what Jesus may have said, 'das Was', the 'what' of revelation. They are employed in the service of mediating that encounter with the word which can take place because of the sheer fact ('das Dass') that in Christ God has broken into the world in a unique way.[33] In this manner not only the event of incarnation, crucifixion, resurrection, ascension, but also Pentecost and parousia, become for the gospel a single event with a single message. This is the 'eschatological event', the moment of ultimate encounter.[34]

The centering upon the eschatological event is so consistently carried through by the evangelist that traditional Christian categories are thoroughly reinterpreted. Thus while Bultmann identifies the notion of vicarious suffering in 1:29, for instance, this idea can no longer be of great importance for the the evangelist.[35] Forgiveness is the gift of the risen one through his word.[36] For the whole life of Jesus is an offering, and then only in the sense that in love he has given himself in the service of making the Father known, even in the final hour when in love he lays down his life.[37]

Similarly traditional notions of eschatology have been reinterpreted by the author, because eternal life and resurrection happen in the encounter with the word already in the person of Jesus.[38] Eschatology is subsumed under christology. Because this is so, Bultmann sees no place within the author's thought for notions of future resurrection or judgement. What awaits the believer at death is the final fulfilment of the oneness already known on earth.[39] The few verses which, by contrast, speak in traditional eschatological terms, Bultmann attributes, on these and other grounds, to later redaction. He sees the author, indeed, deliberately countering traditional eschatology as he identifies the moment of the casting out of the prince of the this world not with a future apocalyptic event but with the event of the cross,[40] just as he has similarly relocated the moment of the Son's glorification to the cross.[41] Bultmann also sees no place in this radical reinterpretation, with its emphasis on encounter with the word, for a sacramental understanding of salvation and accordingly attributes 6:51c-58 and 'of water' in 3:5 to the hand of an ecclesiastical redactor.[42]

Bultmann's presentation of Johannine christology is a consistent whole. His commentary has that quality, rare among exegetical works, of being able to bridge the gap between the reader and the gospel. Bultmann achieves this, not primarily by reading into the gospel his own theological concerns, but by reflecting upon the questions which the text of the gospel raises, not least because of the discrepancies which arise from a literal reading. That Bultmann sees these questions leading in the same direction as his own existentialist theology is not to be denied, but he appears not to compromise the integrity of the text as he perceives it.

There are, indeed, discrepancies in the text. Why does the revealer reveal nothing but that he is sent as the revealer? How can the author narrate the raising of Lazarus, for instance, and present Jesus as speaking of a totally different kind of resurrection available in his person, so that the original story seems little other than a symbol?[43] How can Jesus claim at one time that he proclaims what he has seen and heard and at another that he proclaims what he sees and hears in the present? Is not the idea of pre-existence thereby relativised? Is it merely symbolic? And when life is offered, on the one hand, as the gift of the one who goes and, on the other, as the gift of the one who has come, do not the sayings about coming and going appear to conflict if they are not understood as just two different ways of symbolising Jesus' absolute claims? How, further, is it possible to speak of Jesus' glorification at his return to the Father and at the same time to affirm that the glory was seen in the earthly Jesus?[44]

Bultmann's is a genuine attempt to face these issues. His synthesis is impressive. The 'theologia crucis' is found in the fact of Jesus' earthly, ordinary existence as well as in the suffering on the cross.[45] This authentic human life is the place of divine revelation! The encounter which takes place in the preaching of the word demands not extensive cognitive reception of the historical details of the life of Jesus or of dogma, but faith in the fact that this word has broken through in history.[46] The anthropological correlate of the divine gift is human hunger and thirst, the basic existential, and in that sense, timeless needs of human beings.[47] Accordingly the divine correlate, the gift in the person of Jesus, is bread, light, life.[48] By seeking to show that the evangelist uses the elements of the story to this one end, to focus upon the encounter, Bultmann achieves a presentation of Johannine christology which speaks with timeless relevance. For the evangelist, while using the revelation schema, has in fact abandoned the revelation model or transformed it into an encounter model.[49]

The synthesis, thus achieved, not only presents the Johannine gospel as a contemporary challenge; it also meets many of the questions, which the text raises for the modern reader. Miracles are seen by John as symbols. So, too, are pre-existence, exaltation, glorification, and parousia. And the issue of the Jesus of history becomes irrelevant, for only the fact of his coming, the paradox of the divine glory in human flesh, as as act of divine love, is important for the Johannine Jesus. We need not therefore be concerned at the differences between the Johannine and the Synoptic portrait of Jesus' ministry or the anachronisms in the Johannine account; for it is a post Easter presentation of the Jesus of faith's experience in the time of the church, not a reconstruction of the past. It is a re-presentation of the glory which faith has seen and which abides.

With the exception of the few eschatological and sacramental passages which Bultmann attributes to a redactor, and despite his generally unconvincing theory of disorder in the gospel as the result of displacement of original sheets, Bultmann's synthesis is achieved without sacrificing the integrity of the work as a whole. The key to the synthesis lies in Bultmann's answers to the questions outlined above, especially in his belief that the evangelist must have intended a transformation of the story or myth of the Redeemer-Revealer. To use Bultmann's own terms, the evangelist practised demythologising. Once this demythologising, for which Bultmann marshalls strong arguments from within the gospel, is called into question at any point, the synthesis weakens and the problems are exposed. Criticisms of Bultmann have frequently called into question various points of the synthesis, but have rarely faced the reexposed problems with the thoroughness of Bultmann. It is Bultmann's achievement to have faced these problems and sought for them a consistent explanation. Whenever any point in his synthesis has been questioned, far reaching problems have been thrown up which ultimately demand a totally new synthesis. This may be illustrated in the following overview of elements of the synthesis which have been called into question.

Johannine Christology after Bultmann

Did the fourth evangelist really not believe in miracles? Most likely he did.[50] This is not to deny that they were signs, that they were ultimately words about the Son; but, as Wilkens points out, the suffering which forms part of the paradox of the cross is in part the direct result of miracles, according to the Johannine story; they demonstrate Jesus' glory and are as real as other signs which are not miracles, such as the cross, itself.[51] They were not just symbols.[52] As well as symbolically pointing to the deeper reality, for instance, that Jesus is the bread of life, the feeding of the 5000 also demonstrates Jesus' power which belongs to his being the Revealer. The miracles must accordingly be taken seriously in the presentation of Johannine christology and in their endeavour to do so scholars are divided over their significance. Many, like Schnackenburg, argue that miracle faith is a first step.[53] For Becker it is not faith at all, but rather leads to a christology the evangelist seeks to counter.[54] For Schottroff miracle faith belongs to the irrelevant response to Jesus which sees him in this worldly terms. True faith sees what the miracles symbolise and that alone.[55] For Käsemann the gospel intends miracle faith and emphasises miracles as manifestations of Jesus' divine power and glory.[56]

The question about miracles opens a much wider door. Was the evangelist at all concerned about the details of the earthly Jesus? Bultmann would answer: no. Schottroff also answers: no, but not in a way that denies the reality of the details.[57] On her analysis, Johannine christology considers the earthly Jesus irrelevant except insofar as one sees the heavenly Jesus beyond the human. But most other scholars imply by their response to the miracle question some relevance of the picture of the earthly Jesus for the evangelist. It is not insignificant that Käsemann, who, one could say, reopened the issue of the historical Jesus, was the one who revived the nineteenth century critical description of the Johannine Jesus as a god marching triumphantly across the world.[58] For not only the miracles, but also Jesus' sovereign knowledge in encounter with his opponents,[59] presents a

Jesus who fails to meet Bultmann's ideal of an ordinary human being about whom there was nothing extraordinary except his claim to be the Revealer.[60] Käsemann's analysis was in a sense inevitable once he crossed the threshhold which Bultmann forbad as irrelevant and inappropriate to the Johannine conception and began to ask what kind of Jesus is portrayed here.

In response to Käsemann, Bornkamm pointed to elements of the portrayal which present Jesus as a real man, especially those which centre attention upon his death, including, not least, the final discourses, to which Käsemann gives scant attention, and also the passion narrative.[61] One could, indeed, assert with Thüsing, as Kähler had of Mark, that John is also a passion narrative with an extended introduction.[62] Above all, Bornkamm argued that the Johannine Jesus must be seen in the light of the work of the Paraclete as a post Easter presentation of the Christ of faith.[63] But the issue raised by Käsemann is primarily whether the picture, so produced, has not overlaid the earthly Jesus with post Easter perspectives of a certain developed christology, that beneath it all, the earthly Jesus ceases to be a real human being. This certainly was to happen in gnosticism, which denied Christ a real humanity and a real death. For Käsemann the evangelist is not so blatant,[64] but nevertheless does reflect a naive docetism,[65] a Johannine tendency also noted by Schweizer.[66]

Accordingly Käsemann counters the central role given to 1:14a ('The Word became flesh') in Bultmann's christology and much traditional christology, arguing that it is of subordinate significance in the immediate context and means little more than that the Logos assumed fleshly attire as the vehicle for manifesting divine glory. The focus of the passage lies on 1:14c, 'we beheld his glory.'[67] Bornkamm argued against this the Bultmannian thesis that the manifestation of glory is primarily in the cross as a paradox of real human suffering and divine glory and attacks Käsemann's exclusive dependence on 1:14c.[68] But for Käsemann the manifestation of glory in John is not confined to the cross. Jesus' life and ministry was one long manifestation of glory, the passion narrative, no longer relevant as passion, now portrays a triumphant exit. He also points out that Bultmann went primarily to the antidocetic statements of 1 and 2 John for support of his interpretation of 1:14, not to the gospel itself.[69]

Others have taken this further and suggested that 1:14a, itself, comes from the hand of a later redactor sharing the epistles' concerns.[70] On the other hand, Schottroff argues for taking 1:14 to mean becoming real flesh, but claims that the flesh is irrelevant for the author,[71] while according to U.B. Müller 1:14 belongs to the author's tradition and expresses originally a miracle centred christology, which he then sets in balance with the passion narrative.[72] Others, like Ibuki, while acknowledging Käsemann's valid exegetical observations about the centrality of 1:14c, have explained the manifestation of glory in ways that seek to retain a strong emphasis on 1:14a as expressing a real humanity and have therefore interpreted the glory as the glory of the relationship of love between Father and Son.[73]

The issue of Jesus' humanity is also addressed by those who endeavour to remove pre-existence from the story of Johannine christology altogether. Often noting, as Bultmann had, the discrepancy between statements of pre-existent seeing and hearing as the source of revelation and such passages as 5:19f which speak of the Son's seeing and hearing in the present, these scholars opt not for Bultmann's synthesis of demythologising but for a throughgoing humanised christology. Thus Robinson revives the suggestion that only an anhypostatic pre-existence of the Logos should be presupposed in John, so that Jesus is totally a human being like us and the model for all human relationships with God, and Watson has taken this further, arguing for an adoptionist christology on the theory that the Logos joined Jesus at his baptism.[74]

The question of Jesus' humanity is also closely bound to the issue of faith and history in John. The Johannine Jesus speaks Johannine language. Correspondingly there is a distinctive Johannine way of seeing, as Mussner points out. The Paraclete not only brings to memory, but also inspires interpretation. This results in a portrayal of Jesus in which pre- and post Easter perspectives are merged in the light of Jesus' glory. The gospel is therefore speaking the language of epiphany and the evangelist becomes the mouthpiece for Christ, who speaks Johannine language in response to issues of the evangelist's day.[75] The work of Leroy and others on techniques of misunderstanding and double meaning show that the gospel depends on having an 'in-group' for such techniques to be effective and speaks to and serves the interests of that group.[76] Martyn has shown how at one level of the miracle in the healing of the blind man in John 9 reflects the community's own conflicts with the synagogue.[77] He speaks of the author doubling Jesus with an early Christian preacher.[78] These and other studies raise all the more acutely the question: how did the evangelist intend that we should understand his gospel?

Was it to be understood as an historical account with a few interpretative elements, inevitable in any historical work because of subjectivity and distance, and above all, because of the latter, of even greater value because of the perspective which elapse of time brings? Then we should expect to find evaluative interpretation beside, but separate from, faithfully reproduced words of Jesus. Were words of Jesus which are distinctive to the fourth gospel derived from a special memory tradition, as Riesenfeld suggested,[79] preserving perhaps the private instruction of Jesus, the rabbi? An extreme form of this approach is found in Temple, who argues that a scribe wrote down the core of the gospel shortly after the end of Jesus' ministry and that it came to light only some 50 years later.[80] Can, then, even the pre-existence sayings and those which are most commonly understood to reflect a post Easter situation be explained as expressing Jesus' earthly experience of instruction from the Father and not pre-existence at all, in the one case, and as proleptic foreknowledge, in the other, as Cadman suggests?[81] This is most unlikely. It does not account for the fact that Jesus' language in John is so distinctly Johannine, his words, there, are mostly addressed to a public audience, and they include those which contain the developed Johannine christology of which the Synoptics bear little trace.

Does this mean that the evangelist simply projected back into the setting of the earthly ministry and onto earlier traditions an image of the post Easter Jesus without regard for history, except the all important single fact of the Word made flesh in history, as Bultmann suggests? Would the evangelist have known that he was projecting such a picture?[82] Or was it done unconsciously as the fruit of faith? Schulz argued that the evangelist depends heavily on what had already been developed in apocalyptic Christian material.[83] Grundmann spoke of visionary experiences of the Johannine church being reflected in the speeches of Jesus.[84]

Haacker, in response, notes that many speeches of Jesus are not directed to the disciples.[85] And de Jonge and others have pointed out that the author shows himself fully aware at points that certain insights about Jesus came to the disciples only after Easter (12:16; 2:22; 13:7). Similarly the Paraclete sayings assume an awareness that true knowledge about Jesus came to the disciples only then.[86] Is it the case that the evangelist believed that he was recounting events as they happened with help of the divine 'recall' of the Spirit? Or was it that he believed Jesus gave pointers during his earthly ministry and that post Easter reflection simply elaborated these?[87]

Growing recognition of the author's skilful compositional techniques which touch every part of the gospel, including especially the words of Jesus, suggests that the author must have been aware that his portrait was ahistorical. This is not to say that it was unhistorical, ie. that it did not contain some reference to what the author believed had actually happened. It does suggest that he was governed by another purpose. In that sense Bultmann is right that the details of history are not a priority, but Käsemann is also right to examine the resultant picture for its portrait of the earthly Jesus. The issues of the historicity of the picture of Jesus and of its humanity are not the same as the issue of how the author might have understood the historicity or humanity of his portrayal of Jesus. Both sets of questions must be seen in their distinctiveness and both deserve attention.

There are other important issues related to the question of faith and history. Bultmann bracketted out the historical questions about Jesus and also gave too little attention to the situation of the evangelist and its relationship to christology. Bultmann's tendency to reduce elements of the gospel story to symbol may be observed in his treatment of 'the Jews' in John. They are allegedly mere symbols of the world of darkness which rejects the light.[88] Investigation of the author's situation suggests strongly that the Jews are not just symbols of the world, but reflect in some way the conflicts of the Johannine community with contemporary Judaism.[89] As Bultmann's reduction of the historical Jesus to a simple point in time has been largely given up in favour of a reexamination of the Johannine understanding of the earthly Jesus and his story, so Bultmann's reduction of the Johannine situation is increasingly being surrendered to a more differentiated analysis. This goes hand in hand with an increasing unwillingness to accept Bultmann's view that John's gospel has demythologised the myth of the Redeemer-Revealer sent from heaven.

Schottroff remains close to Bultmann in denying that the evangelist places emphasis upon any temporal development in the story of the Revealer as presupposed in the myth.[90] For her, the evangelist, however, does not deny pre-existence. Nevertheless all the emphasis falls upon the call of the Redeemer. The Redeemer calls his own out of the hostile world.[91] Reality is polarised by the fact of the Redeemer. Like Bultmann's analysis, Schottroff's has a dualism of decision.[92] By decision the two spheres of light and darkness are established. Yet Schottroff also presupposes a modified cosmic dualism, for a real pre-existence implies it, as does the understanding of salvation as escape from this world, and it also lies behind her distinction between faith's vision of the truth about Jesus and the world's seeing him only as a miracle worker.[93] This dualism recalls Dodd's analysis where Platonic thought is employed to distinguish between two levels of reality in John.[94] Schottroff's conclusion is different from Bultmann's also in that it aligns John with gnosticism. This is reflected not only in the role she presupposes for cosmic dualism, but also in the common dualism of decision, shared with gnosticism.[95] As Haenchen had already pointed out, Bultmann's assumption that gnosticism does not know the dualism of decision is questionable.[96]

Here it is interesting to observe that as soon as we give up demythologising as an explanation of the evangelist's method in interpreting the Redeemer's story, Bultmann's analysis drives us in the direction of gnosis, for he had maintained that the Johannine story pattern had been modelled on the gnostic. And once it is recognised that gnosticism also used the dualism of decision, the differences between Johannine christology and the gnostic myth are reduced considerably. Because he shares Bultmann's presuppositions about a gnostic background of the gospel, Käsemann, too, finds himself acknowledging a more direct relationship with gnosticism than Bultmann would allow.[97] Langbrandtner takes this development even further when he argues that notions such as the pre-existence of the soul are not of the 'esse' of gnostic thought; they are myths spun out to underpin what is basically a theology of salvation, according to which faith means acceptance of the Redeemer who offers the way to the heavenly rest; the true gnostic is born only by faith, by decision.[98] Bultmann's position on the relationship of John and gnosticism meets its antithesis in Bergmeier who argues that gnosticism is characterised by the dualism of decision, but that in John's gospel we have determinism![99]

This is not the place to examine the case for the relationship between John and gnosticism, but it is apparent that Bultmann's synthesis was so achieved that removal of the demythologising theory inevitably led to directly gnostic interpretations of the gospel and the Nag Hammadi discoveries, which established the new understanding of gnostic dualism, have hastened the process.

The assertion that the Johannine story or pattern is not to be demythologised gave to pre-existence and sending a far greater importance than ever Bultmann had allowed. Scholars like Käsemann, Schottroff, and Appold have persisted in playing off the idea of Jesus' oneness with the Father against the idea of sending.[100] This is largely a legacy of Bultmann's synthesis. Haenchen and others are right when they recognise that the notion of pre-existence and sending is of central importance for the author and raises crucial questions about how Jesus' relationship to the Father is to be understood.[101] In contrast Blank and Riedl, for instance, strongly emphasise the person of Jesus, his being and nature, as the clue to his revelation, so that to meet him is to meet the divine, and they consider Johannine christology as thus treading a pre-trinitarian path. Riedl even speaks of a binitarian conception in John.[102] That seems a straightforward way of explaining such statements as: 'he who has seen me has seen the Father.' But the gospel does not argue in this way. Rather it relates revelation to what Jesus says and does. He says what he has heard from the Father in his pre-existence; he fulfils a commission given him; he does the Father's works not because of an innate deity, but because of obedience. And, above all, the notion of pre-existence and sending serves to portray Jesus' oneness as the oneness of the sent one who is subordinate. Barrett, in particular, has argued this strongly.[103]

It is at this point that Bultmann's synthesis was at its strongest. For his observation is valid that Jesus does not in fact come with revelations from the Father. Haenchen who stresses the importance of sending and its implied subordination tries to counter this by saying that Jesus reveals more than just the fact that he is the revealer. He reveals the Father's love and offers bread and life.[104] But that was already implied in Bultmann's statements.[105] The problem of the christology of sending lies in its failure to do justice to the fact that in the fourth gospel Jesus is not the bearer of revelation. The information-revelation model has been transformed into a revelation-encounter model. The answer does not appear to lie in the direction of Riedl and others who would say that Jesus was the revelation himself because of his being and nature. For that in turn fails to do justice to the sending and related motifs which are so strongly represented through the gospel.

A new and important way lies in a reexamination of the notion of sending in the light of judicial emissary patterns in Judaism and stereotype emissary and ambassador protocol in the ancient world, which were frequently applied to heavenly as well as earthly figures. In these the messengers present themselves in such a way that they may be much more than the bearers of a message. They are an extension of the person of the sender, so that they mediate the presence of the sender. Earlier Rengstorf and Kühl, and more recently Borgen, Miranda, and Åhner have pointed to this circle of ideas.[106] The recent studies have explored the prophetic, rabbinic, and apocalyptic backgrounds of the sending idea and sought to relate the fourth gospel to them. Bühner, somewhat speculatively, even posits a Johannine christology of a pre-existent ascension for authorisation and finds traces of this in 3:13.[107] This is unconvincing.

Further exploration and clarification is needed not so much of the idea of a heavenly sending of Jesus as of the relationship between statements which imply sending, subordination and the reception of revelation, on the one hand, and those which speak more directly of Jesus' relationship to God, on the other. Is Jesus, analogous to Wisdom,[108] or to apocalyptic eschatological figures,[109] a bearer of God's name and therefore 'God' or a 'second God'? Is he such only because of his representative function? But that would leave open the ontological question. Clearly the author presupposes an ontology which enables him to speak of Jesus' pre-existence and being with the Father in the beginning. How is this perceived in such a way that it is not made the basis of the revelation scheme along the following lines: 'I am God: see me'; but rather is integrated within a story of sending and revealing and representing another?

If the surrender of the Bultmannian reduction of the significance of the earthly Jesus leads in Käsemann to the issue of the reality of Jesus' humanity, the surrender of demythologising in relationship to pre-existence and sending leads to the issues of the relationship between the Father and the Son.

The solution of Bultmann that the revealer does not reveal, but is himself the gift in the fact of his being in the flesh, has been countered with alternative suggestions. Haacker, acknowledging the legitimacy of Bultmann's observations about revelation, opts rather for the idea of Jesus, the founder.[110] But this imports a foreign model into the discussion and in much of his analysis Haacker in fact reproduces the revealer model.[111]

Another alternative focusses upon the statements within the gospel which use the language of vicarious suffering. Jesus is indeed the revealer, but what he reveals is what he does: his work; and his work and commission from the Father is to die on the cross offering his life as a vicarious sacrifice on the basis of which salvation and life are offered to all who believe. T.E. Müller has developed this thesis most fully, but many agree with him in giving the traditional notion of Jesus' atoning death a major role in the gospel.[112]

Bultmann had acknowledged the existence of such tradition in John to a minimal extent, but denied it had any role.[113] There was a certain consistency which demanded this conclusion. If life is available in the encounter with the Redeemer, then what can the sacrifice on the cross add? The whole life of Jesus is an offering of love right to the end; and in that offering life is offered. This is a powerful argument, all the more so because of the paucity of references to Jesus' death as a sacrifice against the dominant emphasis throughout the gospel on eternal life now available in the person of Jesus.

It is possible to argue that the gift of life was in fact available only after and because of the vicarious death, so that all statements about Jesus' offering life during his earthly ministry are proleptic of the post Easter situation and were placed within the ministry by the evangelist in the light of this.[114] But this puts an enormous strain on the text. It might gain some support from 6:51-58 which interpret the bread of life as the eucharistic gift of the flesh and blood of Jesus, but this passage is not typical and its authenticity widely questioned. There are passages which speak of the promise of life in the future, especially those which allude to the future gift of the Spirit (7:37-39), but these are not usually related to the idea of sacrificial death.[115]

Nevertheless a text like 1:29 cannot be ignored, especially because of its place in the gospel, and even those like Forestell, who rule out the notion of vicarious sacrifice elsewhere in the gospel, recognise its presence here,[116] though some, like Hegermann and U.B. Müller, argue for a non cultic interpretation, such as taking away of sin by exposing it or simply by being the saving one.[117] But, should the notion be present here, other more doubtful and ambiguous passages may well have to be seen in the light of it. There remains a tension, but hardly a convincing case that the central salvific act in John is vicarious death, as it is, for instance, for Paul.

Bultmann had also seen demythologising in the way the author handled the elements of exaltation, glorification, and return, in the story pattern of the Redeemer. For Bultmann the death of Jesus is the conclusion of the earthly paradox of divine glory and so the glorification of Jesus. Preiss drew attention in particular to the forensic nature of much of the fourth gospel and since then much greater emphasis has been given to the death of Jesus as the climax of the world's judgement of Jesus and in reality Jesus' judgement of the world.[118] Forestell, too, emphasises the cross as the place of supreme revelation.[119] Similarly Bornkamm points to the repeated references to the death of Jesus from the beginning of the gospel onwards in such a way that it becomes the climax of revelation.[120]

In Bornkamm, and in the work of many others, Bultmann's thesis persists, according to which the elements of glorification and exaltation to heaven are transferred by the author to the death of Jesus and this has been restated in modified form also by Moloney and Lindars.[121] Thüsing retained this view to the extent that he spoke of Jesus' exaltation in the event of the cross; but he saw it as something separate within the total event of his return to the Father, for which he saw the word glorification being used. In that sense he made a distinction between the foci of exaltation and glorification and so broke the connection affirmed by Bultmann's line of interpretation.[122] For Thüsing, glorification, applied in its specific sense to the climax of Jesus' earthly ministry, meant glorification in the presence of the Father. He identified two stages: the work of glorification in the broader sense, by the Son of the Father and by the Father of the Son, in his earthly ministry up to and including death and exaltation on the cross; and secondly, the ministry of Jesus through the Spirit after Easter, glorifying the Father and being glorified by him and in the disciples, in the community of faith.

Blank challenged Thüsing's separation of exaltation and glorification, arguing, as has Nicholson more recently, that exaltation must also include its traditional meaning of exaltation on high to the Father,[123] and Thüsing's response acknowledged the validity of challenge. Yet he has done so in a manner which leaves a certain ambiguity. He retains statements about the distinction, but also speaks of Jesus' exaltation as his elevation to the throne of glory[124] and draws attention to the cross as a symbol of the crowning, the crowning taking place subsequently in heaven.[125] It seems to me that in effect the distinction has almost disappeared. It is true, and frequently ignored, that the passion narrative is just as symbolically suggestive as the rest of the gospel. But the crown of thorns, for instance, and the regal imagery is manifestly symbolic of Jesus' messiahship, not of a post mortal crowning. The author does not use royal messianic imagery in association with Jesus' exaltation, glorification and return to the Father, but uses it in association with Jesus' claim during his earthly ministry to be God's sent one.

The surrender of Bultmann's thesis of demythologising also means, therefore, the surrender of one of the most challenging features of his analysis: the idea of the death of Jesus as the paradox of glory and humanity in suffering. This Pauline insight remains, of course, theologically valid, even though we have to admit it is not intended in John.[126]

Taking the glorification seriously as the return to be glorified with the glory which Jesus had with the Father before the world began raises important issues about the nature of Jesus' revelatory glory on earth as expressed in 1:14 and elsewhere. Here Bultmann had harmonised, arguing that it would be inconsistent to suggest that Jesus received glory when he already had it from the beginning. Hence a demythologised solution: the cross is glorification, in end effect in exactly the same way as the whole life bears glory.[127] Without Bultmann's solution a tension remains. Are we to speak of degrees of glory, the one hidden or more obscured, the other open?[128] But that is not the author's formulation. It is those who have truly seen who testify to the glory of 1:14; and 2:11 scarcely means anything different. Further Jesus' glorification at the climax of his ministry is not an unveiling, but a receiving.[129] These appear to be different uses and need further exploration.

The death and departure of Jesus have also been an important special instance of the problem of the nature of Jesus' humanity, which I mentioned in general terms earlier. Here, having given up Bultmann's premise, Käsemann saw the triumphant exit of the divine being, the transformation of a passion narrative of real suffering, for which the author's scheme, according to Käsemann, could have no place, into a virtual parody of suffering.[130] He is followed by Schulz[131] and U.B. Müller.[132] Jesus comes and goes, having power and authority to lay down his life and take it up again. What they explicate is what Bultmann affirmed as myth, but then demythologised. Here, too, the danger of oversystematisation lies close at hand. Do the texts support this view - even though it may be logically demanded by the myth? For instance, Hebrews assumes Jesus has the power of an indestructible life and makes his return to the Father upon accomplishment of his work (7:16), but it recounts side by side with this the story of one who sheds real tears and knows real suffering (5:7). Is it similar with John's Jesus? Only a careful analysis of the texts will prove to what degree he holds to a human or real view of the passion, perhaps even holds it in tension.

In the story the Son's return is linked with the giving of the Spirit which makes the continuing work of Jesus possible, not by adding to, but by bringing clear understanding of who Jesus was and is. As Thüsing has clearly shown, this means that the work of glorification which marked the earthly ministry continues after Easter.[133] This makes mission possible, the fruit bearing which is achieved through the witness of the disciples who love one another. All this means that the death of Jesus is not seen as simply the 'end', but rather as the 'turning point', as Blank puts it, using the German 'Ende' and 'Wende'.[134] Haenchen, too, emphasises the important hermeneutical function of the coming of the Spirit in the thought of the author.[135] He rejects Bultmann's grouping of parousia, Pentecost, ascension, resurrection, death and incarnation as one single event. Rather the event of Jesus' death belongs with the exaltation, glorification and return complex and issues in the coming of the Spirit. This is a new stage in the story, the real story of God's action in Christ.[136]

Because this 'turning point' makes greater understanding possible of who Jesus is, it makes possible true sight and salvation. It is, in that sense, what makes the gift of life accessible. The logic of the story suggests that this is because of the work of the Spirit enabling true sight because of the completed work of revelation.[137] Others presuppose that this life is available post Easter because it is the result of Jesus' vicarious death, as we have already noted. But that does not seem to be the main line of the story and Bultmann's objection remains that it was in the person of the revealer that this life was available, and therefore already before Easter.[138]

In a sense the problem is not peculiarly Johannine. We might also ask: was the word of life present in its fullness in the person of the earthly Jesus? Was justification, or whatever other term we use to describe salvation, already possible then? The Jesus tradition points strongly in the affirmative direction. If it was all there before Easter in the person of Jesus, then Bultmann's comments concerning the fourth gospel, that in fact the resurrection adds nothing to the content of revelation,[139] touches on a problem that was already implicit in the Jesus tradition. Yet, just as the resurrection of Jesus before the eschaton was celebrated as God's vindication of what he claimed to be in his earthly ministry and so performed for the disciples the all important hermeneutical function that finally made their faith possible, so in John the event death-resurrection-exaltation-glorification-giving of the Spirit has primarily a hermeneutical role. To that role belongs not only the coming of the Spirit who leads the disciples to the truth, but also the Johannine portrait of Jesus' death as the place of judgement by the world of Jesus and by Jesus of the world. In this sense the death of Jesus cannot simply be the end or even just the climax of Jesus' ministry. It is the point at which the conflict and controversy with the world reaches its climax and its verdict. It is therefore the final exposure of the world for what it is and thus the victory over the devil. The ascent of Jesus to the Father is at the same time his vindication and the confirmation that the world has been judged and Jesus has been justified. Yet precisely because this is so for the evangelist, he can point to the gift of life as already being present during Jesus' earthly ministry and at the same time highlight the climax of the story as the means by which this became truly known and, in that sense, available.

The Spirit also brings to light the relationship between Jesus and the Old Testament. Bultmann refers to the Old Testament fulfilment within the gospel,[140] but rejects a salvation historical perspective. This is consistent with his demythologising theory which treats the story or myth symbolically as a statement about a single event in history and not as a narrative of events.[141] The prologue does not, according to Bultmann, tell of the Logos's encounter with Israel, and its activity in creation is symbolic of the inner unity of redemption and creation.[142]

This is not the place to discuss the gospel's understanding of the Old Testament, which it uses mostly from traditions rather than directly, or to examine the role of the history of the people of God in John. But a number of scholars recognise in the prologue some reference to the Logos 'asarkos' in pre Christian history. The abandonment of the demythologising principle for interpreting John inevitably raises the issue afresh. Nevertheless it remains a matter of dispute whether the gospel intends such a continuity with Israel. 4:22 was for Bultmann an oddity with its claim that salvation came from the Jews, who are otherwise so frequently symbols of the hostile world; it was a later gloss.[143] But there has been increasing dissatisfaction with his solution of attributing it to a later hand. Hahn has shown convincingly that the verse belongs well within its context and within the theology of the author.[144]

The opening up of the question of salvation historical perspectives in John, which Bultmann's theory virtually forbad, has also led to a new evaluation of the role both of the Old Testament and of the Jewish traditions in the fourth gospel. We have already noted the works of Borgen, Miranda and Bühner on the background of the sending idea. Borgen especially has drawn our attention anew to rabbinic and Philonic use of early Jewish traditions which appear also to lie behind Johannine material.[145] Meeks argued for a strong Moses typology behind the gospel and sought to trace behind the gospel a prophetic-messianic hope which has left traces both in the Samaritan episode and in 6:14f.[146] Bultmann had already noted similarities between the christological story's words of Jesus telling what he had seen and heard and the picture of the Mosaic prophet of Deut 18:15-18. But, he countered, the Johannine model does not ground Jesus' authority in inspiration and call, but in oneness with the Father and the fact of his person.[147] The alternatives are no longer so simple, as the monograph studies of Bühner and Miranda, for instance, on the sending motif have shown.

With the increasing awareness of the Jewishness of much Johannine material has come an awareness that there is a twofold orientation in the gospel in relation to Israel. There is the strong negative reaction against contemporary Judaism represented in the Jews of the gospel story. This shows all the marks of abreaction of a group which has been forcibly separated from a wider community. Probably the dualistic determinism which comes to expression in parts of the gospel is a fruit of the Johannine community's coming to terms with the break. The same phenomenon repeats itself in the inner divisions of the Christian community evident behind 1 John and recalls the response of the Qumran community to the Jerusalem hierarchy.

On the other hand, there is a strong positive concern to maintain the validity of the Christian cause as fulfilment of scripture and its intention. Scripture witnesses on Jesus' behalf in the great trial carried through in Jesus' ministry. Moses takes the stand against the Jews and Isaiah and Abraham know Jesus in his pre-existence. But the concern seems less with establishing historical continuity as God's people and more with establishing scriptural warrant. Thus the manna story is but a springboard for the claim that Jesus is the bread of life and the temple is left in irrelevance as Jesus goes on to speak of his body temple.

The question of the author's perception of how Jesus is to be understood in history is different from the question what historical factors played a role in the development of the author's christology. Bultmann made important suggestions about the background of the christology, but his synthesis of Johannine christology is primarily won from the text itself. This is the great value of his work. Yet he did posit written sources: a gnostic discourse collection, a source of miracles, and a passion narrative. Of greatest influence has been the Semeia source which has been taken up by a number of scholars and variously defined, the most thorough going attempt being Fortna's.[148] It is not my concern to evaluate these constructions. My question is rather their importance for establishing the christology of the author.

In the works of Boismard, Becker, U.B. Müller, Richter, Martyn, Brown, Haenchen, Langbrandtner and others, attempts are made to lay bare a history of christology within the Johannine community.[149] A development is usually traced from a miracle oriented messianic, prophetic or 'theios anēr' model of christology to a revelational christology (analogous or related to gnostic patterns), mostly also seen in the context of conflict with Judaism, finally to a christology which more carefully avoids docetic characteristics or suggestions. The latter is linked with the stance of the author of the first epistle over against opponents who have followed an alternative development from the second stage.

It seems to me very likely that some such development took place with the Johannine community, but questions arise for me in the way each stage is related to the other and significantly it is here that these scholars are least united. The relevance for understanding the christology of the author of these hypotheses lies in their ability to open a new way of solving the problems and discrepancies within the gospel. But this is a procedure frought with difficulty. How can I know that what does not fit my system of Johannine christology must either be from a later hand or represent the residue of older tradition? And in the latter case what is gained by establishing that this or that saying is traditional when the question to be faced is: how does the author integrate it? The procedure is even more complicated by the distinctive Johannine style which according to Ruckstuhl permeates the whole gospel.[150] And more recently Strecker and Schnelle have proposed what amounts to a reversal of traditional understanding of the order in which the gospel and epistles were written. Schnelle has sought to support this hypothesis in his recent analysis of the gospel on the assumption that it is dealing with the problems of docetism already addressed in the first epistle.[151] To my mind he fails to demonstrate his case. As often happens in Johannine research hypotheses, the thesis is weak where one would want it to be strongest: in the discourse material.

The diversity of reconstructions is evidence of a high degree of subjectivity in such research, but the obverse of this is also true: the persistence of such a range of proposals indicates that the material must be recognised as demanding such a treatment. The strength of the proposals of Martyn and Brown is that they seek to relate source theories, history of the community and development and diversity of christology. Inevitably such reconstructions entail speculation and are vulnerable to criticism on these grounds. Wengst's impressive reconstruction is too harshly put aside as akin to 'science fiction'.[152] There is no question of the importance of seeking the sociological context of Johannine christology. In this regard Meeks's essay on the social function of the myth of the descending ascending redeemer[153] has contributed importantly to the discussion of the nature of the community raising the question of its sectarian character. Onuki's study takes this further detecting a twofold movement of mission and withdrawal reflected in the pattern of coming and returning of the Son.[154] Becker's insistence on the basically dualistic world view of the gospel also has important implications for understanding the community and not least its christology.[155]

Recent studies of the transmitted text from a literary perspective, such as those of Culpepper, Duke, and O'Day,[156] have not only expanded our awareness of the literary forms and devices of the work. They have also raised important questions about the nature of the document itself and its relationship to the community in which it was produced. This is particularly so, when they highlight the importance of irony, double meaning, misunderstanding, and symbolism, all of which function most naturally within a community which 'knows' and so enhance the fellowship of knowing and belonging. These raise, in turn, significant questions about the nature of the gospel itself, its portrait of Jesus, and its use, even in our own day.

Conclusions

These reflections underline the importance of Bultmann's starting point. He sought the central structure of the author's thought. I hope to show that fundamentally he was right in his outline of the Johannine story. But I cannot agree that the author demythologised the story to the extent that Bultmann presumes. It seems to me that Bultmann's insight that the revelation-information model has been transformed into a model of revelation-encounter is fundamentally correct and of abiding worth for interpreting the gospel today. By allowing the story to stand un-demythologised and so by facing anew the author's understanding of pre-existence, sending, oneness with the Father, humanness, death, exaltation, glorification, and return to the Father, both new problems and discrepancies come into focus and also new possibilities are opened for understanding the christology of the author within the gospel and within the context of early Christianity.

The problems include the significance of Jesus' death. Has vicarious sacrifice a place in Johannine christology? In what way does his death relate to his work? Was it real suffering or merely triumphant exit? What is the relationship between Jesus' death, his exaltation, and his glorification? They also include the significance of his earthly life as a whole. What constitutes the saving event in John? In what sense does the revealer reveal? What is the nature of his divinity? What role has pre-existence? How human is the Johannine Jesus? How real his passion? What role do miracles play in John's christology? They also include consideration of the nature of the gospel in the light of its christology. Does the Jesus of history and the details of his life matter any longer to the author? What is the life setting of Johannine christology? Is it still possible to do as Bultmann did and relate it the modern world? We shall return to many of these issues in Part III. The way to these issues must lie first of all in a reexamination of Bultmann's fundamental question: what is the central structure of the author's christology? And to this we turn.

PART II

THE STRUCTURE OF JOHANNINE

CHRISTOLOGY

A. IDENTIFYING THE CENTRAL STRUCTURE

1. Issues of Method

In reviewing research into Johannine christology since Bultmann we have shown that the major issues of dispute which have arisen, often over against Bultmann, have concentrated on elements within the story which Bultmann saw as forming the centre of Johannine christology. Bultmann's interpretation of each element of the story sought to retain a consistency and coherence with the story as a whole. In discussing the major areas of dispute in Johannine christology I want similarly to take into account the Johannine story as a whole, in particular, what I describe as the central structure of Johannine christology. For it is only when we have been able to see the overall structure that we are able to gain a perspective for evaluating the role of individual elements.

The Fourth Gospel contains a wide variety of christological sayings, motifs and narratives. Most have been subjected to minute analysis, both for their role within the gospel and for their background in Christian tradition and in the religio-historical traditions of the day. On the surface of the text of the gospel we see rich and varied expressions of christological thought. The search for the central structure of the author's christology is the search for what holds these various motifs and images together. What structure or structures lie beneath the surface manifestations in the text?

In looking for the basic story of Johannine christology we are not wanting to find a central structure which we can then use to rule out the significance of other motifs or into which we might force other motifs and patterns of thought on the assumption that the author's christology must be consistent and unified. It is rather that we seek an overall perspective, a christological map, which will enable us to see the way particular motifs function within the whole. This is particularly important in a writing which contains a wide variety of christological themes and in which it is very easy to isolate particular motifs, like, for instance, that of Jesus' death as an act of vicarious atonement, and elevate it to the major theme of the gospel. Tracing the christological map that emerges from the text must not be undertaken on the presupposition that there is a single unified structure. That can only emerge from the text itself. We may assume consistency, but with caution.

Our concern at this stage is therefore not with individual motifs but with what integrates them or with the way they are related to one another. Similarly I am not interested at this stage in classifying the Johannine christological material into a systematic arrangement of, for instance, titles or themes. As far as possible I want to listen for structures and patterns that emerge from the text itself.

Some have presented Johannine christology by identifying a key text or texts. The Prologue with the Logos motif might, by its very position, be seen as an appropriate key or starting point for understanding the author's christological thought. We may assume its meaning would have been clear to its first readers for whom it functioned as the overture or key to the gospel, unlocking its messianic secret, the directive for how the gospel should be understood, the window through which it should be viewed, the script for its main character. But for us, as Bultmann points out, it is an 'enigma' which only makes sense after we have read the gospel as a whole. Furthermore, many of its major motifs, including its chief motif, Logos, the theme of Christ and creation, the incarnation of the Word, to name only a few, do not occur elsewhere in the gospel and it contains no direct reference to Jesus' death and ascension. Nor can 'the Word became flesh' (1:14a) on its own function as a summary of the author's christology, as it had for Bultmann, especially since Käsemann challenged its traditional interpretation and suggested that it intended little more than to describe how the glory appeared (1:14b). Similarly Haacker's attempt to make 1:17, with its contrast between Moses and Jesus Christ, 'law' and 'grace and truth', the centre of the author's christology proves an inadequate starting point, because it puts the focus too much on the salvation historical perspective which is not dominant in John. Accordingly Haacker emphasises Jesus as 'founder', though his own expositions make the motif of revealer much more central.

Richter makes the christological formulation in 20:31, 'Jesus is the Christ, the Son of God', into a criteron of the evangelist's concerns and uses it, for instance, in arguing that 1:14a is a redactional addition, but this confession is also too narrow a base for such assertions. Numerous other passages have been described from time to time as embodying the essence of the author's christology. Smalley sees the gospel as a kind of midrash based on the Son of Man saying of 1:51. Similarly the wedding at Cana (2:1-11), as the first sign and as one standing without interpretation, is seen by some as a programmatic statement of the evangelist's theology. Ruckstuhl, arguing for the integrity of 6:51c-58, maintains that it contains within a confined space a summary of the whole gospel in form and content and, more recently, Weder argues that John 6 as a whole should be seen as representative of Johannine christology. Appold focusses on the brief statements in 10:30 ('I and the Father are one') and 17:11f as abbreviations of Johannine christology. Some choose the even briefer formulation, 'It is finished' (19:30), as their centre.

It is not my intention to dispute that these passages or formulations may reflect the centre of Johannine christology. Many are, however, too succinct. They need expanding and this expanded outline or structure needs to be identified. In many ways scholars who have analysed the christology of the fourth gospel, presenting systematic outlines, have also noted patterns and structures in the text.

Wetter, for instance, created a list of Johannine christological statements, above all, of the enormous variety of statements which we have classed under the heading: 'The Son makes the Father known'. He speaks of an almost tiresome monotony in such Johannine material.[18]

Lütgert made similar lists, but tried to force them all into a theory according to which Jesus' claims amounted primarily to a claim to be a man inspired by the Spirit.[19] Bultmann also listed the variations before arguing that the author had a demythologising interpretation of the pattern of coming and sending.[20] Forestell surveys the gospel for statements illustrating the centrality of revelation,[21] and lists motifs which follow the verbs to believe and to know: Jesus is sent by God, the Father; he comes from God; he is in the Father and the Father in him; and the enigmatic statement, 'I am'.[22] The sending sayings have been listed by many.[23] Ibuki places 8:28; 12:49f; and 14:10bc in parallel columns,[24] texts which, as we shall see, reflect the central structure and does the same for 3:32; 8:26; 8:40; 1:18; 6:66; and 15:15b.[25] Schnackenburg lists motifs associated with 'Father' and 'Son';[26] de Jonge and Moloney do similarly, the latter contrasting these with motifs associated with the Son of Man title.[27] Bühner lists the elements which belong to the traditional motif of the envoy and finds the pattern expressed in 13:3 and 3:35.[28] Becker draws on Bühner in applying the pattern to the christological statements in the gospel as a whole.[29] Bornkamm uses 3:31-36 and also 8:21-29 to trace a pattern of christological thought.[30]

Much of the work done thus far has rarely gone beyond listing the elements or focussing upon particular elements (especially the sending sayings). The work of identifying similar material and listing it is essential for any careful analysis of Johannine christology, as is individual investigation of particular elements. But beyond that it is important to identify patterns or structures of thought which show the ways the various elements interrelate. It is particularly valuable if these structures can be shown to exist already within the text itself and not simply be a structure systematised out of the gathered material. This is the strength of the approaches like Bornkamm's. Both the systematic review and the tracing of patterns in particular passages of the text itself are important for identifying the central structure of the author's christology.

In the investigation which follows I have sought to establish the basic structure of the author's christology by noting:

1.   motifs and images occur frequently within the gospel;

2.   combinations or patterns of motifs and images which occur frequently;

3.   summary statements, especially those within which the common motifs and groups of motifs occur;

4.   motifs or groups of motifs made the subject of attention and development, especially in discourses of Jesus about himself.

Any such posited underlying structure should be shown to integrate, or, at least, to relate coherently to, the variety of motifs within the gospel. As well as these general criteria there may also be indications of the author's special christological interests in the way the author structures the gospel, inasmuch as such structures are visible and generally agreed. It is also important to take into account not only the thematic statements in the sayings material, but also the way the narrative material functions.

I have spoken of the author's christology. Strictly speaking it is only the christology of the text before us to which we have access and we assume it reflects that of the author. But a greater problem arises in the light of question whether the text which we have should be treated as a whole or whether it should be seen as a multi layered document in which we can detect a pregospel gospel or miracle source, the gospel itself and redactional expansions and additions. I want to treat the text as it stands as a unity and to take my readings of its christology from the whole text. But I also want to be aware of the (to my mind convincing) view that the present gospel text has behind it a history of development. Rather than frustrate the reader with a maze of 'if's and 'but's in the light of the various source and redaction theories proposed, I shall press ahead with the text as we have it, and return to the consider the author's christology in the light of source theories in IIIC2 below. The viewing of the text for traces of the central christological structure will, in turn, raise questions of tradition and redaction, but they are not the primary subject of this study.

Frequency of motifs alone could be established on the basis of statistics; but then we should be in danger of the losing the individual contours of the text which give each motif its setting and specific meaning. The ideal would be a careful sifting verse by verse and passage by passage of the gospel, but this will have to be assumed as background to what follows. Instead I propose to begin by looking at some sample passages and to examine what emerges as a common christological structure. The elements of this structure will be examined in the light of the criteria of frequency and combination outlined above, including occurrence in summary statements. In a further step we shall review the gospel as a whole for indications of particular attention and development of the structure and finally consider the way in which the structure integrates, or relates to, the various christological motifs of the gospel. On this basis we return in Part III to the wider issues of Johannine christology.

2. Examining Select Passages.

I want to begin with the passage, 3:31-36. It comes at the conclusion of the first major dialogue and discourse and functions as a summary.[31]

Schnackenburg considers the passage a piece of Johannine writing, probably by the author of the gospel, which, together with 3:13-21, has been secondarily added to chapter 3; but at the same time sees in this material a condensation of the principal assertions of Johannine theology.[32] He frequently uses it as such a reference point.[33] Olsson includes this passage and 12:44-50, which we shall consider below, in his list of Johannine 'footnotes' which reflect the author's theology.[34] For Schulz it is the author's composition and reflects his characteristic christology.[35] Sanders and Mastin see in it the author's own meditation.[36] Significantly it was 3:31-36 which Bornkamm used when highlighting the parallel thought structure between the author's christology and his pneumatology.[37] Becker challenges its use as a starting point for investigating Johannine christology, rightly drawing attention to its loose connection within the gospel.[38]

Its usefulness as a starting point is its compactness and summary character. Comparison with the rest of the gospel will indicate how loosely its christology fits within the gospel. It serves as a starting point, not a concluding summary of our investigation.

The following are its major christological statements:

(i) 'He who comes from above is above all' (31a)

This statement is expanded in two ways. Negatively:

> 'he who is of the earth is of the earth
> and speaks of the earth' (31b)

The contrast is not with John the Baptist.[39] That would devalue his informed witness to Jesus in the preceding verses (3:27-30!), not to speak of 1:15. Rather the contrast is with Nicodemus, the teacher of Israel who cannot see because he is not born from above (3:3) and with those like him who involve themselves in disputes about purification (3:25).[40] The first statement is then reformulated:

> 'he who comes from heaven...'

At this point the textual witness is divided between continuing directly into 32 or repeating the formulation from 31a 'is above all'. Whichever text we follow, we can see that 31 contains two major statements about Jesus:

> he comes from above, from heaven;
>
> and he is above all
> (either people or both people and things).

The verse also associates his òrigin with his superiority ('from above' and 'above all') and relates this to his speaking, which follows directly in 32, but is indirectly implied in 31 where the one who is 'of the earth speaks of the earth'.

(ii) 'What he has seen and heard, this he bears witness to' (32a)

With this we may associate:

> 'He whom God sent speaks the words of God' (34a)

The first of these statements casts Jesus in the role of someone reporting what he has experienced. It uses the specifically forensic motif of witness and forensic imagery also lies behind 33 ('seal'; 'true'). The second also alludes to Jesus' speaking, but uses the envoy imagery. Both confirm the focus on speaking, already present in 31. Both are to be seen as relating the validity of Jesus' speaking to his origin in heaven. He has come from there as witness and envoy.

(iii) 'and no one accepts his witness.' (32b)
> 'He who has accepted his witness
> has set his seal to the fact that God is true' (33)

The first is a statement about response to Jesus and his communication (see ii), now expressed in forensic terms as 'witness,' but because of that, also a statement about Jesus and his rejection. The 'no one' cannot be inclusive because 33 tells of those who do accept him (like 1:11f). The seal image is also forensic language.

(iv) 'For he whom God sent speaks the words of God, (34a)
for he does not give the Spirit by measure. (34b)
The Father loves the Son (35a)
and has given all things into his hand.' (35b).

Jesus receives his authorisation as envoy from God (34a). The three statements
which follow expand the meaning of the Son's authority. It is best to take God as
the subject of all three.[41] Jesus' authority rests on God's equipping him with the
Spirit, loving him, and giving all things into his hands. Three further motifs are
thus employed to express Jesus' authority: pneumatic or charismatic authority,
familial or filial authority, and delegated authority. 'All things' echoes 'above all'
in 31. There, too, authority is the focus.

In itself the text, 'he does not give the Spirit by measure', is ambiguous. The following
grounds have been offered for taking Jesus as the subject: (i) the present tense, 'give'; compare
the aorist and perfect in 34a and 35b; (ii) elsewhere *pneuma* and *rhēma* are associated as gifts
of Jesus (6:63), so that 34b should be treated as a parallel to 34b; (iii) 35b can be read as
explaining why the Son can give the Spirit: he has been given it (35b); (iv) one might
expect a *gar* ('for') in 35 if the Father were the giver of the Spirit; (v) the coming of the Spirit
upon Jesus in 1:32f, while reflecting earlier christological traditional, now serves merely as a
sign for John the Baptist to help him recognise the one who was authorised and empowered
already in his pre-existence; (vi) the promise that Jesus would baptise with the Spirit (1:33b) is
being reflected here; (vii) the chapter had begun with reflection on the receiving of the Spirit
by those who are born again (3:5-8). The case is argued strongly by Thüsing and Porsch.[42]

But none of these arguments is finally convincing. 35 uses the present tense of *agapao*
immediately after 34b and the use of the perfect *dedōken* also puts the focus on the present
relationship. It may be that 1:32 is in mind, but hardly as the event when Jesus first received
the Spirit; rather it is a sign that Jesus has the Spirit. *rhēma* and *pneuma* are associated, but this
is so because Jesus has received the Spirit, the word, which he can then give. The conjunction
of the two words in 34 is best explained as a statement, first of all, of Jesus' sending to speak
the words and then of his complete equipping to do so, hence the *gar* of 34b. This best
explains 'without measure'; for, like 34a ('whom God sent') and especially 3:35 ('all things'),
it emphasises Jesus' complete authorisation. The focus of the context is not the giving of the
Spirit and the equipping of the disciples, but the authorisation and equipping of Jesus, though
earlier in the chapter the Spirit is related both to Jesus and to the disciples (3:3-8). Further, the
passage clearly refers to Jesus' earthly work of revelation, not his work as the exalted one who
gives the Spirit or has the Spirit sent. Strictly speaking, the Son is described as sending the
Paraclete (15:26), but only the Father 'gives' it (14:16). However the issue is settled, the
question of the basic structure of thought in 3:31-36 is largely unaffected. A third hypothetical
alternative might take *pneuma* as subject, but this is less convincing and would be without
parallel in John. The variant reading in a few manuscripts (apparently including Vaticanus)
which omit *pneuma* would most naturally require God as subject and this is probably why
other manuscripts include the word 'God' in the text (an impressive number of witnesses, but
probably outweighed by those that omit it, including such as p[66], p[75] and Sinaiticus).

Within these verses we also note for the first time the terms 'Father' and 'Son' for
Jesus and God in the words, 'The Father loves the Son' (35a), and the way the
relationship is described as one of love. 'The Son' also appears twice in 36.

The expression 'giving all things into his hands (literally: 'hand')' (35b) reflects
the Old Testament idiomatic expression, 'to fill the hands', meaning to ordain (eg.
a priest; Exod 29:9,29,35; Lev 8:33); it is used here by extension in the sense of
authorisation.[43] A variant occurs in 13:3 'knowing that the Father had given all
things into his hands' (compare also Matt 11:27a par. Luke 10:22a). The same idea

is reflected in 17:2, 'you have given him authority over all flesh'. *Panta* ('all things') is neuter, though John seems primarily concerned with people, as also the parallel in 17:2 indicates. *Pantōn* in 3:31 may also be neuter, especially if the two references form an inclusio, and not masculine as Schnackenburg and Brown suggest.[44]

(v) 'He who believes in the Son has eternal life;
   he who does not obey the Son shall not see life,
   but the wrath of God abides upon him' (36)

While our concern is christology not soteriology, we note that this is a statement of judgement and so recalls the forensic motifs of 32f. The sentence of judgement falls according to people's response to the Son and his words. The Son's coming and speaking is decisive for the future of people.

Within 3:31-36 we may trace the following christological statements:
1. Jesus comes from above, from heaven.
2. Jesus is above all.
3. Jesus has been sent by God.
4. Jesus tells/bears witness to what he has seen/heard,
    the words of God.
5. Jesus faces rejection, disobedience or belief.
6. Jesus is equipped fully with the Spirit.
7. Jesus is loved as Son by the Father.
8. Jesus has been given all things.
9. Response to Jesus brings judgement to life or death.
10. Jesus is the Son, God is the Father.

When we set these main christological points alongside the findings from other passages, a common pattern emerges. I shall illustrate this first by looking at another passage of summary character, 12:44-50. In its present position within the gospel it carries considerable weight. Olsson lists it as one of the evangelist's 'footnotes'[45], while Brown considers it a variant of 3:31-36.[46] Schillebeeckx considers it a resume of Johannine christology.[47] There are grounds for seeing it as at one time an independent piece of Johannine writing written by the author,[48] perhaps on the basis of earlier Jesus tradition,[49] or by an earlier author of the Johannine school,[50] or by a redactor using gospel's motifs and ideas and added it to the gospel as a summary of the message of the earthly ministry.[51] But without doubt its place within the transmitted text makes it Jesus' final public statement of any length, a summary statement of the purport of chapters 1-12.[52] In taking it as another starting point beside 3:31-36 we are not making a particular claim in relationship to its authorship, but using it to trace patterns within the existing text.

The following points emerge:

(i) 'he who believes in me believes not in me
    but in him who sent me' (44)
    'he who sees me see not me but him who sent me'(45)

Already these opening statements contain much that is repeated or developed in the rest of the passage. We note first the expression, 'him who sent me', repeated in 45 and again in 49: 'the Father who sent me'.

'He who believes in me' (cf. 3:36), in 45: 'he who sees me'; and in 46: 'everyone who believes in me', has its opposite in: 'if anyone hears my words and does not keep them' (47); and 'he who rejects me and does not receive my words' (48).

Of more directly christological interest is the coupling of response to Jesus with response to God: 'The one who believes in me believes not in me but in him who sent me' (44) and 'he who sees me sees not me but him who sent me.' This coupling receives an explanation in 49: 'I do not speak on my own authority, but he who sent me has given me commandment what I am to say and what I am to speak' and in 50: 'in regard to what I speak, as the Father has spoken to me, so I speak.' This recalls the statements in 3:31-36 about Jesus bearing witness to what had seen and heard (32) and speaking the words of God as the one sent and authorised by the Father' (34). Seeing Jesus as seeing the Father may be another way of saying this; it may go beyond it.

(ii) 'I have come as light into the world,
      that all who believe in me may not walk in darkness.'
      'I did not come that I might judge the world,
      but that I might save the world.' (48)

We note the statement, repeated in abbreviated form in 48, that Jesus came into the world. 47 also contains the contrasting imagery of light/darkness and identifies Jesus himself with light. 48 speaks of Jesus' saving and contrasts this with the role of judging, ie: condemning. When 50 speaks of the Father's commandment being 'eternal life', it probably means that, as the Son carries out the Father's commission, he brings to the world the opportunity for people to believe and so have life (like 3:36). The Son brings not condemnation, but light, life, salvation.

'Anyone who rejects me and does not accept my words
has one who judges him.
The word which I have spoken,
it shall judge him on the last day.' (48)

The verse speaks of a future judgement day and 'the one judging' is not God but Jesus' own word. 49f explains (*hoti*,'because') this along the lines that rejection of Jesus' word is nothing other than rejection of God's word. Response to Jesus is response to God.

Within 12:44-50 we may trace the following christological statements:
1.   Jesus has come into the world.
2.   Jesus has been sent by the Father.
3.   Jesus says what he has been commanded to say by God.
4.   To see Jesus is to see the one who sent him.
4.   Jesus is rejected or accepted.
5.   Jesus brings light, life, salvation
      and indirectly also judgement.
6.   God is the Father.

The third passage to be considered, 8:12-19, is typical of much of the material portraying Jesus' dialogue with the Jews. Here their concern is the validity of his self testimony and within Jesus' response a number of christological statements are made.

(i) 'I am the light of the world;
   he who follows me shall not walk in darkness
   but shall have the light of life.' (12)

This recalls 12:46 where Jesus will speak of his coming as light into the world. Instead of 'I have come' here we have one of the 'I am' sayings of Jesus' self presentation. As in the passage just considered response to Jesus determines whether one abides or walks in darkness or has the light of life.

The Pharisees challenge Jesus' claim about himself. Forensic language dominates the discussion that follows: 'witness', 'judging', 'truth', (all three also in 3:31-36). Jesus' witness is true (14; cf. 17) and should he judge, his judgement is true (16). By contrast, the Pharisees make their assessment according to the flesh. Unlike 3:31-36 the 'witness' here refers not to what Jesus has seen and heard (3:32), but directly to his self claim to be light coming into the world. Beyond the evidential dispute is the claim itself, expressed not only in terms of light but also in the following ways:

'If I witness concerning myself, my witness is true.
I know where I come from and where I am going;
you do not know where I come from and where I am going' (14)
'I am not alone,
but there is me and the Father who sent me.'(16)
'I am witnessing concerning myself
and my Father who sent me witnesses concerning me.' (18)
'You neither know me nor my Father.
If you had known me, you would have known my Father.' (19)

Jesus has come from the Father and returns to the Father. The Father sent him and witnesses concerning him. In this sense Jesus is his own authority, but is also ultimately authorised by the Father. Knowing Jesus is knowing God. This a variant of what appears in 12:45, seeing the Son is seeing the Father.
Within in 8:12-19 we may trace therefore the following christological statements:

1.   The Son comes from the Father.
2.   The Son returns to the Father.
3.   The Son knows where he comes from and where he is going.
4.   The Father has sent the Son.
5.   The Son witnesses concerning himself.
6.   The Father witnesses concerning the Son.
7.   The Son presents himself: 'I am the..'
8.   The Son offers the light of life or darkness.
9.   To know Jesus is to know the Father.
10. Jesus as Son speaks of God as the Father.

The most consistent elements to emerge from all three passages taken together are: the use of 'Father' for God and, by implication, 'Son' for Jesus; the sending of the Son by the Father; the coming of the Son into the world from the Father (from above, from heaven) and, by implication, his return; his authorisation by the Father (variously expressed: given the Spirit, 'all things', being commanded, borne witness to, as well as sent); his self claim expressed variously to be the one who represents the Father, speaks his words, bears his message and therefore brings life, light and salvation to those who believe in him. The pattern which emerges may be set out schematically as follows:

1. The Son comes from the Father.
2. The Father has sent the Son.
3. The Father has authorised the Son.
4. The Son makes the Father known.
5. Jesus is the Son and God is the Father.
6. The Son returns to the Father.

We shall use this as a framework for the next section in which we shall explore each of these and, in doing so, take into account other motifs and elements, including those noted in the three passages above. In proceeding in this way, having sampled three brief passages, I am not making the claim that they, alone, are sufficient evidence on which to assert that the outline does in fact represent the central structure of Johannine christology. Only the following steps can establish the extent to which this may be so. In these I will show how extensive this pattern is within the gospel and how the indicators outlined above support the claim. The one element which will be shown to require a more expansive treatment is the sixth element, 'The Son returns to the Father', for it entails a discussion of the very complex variety of images used in the gospel to express the significance of Jesus' death and the events associated with it. This emerges especially when we run through the gospel as a whole in the light of the findings concerning the patterns.

3. Common Elements of the Structure

This section considers the elements of the above structure in turn, examining the ways they are expressed and their frequency within the gospel.

(a) The Son comes from the Father

This takes many forms, but the most common are:

He comes (*erchomai*):
    from above (3:31; 8:23),
    from heaven (3:31; with *katabainō*: 3:13;
        and as the bread also 6:33,41,42,50,51,58),
    from God (3:2; 8:42f; 13:3; 16:30),
    from the Father (16:27,28; cf. 1:14; 17:8).
Similarly, he is not from this world (8:23; 15:19; 17:14,16).
The coming stands on its own
    without a statement of origin (10:10; 12:27; cf. 10:18),

with a denial that he comes of his own
   accord (7:27-29; 8:42f; cf.5:43),
or with the addition that he comes
   into the world (1:9; 3:20; 9:39; 12:46f; 18:37; 16:28),
   or to his own (1:11).
Sometimes the coming is expressed in association with motifs of
   light (1:9; 3:20; 12:46f; cf.8:12,14)
   or judgement (9:39; 12:46f)
The coming is associated with hopes for
   a prophet (6:14)
   or a Messiah who is coming (1:15,27,30; 4:23; 7:27,31,42;
      11:27; 12:13,15).

Often the Son's coming is alluded to in the form of a question about Jesus' origin, usually introduced by *pothen*, 'whence?'. Both in relationship to Jesus' messianic claims (7:27f,42) and more generally (8:14; 9:29f) the Jews are shown to be perplexed about where Jesus has come from. Pilate, too, asks the question (12:9). The issue of Jesus' origin is crucial for the author's christology. This is evident also in the way he introduces it into other narratives: 'Whence do you know me?' (1:48); whence does Jesus get the wine? (2:9), the water? (4:8), and the bread? (6:5; cf.4:33). Often the author associates the 'whence' question with the 'whither' question (3:8; 8:14) or associates a statement about origin with one about his return (8:42f; 13:3; 16:27f; cf. 3:13).[53]

(b) The Father has sent the Son

The words, *ho pempsas me* ('the one who sent me'), are almost a standard formula for God on the lips of the Johannine Jesus (4:34; 5:30; 6:38,39; 7:18,28,33; 8:26; 9:4; 12:44,45; 13:16,20; 16:5), sometimes directly linked with the designation of God as 'Father' (5:37; 6:44; 8:16,18,29; 12:49; 14:24), and usually presuming a reference to Jesus and God as 'Son' and 'Father' (5:23f; cf. 5:30,37 and most of the above references).

Apart from the aorist active participle no other form of *pempō* is used of the sending of the Son by the Father (cf. 13:20; 15:21,26; 16:7; 20:21). Instead the verb *apostellō* is used, either on its own in the indicative with implicit reference to 'Father' and 'Son' (5:38; 7:29; 8:42; 11:42; 17:8,18,21,23,25) or with explicit reference to 'God' (3:34; 6:29; 17:3), to 'Father' (6:57; 10:36; 20:21), to 'God' and 'Son' (3:17), or to 'Father' and 'Son' (5:36; cf.3:34f). But it is never used in the active aorist participial form, the form preserved exclusively for *pempō*.

This makes it likely that the use of one or the other verb is for the author a matter of stilistic preference and that both mean the same thing.[54] I find no evidence in John for Rengstorf's claim that *apostellō* stresses authority and *pempō*, God's involvement;[55] nor for Radermakers's or Seynaeve's opposite respective claims that the former or the latter focusses more on the purpose of the sending.[56] The same two verbs are used in the same way in relation to the sending of the disciples (*pempō*: 13:16,20; 20:21; *apostellō*: 4:38; 17:18; cf. 1:6 and 3:28 of John the Baptist). The words of Jesus' commission to the disciples in 20:21 bring both verbs together: 'As my Father has sent me (*apestalken*), even so I send (*pempō*) you.'

Closely associated with the motif of sending is that of the giving of the Son (3:16; cf. 3:17). Both terms are also associated in the promise of the coming of the Spirit, the Paraklete (giving: 7:39; 14:16; cf.3:34; sending 14:26; 15:26; 16:7).

(c) The Father has authorised the Son

The notion of authorisation belongs closely with that of sending, especially with the envoy motif. Most statements that speak of the Son coming from the Father also assume authorisation. It is also related to statements about the Son receiving something which he can pass on or seeing something to which he can bear witness. We shall turn to these in section (d) below.

Both 3:35 and 13:3 speak of the Father's giving all things into the hand(s) of the Son in association with the task to be fulfilled by the Son. This is best understood as authorisation in much the same way as 17:2 ('you have given him authority over all flesh'). Thüsing and Schnackenburg relate 17:2 only to Jesus' exaltation and its fruit, the giving of eternal life (17:3);[57] but while the giving does indeed relate to the easter event, this need not mean that 17:2a refers to anything other than the authorisation which sent Jesus on his course in the beginning.[58] A distinction must be drawn, as we shall see, between Jesus' authorisation 'authority', and his exaltation and glorification. This is already clear from 17:1, which portrays Jesus as praying for glorification in the immediate future (its hour has come). Similarly 3:31 ('above all') is associated with Jesus as the one who has come from above, from heaven.

The author often uses the word 'given' to express authorisation. Jesus says to Pilate: ('You would have no authority over me except it was given to you from above' 19:11), and of disciples ('no one can come to me unless it is given to him by the Father' 6:65). John the Baptist uses a similar formulation in discussing Jesus' authority: 'No one can do anything except it is given him from heaven' (3:27). The phrase 'from heaven' recurs shortly afterwards in the designation of Jesus as the one who is 'from heaven' (3:31). The verb *didōmi* occurs a number of times in ch. 17 in relation to authorisation. We have already noted 17:2a. Jesus speaks of 'having completed the work the work you gave me to do.' (17:4). Authorisation is also present where Jesus speaks of being given the Father's name (17:11f) and is also associated also with Jesus' being given God's word (17:8,14) and glory (17:22,24). The same chapter also speaks of believers as given to the Son in a way that recalls 6:65, already noted, which speaks of authorisation of disciples to come to Jesus (17:6,9; cf. also 6:37,39; 18:9). Disciples may also be meant in the enigmatic phrases, 'all that you have given him' in 17:2, 'all that you have given me' in 17:7 and 'what you has given me' in 10:29. Jesus also refers to his commissioning in these words in 18:11 'The cup which my Father has given me, am I not to drink it?'

In 5:26f being authorised and being equipped are linked: the Son is given life in himself and the authority to judge. 5:20f expresses this authorisation in close association with the Father's love for his Son, as in 3:35 ('the Father loves the Son and has given all things into his hands'; cf.3:34 which speaks of the giving of the

Spirit). Love and authorisation are also linked in 10:17f, where the Son speaks of his authority to lay down and take up his life again in accordance with his Father's will. In 15:10 the Son's remaining in the Father's love is linked with his keeping the Father's commandments. Authorisation and receiving commandments are also closely linked and will be dealt with in the following section. Authorisation is also expressed where Jesus emphasises that he has not come of his own accord (7:27-29; 8:42f) nor does anything of his own accord (7:17; 8:28; 5:30; 14:10).

(d) The Son makes the Father known

This idea is fundamental and widespread, but expressed in a variety of ways. There are two aspects: receiving and giving. Under receiving we may list statements which speaks of the Son knowing, having seen, having been told, taught, given, commanded. Under giving we might list: making known, giving, witnessing, teaching, and doing works which function in these revelatory ways.

The following illustrate the bringing together of both aspects:

The Son witnesses to what he has seen and heard (3:32),
tells of what he has seen (8:38; cf. 1:18; 5:37; 6:46; 3:11),
      of what he has heard (8:26,40; cf. 5:37; 3:8)
or makes it known (15:15).

He speaks as he has been taught (8:28: cf. 7:16,35; 3:2),
            been told (12:50)
            or commanded (12:49).

As he has been given, so he gives the Father's words (17:8),
                  the Father's name (17:6,11f,26),
                  the Father's glory (17:22,26).

He also does on earth what he has been commanded to do by the Father (15:10; 17:4; 5:36).
This includes laying down his life and taking it up again (10:18; 14:31; 18:37).
The Son does the works of the Father (6:38-40; 10:32,37; cf. 5:17,20).
The Son's concern is to complete the work given him to do (4:34).
This he does (17:4; 19:30 'it is finished').
Thus the Son does not act of his own accord (7:17; 8:28; 5:30; 14:10).

Because it is in the authority and the power of the Father that the Son does the works he has been commanded to do, it can equally be said that the Father is doing the works (14:10). Accordingly to have seen and known the Son is to have seen and known the Father (14:7-11; cf. also 1:18).

The unity of the Father and the Son is expounded in association with this christology of revelation, both in 10:32-38 and in 14:7-11. Jesus' being one with the Father (10:30) and his being in the Father and the Father in him (10:38; 14:10f cf. 14:20) is argued on the basis that he does the works of the Father, which he had been given to do (similarly 5:17f,20). Other factors play a role in the author's understanding of Jesus' relation to God and these will be examined below, but it is noteworthy that the author consistently returns to the model of the Son making the Father known.

This is also both the central thrust and the climactic claim of the prologue.
Jesus is the Word.
He has seen God and makes him known (1:18).
He was with God, was *theos* (1:1), *theos*, the only Son, in the bosom of the Father (1:18), and, as only Son from *(para)* the Father (1:14), he became flesh, manifested his glory (1:14) and made the Father known (1:18).

Correspondingly the gospel frequently records that a response to the Son is a response to the Father.
To believe in (12:44), see (12:45), honour (5:23), receive (13:20), know (14:7) or hate (15:23) the Son is to believe in, see, honour, receive, know or hate the Father who sent him. For the Son knows the Father and has made him known (14:7; 15:24; cf. 16:3; 17:3; 8:19; 15:21).
In this sense the Son has made known the truth (8:32,40; 17:17; cf. 5:33). For this purpose he came (18:37f). Grace and truth came through him (1:14,16). Therefore he can be identified as 'the truth' (14:6).

Here, too, belong the enigmatic 'I am' sayings in which Jesus presents himself as the revealer.

Within the variety of motifs listed there is a consistent pattern. It is that the Son makes the Father known. The Son has come as revealer, sent by the Father and authorised by him to speak and act in accordance with what he has been shown and been commanded. He does this in the power and authority given him by the Father and in unity with him. The effect of his making the Father known is to provoke crisis, to bring a turning point, for some to life, for others to death. Because the Son comes from the Father, as the one sent and authorised to make the Father known, he can claim: I am the source of water, the bread, the light, the shepherd, the door, the bread, the resurrection and the life, the way, the truth and the life for those who believe. For those who do not believe he is the bearer of judgement.

(e) Jesus as 'Son' and God as 'Father'

It is beyond dispute that these terms occur with great frequency throughout the gospel, so that I see no need other than to state this fact and point to the evidence of a concordance.

(f) Review

The elements of the structure identified initially in the three passages considered occur extensively within the gospel and often take a variety of forms. They also occur frequently in association with one another in much the same way as in the three passages considered earlier. This can be shown by considering first the summary statements within the gospel.

4. Summary Statements illustrating the Christological Structure

We have already considered the summary passages, 3:31-36 and 12:44-50. Apart from these the following illustrate the conjunction of the elements of the christological structure noted above.

At the beginning of the second major section of the gospel after the conclusion of the public ministry Jesus is introduced as:
'knowing that the Father had given all things into his hands and that he had come from God and was going to God,' (13:3)

In his dialogue with the Jews Jesus says that after they have lifted up the Son of Man they would come to a understand who Jesus is:
'Then you shall know that I am the one and that I do nothing of myself, but as the Father taught me, these things I speak. And he who sent me is with me. He has not left me alone, because I always do what is pleasing to him.' (8:28f)

A little earlier Jesus had cried out in similar terms:
'You do not know me and you do not know where I come from. I have not come of my own accord, but he who sent me is reliable, whom you do not know. I know him, because I came from him and he sent me.' (7:28f)

At the conclusion of his first farewell discourse Jesus says:
'but, that the world may know that I love the Father and as he has commanded me so I act, arise, let us go hence.' (14:31)

At the climax of the second farewell discourse he says:
'The Father loves you, because you have loved me and believed that I came from God. I came from the Father and have come into the world. Again I am leaving the world and I am going to the Father.' (16:27f)
The disciples find in this previous statement a clarity no longer masked in parable. Accordingly they declare that Jesus knows all things and has unquestionable credentials. They add: 'In this we believe that you are from God' (16:29f).

Within the passion narrative there are few utterances of Jesus, so that it is all the more significant that before Pilate Jesus declares:
'I was born for this and for this I came into the world to bear witness to the truth.' (18:37)

Jesus final words on the cross are:
'It is finished'. (19:30)
Near the beginning of his ministry Jesus had declared to his disciples:
'My food is to do the will of him who sent me and to finish his work.' (4:34; cf. also 9:3f).
Jesus' prayers sometimes summarise the aims of his ministry such as the one before Lazarus's grave. He prays,
'that they may believe that you sent me.' (11:42)

Jesus' prayer for his own also contains similar summaries:

'Now they know that all that you have given me is from you, because the words which you gave me I have given to them, and they have received and know truly that I came from you and they have believed that you sent me.' (17:7f; cf. also 21,23,25 and the discussion of this chapter below).

Nicodemus is also unwittingly the bearer of the christological statement if his words are understood at the Johannine level of faith: 'Rabbi, we know that you have come as a teacher from God. For no one can do the signs which you do unless God is with him.' (3:2)

These are by no means all the summary statements of the gospel, but they represent a significant portion.[59] Of those which remain perhaps the most distinctive are:

'These things are written that you may believe that Jesus is the Christ, the Son of God, and that believing you may have life in his name.' (20:31)
'I have believed that you are the Christ, the Son of God, coming into the world.' (11:27)
Later I shall show that such messianic confessions are consistently interpreted by the author within the framework of his basic christological structure. This is also the case with Thomas's acclamation (20:28) and the Johannine Petrine confession, where already the focus falls upon the words of eternal life which Jesus brings (6:68f).

Statements within the prologue, as well as the prologue as a whole, reflect the same basic structure:
'The Word became flesh and dwelt among us and we beheld his glory' (1:14);
'God, the only Son, who is in the bosom of the Father has made him known' (1:18).

Within the summary statements considered we have clear evidence that the elements of the christological structure identified above frequently occur in combination. In no one brief summary do they all occur. But what we do find is that the basic thought structure is presupposed and the fact that this is so in clearly summary statements at strategic points within the gospel indicates that we are dealing with an important outline of the christology underlying the gospel. This becomes even clearer when we examine specific passages.

5. John 17

In examining selected passages, finding a common underlying structure of christological thought, and testing its frequency within the gospel as a whole, we have been able to support the claim that this structure underlies the gospel's christology. This does not exclude the possibility that there are other such structures nor does it mean that the structure itself does not need expanding with further elements. Before turning now to a review of the gospel as a whole I want first to test our findings in relationship to John 17, the passage Käsemann took as his starting point for discussing Johannine christology and Ritt describes as a compendium and summa of Johannine theology.[60] By its position as the climax of

Jesus' words before his disciples, it carries significant weight. In it we find not only strong confirmation of what we have defined so far as the central structure but also focus on the significance of Jesus' death and return to the Father.

(a) John 17 - Review

The prayer begins with the address to God as 'Father' and immediately focusses upon the 'hour' of Jesus' death and glorification: 'Father the hour has come, glorify your Son, that your Son may glorify you' (17:1). The request is repeated in 17:5 'And now, Father, glorify me with the glory which I had with you before the world began.'

In the christological structure we have traced thus far the focus has not been upon Jesus' death and departure, but on his coming and earthly work. But we have already noted that statements about 'whence' are often linked with statements about 'whither' he goes, and ones about his coming with ones about his going. Here Jesus looks forward to his death and return to the Father, using the motif of glorification. The motif of pre-existent glory also appears in 17:24.

In 17:2 the revealer envoy pattern appears in the words: 'as you have given him authority over all flesh' (2a). This refers not to an authorisation yet to come as a result of Jesus' death and return, as Thüsing and Schnackenburg suggest, much along the lines of Matt 28:18,61 but rather, with Barrett and Becker,[67] to the fact that as the sent one Jesus was authorised 'that he might give eternal life to what was given to him' (2b), his disciples. It carries much the same meaning as the giving of all things into the Son's hands in 3:34f and 13:3. We have noted the two uses of 'give', one more directly christological and referring to authorisation of the Son, the other related to the granting of disciples to Jesus.

The 'eternal life' (2) comes according to Jesus from knowing 'the only true God and Jesus Christ whom you have sent' (3). Knowing the Father and knowing the Son are not two separate acts, but to be understood in the light of the basic christological structure. The Son is the Father's envoy. Similarly 4 reflects that structure when it speaks of Jesus finishing the work he had been given to do and having so glorified the Father.

6 continues to draw upon the revealer envoy structure: 'I have manifested your name to the people whom you have given me from the world.' 'Name', like 'glory', entails something of the power and the person of the Father. This is how the disciples know the Father. This is the 'word' of revelation to which they hold (6b). The extrapolation of the central structure is also evident in 7f. 'Now they know that all that you have given me is from you, because the words which you gave me I have given to them, and they have received and know truly that I came from you and they have believed that you sent me.'

The following verses contain Jesus' prayer for his disciples and their future protection and unity. But here, too, the structure surfaces. When 10 begins by affirming that all that belongs to the Father belongs to the Son, it does so with a view to the disciples' belonging both to the Son and to the Father; but the broader statement with which the verse begins (using neuter forms: 'all mine is yours and

yours is mine') may well reflect the motif of the structure according to which the
Father has given all things into the Son's hands. This element is certainly present
in 11f when Jesus speaks of having been given the Father's name.

In 11 Jesus refers again to his return to the Father, 'I am coming to you' and
repeats this in 13. The revealer envoy structure is also apparent where the Son and
disciples are compared. As the Son, who gave them the Father's word, is hated, so
the disciples will be hated; as the Son is not of this world, so the disciples do not
belong to this world (14,17). The Son came from the Father and is therefore not of
the world. But because the disciples received his word, they, though coming from
the world, now no longer belong to it. The analogy is not exact, but sufficient for
the structure to be used also of the sending of the disciples into the world: 'As you
sent me into the world, so I sent them into the world.' (18). The motif of
sanctification, also applied both to Jesus and to his disciples (17f), should be taken
in close association with the sending and thus echo the notion of equipping (cf.
10:36). What equips the disciples is the word the Son has given, the truth to which
he came to bear witness (17,19; cf. 18:37). In the case of the disciples there is no
indication that what they will achieve should be interpreted cultically, nor need
this be the case when Jesus sanctifies himself (18), though some see here an
allusion to his death as a sacrifice.[63]

In 20-23 the parallel is continued in the prayer that the unity which exists between
Father and Son may exist between Son and disciples and among the disciples
together, all with the common goal expressed in terms of the structure: 'That the
world may know that you sent me and that you have loved them as you have loved
me' (23).

The climax of the prayer expresses the desire that the disciples might join the Son
in the glory and love given him before the world began. This reflects the equipping
and authorising of the Son, but in a manner consistent with the basic christological
structure which sees the Son not as an impersonal emissary, but as the one who has
been loved, authorised and commissioned (cf. 3:34f). The structure surfaces also in
the concluding two verses which speak of the Son's knowing the Father, and, as
the one whom the Father sent, making his name known.

Jesus twice referred to his coming to the Father (11,13). In this final segment Jesus
desire that his disciples might be where he is and see his heavenly glory to which
he returns forms an inclusion with his prayer for glorification in 17:2 and 5.

(b) John 17 - Conclusions

The review of ch 17 confirms that the christological structure we have outlined
functions as the basic structure beneath the text. At the same time we have noted
that the events forming the climax of Jesus' ministry are described in two ways:
one speaking simply of his return to the Father and the other of his glorification.
None of the passages considered thus far had thematised this element in relation to
the central structure beyond speaking simply of the Son's return to the Father.
Associated with Jesus' death and return is his commissioning of the disciples and
his concern for their unity in the future. In the context of speaking of their
sanctification and sending, Jesus speaks of sanctifying himself. A cultic

interpretation of Jesus' death (eg: vicarious sacrifice) may, but need not, be implied by this. In the review of the gospel which follows we shall find further expansion or different ways of speaking of Jesus' death and return.

IIB. THE STRUCTURE OF JOHANNINE CHRISTOLOGY

A SURVEY OF THE GOSPEL

1. John 1 - 5

John 1 - 5 Review

The Prologue, the gospel's 'overture', reflects the underlying structure of the author's christology. The Logos/Son, with the Father, in the bosom of the Father, even bearing the name 'God', comes into the world, becomes flesh and tents among us, manifests glory, and makes the Father known. Many of the surface manifestations here are unique and may add nuances of meaning not found elsewhere. These include: the Logos motif itself, his being 'in the beginning with God', that he 'was God' (cf. 20:28), his mediatorship of creation, his possible other activity 'asarkos' in salvation history (if this is present); his becoming flesh, his tenting among us, his being 'full of grace and truth', his fullness, his being in the bosom of the Father and the 'God, only Son', *monogenēs theos*. To many of these we shall return in Part III, but the structure beneath the unusual text as it stands in the gospel is clearly and predominantly that of the revealer pattern. The focus on the Son's making the Father known is so much the centre of attention that the prologue does not even mention Jesus' death, return to the Father and events associated with it. The references to John the Baptist will be taken up in what follows.

In 1:19-34 John the Baptist witnesses that he, himself, is neither the Christ, nor Elijah, nor the Prophet. Instead he points to Jesus, the one who comes after him. Jesus is 'the lamb of God who takes away the sin of the world' (1:29). He comes after John, but is before him in rank and time (1:30; cf. 1:15). Through John he becomes manifest to Israel (1:31). John knows who he is only after he sees the Spirit descend and abide upon him: he is the one who will baptise with the Spirit; he is the Son of God or the elect one (1:33f). The Son's pre-existence, coming and being manifest to Israel, reflects generally the central structure. The messiahship of Jesus will be shown below to be fully integrated within it.

Two features of the text do not relate to the central structure as we have delineated it: the lamb of God taking away sin and the giving of the Spirit. The former may function as an inclusio with 19:26 if it contains passover allusions in relation to Jesus' death. We shall see that both relate to the significance of Jesus' death and will be treated in detail in that context.

In 1:35-51 Jesus' first disciples come to him. John repeats, 'Behold the lamb of

God!' (1:36). The two disciples ask where Jesus stays and are invited to come and see (1:38f). Probably more than the literal sense is intended by the narrative. Messianic affirmation is the focus of the encounters which follow, depicting Jesus as fulfilment of scripture promise (1:45). The narrative of Jesus' meeting with Nathanael employs irony. Both Nathanael's words about Jesus' town of origin and his question about where Jesus obtains the ability to know about him suggest to the reader the truth of the central structure: Jesus is the Son who has come from the Father. Jesus accepts Nathanael's messianic affirmation: 'You are the Son of God; you are the king of Israel' (1:49). It will find its echo in the passion narrative with the superscription of the cross.

But 1:50f suggests there is more to be seen: '"You shall see greater things than these." And he said, "Truly truly I say to you, you shall see the heaven opened and the angels of God ascending and descending upon the Son of Man."' We shall discuss this passage in more detail in IIIA4 below, but for the present we may note two main interpretations. The one sees Jesus promising Nathanael that he will see Jesus as the medium of revelation between heaven and earth in the ministry that is to follow. The other sees here a reference to Jesus' death and exaltation. The former interpretation would interpret this saying as giving expression to the central thrust of the christological structure we have identified. The other would need to include this saying as another example of the variety of motifs, yet to be examined, which speak of Jesus as Son of Man and expand upon the meaning of Jesus' death and return to the Father, to which we return in IIC9 below.

The narrative of the wedding feast at Cana and the account of the temple expulsion both appear to interpret Jesus' death and resurrection.[1] The clues in the former are probably the dating 'on the third day',[2] and certainly the reference to Jesus' hour as having not yet come,[3] and perhaps also a eucharistic allusion in the wine imagery.[4] In the latter it is explicit in the reference to Jesus' being consumed because of his zealous act in regard to the temple (2:17) and in the author's interpretation of Jesus' saying about the destroying and raising of the temple (2:21f; cf. 2:19). The symbolism of the wedding feast also suggests that eschatological hope, often expressed as a feast, sometimes a wedding feast, is fulfilled. The mention of jars for purification may indicate that both passages have to do with the replacement of the Jewish cult through Jesus.[5]

While both passages serve to expand symbolically the meaning of Jesus' death and resurrection, there may be traces of the structure in the irony concerning the origin of the wine, unknown to the chief steward, but known to the servants (2:9).[6] This is more likely to be so if a directly eucharistic allusion is not present and what is being celebrated under the symbol is the nourishment that Jesus brings as the revealer. An allusion to both is possible, as both are present in the use of the bread imagery in ch. 6. The structure is, however, reflected in 2:11 where the author remarks that in this first Cana sign Jesus manifested his glory. This is doubtless the same as the 'glory of the only Son of the Father' of 1:14 and thus interprets the miracle at one level as part of the Son's revelation. We shall consider in IIC6 below the way the author integrates signs within the structure of his christology. Perhaps Jesus' behaviour in the temple should also be seen as an expression of judgement in fulfilment of Malachi's warning that Lord would suddenly appear in his temple in judgement (Mal 3:1) and so interpret his coming as confrontation.[7]

The concluding verses of ch.2 show Jesus refusing to acknowledge as true faith those who respond to him merely at the level of the miraculous. Ch. 3 begins with the Pharisee, Nicodemus, making an equivalent response: 'You are a teacher come from God, because no one can do these miracles which you do unless God is with him.' (3:2). This is another example of Johannine irony. For, understood at the right level, they do indeed express the truth about Jesus and echo the basic structure. He is indeed a teacher come from God and does indeed do the signs because God is with him (3:2). But this statement must be understood in the light of 3:11-21,31-36.[8]

The teacher motif remains important in what follows, where attention is being drawn both to Jesus and his disciples at the same time. Thus the true teacher is the one who can see the kingdom of God because he is (born) from above (3:2f). Nicodemus is not a true teacher (3:10); a person born of the Spirit is (3:8). The contrast from 3:3 onwards is between Nicodemus and anyone who is born of the Spirit. But implicitly there is also a link between those born of the Spirit and Jesus of whom this is uniquely so.[9] This association with Jesus explains the use in the wind/spirit image of the 'Whence - Whither' motif, employed ironically elsewhere to express the christology of the central structure. People like Nicodemus hear the sound of Jesus' words, but do not know where he comes from or where he goes (he is 'from above'! 3:31); nor do they comprehend the witness of people of the Spirit. They bear witness to what they have known and have seen (3:11). In 3:32 a similar formulation is used directly of Jesus. The central structure is of major importance in 3:1-11, as it is also in 3:31-36 in which a number of its themes are echoed.

3:12 introduces a contrast between what Jesus has been saying thus far, about his coming to earth, and what he might say about 'heavenly things' (3:12). This recalls the promise to Nathanael of 'greater than these'. The heavenly things are the events associated with his death (3:13-15). We explore these, including the post Easter perspective represented already in 3:11 and 3:13 and their relationship to the argument of the context, in IIIA4 below, but for the present we note: ascent and descent of the Son of Man; the lifting up of the Son of Man. Descent refers to Jesus' coming to earth; the rest add to a range of motifs associated with Jesus' death and return.

In 3:16-21 the motifs of the coming and the sending of the Son into the world reappear in passages highlighting the crisis of life and condemnation which the Son brings. In IIIA2 we shall explore the extent to which 3:16 is primarily a reference to Jesus' coming to earth as revealer, as in the central structure and the previous reference to him as the only Son (1:14, 18) or whether it does not (perhaps, also) make reference to Jesus' death and its significance, possibly with allusion to the sacrifice of Isaac. 3:17 refers directly to God's sending his Son into the world; 3:18 refers to faith in him as the only Son and 3:19 repeats the reference to his coming into the world, using the imagery of light, a further echo of the prologue and of a common motif in passages in which the underlying christological structure of the gospel comes to expression.

Ch.4 continues the contrast between the old and the new, above all in the assurance that now old centres of worship are superfluous and true worship is in spirit and is now possible. The Samaritan makes her faltering journey of faith from acknowledgement of Jesus as a prophet (4:19), to tentative, but nevertheless missionary proclamation of his messiahship (4:29), which leads to the acclamation by her kinsfolk that he is 'the saviour of the world' (4:42). Apart from these messianic affirmations the narrative subtly portrays Jesus as the giver of the water of life and its brilliant irony has been well set out recently in Duke's study.[10] This is the life he brings as the one sent from the Father. In the dialogue with the disciples the structure is also apparent when Jesus refers to his food as doing the will of him who sent him and completing his work. The context relates this work to mission and speaks in turn of Jesus' sending the disciples.

The episode of the healing of the official's son (4:46-54) illustrates the life Jesus brings as well as appropriate and inappropriate faith. The miracle story which follows in ch. 5 illustrates the same healing life, but also leads to major controversy with the Jews. In reply to the accusation that he had caused someone to break the sabbath, Jesus says: 'My Father is working up till now and I am working' (5:17). The Jews accuse him further of calling God his own Father and making himself equal with God (5:18). Jesus' reply speaks of himself in family apprenticeship terms: 'The Son cannot do anything of himself but only what he sees his Father doing. For what he does, this the Son likewise does. The Father loves the Son and shows him all which he himself is doing, and greater works that these will he show him, that you may marvel' (5:19f). Thus the central structure is visible where the Son argues his 'equality' with the Father on the grounds of his obedient subordination. The family apprenticeship motif, which is developed christologically in 19f, probably explains the change to the present tense, where the usual model of Jesus doing or telling what he has seen and heard is replaced by one which speaks of continuing observation and instruction during Jesus' earthly ministry. In addition the focus here is not on giving of revelation once received, but on unity of will and action in the present. This change has occasioned considerable discussion in treatments of Johannine christology and we shall address them in IIIB2 and 3 below.

The structure is also apparent when the Son speaks of his being authorised to judge and to give life (5:22,26f), and of his doing the will of him who sent him (5:23f,30). The activity of the Son in giving life encompasses his present ministry. In that sense raising the lame man has become the springboard for a discourse about Jesus' raising the dead and giving life. But 5:28-29 extend the focus to the eschaton, one of the few such references to Jesus' activity in the future resurrection. The central structure of the author's christology does not extend to include references to future parousia, resurrection and judgement, though these need not be seen as incompatible with it. We shall return to this theme in IIIB1 below.

Finally two further elements are to be noted. The words 'Son of Man' appear in 5:27 in reference to Jesus as judge. We shall note elsewhere the association of the title 'the Son of Man' and judgement motifs in John. The other feature is the promise to which the Son alludes when he says that the Father 'will show him greater things than these that you may marvel' (5:20). Could the contrast here be similar to the one in 3:13 and possibly behind 1:50f, so that present ministry and the events associating with the Son's death and return to the Father are being alluded to here as well?[11] The difficulty here is that the 'greater things' must refer to what immediately follows, namely the Son's giving life to whom he will. It is unlikely that this should be taken to refer to Jesus' post Easter activity and not his earthly ministry. The present tense is used to describe this activity: the Son makes alive (5:21). The contrast here is probably between the miracle as a literal act of healing and the resurrection life the revealer offers.[12] This would correspond, in turn, to the interpretation which sees in 1:50f a contrast between seeing Jesus as Messiah because of miracles and seeing him as the ladder between heaven and earth.

In the discourse about Jesus' self-testimony and the testimony borne to him by others (5:31-47), the content of each testimony is expressed using the language of the central structure. 'The works which the Father has given that I should complete, the works themselves that I do, bear witness that the Father sent me.' (5:36). Unlike the Son the Jews have never 'heard his voice or seen his form' (5:37). They have not believed in 'him whom he sent' (5:38). Jesus has come in the name of his Father (5:43). But they do not accept him nor do they accept the glory which comes from God alone (5:44). The Son will not be their accuser before God; Moses will, who bears witness to the Son (8:45). This recalls 12:47f according to which Jesus will not judge, but his word will. The passage as a whole also recalls 8:12-19 considered above and similarly reflects the basic christological pattern.

John 1 - 5   Conclusions

1. Within these chapters the revelation pattern clearly underlies much of both the discourse and the narrative material. From the prologue we learn that the Son may be described as the Logos, with God in the beginning, in the bosom of the Father, 'God', mediator of creation, the only Son, and possibly active in salvation history. The pre-existence is reiterated by John the Baptist (1:15,30) and presupposed by the many statements which reflect the revelation pattern of christology. The Son comes as the one sent by the Father to make him known (1:18; 3:2,16-19, 31-35; 4:34; 5:17-20,22-24,26f,30,36-38,43f). In 4:34, and especially in 5:17-30, Jesus' mission is described as doing the works of the Father (cf. also 5:36; 3:2). The uniqueness of the Son is also expressed in 3:16,18. 5:17-20 reflects in particular on the relationship of the Son and Father, explaining it in terms of an equality in which Jesus shares the Father's tasks in obedient submission to him, and speaks also of a present relationship on earth, rather than the usual pattern of the revelation model where the Son reports what he has seen and heard. This reflects the focus in the context upon the exercise of judgement rather than revelation. Sometimes the author playfully alludes to Jesus' origin (in Nathanael's comment about Jesus' town of origin and the source of his knowledge about him, 1:46,48; in the origin of the wine, 2:9; in Nicodemus's 'from God', 3:2; in the mysterious whither and whence of the wind/Spirit, in the Samaritan woman's question whence Jesus draws his water, 4:11).

What Jesus brings is represented in the prologue as word, light (also 3:19-21), life, authority to become God's children (also 3:3,5), glory (also 2:11), grace and truth, and, supremely, knowledge of God. It is also symbolically represented in the wine of a wedding feast replacing the jars of purification water (2:1-10), the living water

(4:10), the raising of the near dead (4:46-54), and the healing of the lame (5:1-9). The miracles display the glory of the Son of the Father (1:14; 2:11) and this is understood within the framework of the revelation pattern, so that true faith goes beyond hailing the miraculous quality of deeds and sees in them a sign that he is the Son come from the Father (cf. 3:23-25; 3:1-3; 4:48). By contrast even with simple faith in miracles which may move on, unbelief means refusal of light and condemnation to judgement (3:18-21,36).

At a number of points the motif of messiahship appears (1:20,25,41,45-49; 4:29; cf. the Son of God, 1:34,49; a prophet, 4:19; the prophet or Elijah, 1:21,25; saviour of the world, 4:42). The episode with the Samaritan shows clearly that ultimately all such expressions mean: Jesus is the bearer of life in terms of the revelation pattern.

2. At some points the material goes beyond the revelation pattern and focusses on the significance of Jesus' death, his return to the Father, and events associated with it. In particular we noted two places where a contrast is made between what is now available or to be seen during Jesus' ministry and something greater which lies ahead. The first is 1:51 which we take to refer not to Jesus' earthly ministry of revelation, as some do, but to his coming exaltation as Son of Man. The second is 3:12 which introduces a contrast between earthly things and heavenly things in Jesus' words and in the latter includes: the ascension of the Son of Man, who descended, and the exaltation of the Son of Man, so that all who believe may have life. It is unlikely that the other verse which speaks of something greater to be shown to the Son (5:20) also refers to this event, for its specific reference is to Jesus' authorisation for judgement to life and death, even though we also note the presence of Son of Man (5:27), but here it refers to his judging role in the future (also reflected indirectly in 5:45).

The event of Jesus' death and return to the Father is heralded in the words about the hour yet to come in 2:4 and Jesus prophesies his death in the words of Ps 69:10 in 2:17. The resurrection of Jesus, probably hinted at in 2:1, is also prophesied in the temple saying (2:19).

The author notes also that after this event the disciples would remember both Jesus' words and the applicability to him of the scripture in which he prophesied his death because of his zeal for God's house (17). Other benefits associated with this coming event include the sending of the disciples, alluded to in 3:11; 4:35-38, and, perhaps, given a model in mission by the Samaritan woman (4:29); possibly the eucharist (if the wine also refers to it in 2:1-11) and the gift of the Spirit (1:33), which in ch. 3 is spoken of in association with new birth imagery in such a way that the conversation moves from Jesus the true teacher, in contrast to Nicodemus the teacher of Israel, to the disciples as true teachers born from above, an anachronistic allusion to the witness they would fulfil after Easter.

In addition there is a saying which highlights the significance of Jesus' death in itself (1:29). In speaking of Jesus as the lamb of God taking away the sin of the world a sacrificial interpretation of Jesus' death is likely. Possibly passover imagery is implied. The full significance of the verse must be considered in the light of the gospel as a whole because nothing in the context develops the theme further. Some also see a sacrificial reference in 3:14 ('lifting up of the Son of Man') and 3:16 (given up to death, perhaps like Abraham giving up Isaac). So much depends, here, too, on use of terms elsewhere in the gospel ('lifting up', 'Son of Man'), so that we will consider all three passages within the systematic survey of alleged references to vicarious atonement and its role in the gospel in IIIA2 below.

2. John 6 - 12

John 6 - 12 Review

The feeding of the 5000 in ch. 6 forms the basis for a presentation of Jesus as the bread of life in the discourse which follows. The messianic response of those who were fed in the miracle (6:14f) fails to grasp Jesus' true significance. It remains at the level that Nicodemus reached, the level of the material. There is a faint echo of the deeper reality when Jesus is hailed as the prophet 'coming into the world' and faith would have its deeper understanding of messiahship, as the passion narrative shows. The feeding miracle is primarily a sign of the true nourishment which comes from God.

The narrative of Jesus walking on the water confirms to the eyes of faith that Jesus acts with divine power. As in Mark Jesus presents himself to his anxious disciples with the declaration, 'It is I (egō eimi). Do not be afraid' (6:20; cf. Mark 6:50). He is not a ghost or the like.[13] Nothing in the immediate passage (nor its parallel in Mark) suggests egō eimi specifically alludes to the divine name,[14] even though a divine claim is implied by Jesus' miracle, expressed in the Matthean parallel by acclamation of Jesus as Son of God (Matt 14:33).[15] Whether such a meaning would be given to the text by the author or the first readers depends upon wider consideration of its use throughout the gospel.

In the present state of the text the discourse presents two foci when expounding nourishment symbolised in the feeding miracle. In 6:27 Jesus speaks of 'the food which endures to eternal life, which the Son of Man will give you; for on him the Father has set his seal.' This corresponds to 6:51-58. Here Jesus speaks of the bread which he will give (51). It is the flesh and blood of the Son of Man (53), the true food and drink (55). The eucharistic allusions here and probably elsewhere in the chapter (6:11,23) confirm that the use of the future 'he will give' (27, 51) is intentional.[16] Probably the occurrence of the title 'Son of Man' suggests the same, namely, that these passages refer to Jesus' post Easter activity. The words, 'and the bread which I give is my flesh for the life of the world' (6:51), may refer primarily to Jesus' eucharistic gifts of his flesh (and blood);[17] they may also,[18] or perhaps primarily,[19] refer to his death as a vicarious act. We shall return to this question in IIIA2 below. In terms of our analysis, the sayings which represent this first focus belong among the motifs associated with Jesus' death and return to the Father and not with what we have delineated so far as the central structure.

There is another focus of the text, found in particular in the contrast made between the manna which came down from heaven and Jesus as the bread come down from heaven (6:31-51b).[20] Jesus offers this bread now in his person, much as he had

offered living water to the woman of Samaria. Within the discussion elements of
the structure appear frequently. The Son has come, has descended, as bread from
heaven (6:33,38,41,42,50,51). Irony underlines Jesus' heavenly origin, when the
Jews claim to know his parentage (6:41). Jesus declares: 'I have not come from
heaven to do my own will, but the will of him who sent me' (6:38). The sending
motif occurs frequently (6:38,39,44). The structure also surfaces in the words:
'Not that anyone has seen the Father except the one who is from God, he has seen
the Father' (6:46). Jesus, the Son, sent by the Father, has come into the world with
the offer of life, presenting himself as God's representative, and using the 'I am'
presentation formula.

The sequel to the discourse (6:59-71) presents a reaction of certain disciples to
Jesus' 'hard saying' (6:60). This may refer to Jesus' requirement that people eat
his flesh and drink his blood (6:53-57);[21] or it may refer to Jesus' claim to have
come down from heaven (6:31-51,58).[22] In 6:62f Jesus contrasts what offends them
with something greater: 'What if you were to see the Son of Man ascending where
he was before? The spirit is what makes alive, the flesh is not at all profitable. The
words which I have spoken to you are spirit and life.'

These words recall the dialogue with Nicodemus and represent a challenge to a
way of perceiving Jesus which sees him only at the level of the flesh, as
Nicodemus had done. In this sense they pick up the response of the Jews who
failed to see the meaning of the sign, earlier in the chapter (6:14f,26). Jesus' words
are spirit and life because Jesus has come down from heaven. This, then, is another
way of saying his words are bread from heaven. This recalls the contrast in 3:31
between the one from heaven and the one from the earth. It would seem that the
second focus forms the immediate background for the saying. They refer primarily
to the words of the Son come from the Father and not directly to the promised
offer of life in Jesus' flesh and blood.[23] A reference to the latter would have been
awkward because of the two different uses of the word, 'flesh'.

This means that probably what offended the disciples is the notion of Jesus'
descent from heaven. This receives confirmation in the fact that Jesus sets in
contrast to it a reference to his ascent as Son of Man to where he was before. If
they cannot 'stomach' his claim of descent, what will they do when he ascends?
The presumed reader knows well that this ascent will be by way of the cross: the
offence will then be even greater;[24] the reader also knows that the ascent will bring
greater benefit,[25] including an understanding through the Spirit of Jesus' words.
Both levels operate here: greater offence at the level of the flesh, greater benefit at
the level of the spirit. Accordingly we find here a further example of the other,
more positive, contrast in ch. 3 between Jesus' earthly revelation and the heavenly
things related to his ascent and exaltation as Son of Man. What we have described
as the central structure describes primarily the coming and revealing; consistently
we also find another field of concepts describing what comes next, the events
surrounding Jesus' death and return, as something greater.

Peter voices the faith of those who perceive Jesus in his true role as the revealer
envoy: 'To whom shall we go? You have the words of eternal life, and we have
believed and know that you are the holy one of God' (6:68f). Probably related to
the tradition of Peter's confession in the synoptic gospels, the confession is

understood fully within the frame of reference of the revelation pattern.

Jesus' brothers operate at the level of the flesh in suggesting Jesus go to Judea to display his wonder working powers. Jesus responds with reference to his 'time' not yet having come (7:6,8). While the immediate reference is to when Jesus will go to Jerusalem, readers would doubtless recall the use of 'hour' in Jesus' response to his mother at Cana: 'My hour has not yet come' (2:4) and connect this, in turn, with the hour of Jesus' death, exaltation and glorification referred to explicitly later (12:23,27,31f; 17:1). Perhaps even the use of the word 'to go up, to ascend' contains hints of Jesus' ascension (7:8).[26] The narrative contributes thus to the material concerned with Jesus' death and return to the Father.

In the Jerusalem scenes which follow, the Jews voice their questions and their objections to Jesus and in both the questions and the answers the central structure has been determinative. 'My teaching is not mine but his who sent me' (7:16). Jesus 'seeks the glory of him who sent him' (7:18). The author's use of irony is present, when he pictures some Jews wondering if Jesus is the Christ, but being disturbed that he did not fit the expectation that the origin of the Christ was to be unknown (7:27). Jesus responds: 'You know me and you know where I come from; I have not come of my own accord, but he who sent me is true, whom you do not know. I know him, because I am from him and he sent me' (7:28f).

Noting Jesus' escape from the Jews' hostile response, the author refers again to Jesus' death: 'His hour had not yet come' (7:30). And in response to a delegation sent to arrest him Jesus continues: 'A little while I am with you and I am going to him who sent me. You will seek me and not find me, and where I am you cannot come' (7:33f). The perplexed Jews speculate whether Jesus is going into the diaspora to teach the Greeks (7:35f). The irony of this is that the Christian mission will indeed reach the Gentile world, but the reader knows that this will happen as a result of Jesus' death and return to the Father. The promise of the Spirit which follows in 7:37-39 also belongs to this complex of events to come, as the author indicates by the explanation in 7:39 that the promised Spirit was not yet available to the disciples at the time of speaking because Jesus was not yet glorified. Yet the saying of Jesus also offers something to the listeners of the time: 'If anyone thirsts, let him come to me and drink'. As in ch. 6 we find here a double focus, one which views the gifts brought by the revealer (37); the other (38) takes this further and overlays it with reference to the post Easter gift of the Spirit. The former belongs within the revealer pattern traced out in the central structure; the second belongs to the material associated with Jesus' death and return to the Father.

Irony features again in the discussions among the Jews of Jesus' origin in 7:40-52. We have already considered 8:12-19 and traced in it the emergence of the central structure. 8:20 again refers to Jesus' hour not yet having come. The following verses show Jesus returning to the theme of his going away and using again the language of the central structure: 'You are from below, but I am from above; you from this world, I am not from this world' (8:23); 'He who sent me is true and what I heard from him, this I speak to the world' (8:26). In the same context Jesus warns: 'If you do not believe that I am, you will die in your sins' (8:24). When the Jews reply, 'Who are you?', they understand Jesus to have meant something like: 'I am who I claim to be.' This may be an ironical allusion to Jesus as 'I am', ie:

bearing the name of Yahweh.[27] But Jesus responds by saying he is what he has
been saying to them all along from the beginning (8:25)[28] and obviously alludes to
the repeated variant explanations that derive from the central structure and must
mean something like: 'I am the sent one,' as in 8:28.[29]

8:28f gives an answer to the question who Jesus is by using the central structure:
'Then you shall that I am (who I claim to be), and I do nothing of myself, but as
the Father taught me, so I speak and he who sent me is with me; he has not left me
alone, because I always do what is pleasing to him.' The introduction to this
formulation is equally interesting. It should not be read with Bultmann to indicate
that Jesus' response implies that they will see him as Son of Man and judge.[30] The
rest of the verse shows that the focus is on coming to know he is the sent revealer.
It speaks rather of the lifting up of the Son of Man as the event which will make
such knowledge available. Again two levels operate. At one level the verse refers
to the Jews' crucifixion of Jesus. At another, it refers to Jesus' exaltation. Again,
as in 3:14 and 6:62, where this greater event is looked forward to, we have the Son
of Man title. Again the affirmation of the central structure is set beside a further
complex of ideas which concentrate on Jesus' death and return to the Father.

The dispute with the Jews heightens in the rest of ch. 8. Again Jesus defends
himself, using terms familiar to us from the central structure: 'What I have seen
with the Father, I speak and what you have heard from the Father you do not do'
(8:38); 'now you seek to kill me, a human being, who has spoken the truth to you
which I heard from God' (8:40); 'If God were your Father, you would love me,
because I came out from the Father and have arrived here; I have not come of my
own accord, but he sent me' (8:42). Jesus does not seek his own glory, but God's
(8:50,54). 'The Father is the one who glorifies me, of whom you say, "he is our
God", and you have not known him, but I know him. If I were to say I do not
know him, I should be a liar like you. But I do know him and I keep his word'
(8:54f). The conflict reaches its climax when Jesus asserts his pre-existence:
'Before Abraham came into being, I am' (8:58). Again the precise meaning of 'I
am' will depend on factors outside the immediate passage. The attempted stoning
(8:59) might suggest blasphemous utterance of the divine name,[31] but need not
either here or elsewhere. Need it mean more than the stupendous claim: I am in
existence since before Abraham?[32]

Ch. 9 is primarily narrative material, though within it the central structure appears
explicitly in Jesus' affirmation that he must works the works of him who sent him
while it is day (9:3f) and is implicit in the ironical treatment of the Jews'
discussion of Jesus' origins ('this man is not from God' 9:16; 'we know that God
has spoken to Moses, but this man, we do not know where he comes from.' 9:29)
and the blind man's response, 'If he were not from God, he could not do anything'
(9:33). It should also be seen in the etymology of Siloam: 'the sent one', as a
symbolic reference to Jesus as the fount of healing. The symbolism of light and
darkness, blindness and sight, lifts the story into being a proclamation of Jesus, the
light come into the world (so explicitly, 9:5) and by implication also the bearer of
judgement when people refuse the light: 'For judgement I have come into this
world, that those who do not see may see and that those who see may become
blind' (9:39). The chapter also contains an affirmation of Jesus as 'a prophet'
(9:17) and mention of confessing Jesus as the Christ (9:22), only here in John the

faith called for ultimately by Jesus is faith in 'the Son of Man' (9:35). The presence of the judgement theme probably explains this somewhat sudden appearance of the Son of Man (9:35), linked already with judgement in 5:27 and in tradition.[33]

Ch. 10 is marked by its use of shepherd imagery. Beneath it we detect the basic christological pattern when Jesus speaks of his coming (10:10), of his being recognised for who he is (10:2,4,5,14,27), of his knowing the Father and being known by him (10:15) and of his receiving authority to lay down his life and take it up again (10:11,17f). Jesus, the shepherd, lays down his life for the sheep (10:11,15) and promises a future gathering of sheep not of this fold into a single flock (10:16). Both of these statements belong to the complex of events concerned with Jesus' death and return to the Father. Their possible relation to Jesus' death understood as vicarious atonement will be discussed below in IIIA2.

10:19-39 contains many christological statements and again they reflect the central structure. Jesus responds to the question about his messiahship (10:24) by appealing to the works he does in his Father's name (10:25). The Jews do not believe and are not Jesus' sheep. Those who are Jesus' sheep will kept by the Father (10:29). Immediately there follow Jesus' famous words: 'I and the Father are one' (10:30). The preceding context relates these words to at least a common interest between the Father and the Son as the basis for the Son's claim that the Father will look after his sheep. The Jews sense blasphemy and gather stones. Jesus responds by appealing again to the many works which he has shown them from the Father (10:32). The Jews specify the grounds of their charge: 'You, being a human, make yourself God' (10:33).

We shall be exploring more fully the possible meanings of both the accusation and Jesus' reply in IIIB3. At this stage we note however that Jesus uses the language of the central structure in making his reply, as he had done earlier in drawing attention to the work he had done in the Father's commission (10:25,32). Jesus appeals to the use of 'gods' in Ps 82:6 to address those to whom the word of God came (10:35), then continues in typically Johannine christological terms: 'Of the one whom the Father sanctified and sent into the world you say, "You blaspheme", because I said I am son of God. If I do not do the works of my Father, do not believe in me. If I do, and you do not believe in me, believe in the works, so that you may come to know and realise that the Father is in me and I in the Father' (10:36-39). For the first time we have the language of mutual indwelling as a way of expressing the relationship between Father and Son. The same language is used in the first farewell discourse (14:10f,20) and the final prayer (17:21,23), both of the Father Son relationship and of the relationship between disciples and the Son and the Father. We shall return in IIIB3 to a discussion of the implications of such unity statements for the author's christology.

Ch. 11, like, ch. 9, is primarily discourse, but again we can understand it within the framework of the central structure. Martha's messianic affirmation, 'I have believed that you are the Christ, the Son of God coming into the world' (11:27), follows Jesus' summation of his mission as an offer of resurrection and life. Like earlier miracle stories, the raising of Lazarus is made to symbolise the gift which Jesus brings. Jesus' prayer functions as a demonstration of his relationship with the Father: 'Father, I thank you that you have heard me. I knew that you always hear me, but I am speaking because of the crowd standing around, that they may believe that you sent me' (11:41-42). In the miracle the crowds can see the glory of God which Jesus had predicted, at the beginning of the narrative, would be seen (11:4) and of which he reminded Martha before the tomb (11:40). To see the glory of God in the miracle and to read it as a manifestation of the Son sent from the Father to bring life, is to read the story in the light of the central structure.

The references to glory almost certainly function at two levels. One relates to the revelation of glory in the miracle just mentioned. The other relates to something yet to come, namely Jesus' death and return to the Father. For in John's account it is this miracle which leads ultimately to Jesus' arrest and thus to his crucifixion, and, through his death, to his return to the glory of the Father. In other words we meet here the same twofold structure, presenting Jesus as the revealer and Jesus as the one who will die and return to the Father. The latter focus of the Lazarus episode finds confirmation in the account of the Sanhedrin meeting in 11:47-54 where with splendid irony the author portrays the high priest Caiaphas unwittingly prophesying that Jesus' death would be for the nation and for the gathering into unity of all God's children (11:51-53). Does 'dying for' imply vicarious atonement or indicate representative action in some other way? The immediate context offers no answer. We shall return to this in IIIA2 below.

Ch. 12 continues the focus on Jesus' death and resurrection as the reader is reminded in the first verse of Lazarus' resurrection and again in 12:9. The anointing at Bethany is symbolic preparation for Jesus' burial (12:7). Jesus enters Jerusalem as Zion's king upon a foal. The royal messianic overtones are also present in the crowd's acclamation, 'Hosanna. Blessed is he who comes in the name of the Lord, the king of Israel' (12:13). This imagery runs strongly through the Johannine passion narrative and, as we shall see, the author interprets it within the framework of the central structure (see IIB5 and IIC6 below).

The author makes the important footnote: the disciples did not understand the messianic significance of what the crowds did nor the fulfilment of messianic prophecy in this event until after Jesus was glorified (12:16). This is similar to 2:22 where the author notes that understanding of scripture and of Jesus' words in relation to the expulsion from the temple did not come to the disciples until after Jesus was raised from the dead. The same idea was present in the claim that the Jews would be able to know who Jesus was after his exaltation (8:28).

The significance of events associated with Jesus' death and return to the Father form the central focus of 12:20-33. The Pharisees' fear that the world was going after him (12:19) and the request by Greeks to see Jesus, relayed through two disciples, Philip and Andrew (12:20-22), point, through the author's irony and symbolism, to the Gentile mission which would come as a fruit of Jesus' death and return to the Father and be carried out through such disciples.[34] That hour has come. It is the hour of Jesus' glorification (12:23). Continuing the metaphor of bearing fruit, Jesus interprets his death as the falling of a seed into the ground, which should bear fruit (12:24). Appropriately the disciples are also encouraged to follow their master on this path and promised the same shared honour with the Father (12:25-26).

In 12:27 the author returns to Jesus' facing his 'hour': 'Now is my soul troubled, and what shall I say? Father, save me from this hour? But for this I came to this hour. Father, glorify your name.' The Son came to this hour to face death and does not ask to be saved from it,[35] but that what he will do will bring glory to God. In what way Jesus' facing death fulfils the task (eg: as an act of revelation or of atonement) is not stated and will engage us in IIIA2 and 3 below. God's reassurance follows: 'I have glorified it and will glorify it again' (12:28). This reflects the same twofold character of Johannine christology: the earthly ministry up to the passion and the passion and return to the Father.[36] The author has these words function as christological commentary when he has Jesus declare that they were spoken not for his sake but for the crowd's (12:30).

The focus returns to the event itself, the 'hour'. It is the hour of the judgement of this world when the ruler of this world will be cast out (12:31). It is also the hour for Jesus to be lifted up, resulting in the drawing to himself of all people (12:32). This picks up again the motif of mission already expressed through the metaphor of bearing fruit and the symbolic use of the coming of the Greeks. Finally the literal truth of the saying about Jesus' being lifted up is underlined: it indicates crucifixion. 18:32 will make reference back to this as a prophetic prediction. The following verses in ch. 12 show the crowd understanding 'lifting up' to mean death. It does not fit with their ideas of messiahship. Interestingly they report Jesus as saying, 'The Son of Man must be lifted up' (12:34), and then ask who this Son of Man is. The title does indeed occur in association with 'lifting up' in 3:14 and 8:28 and the narrative presupposes it also behind 12:32.

There emerges from this passage in ch. 12 a range of images associated with Jesus' death and return to the Father which we have met already. They will be drawn together and explored in detail in IIC9-14 and IIIA. The elements of the central structure reappear in the remaining verses of ch. 12 where response to Jesus' ministry is in view. Jesus has come into the world as the light (12:35f). The invitation to believe in him has been refused, despite the signs (12:37). The author uses Isa 53:1 to bemoan this lack of response: 'Lord, who has believed our report (what we have heard) and to whom has the arm of the Lord been revealed?' We should probably interpret this within the framework of the central structure as the words of Jesus so that it means: Who has believed the report the Son has brought of what he heard from the Father and who has accepted the revelation he offered? This is in contrast to the prevailing interpretation which treats the words as those of Christian preachers bemoaning response to what they have heard from Jesus.

Using Isa 6:10, the author explains the inability to believe and alludes to the wider context of this passage, identifying Isaiah's temple vision as a vision of the pre-existent glory of the Son (12:41f).[37] 12:43 berates those who through fear fail to confess Christ, as preferring the glory (praise) from people (ie., that people give) to the glory of God. It is possible that 'the glory of God' may not mean any more here than praise from God, though the immediate parallel suggests this. In the light of the reference to Isaiah's seeing Christ's glory in the temple it is tempting to see here another reference to the glory of God seen in Jesus' earthly ministry by the eyes of faith: we beheld his glory, glory as of the only Son of the Father' (1:14).[38]

The concluding passage, 12:44-50, functions as a summary statement of the meaning of Jesus' earthly ministry. We have already seen the way the central structure emerges underlies its statements.

John 6 - 12   Conclusions

Two things have emerged clearly from the review of John 6-12.

1. The 'central structure' has been confirmed as underlying the statements about Jesus' coming and his earthly ministry. The pre-existent Son (with the Father before his descent, 6:62; before Abraham, 8:58; seen by Isaiah, 12:41), was authorised and sent by the Father into the world. The Son who knows the Father comes from the Father and makes him known (7:16,18; 8:28); and returns to the Father. These motifs occur frequently throughout, fuelling irony concerning Jesus' origin (eg: 6:41f; 7:27, 40-52; 9:16,29,33) and destination (7:33f; 8:21f). It is Jesus prayer that people will know he is sent by the Father (11:41f; cf. 12:30).

The oneness of the Father and Son is asserted and argued along the lines we found in ch. 5, namely, that the oneness finds expression in the Son doing the the works of the Father and so remains within the framework of the revelation pattern of christology (10:29-39). The same is true of the concepts of mutual knowledge (10:15) and indwelling (10:36-39).

Jesus' messiahship (7:27: 9:22; 10:24; 11:27; 12:13-15) and occasional references to him as prophet (9:17; 6:14f) are understood within the framework of the revealer envoy pattern, when they are correctly interpreted (cf. 6:14f; 12:34). The reworking of Peter's traditional confession illustrates this also (6:68f).

In 6:20, 8:25,28 and 58 Jesus uses the absolute, *egō eimi* (lit. 'I am'). In 8:25,28 the context favours the meaning, 'I am what I claim to be', understood in terms of the revealer pattern (so: esp 8:28). In 6:20 Jesus is identifying himself: 'It is I (not a ghost or the like)' and in 8:58 the text need mean no more than I am and was in existence before Abraham, still a majestic unique claim but not an allusion to the divine name. Wider meanings may be present, but this will be determined by other uses in the gospel.

In particular the coming of the Son brings nourishment (6:31-51b,58), light (8:12; 9:5; 12:35f, 46) and life (7:38; 11:25). The sent one 'Siloam' (11:7) is the source of healing. Of these gifts the miracles are signs. In them God's glory is seen (11:4,40), but ultimately they are not believed (12:37) or they are responded to inappropriately (6:14f). Isa 53:1 expresses what could be the words of the revealer envoy himself: 'Who has believed what we have heard?' (12:38) and Isa 6:10 explains it. Faith is to recognise Jesus as the true shepherd and this too means seeing him as the revealer sent by the Father (10:2,4,5,14,27).

2. The death of the Son and his return to the Father is an event looked forward to during the Son's earthly ministry and his revelatory activity expressed through the central structure. As a total event it is portrayed as something greater and more significant yet to come (6:62). The total event, signalled by 'the hour' (12:23,27; cf. 7:6,8; 12:31) encompasses Jesus' death (12:24,27,33f), resurrection (12:24; cf. 2:22), exaltation (8:28; 12:32-34), glorification (7:39; 12:16,22; cf. 11:4,40;

12:28), ascent (6:62), and the judgement of the world (12:31; cf. 9:39,35). The event is also associated with the sending of the Spirit (7:39; cf. 6:63), with mission (7:35f; 10:16; 11:51-53; 12:19-24,32), eucharistic nourishment (6:51-58; cf. 6:27), and a new understanding of scripture and the events of Jesus' life (12:16; cf. 6:62; 8:28f). The title, 'Son of Man' occurs often in these contexts (6:27,53, 6:62; 8:28; 9:35; 12:23,32).

Some passages speak of Jesus' dying as an event in itself 'for' (*hyper*) the sheep (10:11,15), 'for' the nation (11:51) or 'for' the world (6:51c); and in 12:27 Jesus states that for 'this' (suffering death) he came to this hour. These formulations raise the question of the extent to which the author thinks of these texts as expressing a notion of vicarious atonement or whether they should be seen as expressing a representative action of some other kind on others' behalf (eg: act of revelation?). To this we shall return when we consider all such passages.

3. John 13 - 14

John 13 - 14 Review

Ch. 13 begins with two statements about what Jesus 'knew' as he faced his disciples for the last time: 'Jesus, knowing that the hour had come for him to depart from this world to the Father' (13:1) and 'knowing that the Father had given all things into his hands and that he had come from God and was going to God' (13:3). Both reflect the central structure, yet both focus on the implications of Jesus' impending death, as the context demands. Schnackenburg takes the reference to the Father giving all things into the Son's hands as more directly a statement about power and control in the light of the assault of the devil through Judas, just mentioned in 13:2, and, like Becker, sees 13:3 as a redactional addition.[39] Brown refers it rather to Jesus' salvific mission.[40] The fact that the phrase occurs in 3:35, also in association with elements of the revealer envoy pattern, suggests that this context should also be borne in mind here. Authorisation for mission and being given authority over all for that purpose need not exclude here some reference to the devil's threat. But the verse is primarily saying that nothing will prevent the obedient fulfilment of the commission given in pre-existence.

Jesus washes his disciples' feet. Peter questions Jesus, who replies: 'What I am doing you do not understand now, but afterwards you will understand' (13:7). The 'afterwards' indicates that what we have here follows the pattern we have already observed: only after the event of Jesus' death and return to the Father is the meaning of some words and events in Jesus' ministry able to be understood. Will he understand then because of a better knowledge of who Jesus was? Will it be because of Jesus' atoning death as the basis for the granting of forgiveness? The answer cannot be considered in isolation from other passages in the gospel and we shall return to it in IIIA2.

The second interpretation (13:12-17), which sees in the act an example to be followed, uses the familiar language of the central structure in saying that 'the apostle is not greater than the one who sent him' (13:16). In 13:19 Jesus comments on his prediction of Judas's betrayal: 'From now on I am telling you before it happens, so that you may believe, when it happens, that I am'. This is another example of the enigmatic 'I am' use we shall consider below. It need mean no more than 'I am the one I claim to be.'[41] It could be a deliberate self identification using the divine name.[42] In 13:20 the envoy language is used in making a parallel between response to Jesus and response to his disciples: 'He who accepts anyone I send accepts me and he who accepts me accepts him who sent me.'

On the exit of Judas, the event which sets the events of the passion night in motion, Jesus declares: 'Now is the Son of Man glorified and God is glorified in him. If God is glorified in him, God will also glorify him in himself, and will glorify him immediately' (13:31f). These words echo 12:23 'The hour has come for the Son of Man to be glorified.' The simplest explanation of the use of the word 'glorify' in the aorist in 31 and the first clause of 32 and in the future in the remaining two clauses of 32 is that they relate to the one single event. 31 views it as having happened, now that Judas has departed, even though Judas' activities are but its beginning; for Jesus now sees his death as inevitable. 31 and 32a use the punctiliar aorist. 32a repeats 31b and reflects back on both how and when 31a will take place.[43] This is preferable to delineating two events in 31 - 32a and 32b, finding here, as Thusing does, glorification through the cross and glorification through future mission,[44] or glorification through Jesus' ministry up to this point, including the footwashing and glorification through the event of the cross.[45]

'Now is the Son of Man glorified' (13:31a). Beside this the author places the words: 'and God is glorified in him' (13:31b). 32a reflects on 31b, repeating its substance, 'if God is glorified in him', to suggest that God's glorification of Jesus is a response to his glorification of God: '(then) God will glorify him in himself', that is, God will reward Jesus by taking him into his own intimate glory. Caird suggests 'glorified' in 13:31b and 32a is not a true passive, but expresses the idea that God has revealed himself in him.[46] While this is linguistically possible and would be consistent with the central structure of the author's christology, it is best to understand it as a genuine passive and to take 'in him' as local in the sense that God has been glorified in and through Jesus' obedience and will in turn glorify him in the glory of his own being.[47] 32c adds: this will happen immediately. The way this text relates to others which use the glorification motif is subject of a separate discussion in IIIA4.

The following verse speaks of Jesus' departure: 'Little children, yet a little while I am with you; you shall seek me, and as I said to the Jews: where I am going you cannot come, so I am telling you now' (13:33). The Jews had heard (7:33f) and misunderstood the saying (7:35f; 8:14,21f). It belongs with the 'whence-whither' sayings, for to know where Jesus is going is to know where he came from (8:14). It reflects the 'revelation pattern'.

The differences between 7:33f and 13:33 are noteworthy:

7:33f	13:33
	Little children,
yet a little while I am with you;	yet a little while I am with you;
and I am going	

to him who sent me.	
you will seek me	you will seek me
and you will not find me	
and	and, as I said to the Jews,
where I am going	where I am going
you cannot come	you cannot come

The author adds 'little children' because these are his disciples. He omits the reference to where Jesus is going because this becomes a major question which will dominate the discourse to follow (13:36a; 14:5). He also omits 'you will not find me', because this will not be true of the disciples. The Jews will die in their sins; the disciples will indeed find Jesus. The final part of the saying is modified in Jesus' answer to Peter's question two verses later, 'Lord, where are you going?' Jesus replies: 'Where I am going you cannot follow now, but you will follow later' (13:36). At the level of literal meaning this connects with the description of Peter's death in 21:18f: 'When you become old, you will stretch out your hands and another will gird you and carry you where you do not want to go. He said this indicating by what death he would glorify God. And having said this he says to him, "Follow me!"' But at a deeper level it is true for all disciples, for Jesus goes to prepare a place for them (14:2) and prays that they may be where he is (17:24).

The announcement in 13:33 has therefore important sequels. The first is an instruction about loving one another (13:34f), a typical instruction by a parting one to those who are left. There follow Peter's question, Jesus' answer, and his prediction of Peter's denial. With typical Johannine irony the narrative tells how Peter wants to go so far as to lay down his life. The irony works because of what we know from 21:18f, but the readers may well have known this independently. The denial warns of the difficulty in following Jesus.

Ch. 14 begins with Jesus addressing the disciples' grief, which is assumed to have arisen because of his words in 13:33. The basis of their comfort is to be their belief in the Father and the Son: 'Believe in God and believe in me' or possibly: 'You believe in God, believe also in me' (14:1). The 'and' which joins these two statements (or alternatively the 'also') is more than a means of simple juxtaposition. For the 'revelation pattern' makes it clear that we can know the Father only by knowing the Son. The 'revelation pattern' speaks not only of the Son's coming, but also of his return to the Father and it is the latter which is immediately expounded here. The Son goes to the Father to prepare a dwelling place for his own. He will then come again and take them so that, as he was with them on earth ('a little while I am with you' 13:33), so he will be with them in the presence of the Father (14:3). We are not told in these verses when or how the Son will come again, but just that he will do so and that the ultimate goal of that coming will be to take the disciples to himself, to where he has gone, to his Father's house.

The comfort is twofold: the hope of a place with the Son where he goes and the coming again of the Son; not only the place, also the coming; in fact, because he goes to prepare a place, he comes again. This emphasis returns in 14:18-23. But first, in a way characteristic of the dialogue in ch. 14, Jesus concludes response to one issue by opening another: 'And where I am going you know the way' (14:4;

further issues are introduced similarly in 14:7b,11b,21b). 14:5-11 expounds the issue, using the 'revelation pattern': Jesus the revealer is the way, the truth and the life (14:6), because to know him is to know the Father (14:6f). Philip's request to be shown the Father (14:8) is used to underline the central theme of the revelation pattern: to have seen the Son is to have seen the Father (14:9). 'Do you not believe that I am in the Father and the Father in me; otherwise believe me because of the works themselves' (14:10). This is the same mutual indwelling formula and appeal to the works which we found already in 10:38. To believe in the Son is the way to the Father, so that he is the way, the life, the truth. In these verses we have an expansion therefore of what is meant in the opening exhortation: 'believe in God and believe in me' (14:1).

Comfort consists in the promise of a place with the Son in the Father's presence. That is future. It also consists in Jesus' coming and in comfort for the disciples as they face life on earth. It is this need which the author addresses from 14:12 onwards. Because Jesus goes to the Father, the disciples will do the works of Jesus and will do even greater works (14:12). This is another of the occasions where Jesus contrasts his earthly ministry with something greater that will come as a result of his death and return to the Father (cf. 3:12; 6:62). The works of Jesus were to make the Father known. The works of the disciples will do that to an even greater extent. The primary focus is not greater miracles, but mission, not in the sense of winning larger numbers or of achieving greater geographical spread, but in the sense that the Spirit will cause new fruit, the fruit of a community of faith bearing witness in accordance with its commission.[48]

Immediately associated with this promise is a saying which features also in the later discourses: 'Whatever you ask in my name I will do it, that the Father may be glorified in the Son. Whatever you ask of me in my name I will do' (14:13f; cf. in variant forms: 15:7; 16:23f,26). This is not a blank cheque to fulfil all manner of whims and wishes, but a promise related to the 'works'. As Untergassmair points out, 'in my name' means more than motivation; it refers also to the commission undertaken by the community in love and obedience.[49] The Father is glorified by the Son's fulfilment of his Father's commission and also by the disciples' fulfilment of theirs. The commission is understood according to the revelation pattern and this pattern also influences the way he perceives the disciples' role.

The introduction of the love theme in 14:15 continues the focus on commission: 'If you love me, keep my commandments.' The same thought complex, linking mission, prayer, glorification of the Father, and love, is present in 15:7-10 'If you remain in me and my words remain in you, ask what you want and it shall happen for you. In this is my Father glorified that you bear much fruit and become my disciples.' To be a disciple means following Jesus in fulfilling the commission he had and passed on. A similar connection to the one found in 15:9f, between the love commandment and the result that people recognise the disciples for who they are, occurred already in 13:34f. In 14:15 the commandment is more directly related to keeping the commission. The commission is to make the revelation known and so to bear fruit. This the disciples are to do in Jesus' name, that is, with the authorisation that belongs to the commission.

The promise and the commission to do the same and greater things than the Son relates closely to the promise of the Paraclete which will give the disciples the sure knowledge they will need for mission. 'I will ask the Father and he will give you another Paraklete to remain with you forever, the Spirit of Truth whom the world cannot receive because it neither sees nor knows it. You know it, because it remains with you and shall be in you' (14:16f). Jesus, who was with the disciples a little while (as 13:33), is contrasted with another Paraclete who will be with them forever. The disciples are being comforted for the Son's absence by the promise of the Spirit's presence. They are not abandoned as orphans (14:18a). Yet at the point where we might want to see the Paraclete as a replacement for Jesus, the author has Jesus assert: 'I will come to you' (14:18b) and returns to the saying which introduced the discourse in 13:33, 'Yet a little while and the world will see me no more, but you will see me, because I live, you will live also. In that day you will know that I am in my Father and and you in me and I in you' (14:19f).

The statements concerning the the Paraclete and those concerning the Son can be parallelled:

he will give you another Paraclete	I will come to you
(the world) neither sees nor knows it (the Spirit)	the world shall see me no more,
you know it,	but you will see me
because it remains with you	you will know
and shall be in you.	that.... I am in you

Both the Spirit and the Son come. Neither will be able to be seen by the world, but each will be seen or known by the disciples. Both are currently with the disciples: the Paraclete 'remains with *para* you' and Jesus is with the disciples for 'a little while' (14:19; alluding to 'a little while I am with you' 13:33; see also 14:25 'while I remain with *para* you'); and both will be in them.[50] Beutler relates the promise of the indwelling of the Spirit to the covenant hope of Jeremiah.[51] There is no indication here that the promise should refer to the Spirit's presence only among the believers, such as through the activity of Christian prophets, and not in them, as Boring suggests.[52] 14:3 had promised the Son's coming. In 14:18-24 this coming coincides with the coming of the Spirit. 'Because I live' (14:19) probably includes an allusion to the resurrection, but, as Porsch rightly points out,[53] the promised presence of the Son is not limited to the time of resurrection appearances. Primarily it refers to the life he has in himself which enables him both to lay down and to take up his life again. Because he lives, the disciples will live. Nor does this refer primarily to life with the Son in the heavenly mansions promised in association with the Son's coming in 14:3, but to life through the gift of the Spirit and the risen Christ.[54] The extent to which Johannine eschatology still had a place for parousia eschatology will be discussed in IIIB1 below. This passage implies that it is the Spirit who mediates this presence of the Son and the Father to the believer.[55]

These promises are all seen within the context of the Son's commission so that 14:21 returns us to the theme of loving the Son by keeping his commandments: 'He who has my commandments and keeps them, he it is who loves me; and he who loves me will be loved by my Father and I will love him and manifest myself to him' (14:21). The words, 'manifest myself to him', are the cue for Judas's question and for wider exploration of the theme of the Son's manifestation. 14:23 rephrases 14:21, 'If anyone loves me, he will keep my word and my Father will love him and we shall come to him and make our dwelling with him.' The author then expounds the meaning of keeping the word of the Son by using the familiar revelation pattern: 'He who does not love me does not keep my words; and the word which you hear is not mine but the Father's who sent me' (14:24).

In 14:25 Jesus returns to the thought of 13:33 in saying: 'These things I have spoken to you while remaining with you.' The 'these things' could refer to 'the word' received from the Father, following the revelation pattern. More likely they refer to the content of the discourse as a whole. In the light of 14:18-23 we might expect the author to have Jesus continue: 'but when I come to you and dwell in you...' Instead the author has Jesus return to speak of the Spirit: 'The Paraclete, the Holy Spirit, whom the Father will send in my name, he shall teach you all things and remind you of all I have said to you.' The elements of the revelation pattern are present: 'the Father', sending, the teaching role; but the Spirit is not a second revealer. He acts on Jesus' authority ('in his name') and reminds of his words. Only the statement 'he will teach you all things' could suggest something more.

With 14:27 we come full circle. Jesus gives his disciples peace. The words, 'Let not your heart be troubled, neither let it be afraid' (14:27c), echo 14:1. 14:28 is a summary: 'You heard that I said, I am going away and I am coming to you. If you love me, you would rejoice that I go to the Father, because the Father is greater than I.' In it, as in the discourse as a whole, the departure motif of the revelation pattern, which had been introduced through the saying in 13:33, is expanded in two ways: by the promise of Jesus' coming (as 14:3,17b-23) and by the fact that Jesus is going to the greater one. In the summary this reference to the Father as the greater one picks up the promise of 14:12; for on the Son's return the Father will enable the disciples to do greater things, will send the Paraclete which will enable true knowledge of who Jesus is and of his abiding presence with the disciples. Jesus will refer back to this promise when he tells Mary Magdalene of the good news for the disciples that he is going to his Father (20:17). The perspective of something more, which will come through the death and the return of the Son, is also expressed in the words that follow: 'I have spoken these things to you now before they happen, so that when they happen you may believe' (14:29). They are almost an exact echo of 13:19, but there they refer to the prediction of Judas' betrayal. Here they relate to the promise of greater things to come.

The closing verses allude to the coming confrontation with the ruler of this world (14:30), already mentioned in 12:31 (cf. also 16:8-10, 33), and have Jesus summarise his purpose, using the revelation pattern: 'that the world may know that I love the Father, and as the Father commanded me, so I act' (14:31).

John 13 - 14   Conclusions

In these chapters the revelation pattern has continued to determine the way the author expounds the coming of the Son into the world. This is so in the opening verses (13:1,3), in the final words of the discourse (14:31) and throughout. It is particularly present in 14:5-11 and is doubtless in mind in the command to the disciples: 'Believe in God and believe in me' (14:1). Elements of the pattern are also applied to the sending of the Spirit (14:26) and the disciples (13:16,20). Behind much of ch. 14 is the assumption that the disciples are entrusted with a commission to do the works Jesus did and to spread them more widely (14:12,15,21,24).

Much of these two chapters concentrates on the event of Jesus' death and return to the Father. The return belongs with the revelation pattern as 13:1,3 indicate, but it comes to particular expression in 13:33, a saying already used in conflict with the Jews. This is almost like the preaching text for the discourse and its elements keep recurring throughout. It is used by the author as a starting point for interpreting this event. Jesus' return is to prepare a place with the Father in heavenly dwellings for the disciples who will follow the path of his return if they believe in him (14:3; 13:36b; 14:6). This might be little more than an exposition of the revelation pattern and recalls sayings such as Jesus is the door. But the author expands the meaning of Jesus' return in two ways.

First he shows that the Son's return will enable the disciples to do greater things than Jesus, as they fulfil their mission at his command (14:12) and rely on his help in answer to their prayers in this regard (14:13f). Then the return also brings the Paraclete, the Spirit, already present among the disciples during Jesus' ministry, but in future to be in them (14:15-17) and to inform them of all things, especially the words Jesus had spoken to them (14:26). The Father to whom Jesus goes is 'greater' according to the summary in 14:28 and this doubtless connects back to the promise of the Spirit which will make the achievement of greater works possible.

The second and surprise development is that the Son's return to the Father will be followed by the Son's return with the Father to dwell in those who love him and carry out his commission (14:18-24). The context suggests strongly that the presence of the Son is made possible by the presence of the Spirit. The disciples' life will derive from Jesus' life (14:19) and the day of Jesus' coming will be the day of greater understanding both about the relationship of indwelling of the Father in the Son and mutually of the Son and the disciples.

Other elements related to Jesus' death and return to the Father which feature briefly are the motif of mutual glorification between God and the Son of Man (13:31f) and the two occasions when Jesus makes predictions so that their fulfilment may confirm the disciples' knowledge. In the case of the prediction about Judas (13:19) it is that they may know 'that I am.' This could mean I am who I claim to be or it could be a revelatory claim in itself through use of the divine name. The second (14:29) expresses no object of what the disciples will come to believe, though the context suggests something along the lines of what is expressed in the revelation pattern (so 14:31).

4. John 15 - 16

John 15 - 16   Review

15:1-8 is dominated by the motif of the vine and emphasises the need for the disciples to abide in the Son. 14:20 had spoken of a future perception made possible for the disciples through the Son's return: 'On that day you will know that I am in the Father and you in me and I in you.' The 'I in you and you in me' is now subject of further reflection and exhortation. It is assumed that the disciples are not diseased unfruitful branches (15:2f), because they have received Jesus' word: 'you are clean through the word which I have spoken to you' (15:3). The revelation pattern also informs the use of this imagery. Being clean means receiving the Son's revelation. This is evident also in 15:7, 'If you abide in me and my words abide in you, you shall ask what you want and it shall happen for you.' The goal of such abiding is the glorification of the Father through the bearing of much fruit: 'By this is my Father glorified that you bear much fruit' (15:8).

In ch. 14 the author links glorification of the Father, the promise of answered prayer and the disciples' future greater works, a reference to their mission (14:12-14). Here the same motifs are present, only mission is expressed through the image of bearing fruit (as already in 12:24; 4:35-38). Thus Borig's dichotomy here between fruit as deeds of love and fruit as mission, with the suggestion that primarily the former are intended in this passage,[56] must be rejected. Thusing shows how the notion of fruit bearing and mission are interrelated. Fruit bearing is not primarily about numbers but about manifesting the life which by its quality continues the mission of Jesus the vine.[57] The vine image is being used not primarily with a focus on Jesus as the source of life, though without this the image scarcely works. Nor is its focus on the office of ordained ministry alone, as Mussner suggests,[58] or at all, nor on a select group of charismatic leaders, as Minear suggests,[59] to whom he sees the last discourses primarily addressed. Its focus is on the fact that, for all, abiding in the vine and its life makes fruitbearing possible.[60]

The connections with the passage in ch. 14 continue with the reference to the love theme and the commands in 15:9 (cf. 14:15). In 15:10 abiding in the Son's love is defined as keeping his commands and grounded by using the language of the revelation pattern: 'as I have kept the commands of my Father and remain in his love.' 15:11-17 recalls 13:34f when it calls for the disciples to love one another, as the Son has loved them. The Son's love is illustrated: 'No one has greater love than this, that someone lays down his life for his friends' (15:13). We note a possible reference to Jesus' atoning death here, but it is not the subject of further reflection. The statement could simply mean that in carrying out the task of revelation on their behalf Jesus went even so far as to die. As a generalisation it means little more than the extent to which people go to benefit others. It is therefore hard to be sure from the context to what extent expiatory ideas may be present. We shall return to this in the context of discussion of similar statements in IIIA2. In what follows the author stays close to the revelation pattern: 'I have called you friends, because all that I heard from the Father I made known to you' (15:15). The imagery of 'master', 'servant', chosenness, and the example of Jesus' love, recall 13:12-20, where similar focus is given to the way the commissioned ones relate to one another. 15:16f return directly to the commission to bear fruit and the promise of answered prayer associated with it (as already 15:7f).

The parallels between the Son's commission and that of the disciples continues through 15:18-25 and the elements of the revelation pattern feature throughout. The world hated the Son and hates them (15:18). Like the Son, they are not of the world, for he has chosen them (15:19). The issue is whether people respond to and keep the word, whether the Son's or theirs, for it is the word of revelation (15:20). The disciples will operate with Jesus' authority, so that their rejection will be on account of that authority, that name: 'They will do these things to you because of my name, because they do not know him who sent me' (15:21). Jesus has come and has spoken the word and done the deeds of revelation (15:22,24); negative response to this revelation constitutes sin: 'If I had not come and spoken to them, they would have no sin' (15:22). Such rejection is rejection of the Father (15:23f).

15:26f shifts the attention from rejection to the coming of the Paraclete: 'When the Paraclete comes, whom I shall send from the Father, the Spirit of Truth which proceeds from the Father, he will bear witness concerning me; and you will bear witness, because you have been with me from the beginning.' As in 14:26, the sending of the Spirit reflects the revelation pattern. Here the forensic language of evidence, 'witness', and the fulfilment of the formal legal requirement of two witnesses for valid testimony, may reflect forensic concerns in the rejection of the disciples, just mentioned, and this may reflect the original setting of the Paraclete motif in relation to the Spirit.[61] It may however simply reflect John's wider use of the term, such as in 3:32f. Bearing witness is another way of speaking about bearing the word of revelation. Both the witness of the Paraclete and that of the disciples are firmly tied to Jesus. Both are sent by Jesus, the former directly from the Father and bearing the designation, 'Spirit of Truth', the latter through historical association with the earthly Jesus.

The persecution theme continues into ch. 16. Persecution occurs, 'because they have come to know neither my Father nor me' (16:3). Jesus makes these predictions 'so that when their hour comes, you may remember that I told you of them' (16:4a). This is not unlike the statements about prediction in 13:19 and 14:29, except that the purpose remains simply remembering that Jesus had said so. Presumably this is to function as comfort.

The following statement is enigmatic, almost as if the exalted Jesus speaks: 'These things I did not tell you from the beginning because I was with you.' Read in the present context, it must mean that Jesus had not spoken of such things earlier in the ministry when the prospect of his departure was still some time away. Now departure is imminent and Jesus continues: 'But now I am going to the one who sent me' (16:5a). This is a return to the statement of 13:33. It is as though the former conversation begins all over again. 'No one asks me, "Where are you going?"' (16:5b). It is as though Thomas's question, using exactly these words (14:5), had not occurred. In 16:6 there is a similar assumption that Jesus' departure would distress the disciples as we find behind 14:1. A similar comfort is offered: the coming of the Paraclete (16:7; cf. 14:16f). Within the present text of the gospel Jesus the evangelist (or a later hand) is repeating themes of ch. 14 with variation. 16:8-11 offers a succinct summary of the Paraclete's work. The language is forensic (as already in 15:26) and this is consistent with forensic use of the word, Paraclete, itself, meaning advocate. Here the world is on trial and the Paraclete presents convincing evidence so as to lead to a conviction of the world in relation to three themes.[62] It will establish the world's guilt on the basis that it has not believed in Jesus. This is similar to 15:22 which defines guilt as negative response to the revelation Jesus brings. Second, it will provide convincing evidence of Jesus' righteousness. This evidence lies in the fact of Jesus' return to the Father and of people's (including the disciples') no longer seeing Jesus as he was on earth. Why this counts as evidence of righteousness is that Jesus' return to the Father shows the Father has vindicated him.[63] Third, evidence will be laid on the table proving that the world's judgement has taken place. The cross on which the world condemned the Son is the place where the world is condemned. The hour of Jesus' judgement is the hour of the judgement of the world, when the ruler of this world would be cast out, as already 12:31 suggests (cf. also 16:33).

The author has constructed a neat summary of the gospel,[64] using the revelation pattern and the theme of the cross as the hour of judgement. In effect the Paraclete will hold before the world the implications of its response to Jesus' coming, understood in accordance with the familiar envoy revelation pattern. The primary focus of the Paraclete's work here is, as the text explicitly states, the confrontation of the world,[65] not a court action in the consciences of the disciples for their comfort and reassurance.[66] The disciples will indeed share the verdict, but the focus is the address to the world, the work of the Paraclete doubtless through their preaching.

In the verses which follow, the author has Jesus use the language of the revealer envoy pattern also to describe the role of the Spirit of Truth: 'He shall not speak on his own authority, but what he shall hear he shall speak....He shall glorify me, because he shall take from me and announce it to you. All that the Father has is mine; therefore I said, he shall take what is mine and announce it to you.' The Spirit's revelation is derivative and the author emphasises its secondary role in subordination to the Son. At two points this dependence may seem to falter: 'When he, the Spirit of Truth, comes he will lead you into all truth;' and 'he will announce to you what is to come.' (literally: 'the coming things') (16:13). They echo 14:26 which spoke of the Paraclete teaching the disciples all things. But the context in which these are set demands that such truth and prediction will not come without being authorised by the Son. In IIIC1 we discuss the implications for our understanding of the gospel writing itself.

Taken as a whole, 16:7-15 shows the Paraclete fulfilling a crucial role in relationship to both the world and the disciples. He expounds the meaning of Jesus' coming. Both in the exposition of Jesus' coming and in the manner in which the Paraclete exercises his ministry the author employs the familiar revelation pattern. The openendedness of the Paraclete's ministry to the disciples leaves room for creative developments and growth in understanding and exposition of 'the things' of Jesus, past, present and future.

16:16 returns us again to 13:33 except that the 'little while' is now related to the interim between Jesus' departure and the disciples' seeing him again. The transition from the coming of the Paraclete (16:7-15) to the coming of the Son recalls the similar abrupt transition in 14:18. The manner in which the author has the disciples puzzle over the departure saying recalls the Jews' puzzlement after its first use in 7:33 (cf. 7:35; 8:21f). Jesus addresses the grief of the interim by using the motif of birthpangs which are fulfilled in the joy of the birth of a child. He promises his disciples similar joy (16:22).

As it stands, 16:16-22 is unusual in that it purports to address the problem of the days between Jesus' departure from the disciples and his resurrection appearance to them, a problem of only very indirect relevance to the readers. It is probably dealt with here with such emphasis (the repetition of the question!) because other disciples may feel themselves in a similar situation later.

In 16:23-27 the author returns to the other logion which occurs frequently in the last discourses, the promise of answered prayer. Like the variant of 13:33 in 16:16-22, this saying is repeated a number of times. In 14:13f Jesus had said that he himself would answer prayer requests. In 15:16 it is the Father who does so. Here the emphasis falls upon the fact of the disciples' having direct access to the Father independent of Jesus (16:26f). This is not in any way meant to denigrate Jesus. Rather it demonstrates to the disciples the Father's love. This love is then explained as the Father's response to the way the disciples have responded to Jesus. Predictably we meet the revelation pattern again: 'The Father himself loves you, because you have loved me and believed that I came from God. I came from the Father and have come into the world. Again I am leaving the world and am going to the Father' (16:27f).

Jesus had introduced this promise of a direct relationship with the Father by announcing that he was now going to speak plainly and not in a veiled way as before (16:25). The disciples respond to Jesus' clear word of promise with a somewhat baffling affirmation: 'Now we know that you know all things and have no need for anyone to ask you. In this we believe that you have come from God' (16:30). In 16:29 the disciples indicate that this awareness has come to them since Jesus announced he was speaking plainly to them, namely, from 16:25 onwards. Having no need to be asked sounds similar to the language of the prayer requests, but there is no apparent connection between Jesus not being prayed to directly, the theme of 16:26f, and his knowing all things. Jesus has already affirmed their adequate faith in 16:27f. It is hard to interpret 16:30 as an improvement beyond that.

Probably the author is deliberately presenting the disciples as expressing their faith inadequately at this point in order to explain Jesus' prediction of their imminent failure. Their affirmation that Jesus has come from God on the basis of knowing all things could be seen as the kind of inferior faith exhibited by Nicodemus and by Peter in 21:15-17, a miracle based faith responding here to Jesus' supernatural knowledge.[67] Such faith will not stand. They will be scattered to their homes and will abandon Jesus. The Father will not abandon him. Alternatively their faith had grasped Jesus' descent (16:30b), but not the meaning of his ascent.[68] Within the transmitted text of the gospel the disciples have advanced beyond miracle based faith, so that this second alternative is to be preferred.

The discourse concludes abruptly after this warning. Jesus explains that their peace is the intention of his words and encourages them to face persecution in the world confident that ultimately it has been overcome. This functions as a rudimentary summary, recalling the persecution theme and the interpretation of the cross as the world's judgement (16:11).

John 15 - 16   Conclusions

The christological revelation pattern features often within these two chapters (directly 15:10,15,22,24; 16:27f) and it lies behind the image of clean and healthy branches (15:3,7), the way the Paraclete presents evidential content in 16:7-11, and the parallelling of response to Jesus and response to disciples in 15:18-25. Its structure also determines the way the commission of the Paraclete is described, especially in 16:12-15 (see also 15:26). Twice the revelation pattern is used in defining sin as rejection of Jesus as the sent one (15:22,24; 16:7f).

As in chs. 13-14, much of the material focusses on the events surrounding Jesus' death and return to the Father. We find again an extensive use of the saying found in 13:33, especially from 16:5 onwards where a lot of the substance of the discussion in 13:33 - 14:31 is repeated in variant form (16:16-19; cf. 16:7, 28). In 16:19-22 it is primarily the distress of the disciples between the passion and Easter which is addressed. Mostly however the departure is shown to be the basis for new promising events, like the coming of the Paraclete (16:6-11,12-15).

This is the fullest exposition of the Paraclete's role. The Paraclete presents convincing evidence about Jesus' coming as constituting what sin is and about the significance of his death and departure as vindication and judgement. The Paraclete will also be the source of knowledge both about and from the Son (16:12-15). This is a key passage for understanding how the author would understand the source of the material presented in the gospel.

Already 15:26 connects the witness of the Spirit and the witness of the disciples, the latter's witness tied to their having been with the earthly Jesus. The discourse also assumes that the disciples receive the Paraclete's wisdom. This enables them in mission. 16:7-11 assumes missionary confrontation with the world and 15:18-25 assumes rejection and persecution (very specifically: 16:1-3). Missionary fruit bearing also underlies the vine image (15:2,4,5,7f,16) and the exhortation to mutual love in the community (15:12-17; cf. 13:34f).

Altogether 15:1-17 reads as a direct address to the post Easter community. The vine image assumes the mutual indwelling promised by 14:20 for the future, speaks of the fruit bearing as a present reality, and looks back on Jesus' self sacrifice (15:13). It lacks any reflection on the difference in time perspective. As it stands in the text it is timeless advice to the disciples applicable already pre-Easter. Time specific references are otherwise common from 15:18 onwards and quite extraordinarily so in 16:16-22 and possibly in 16:29-32 where the disciples seem to be shown as having an incomplete faith which will lead to their downfall in the face of the immediate crisis of the passion.

The other saying beside 13:33 to appear a number of times in these chapters is the promise of answeered prayer. In 15:1-18 it relates directly to the tasks of mission in much the same way as it did in 14:13f (15:7f,16). In ch. 16 it is used quite differently as a way of describing the new relationship disciples may now have with the Father (16:23-26).

We note a further use of the judgement motif to describe the death of Jesus, first encountered in 12:31 (16:11 and probably 16:33). Apart from that there also occurs the brief generalised reference to Jesus' death in the word, 'someone lays down his life for his friends' (15:13). How it should be weighted (vicarious atonement? total commitment to benefit others?) cannot be decided from the context. It is not the subject of further reflection in the context.

5. John 18 - 21

John 18 - 21   Review

In the account of Jesus' arrest in the garden (18:1-11) the outstanding feature is the way those who had come with Judas to arrest Jesus backed away and fell to the ground when he identified himself. Twice Jesus asked them whom they sought (18:4,7); twice they answered, 'Jesus of Nazareth' (18:5,7); and twice Jesus replied: 'I am (he)' (18:5,8). After the first exchange the author mentions the falling to the ground in response to Jesus' words, 'I am' (18:6). On the second occasion Jesus continues after the words, 'I am', to say, 'If you are looking for me, let these go!' (18:8).

Is this the effect of the overwhelming numinous power of the presence of him, whom the reader knows to be the revealer, so that 'I am' was the point of the identification and therefore the point when its impact struck the bystanders? In that case 'I am' means: 'I am Jesus of Nazareth whom you seek.' The reaction of the bystanders was occasioned, therefore, not merely by surprise, but by a holy presence outside their control, the holy presence of the revealer.[69] Or, is it that the expression, 'I am',ₐ itself, represents a statement of divine revelation, a statement of the divine name?[70] The revealer would then be presenting himself as the presence of Yahweh.

It is in this event that Judas betrays Jesus and it may be of significance that Jesus appended to the prediction the words, 'From now on I tell you before it happens, so that you may believe, when it happens, that I am (he)' (13:19). Is the 'I am' here meant to connect with the 'I am' in the arrest scene? It could however be nothing more than the claim that when my prediction comes true, then you will know that I am who I claim to be. Nothing in the text forces one to conclude one way or the other, including the repetition of the event twice and of the words, 'I am', three times in the text. Only if the second use is evident elsewhere in the gospel, and particularly if it is already established by this point in the gospel, is the case for the second interpretation strong and this has not proved so. For the present we can note that, one way or other, the dignity of the revealer is presupposed here.

In 18:11 Jesus employs a metaphor of commissioning: 'The cup which the Father has given me, am I not to drink it?' Jesus sees therefore not only the passing on of the words of the Father, following the revealer pattern, as his commission. He must also face suffering and death. Only then is the task complete (cf. 'It is finished' 19:30). In 18:14 the author recalls the prophecy of Caiaphas, 'It is fitting that one man die for the people' (cf. 11:49). The reader is receiving an interpretation of the task which lies ahead. As with 15:13, the precise interpretation depends upon factors which lie outside the immediate context of the passage. I shall therefore return to the question of whether this belongs to vicarious atonement thinking and of the role it has in the gospel's christology in IIIA2 below.

In the interview with Annas (18:19-24) the focus is entirely upon Jesus as teacher. Jesus refuses to refer to the content of his teaching and remains with the affirmation that he has spoken openly for all to hear. This is consonant with the strong emphasis, following the revealer model, on the centrality of Jesus' words. Meanwhile Peter has been denying Jesus three times, as predicted (13:38b). Neither here, nor in Judas' fulfilment of Jesus' prediction concerning him (cf. 13:18f), is direct reference made back to the fulfilled prediction. But both confirm for the reader Jesus' supernatural knowledge (also 18:4).

The trial before Pilate (18:28 - 19:16) is a carefully structured narrative highlighting the theme of Jesus the royal messiah, the king of the Jews. The author notes in the introduction that the Jews remain outside the praetorium, so that they would not defile themselves before eating the Passover (18:28). Already 13:1 made reference to the Passover and further references will follow. They may carry more weight than simple indicators of time, but an evaluation can be made only in the light of all such references and allusions.

The first scene (18:29-32) has Pilate ask the Jews the grounds of their accusation. They give a very shifty, indirect answer, part of the extremely negative characterisation of the Jews during the trial. Their assertion that Jesus has committed a capital crime for which only the Romans could carry out the sentence allows the author to note Jesus' prediction about the manner of his death, deduced in 12:33 from the words 'lifted up'. The particular phrase is not repeated in the passion narrative, neither in its literal nor in its metaphoric sense, nor are the other terms associated with it (Son of Man, glorification).[71] This makes it very unlikely that the author has in mind to portray the passion events as an act of exaltation,[72] or as the prefigurement of a heavenly exaltation or enthronement,[73] or as the simultaneous earthly representation of a heavenly event.[74] The Son of Man, exaltation and glorification motifs should not be synthesised with the messianic kingship motifs in this way and, in any case, the kingship motifs of the trial function as they do elsewhere in the gospel: they focus on Jesus as the revealer, who, as such, is already the messiah, the king.[75] The king motif in the trial belongs, therefore, within the language of royal messianic expectation, as the sequence of images to follow amply testifies.

Pilate asks Jesus if he is 'the king of the Jews' (18:33), a phrase recalling Nathanael's messianic affirmation: 'You are the Son of God. You are the king of Israel!' (1:49). Jesus effectively affirms the question with reservations and safeguards it against misinterpretation: 'My kingdom is not of this world; if my kingdom were of this world, my servants would fight so that I might not be handed over to the Jews. But now my kingdom is not from here' (18:36). This is not a reference to impending enthronement of Jesus in heaven, but to Jesus' present messianic status. It does refer to the heavenly world, the world above, in the sense that Jesus has come from above, but the reference is not primarily topographical, but qualitative. The kingdom to be seen and entered by those born from above (3:3,5) is the realm of the Spirit present in the exercise of Jesus' ministry, his words and deeds, but invisible to those who like Nicodemus see only at the earthly level.

In response to Pilate's reply, 'Then you are a king,' the author has Jesus underscore the nature of his kingship by using words which reflect the revealer envoy model of his christology: 'You say I am a king. I was born for this and came into the world for this, to witness to the truth. All who are of the truth hear my voice' (18:37). Beutler and Ibuki draw attention to the similarity between 18:37 and 3:31.[76] When Pilate asks, 'What is truth?', the reader knows it is the revelation brought by the Son from the Father. This confirms what we have already found elsewhere: the author interprets the royal messianic confession within the framework of the revealer envoy pattern which forms the central structure of his christology. Similarly Hahn and Dauer, who both emphasis the importance of royal messianic motifs in the passion narrative, stress that the focus of the messianic claim in the passion narrative is not rule but revelation.[77]

In 18:38b-40 Pilate offers the brigand Barabbas in exchange for Jesus. The royal messianic pretender motif thus continues to dominate. Jesus' claim to kingship is also the focus of the mockery and presentation which follow (19:1-5). Pilate repeats the affirmation of Jesus' innocence (19:4; cf. 18:38b) and presents the mock king with the words: 'Behold the man!' (19:5). At the level of Pilate within the narrative the statement must mean something like: 'Look at the man. Here he is, your king!' The force of this comment is that it is spoken of Jesus in a state of humiliation and ridicule. He is just a pathetic human being. The Jews are also being ridiculed in the act. The power of this scene for the reader is twofold. Precisely this mocked king is the only true king and messiah and precisely this human person is the Son come from the Father.

For this reason, while the mockery plays on enthronement ritual, we agree with Schnackenburg, against Blank, Dauer, and Hahn, that at the level of the author's christology this is not an enthronement of Jesus as messiah.[78] The scene also recalls the abject suffering servant of Isa 53,[79] but we cannot be certain that this lies behind the passage. Baum Bodenbender has recently emphasised afresh the aspect of humiliation in the Johannine passion narrative, but does so at the expense of playing down the motifs of kingship which are equally present.[80] There is also nothing here to suggest that 'man' should be read as an alternative way of saying 'Son of Man' and so to see here a Johannine instance of the suffering, humiliated Son of Man,[81] nor that this scene fulfils Jesus' prediction of 1:51, as Moloney suggests.[82] The author uses 'Son of Man' frequently and in association with concepts quite absent from the passion narrative and no indication exists within the gospel of an alternative use of 'man' for 'Son of Man'. Nor does the gospel elsewhere indicate that 'the man' here presents Jesus as the human being par excellence (not even because 'the man' occurs six times),[83] or as the new Adam,[84] or the Man-Messiah,[85] or the counter to the Gnostic Anthropos.[86]

Pilate repeats his statement of Jesus' innocence a third time (19:6) and the Jews for the first time name their accusation: 'He made himself Son of God' (19:7). The numinosity of this claim frightens Pilate; the numinosity had already thrown his captors back at the arrest. Introduction of the sonship theme brings us more directly within the framework of the revealer pattern. Accordingly we note the irony in Pilate's next question: 'Where do you come from?' (19:9). Similarly Jesus asserts his awareness of Pilate's relative authority: 'You would have no authority over me, unless it had been granted you from above' (19:11). The royal messianic theme returns when Pilate seeks to release Jesus and the Jews respond: 'Anyone who makes himself a king speaks against Caesar' (19:12).

Pilate succombs. He takes his seat to declare the verdict (19:13). It has long been noted that the Greek could be read to mean either that Pilate himself sat down or that he made Jesus sit down on the seat. The latter could mean that Jesus himself is being portrayed as the judge (cf. similarly, Gosp Peter 3:7; Justin Apol I 35:6).[87] This would cohere with the tenor of the narrative which in effect has Pilate and the Jews on trial before Jesus, an orientation of the narrative brought out strongly by Dauer and Hahn.[88] Alternatively, or perhaps in addition, it would effect the powerful irony of Pilate enthroning Jesus, with the seat understood not as the tribunal seat itself but as a mock throne.[89] Perhaps the author intends us to see in Pilate's act a further act of mockery of Jesus' kingship, following it, as had the first, by a statement of presentation: 'Behold your king!' (cf. 'Behold the man!' 19:5). Both acts of mockery are also a mockery of the Jews and their response is the same: 'Away with him, away with him! Crucify him!' (cf. 19:6 'crucify him! crucify him!').

The motif of setting Jesus up as judge coheres broadly with the tenor of the narrative but is not supported specifically, apart from the suggested action itself, by any further gesture of Pilate, Jesus, or the Jews. There is more to be said for the second interpretation which sees the seating as a further act of mockery, particularly because the events which follow reflect the same structure as the earlier mockery. On this interpretation the seat is not a judgement seat and the judgement motif is not in focus. Had Pilate taken this seat to declare a verdict, why does he not do so immediately? On the other hand, the preceding exchange had reached a point where Pilate was forced to declare judgement so that, at least from what precedes, we should take *bēma* (seat) to be a seat of judgement. In support of this is the formal characterisation of its setting in the Gabbatha. No such concern about location is evident in the first mockery (19:1-5). Similarly the dating given in 19:14 suggests a formally significant event has taken place. On balance, therefore, it is best to read the text as describing how Pilate took his seat for judgement.[90]

We note the further reference to the Passover, which together with 18:28 forms an inclusio and we will return to it below. Pilate mockingly presents Jesus a second time to the Jews as king, this time using the word, 'king', explicitly (cf. 19:5): 'Behold your king.' We have already noted the similarity in structure between the two scenes. The Jews reject their king, their Messiah, and Pilate hands him over to crucifixion.

The royal messianic imagery continues in the account of the crucifixion, especially in the insistence by Pilate that the superscription, 'Jesus of Nazareth, the king of the Jews', should stand (19:19-22). Pilate's 'What I have written I have written' has a finality about it which speaks to the reader at a level Pilate himself would not have realised.

The author emphasises that Jesus' robe was seamless (19:23), perhaps only to explain why lots were cast, perhaps to emphasis his perfection. Some suggest it is, like the unbroken net in 21:11, an allusion to the unity of the Church,[91] or that it alludes to the seamless robes of high priests (cf. Josephus, Ant. III 7:4) and so to Jesus as high priest,[92] but there is no convincing evidence of this motif in the gospel and certainly none that it played a central role in the author's christology.[93] Jesus commends his mother to the care of the beloved disciple, an enormous credit to and benefit for the disciple's community (19:25-28) and thus also for the reader indirectly, who will benefit from this gospel's community. Having not only the Paraclete but also this disciple with his special connection with Mary assures the reader that the portrait of Jesus in the gospel is true. A similar reassurance comes a few verses later in the author's noting of an eye witness report (19:35).

In 19:28-30 the author describes how Jesus, knowing he had completed all, fulfilled scripture by declaring his thirst, announced the mission complete: 'It is finished', bowed his head and gave up his spirit (19:30). The 'It is finished' might mean little more than 'I am dying' (colloquially: 'I am finished!'), but the repetition in the narrative and the underlying revealer pattern of the author's christology determines that we should see in these words Jesus' declaration that he had completed his commission (cf. 17:4 'I have glorified you on earth, having completed the work you gave me to do'; also 4:34). This passage forms an inclusio with 13:1, where the author notes that Jesus loved his own to the end.[94] There is no indication that his death is being singled out as an accomplishment on its own, for example, as an act of sacrifice or atonement.[95] Rather it is best to see these words in relation to the total commission, which, of course, also included his suffering and death (so, specifically, 18:11). We shall return to the question of how elements of that commission were understood in IIIA2 and 3.

Some read the words *paredōken to pneuma* not as 'he gave up the (his) spirit', a reference to death, but as 'he handed over the Spirit'.[96] Should this be so, it is extraordinary that nothing further in the context, before or after, reflects such a meaning. It is best to read the promise of the Spirit being fulfilled in 20:22, not here.[97]

In 19:31-37 two further motifs appear and the meaning of both is disputed. The first is that Jesus' bones are left unbroken, fulfilling a scripture quoted in 19:36. The scripture is either Ps 34:21 which refers to the righteous sufferer[98] or Exodus 12:10,46 referring to the Passover lamb.[99] It is unlikely to be both,[100] much as both might be applicable christological interpretations. Some suggest a former reference to the Psalm has now been overlaid by the author's concern to emphasise Jesus as the Passover lamb.[101] In favour of reference to the Psalm is the frequency of allusions to the suffering righteous of the psalms in passion narratives of the gospels generally and the marked omission of any reference to the Passover imagery in the immediate context here. Should a Passover reference have been intended, it is hard to see why the author missed the opportunity in 19:31 to mention that the great sabbath was the day of the Passover, and this, immediately before Pilate's command to break the legs!

The case for a Passover reference lies wider afield. On the distinctive Johannine dating, Jesus dies about the time when the Passover lambs were slain and not on the Passover itself as in the Synoptics. The author does refer to the feast of Passover as the setting for the events of Jesus arrest, trial and sentencing (13:1; 18:28; 19:14) and the time of sentencing seems deliberately noted as 'the day of preparation of the Passover, at the sixth hour' (19:14). Passovers are also mentioned earlier in the gospel narrative and at least in 6:4 may symbolically allude to a Passover significance of Jesus' death and the eucharistic meal it provided. Above all, John's acclamation of Jesus as 'the lamb of God who takes away the sin of the world' (1:29; cf. 1:35) could refer to Jesus under the image of a Passover lamb. Originally not vicarious, Passover lambs had come also to share atoning qualities. 1:29 would then form an inclusio with 19:36.

The evidence is not conclusive. The timing fits, but this may not carry great weight for the author who makes nothing of it in 19:31 where we should most expect it if 19:33,36 were meant to refer to Passover imagery. Similarly 1:29 does not demand a Passover interpretation, though it could be present. If it is present there, this would add some support to the case for finding it present here in ch. 19. We then have to reckon with the possibility that it may have been significant in the author's tradition, yet not of major significance for the author himself. The failure to make anything of the date, precisely at the point of the passion narrative where the motif might have been uppermost in his mind, counts ultimately against a Passover interpretation being present here.[102]

The second disputed image is the spear thrust and in particular the words of 19:34 'there immediately flowed out blood and water'. The matching scripture is in 19:37 'They will look on him whom they have pierced.' The weight lies on the details of what was seen, blood and water, as the elaborate guarantee of the eyewitness report in 19:35 confirms. This is not the place to enter a detailed discussion of the numerous interpretations, for which I refer to the commentaries, but there are certain major options.

The blood and water may symbolise eucharist and baptism, which in a sense come to the Church as a result of Jesus' death.[103] Or they may symbolise the blood of redemption and the gift of the Spirit often represented by water (cf. 7:37-39),[104] or the gift of life and of the Spirit.[105] These symbolic interpretations seem not to give sufficient weight to the importance of the eyewitness claim in 19:35 which appears to be concerned also with what literally happened, as if to disclaim something else that might have happened. Probably, therefore, the author is emphasising that Jesus really did die and therefore really did rise again from the dead[106] or really was a human being[107] and did not in any docetic sense escape real human death.[108] This is similar to, though also different from, 1 John 5:6 'This is he who came by water and blood, Jesus Christ, not by water only but by water and blood.' With the Spirit these are then the three witnesses, testifying that Jesus is the Son of God and the source of eternal life (1 Jn 5:7-12). Behind both texts may lie a concern to say that Jesus was no bloodless non human person against those who deny his full humanity or a concern to argue in two slightly different ways that Jesus really did die. 1 Jn would be saying he was not only baptised, but also died.[109] Some such direct concern with the human reality of Jesus seems a more convincing background to both texts than symbolism of the sacraments or Jesus' spiritual gifts, especially in the light of 19:34.

The sacramental or spiritual gifts interpretation would connect to other passages in the gospel which promise life to come and food (especially 6:51-58). The concern with Jesus' humanity or real death would represent a concern which may have left traces elsewhere and we shall pursue this possibility in the discussion of the nature of Jesus' humanity below.

Jesus is placed in the tomb (19:38-42). Two days later, Mary Magdelene, finds the stone removed, the body gone, and tells Peter and the beloved disciple. Both run to the tomb, the latter arriving first, peering in and seeing the lying graveclothes. Peter goes right in and observes enough detail to suggest Jesus himself might have arranged them. The beloved disciple enters, sees the same and the head band in a place on its own and believes. The author hastens to add: 'For they did not yet know the scripture, that he must rise from the dead' (20:9). This reflects the notion expressed earlier in the gospel that the applicability of scripture to Jesus comes to the disciples only after Easter (2:22; 12:16), doubtless in particular: after the Spirit was given.

The narrative leaves us up in the air about the extent of the disciples' understanding. At this point Peter does not seem to have read what he saw in such a way as to believe Jesus has risen, whereas the beloved disciple, seeing the same evidence (or did Peter not see the headband?), does believe. The interposition of 20:9 makes good sense after Peter's response, but is difficult after that of the beloved disciple. Either we must reduce the meaning of 'believed' in 20:8,[110] or 20:9 means only the disciples' scripture understanding.[111] The beloved disciple already fully believes without it; Peter does not.[112] Byrne links the disciple's faith with 20:29 and sees in the beloved disciple a model for the later church which will have to believe without encountering appearances of the risen Lord.[113] Perhaps we should be pressing the narrator too far if we ask why the beloved disciple did not tell Peter what he was thinking or what he saw if it was that which made the difference!

Mary Magdalene's dramatic encounter with Jesus concludes with the enigmatic words of Jesus: 'Do not hold on to me (or 'touch me'), for I have not yet ascended to my Father; but go to my brothers and say to them, "I am ascending to my Father and to your Father, to my God and to your God"' (20:17). Jesus had already spoken of his ascent to the Father in the gospel (3:13; 6:62) and of his going to the Father many times. This must be our guide, and not Luke's story of Jesus' visible assumption into heaven on the fortieth day (Acts 1:11), for the fourth gospel nowhere indicates that Jesus' ascent or return to the Father is an observable event.

Within the Johannine context, therefore, the most natural reading is that Jesus is in the process of completing his return to the Father and has not done so yet. The person he is, able to be touched at this moment, has yet to complete the journey. The emphasis on God being God and Father of both Jesus and the disciples must allude to the benefit which will come to the disciples because of Jesus' return. In the light of the last discourses this benefit would include at least the gift of the Paraclete. Accordingly the message to the disciples is the promise of greater things to come, once Jesus has returned. Jesus must therefore be referring here to an event soon to be fulfilled, after which and as a result of which blessing will come to the disciples. In the context of the gospel this most naturally refers to an event which will take place before Jesus appears to his disciples in the following episode (20:19-23). We shall return to a fuller discussion of alternative views in IIIA5 below.

The fact that Jesus was willing to be touched in 20:24-29 might be confirmation that this has by that time happened, since it contrasts with Jesus' command to Mary not to touch him.[114] It is more likely that Mary is being told not to hold on and therefore the possible touching in 20:24-29 is irrelevant to the interpretation of 20:17.[115] There may also be the message here that true Easter faith does not try to hold onto the form of the earthly visible Jesus,[116] so that there emerges a certain similarity between the behaviour of Mary and that of Thomas.[117]

The miraculous appearance of Jesus (despite closed doors) to his disciples (20:19-23) establishes once and for all his resurrection. Seeing the Lord alive with the marks of his ordeal in hands and side ensures secure identification; they rejoice. The double greeting of peace recalls the peace given in 14:27. Jesus then uses the sending language of the revelation pattern and applies it, in turn, to them: 'As my Father has sent me, so I send you' (20:21). This recalls 17:18 and the consistent way in which the author applies the pattern of the Son's commission to the disciples.

Jesus then gives the Spirit, thus fulfilling the promise made in the last discourses where the Spirit is described as the Paraclete and Spirit of Truth, and echoing the breathing of the Spirit at creation (Gen 2:7). It also fulfils the reader's expectation from texts like 7:39 which indicated the gift of the Spirit would come after Jesus was glorified. It connects, too, with 3:34 where Jesus' own authorisation is associated with his full endowment with the Spirit (symbolised already in the descent of the dove at his baptism, 1:32f). Here Jesus also fulfils the divine message to the Baptist that the one on whom the Spirit descends and remains would baptise with the Spirit (1:33), so that the two references function as an inclusio. The authorisation relates to the sending. It relates also to the releasing and withholding of sins (20:23).

The episode with Thomas focusses primarily on the nature of faith and reaches its climax as a statement about faith in the conclusion: true faith is not dependent primarily upon literally having seen, even though that was Thomas' experience and the experience of those who first passed on the witness of the gospel. The theme of faith and its basis continues in the two verses which follow. They should be taken therefore closely with what precedes. The readers do not have Thomas' advantage and there are many signs which Jesus did, which are not recorded in this gospel, but what is written here is with the intention that 'you may believe that Jesus is the Christ the Son of God and that believing you may life in his name' (20:30-31).

We have passed over Thomas' acclamation, 'My Lord and my God', because it, too, should be seen within the connection between the Thomas episode and what follows. Sometimes such heights are supposed to have been reached in Thomas' words that the confession sought in 20:31 would represent a sudden anticlimax. This is surely not the case. 'My Lord and my God' will not have been sensed as being any more or less adequate than 'Jesus is the Christ, the Son of God.'[118] Both belong within the framework of the revelation pattern and in various ways give expression to its central affirmation that Jesus is the Son who has come from the Father to make him known. In this sense he bears the designation *theos* already in the prologue within which it forms an inclusio and from which it forms one here within the gospel. And 'Christ, the Son of God', the language of royal messianism which so dominates the passion narrative, means also nothing other than that Jesus is the one who has come into the world to bear witness to the truth.

The final chapter points in particular to the nature of the Christian community after Easter. There are symbolic references to universal mission in the fish catch (21:11), to the unity of believers in the untorn net (21:11), and to the eucharist in the meal shared on the lakeside (21:13). They occur within a narrative which is also emphasising Jesus' resurrection (21:14) and his appearing (21:1; 'the third time' 21:14). The second half of the chapter regulates the community's leadership and relates it to the leadership of the wider church. Jesus commissions Peter with pastoral leadership and foretells his death. He also indicates to Peter the longevity of the beloved disciple, doubtless indicative also of his enduring influence. The author notes that this had led some to think the beloved disciple would not die before the parousia, but had obviously been proved wrong by events. He then claims the enduring influence of the disciple as witness, 'the one having written these things', and does so in much the same way as he appeals to the eyewitness in 19:35. The gospel ends with a note indicating the necessarily selective nature of what is presented because of the abundance of what is available. Of course the very selection and its ordering are in themselves important statements about the author's christology and this review has sought to bring them out.

John 18 - 21   Conclusions

Reviewing the passion narratives we note first the extensive use of royal messianic imagery in the trial and crucifixion scenes and the way it is thoroughly integrated within the revelation pattern of the author's christology. This is the point of the irony throughout, in Pilate's questioning, the mockery, the two presentations of Jesus as king, the offer of Barabbas, the contrast with Caesar, especially the supreme irony of the superscription. The royal messianic imagery of the passion narrative is not presented as depicting an enthronement of Jesus at his trial or in his crucifixion nor as foreshadowing a heavenly enthronement of Jesus as king on his return to the Father. The language usually associated with Jesus' return to the Father, exaltation, glorification, ascent, Son of Man, is absent and conversely the royal messianic language is nowhere used to describe Jesus' return to the Father.

The only use of exaltation language is in the literal sense of lifting up as a reference back to the prediction of the manner of Jesus' death (18:32; cf. 12:33).

Messianic language also appears in the confession, 'the Christ, the Son of God', in
20:31. Here, too, we saw, that comparison with the equally valid confession of
Thomas, 'my Lord and my God', indicated that both are to be understood as
different ways of giving expression to the same underlying faith, namely that
expressed in the revelation pattern of the author's christology.

Sometimes the revelation pattern surfaces directly in the passion narrative,
especially where Jesus speaks of who he is. He translates kingship into a statement
about coming into this world to bear witness to the truth (18:36f). Similarly at the
end he views his task as finished (19:30). 18:11 had already expressly included his
suffering as part of that commission. The revelation pattern also appears in Pilate's
question: 'Where are you from?' (19:9) and in the Jews' accusation that he made
himself Son of God (19:7), this recalling the discussion in 5:17-23; 10:31-39.

At a number of points exegesis is divided or uncertain. 'Behold the man' in 19:5
we saw primarily as mockery of both Jesus and the Jews that their king looked
such a pathetic figure and not as symbolic of Jesus as Son of Man or representative
man. We understood 'Pilate sat' intransitively and not as reference to Jesus' being
made to sit down. If at all, the case for seeing the transitive expressing mock
enthronement is stronger than suggestions that Jesus is being made judge. 'Giving
up the spirit' (19:30) refers to Jesus' death not the gift of the Spirit. The possibility
of Passover interpretation of Jesus in 19:37 we held to be inconclusive and, on
balance, unlikely, and we were similarly uncertain about the reference of 'blood
and water' in 19:34, though these probably serve to emphasise either Jesus' real
death or his real humanity. The arrest of Jesus raised again the question of what
meaning 'I am' conveys in the author's christology. The numinosity seems best
understood as relating to the person of Jesus as revealer than to an alleged
pronouncement of the divine name. A similar fear overcomes Pilate when he hears
the title 'Son of God' in relation to Jesus (19:7).

A number of passages related to the benefits of Jesus' death and return to the
Father. These included Jesus' words to Mary in which the familiar ascension
language reappears (20:17). These are most naturally understood to refer to an
event about to occur as a result of which God would bring blessing to the disciples.
The sending of the disciples for mission (following the model of the revelation
pattern) and the gift of the Spirit (20:21f) reflect promises made in the last
discourses. Mission is also symbolically represented in the fish catch in ch. 21.
The benefit of the Son's return is also implied in the note that the disciples would
come to understand how scripture foretold the resurrection (20:9).

It is not surprising that the concluding chapters, especially those depicting the
appearances, should contain much that pertains to the life of the post Easter
community and the Johannine community in particular. These include the benefits
mentioned in the previous paragraph. We also note the symbolism of unity, the
untorn net (21:11), the eucharist (21:13), and Peter's pastoral leadership (21:15-
17). The author also includes more particular references relevant to the gospel and
the first readers. They assure the reader of the authority and integrity of the gospel
material and include the beloved disciple's commission to care for Jesus' mother
(19:25-28), his longevity and his function as guarantor and witness, having been
the beloved disciple and the who leant on Jesus breast (21:21-24), and the full

adequacy of faith on the basis of the gospel report alone (20:29-31) which represents the author's selection from a vast quantity of available material (21:25).

IIC   THE STRUCTURE OF JOHANNINE CHRISTOLOGY

AN OUTLINE

What has emerged from the review and the earlier investigations of the revelation pattern may be set out in the following structure:

The Father

sends and authorises the Son,

who knows the Father,

comes from the Father,

makes the Father known,

brings light and life and truth,

completes his Father's work,

returns to the Father,

exalted, glorified, ascended,

sends the disciples

and sends the Spirit

to enable greater understanding,

to equip for mission,

and to build up the community of faith.

I shall use this structure to integrate the findings of Part IIA and B. In doing so, I am concerned to list the salient features and, where interpretation of particular motifs have demanded consideration of their use in a number of passages, to give an overall assessment of their likely meaning. These findings will then form the basis for the systematic consideration of issues of Johannine christology in Part III. The earlier clauses of the statement have to a large degree already been the subject of attention in IIA above, so that these will be of brief summary nature, while later clauses will demand fuller consideration.

1. 'The Father...'

The Son was in the beginning with God (1:1f; 17:5), in the bosom of the Father (1:18), yeos (1:18), only Son of the Father (1:14; 3:16,18), sharing the Father's glory and his love before the foundation of the world (17:5,24), mediator of creation (1:3,10), was before John the Baptist (1:15,30), before Abraham (8:58) and seen in his pre-existent glory by Isaiah (12:41).

The terms, 'Father' for God and 'Son' for Jesus, are most common throughout the gospel, particularly in describing the relationship of the two and the Son's revelatory task. While pre-existence is presupposed throughout when the author speaks of the Son's coming and being sent, the direct references are the few noted above and are found especially in the prologue in association with motifs not recurring later in the gospel.

2. '...sends and authorises the Son...'

The references to the Father sending the Son are extensive and have been listed above. 3:16 also speaks of the Father giving the Son. Because sending entails authorisation I include here other authorisation motifs. The Father has given all into the Son's hands (3:35; 13:3), given him authority over all flesh (17:2), given him authority to judge and to give life (5:22), given him his name (17:11f), given him command (10:18; 12:49f; 15:10), instruction (8:28), and a task to complete (4:34; 5:36; 17:4; 18:11; 19:30). Accordingly the Son does not act of his own accord (5:30; 7:17; 8:28; 14:10).

3. '...who knows the Father...'

This is primarily related to the Son's having been with the Father. Jesus refers to what he has seen and heard (3:32; 6:46; 8:26,38,40; 15:15). No one has seen God, but the Son has (1:18; 5:37; 6:46). This relates also to his having been given instruction in the context of authorisation and to his receiving the Father's name and words (see above).

This follows the envoy revealer model, where the sent one comes from, reports, and acts, for the sender. This is also the framework within which the unique relationship of Father and Son is usually expounded (so mostly in 10:32-38 and 14:7-11). Jesus is one with the Father and to have seen him is to have seen the Father because he does the works the Father has given him to do. 5:17-20 is similar in emphasising unity expressed through the Son's obedience to the Father, but it departs from the revelation envoy model by speaking of the Father showing the Son in the present what he is doing and thereby giving him a pattern to follow (an apprentice model). The Son's knowing the Father is also implied in the concept of mutual indwelling (10:38; 14:20) and is stated explicitly as mutual knowledge in 10:15 (cf. also 17:25).

4. '...comes from the Father...'

The references are extensive and have been gathered above. The Son comes from the Father, from God, from above, from heaven into the world. Coming thence is more than explanation of change of place; it implies authority and superiority in contrast to those who are of the earth and so relates closely to the elements of the statement we have already dealt with to this point. The coming is often linked with the going, as we shall see below. Failure to perceive the one is the same as failure to perceive the other. In association with the manna imagery the author also speaks of the descending of Jesus from heaven as bread, a motif used of Jesus elsewhere only in 3:13, which speaks of descent and ascent of Jesus as Son of Man. The other distinctive formulation for the Son's coming as revealer is in the prologue: 'The word became flesh and tented among us and we beheld his glory' (1:14). The author is particularly fond of irony in relation to Jesus' origin and frequently portrays unknowing questioners discussing Jesus' origin, while the reader knows all along the true answer (1:46,48; 2:9; 3:2,8; 4:11; 6:5,41f; 7:27,40-52; 9:16,29,33; 19:9). Sometimes both the whence and the whither questions occur together in this way (8:14; cf. 3:8).

5. '...makes the Father known...'

The extensive and varied formulations by which this is expressed and the references are listed in IIA above. This is the climactic statement of the prologue (1:18) and appears throughout the gospel as Jesus is portrayed as speaking, telling, witnessing to, or making known what he has seen and heard, been commanded, told, and instructed. Accordingly to have seen the Son is to have seen the Father, for he has made him known (1:18; 14:7-11). Response to Jesus is thus response to the Father. This is the revelation model and is primarily expounded within the framework of the revealer envoy pattern. Closely associated with it are the two elements which follow.

6. '...brings light and life and truth...'

This is a selection of the most important images and within the statement they also represent many others which occur within the gospel. Jesus has come as light into the world (1:4f,7-9; 3:19-21; 8:12; 9:5; 11:9f; 12:35f,46). Light and life are sometimes linked (1:4; 8:12). Jesus comes as life into the world. References to people receiving 'eternal life' through faith in the Son are common throughout the gospel and this corresponds to the gospel's aim (20:31). Eternal life or life (they mean the same as 5:39f shows) is a gift given by the Son during his ministry. Sometimes it is spoken of as a future gift available after Jesus' death and return (3:15; cf. 6:27,51c-58). But mostly it represents what Jesus brings in his person. He offers living water (4:10) and he is also the bread of life, the light of life, the resurrection and the life, the way, the truth and the life. 17:3 explains that this life is to know God and Jesus Christ whom he sent. 6:63 identifies Jesus' words as spirit and life and Peter's confession is introduced with the affirmation that Jesus has the words of eternal life (6:68). The link between the gift of life and the giver as life is evident in 5:26f where the Father has granted the Son to have life in himself, as he has life in himself, and given him authority to bring judgement (to death or life). Life is a gift brought by and also inherent in the Son and derived from the Father and to offer this life is the purpose of the Son's coming (10:10).

The offer of life, when refused, brings judgement. The Son did not come to judge the world (3:17-21; 5:45; 8:15; 12:47), yet his very coming brought judgement, so that sometimes in apparent contradiction Jesus can affirm that it is for judgement that he has come (9:39). The word he has spoken (12:47), and even the word bearing witness to him (5:45), effectively condemns those who refuse its truth (3:18-21,36). Accordingly the final rejection of Jesus on the cross becomes the final act of judgement for the world. It thinks it judges Jesus; but in the cross God judges it and its ruler (16:11; 12:31; cf. 16:33), manifests its sin as rejection of the Son (16:9) and demonstrates Jesus' righteousness, because his return to the Father through death has vindicated him (16:10). The Son's offer brings therefore the judgement of life or death now to people (5:21-27), as well as judgement in the future (5:28f).

Truth (and grace) also came through the Son (1:14,17). Jesus has come to bear witness to the truth (18:37) and is the truth (14:6). This is closer to the revelation imagery, but has the same basic structure as the statements about light and life. These are all ways of expressing what the Son brings by his very presence. They present his salvific significance and do so within the framework of the revealer envoy pattern.

The 'I am' statements with a simple predicate (without a qualifier such as 'true' or 'good') belong here. In each case they are to be understood within the framework of the revealer envoy christology and frequently this is quite explicit (eg. 6:35; cf. 6:36-51b; 8:12; cf. 8:13-19; and 14:6; cf. 14:7-11). There are also parallels for the use of 'I am' in this way by envoy and emissary figures outside the gospel which confirm the likelihood that this is its context here.[119] The two with qualifiers may be in part polemical,[120] but also represent Jesus as the source of life, almost in a popularly Platonic sense,[121] even though more, it seems, from the perspective of the time after Jesus' death and return to the Father. The simple 'I am' of 8:24,28 and 13:19 is also best understood as a statement that Jesus is the one he claims to be: the one sent from God. Of the other absolute uses, 6:20, like its Markan parallel, has Jesus simply identify that it is he, not a ghost. In the account of the arrest, Jesus uses the words, 'I am (he)' (18:5,6,8), to identify himself as the one whom they are looking for in much the same way as the former blind man also owns up to his identity in 9:9 by saying, 'I am (he)'. This is in no way to diminish the impact on the bystanders; but it explains 'I am' as the self identification which triggered it. In 4:26 Jesus identifies himself with the Messiah, just as, by contrast John the Baptist had rejected such an identity for himself with the words, 'I am not' in 1:21. Finally 8:58 means the equivalent of 'I was and have been in existence since before Abraham.'

None of the so called 'I am' sayings demands the explanation that Jesus is pronouncing the divine name and such an interpretation reads most unnaturally in contexts where it is supposed to occur.[122] On the other hand, some influence from Isa 43:10 must not be ruled out in the sense that Jesus speaks in the same manner as Yahweh does when identifying himself as the one who will save Israel.[123] This manner of self claim is being used by analogy. It was also used by analogy negatively of demiurges in gnostic literature, but not as a statement of the divine name itself; it also occurs there frequently in a positive sense with predicates.[124] This usage is consistent with the revealer envoy background noted above.

Here, too, belong the messianic statements of the gospel. Jesus is presented as the Messiah (1:41,45-49; 4:29; 7:27; 9:22; 11:27; 12:13-15; 20:31) and this theme is developed with powerful irony in the passion narrative. When we look for clues about how this messiahship is understood, we find that Jesus' messiahship is consistently expounded in terms of his being the Son sent from the Father and come to make him known.[125] Sometimes there is a movement from messianic titles to Son of Man (eg: 1:49-51; 12:34), as Martyn has shown especially in relation to ch 9.[126] But it is wrong to understand this simply as a taking up of messianic into Son of Man christology, since the latter has its particular focus within the wider Johannine christology, especially in relation to Jesus' death and return to the Father.[127] The author employs confessional messianic statements that Jesus is the Christ and the Son of God, but integrates them primarily within his overall christology of Jesus as the Son of the Father whose coming was the event of revelation.[128] I see no convincing evidence that he is concerned to pit a prophetic Mosaic messianism against a Davidic one, as Schillebeeckx argues,[129] nor that he seeks to do the reverse, as Bittner has suggested.[130] The confession of 20:31 cannot mean less than Thomas's acclamation of 20:28. The same is true where acclamations of Jesus as prophet or saviour of the world are given expression; they are to be understood after the revealer envoy pattern of christology.

7. '...completes his Father's work...'

The words, 'It is finished' (19:30), issue from Jesus on the cross. He had expressed himself similarly in 17:4; and in 4:34 Jesus describes his task as completing the work he had been given to do. We have listed references above which describe how the Son does on earth what he has been commanded to do by the Father, doing the works of the Father, and so not acting on his own authority. Accordingly it may also be said that the Father, himself, is doing the works in the Son (14:10).

What is the work and what are the works? The work refers to the commission to be the revealer envoy and to return to the Father. The work of the revealer envoy is to make the Father known, and the goal of his ministry is that people may come to believe that this he God's envoy, at least on the basis of his deeds, his works, even if not on the basis of his direct claims (5:36; 10:37; 14:11).

The works refer to Jesus' deeds. They include in particular Jesus' miracles. The miracle at the wedding feast and the miracle of the raising of Lazarus are both said to manifest Jesus' glory and, while this word does not appear in other miracle stories in John, the same basic idea is present. The miracles manifest, for eyes that can see, who Jesus is, namely the one sent from the Father (so explicitly as Jesus' purpose for the miracle, 11:42; cf. also 5:36). Therefore the author describes them as signs. Failure to read them as signs reflects an inadequate faith which sees, like Nicodemus, only at the earthly level.

At this point I want also to mention those texts scattered throughout the gospel which, with varying degree of probability or uncertainty, may refer to Jesus' death as a vicarious sacrifice. They are 1:29; 6:51c; 10:11,15; 11:51-53 (cf. 18:14); and 15:13. Others sometimes linked with such an interpretation are 3:14; 3:16; 12:27; 17:19; 18:11. Accordingly some would include this act of atonement as a major part of Jesus' work which he had to complete, and so find it also alluded to in 19:30 ('it is finished') and in 17:4 ('I have finished the work you have given me to do'). The context of 17:4 suggests that the work of revelation is primarily in view, not the work of atonement and the association of the two texts makes it therefore likely for 19:30. Similarly in 10:17 Jesus says that his Father loves him because he lays does his life that he might take it up again. This suggests the task lies in passing through death and returning to the Father rather than in an act of atonement. Nevertheless the presence of the texts, at the very least, one of which probably assumes vicarious atonement (1:29), means that this may also be seen to belong to the Son's work. The extent to which this is so will be discussed below in IIIB2. The primary focus of the Son's work is as the previous two sections have indicated: to make the Father known and so to bring life to the world (17:3).

8. '...returns to the Father...'

Often Jesus' going is mentioned in the context of coming, as in the summary statement of 13:1 ('knowing that the Father had given all things into his hands and that he had come from God and was going to God'; cf. also 13:3). The Son knows whence he came and where he is going (8:14). Jesus tells his disciples: 'I have come from the Father and have come into the world; again I am leaving the world and going to the Father' (16:28). In the last discourses in particular and in the final prayer Jesus speaks of his going to the Father (14:12,28; 16:7; 17:11,13).

As with the theme of Jesus' origin, so also with that of his destination, the author makes full use of irony. In particular the saying 7:33 ('where I am going you cannot come; you shall seek me and not find me') is used in this way with the Jews (7:34,36; 8:21f). We saw that in the last discourses a variant of the same saying becomes the subject of reflection at a number of points from 13:33 onwards, and in particular in chs. 14 and 16. By contrast with the use of the saying in relation to the Jews, Jesus promises Peter and the disciples that where he goes they will come later. 14:2f uses the image of heavenly dwellings. In 17:24 Jesus prays that his disciples may come to be where he is and see the heavenly glory he shares with the Father. The same thought also lies behind 12:26, 'If anyone serves me, let him follow me, and where I am, there also will my servant be.' This is true, notwithstanding the promise that the Son and Father will also take up their abode in the disciples after Easter (14:20-23), since they refer to two different modes of being.

The author associates other benefits with the return of the Son to the Father, benefits which result from it and I shall consider these below. The return completes the Son's movement undertaken in fulfilling the task of revelation on which he was sent. But our survey of the gospel also demonstrated that this is of much greater significance than the completion of a cycle. Throughout the gospel some significant patterns and motifs occurred which interpreted the significance of this event and to these we turn in the remaining elements of our summary.

9. '...exalted, glorified, ascended...'

Under this heading I want also to gather associated motifs.
(a) The first is 'the hour', sometimes 'the time' or referred to simply as 'now'. These terms refer throughout the gospel to the moment of Jesus' death and return to the Father, and to events associated with it. The salient texts are:

'My hour has not yet come' (2:4)
  (Jesus, speaking to his mother at the wedding feast)
'My time is not yet here'; 'My time is not yet fulfilled' (7:6,8)
  (Jesus, speaking to his brothers, referring to his going up to Jerusalem and possibly indirectly to his ascent to the Father)
'His hour had not yet come' (7:30 and again identically in 8:20)
  (The author, telling us why the Jews were unable to arrest Jesus)
'The hour has come for the Son of Man to be glorified' (12:23)
  (Jesus in Jerusalem and in response to the approach of the Greeks)
'Now is my soul troubled. And what shall I say? Father, save me from this hour? But for this I came to this hour. Father, glorify your name!' (12:27f).
  (Jesus in the same setting, facing the prospect of death)
'Now is the judgement of this world, now shall the ruler of this world be cast out; and I, if I am lifted up from the earth, will draw all people to myself' (12:31f).
  (Jesus in the same setting. The author adds: 'he said this to indicate by what kind of death he would die' 12:33).
'Jesus, knowing that the hour had come for him to pass out of this world to the Father...' (13:1)
  (The author, introducing the scene of the footwashing and the farewell discourses)
'Now is the Son of Man glorified and God is glorified in him. If God is glorified in him, he will glorify him in himself and will glorify him immediately' (13:31f)
  (Jesus at the beginning of the farewell discourses)
'Now I am going to him who sent me' (16:5)
  (within the second discourse though really this sense of time is present throughout especially ch. 14 and ch. 16)
'Father the hour has come; glorify your Son, that your Son may glorify you' (17:1); 'And now glorify me, Father, in yourself with the glory which I had when I was with you before the foundation of the world' (17:5); 'But now I am coming to you' (17:13)
  (Jesus, in his final prayer).

There is a remarkable consistency in usage here of the 'hour', 'time' concept. We note in particular the presence of the following motifs in association with it:

  Son of Man
  glorification
  lifting up/exalted
  ascension
  judgement

going to the Father

(a) The second motif consists more of a structure of thought, whereby the present of the speaker is compared with something greater to come and this something greater is associated with Jesus' death and return to the Father.

'Because I said to you (sg), "I saw you under the fig tree," do you believe? You shall see greater things than these.' And he said to him, 'Truly, truly, I tell you (pl), you shall see the heaven opened and the angels of God ascending and descending upon the Son of Man' (1:50f)
(Jesus, responding to Nathanael's confession of Jesus as Son of God and king of Israel)
'If I told you earthly things and you do not believe, how will you believe if I tell you heavenly things. (13) And no one has ascended into heaven except he who descended from heaven, the Son of Man. (14) And as Moses lifted up the serpent in the wilderness, even so the Son of Man must be lifted up, (15) so that all who believe might have eternal life in him' (3:12-15)
(Jesus, having faced Nicodemus with his word of revelation on earth)
'Does this offend you? What if you were to see the Son of Man ascending where he was before?' (6:61bf)
(Jesus, responding to the disciples' difficulty with his claim to have descended and become a human being)
'Truly I say to you, he who believes in me, the works which I do he also shall do and greater works than these shall he do because I go to the Father. And whatever you ask in my name I shall do it, that the Father may be glorified in the Son' (14:12f)
(Jesus, speaking during the last discourse about the disciples' future work and about to promise the Paraclete)
'You have heard that I said to you, "I go away and I am coming to you." If you loved me you would rejoice that I go to the Father, because the Father is greater than me' (14:28)
(Jesus, at the conclusion of the discourse in ch. 14, having assured the disciples of the gift of the Spirit)

These passages bear similarity with those concerning the 'hour'. Both refer to the event associated with Jesus' death and return to the Father. These promise in different ways that this event will bring something greater for the disciples. There is also a striking similarity in many of the motifs associated with both sets of passages. In particular the following should be noted:

Son of Man
ascent (and descent; present also in 1:51 re: angels)
lifting up/exalted
going to the Father

(c) In turning to the motifs 'exalted, glorified, ascended', we note that these have already appeared in the texts considered and within them form a cluster of motifs together with the title Son of Man. The following are passages not cited thus far in which these motifs appear.
'When you have lifted up the Son of Man, then you shall know that I am the one

and I do nothing of myself, but as the Father taught me, so I speak' (8:28)
   (Jesus, addressing the Jews)
'How can you say, that the Son of Man must be lifted up?' (12:34)
   (The Jews, perturbed by Jesus' prediction of being lifted up because it does not
fit their messianic expectation)
'For the Spirit was not yet (present), because Jesus was not yet glorified' (7:39)
   (The author, noting that Jesus' promise in 7:38 of rivers of water from within
could apply only after Easter)
'This sickness is not to death but for the glory of God, so that the Son of God
might be glorified through it' (11:4)
   (This refers initially to the glory manifest in the raising of Lazarus but also to the
ultimate glorification through Jesus' death and return to the Father, the event to
which the Lazarus miracle leads in John's account. 11:40 refers to 'seeing the
glory of God' in the same way.)
'His disciples did not understand these things at first, but when Jesus was
glorified, then they remembered that these things were written concerning him
and that they did these things to him' (12:16)
   (The author's comment about messianic fulfilment of scripture and messianic
implications of the behaviour of the crowd at Jesus' entry into Jerusalem)
'"Father, glorify your name." A voice came from heaven: "I have glorified it and
will glorify it again"' (12:28)
   (Jesus' prayer concerning his hour and God's response)

The motif 'glorify' also occurs in 8:54 (Jesus does not glorify, seek honour for,
himself, the Father does that; similarly using the word 'glory', 5:41,44; 7:18; 8:50;
12:43); 15:8 (the Father is glorified through the disciples' bearing fruit); 16:14 (the
Paraclete will glorify Jesus); 17:4 (Jesus has glorified God on earth); and 17:10
(Jesus has been glorified among his disciples). 'Glory' is also used to describe the
revelation Jesus brought (1:14; 2:11; 11:4,40; cf. 12:43). 12:41 refers to Jesus' pre-
existent glory (cf. 17:5,24).

The only other reference to ascent outside the passages already quoted is:

'Do not hold onto me, for I have not yet ascended to the Father; but go to my
brothers and tell them, "I am ascending to my Father and your Father, to my God
and your God"' (20:17)
   (The risen Jesus, addressing Mary Magdalene)

The passages, taken all together, show how 'hour', the promise of greater things,
exaltation, glorification, ascent (descent), and the title 'Son of Man', form a
distinctive semantic cluster in the author's language and he uses them to describe
Jesus' death and return to the Father. Some of the texts are the author's footnotes,
so that we may be confident in speaking of the author's particular interest in using
this language in this way. The only motif in this cluster not yet considered is the
title, 'Son of Man'. Outside the texts cited above it occurs in 5:27 (where the
author speaks of Jesus' role in judgement), in 9:35 (also linked with Jesus in a
judging role. cf. 9:39) and in ch. 6. Here we saw it is used of future nourishment
(6:27), in particular of the eucharist (6:53). The judgement motif, already
appearing in 12:31, may also belong to the semantic cluster. The ch. 6 sayings are
consistent with the use of Son of Man in most of the texts cited above to refer not

primarily to Jesus' ministry, but to the greater event and what flows from it.

In Part IIIA4 we shall examine a number of these motifs in greater detail. In what follows we shall examine the result of Jesus' death and return. Already a number of elements in this have appeared in the texts cited, illustrating that the motif of Jesus' return, the Son of Man cluster, and the fruits of the event should be considered together.

10. '...sends the disciples...'

The commissioning of the disciples occurs when the risen Jesus appears to them on the evening of the resurrection day and declares: 'As my Father has sent me, so I send you' (20:21). A similar analogy between the Son's own sending and that of the disciples is expressed in 17:18. The same parallel structure lies behind 3:3-11, where there is a shift from Jesus the teacher come from God to a generalised discussion of all who are born of the Spirit and so qualified to be teachers and to bear witness. The wind metaphor in 3:8 uses language elsewhere associated with the Son: people hear his voice, but no one knows where he comes from or where he is going; 'so is everyone who is born of the Spirit.' The distinction lies within the use of the birth metaphor in 3:3,5. Whereas Jesus is the only Son who has come from above (3:31; cf. 3:16,18), the disciples are born (3:3,5), given the authority to become children of God (1:12f). They are from above, but not in the same sense. Nevertheless ch. 3 shows how the author interprets the sending of the disciples within the framework provided by the envoy revelation (-bearer) model.[131]

Accordingly they are not of this world and will face the same hatred and rejection the Son has faced (15:19; 17:14,16). They, too, have been authorised (20:21,23). Their authorisation is associated with the giving of the Spirit (20:22; 3:5) and it is with the Spirit's authority they will bring to the world the evidence concerning Jesus (esp. 16:8-11). They, too, have been loved by the Father (17:23,26), been given the Father's glory (17:22), his name (17:6,26; cf. 17:11f), his words (17:8,14), his command (15:10) and in their own way know the Son as the Son knows the Father and therefore also know the Father (14:7-11; 17:3,25). They, too, bear witness (15:27). They, too, manifest oneness to the world that the world may know the Son by knowing them (17:20-23; cf. 13:34f). They, too, must be willing to follow their master to death (12:25; cf. 13:36; 21:18f) and know the reward that their path will finally lead to his heavenly presence (12:26; 17:24). We shall explore further the purpose of their sending under 'mission', below.

11. '...and sends the Spirit...'

Jesus gives the Spirit directly after commissioning of the disciples: 'Saying this, he breathed on them and said to them: "Receive the Holy Spirit; whoever sins you release they are released, and whosoever you retain they are retained"' (20:22f). The authority to release or retain sins is referred to here only; the giving of the Spirit, on the other hand, has been prepared for at a number of points in the gospel. Already 1:33 designates Jesus the one who will baptise in the Spirit and 3:3-8 assumes the situation when it will be fulfilled. 7:39 identifies the rivers of water (7:38) as a reference to the Spirit, noting that it will be given after Jesus' glorification. This promise is to all who believe and this counts against those who suggest that the promise of the Spirit Paraclete is for an apostolic[132] or prophetic[133] office or only for the disciples as distinct from the wider circle of believers.[134]

It is above all in the last discourses that the promise is expounded in detail. In 14:16f, as in 20:21f, it is associated with the mission of the disciples and doubtless explains how their greater works will be possible. In particular the Spirit is designated the Paraclete (14:16,26; 15:26; 16:7) and the Spirit of Truth (14:17; 15:26; 16:13) and in 14:16 as 'another Paraclete'.

This signals a similar analogy between the Son and the Spirit to the one which exists between the Son and the disciples and a similar use of the envoy revealer pattern. The analogy has been emphasised by Bornkamm,[135] who also suggests that behind it lies an adaptation of the forerunner successor model.[136] Burge puts it well when he writes that Johannine christology is the 'template' for the Spirit in the gospel.[137] The revealer envoy pattern is evident in the following statements. The Spirit also comes from the Father (15:26), is sent (14:26) or given (14:16) by the Father, but also by the Son (15:26; 16:7). When the Spirit comes (16:7), he will expound to the world the significance of the Son: the world's rejection of him as sin, his vindication before God, and the meaning of the climax of Jesus' life as judgement of the world (16:8-11). Thus, as the Son makes the Father known, so the Spirit makes the Son known.

The coming of the Son (and the Father) to dwell in the disciples after Easter is almost certainly to be seen as something the Spirit makes possible (14:16-23). Similarly the Spirit will represent the Son according to 16:12-15. 'When he comes, the Spirit of Truth, he will lead you into all truth; for he will not speak of his own authority, but what he hears he will speak' (16:13). Similarly the Son did not speak of his own authority, but only what he had heard from the Father (8:26,28). The similarity continues: 'He will glorify me, because he will take what is mine and declare it to you' (16:14). The pattern of coming, being sent, receiving and giving knowledge, is clearly discernible. The witnessing (14:26) and teaching (14:26) functions are as central as they are for the Son. The Spirit is the second Paraclete; the Son was the first.

The Spirit is, however, not another revealer envoy independent of Jesus, but as, above all, 16:13-15 carefully points out, the truth into which he leads, including his words about things that are to come, are not original. They all derive from Jesus. This means, however, in turn, that the Spirit calls Jesus' words and deeds into remembrance, but also tells more truth about (and from) Jesus. The Spirit, beside the disciples who also bear witness (15:26), is the explanation of what lies before us in the gospel. It enables us to know the heart of the gospel: the message of the Son come from the Father, sent to make him known. It is because Jesus goes away and the Spirit is sent that the full import of who he was may be known (16:7-11).

12. '...to enable greater understanding...'

In the previous section we noted how it is above all through the Spirit Paraclete that greater understanding comes of who the Son was and is, what he said and is saying. This belongs together with other statements which indicate a change of understanding which will follow the event of Jesus' death and return.

In 2:22 the author notes that Jesus' temple word was remembered and understood only after Easter: 'When Jesus therefore was raised from the dead, his disciples remembered that he said this and believed the scripture and the word which Jesus said.' 'The scripture', Ps 69:10, formulated in the future tense, was read as a prediction of Jesus' death. This, too, was remembered by the disciples (2:17), and again it is likely this refers to remembering after Easter, as the link with 2:22 suggests. 12:16 is very similar. Referring to the messianic application of Zech 9:9 to Jesus' entry into Jerusalem and to the crowd's welcoming him as Messiah, the author notes: 'His disciples did not understand these things at first, but when Jesus was glorified, then they remembered that these things were written concerning him and that they had done these things to him.' Both verses refer to knowledge of two kinds gained after Easter: greater understanding about Jesus and about scripture in relation to Jesus.

A similar prediction of greater understanding comes in the words of Jesus to the Jews in 8:28f, 'When you have lifted up the Son of Man, then you shall know that I am the one and that I do nothing on my own authority, but as the Father taught me, so I speak these things. And the one who sent me is with me. He has not left me alone, because I always do what is pleasing to him.' What the Jews will (may) come to know is spelled out in the language of the revealer envoy christology. In 14:19f Jesus promises special knowledge to the disciples: 'A little while and the world will see me no more, but you will see me; because I live you will live also. And in that day you will know that I am in my Father and you in me and I in you.'

A similar idea seems present in the prediction of Judas' betrayal which is given, Jesus says, '...so that when it has happened, you may believe that I am the one' (13:19). Jesus speaks similarly in 14:29, 'And now I have told you before it happens, so that when it happens you may believe.' What they should believe is doubtless not just that Jesus was right in his predictions, but that he is the one he claims to be (so 14:31).

The prediction that the disciples will come to understand the application of scripture to Jesus, noted already in discussing 2:17,22 and 12:16, occurs also in 20:9 in a note of the author about the disciples' not yet achieving resurrection faith, 'For they did not yet know the scripture that he must rise from the dead.'

Taken together with the Paraclete sayings, these passages indicate that the event of Jesus' death and return, taken as a whole, will bring about greater understanding of who Jesus was and of the way scripture is fulfilled in him and that this knowledge comes in particular through the gift of the Spirit.

Perhaps this is already hinted at in 6:62f, where, after challenging the disciples with the words, 'What if you see the Son of Man ascending where he was before?', Jesus says, 'The Spirit is the life giver, the flesh is of no profit; the words which I have spoken to you are spirit and life.' While the primary reference is to Jesus' words during his earthly ministry (he is bearer of the Spirit!), there may also be the suggestion that after his ascension the Spirit would help them remember his words. When 3:3 speaks of 'seeing the kingdom of God' and relates it to those born from above, born of the Spirit (3:5,8), we also have reference to this special post Easter knowledge.

So far, we have related the greater understanding primarily to the sending of the Spirit. Indirectly the sending of the disciples also increases knowledge. Both are witnesses according to 15:26 and the author takes particular care to emphasise the importance and reliability of the disciples' knowledge of the earthly Jesus. Faith can trust fully in their witness and thus the witness of the gospel and need not be preoccupied, as Thomas was, with material, first hand, evidence. The author emphasises that his gospel is only a selection of much more material that is available (20:30; 21:25). He stresses especially the role of the beloved disciple who 'wrote' the gospel and may be identified as the source of special eye witness tradition. He is portrayed as the one who leant on Jesus' chest at the last supper, so that he is almost pictured as relating to Jesus the way Jesus related to God ('in the bosom of the Father' 1:18). Certainly he was privy to special knowledge on that occasion. A similar special claim to knowledge lies behind his receiving the commissioning to care for Jesus' mother, his inside knowledge of the high priestly courts, his racing first to the tomb and first looking in, and his position of special honour independent of Peter. His is also probably the eye witness report of the piercing of Jesus' side.

The knowledge claim of the gospel combines therefore recall and understanding given by the Spirit, on the one hand, and the connection of tradition through the disciples, the beloved disciple in particular, on the other. It is not the case that the disciples had no knowledge of Jesus during his earthly ministry, any more than it is the case that the gifts of light and life were not to be had then. What comes through the event of Jesus' death and return is greater understanding of what was already there. In particular Jesus' death focusses the issue of who he was and so becomes an act of judgement and an occasion for discernment (so 16:7-11). The Son carries his claim to the end and in the passion narrative this claim is driven to its climax particularly through ironic use of messianic motifs. Jesus' vindication (return to the Father) is a revelation of the rightness of his claim. The Spirit, therefore, not only aids recall and works beside the disciples in this; it also presses home the implications of the death and return of Jesus for understanding who he is. The ultimate focus is therefore who he is, that he is the Son, sent from the Father, who came as the revealer envoy offering the gift of life and then returned.

13. '...to equip for mission...'

Both the sending of the disciples and the sending of the Spirit are closely related to mission. The theme of the disciples' mission appears at a number of points through the gospel. It is present in ch. 4, both in the Samaritan woman's 'mission' to her townspeople (4:29) and in Jesus' words to his disciples about sowing and harvesting (4:35-38). It is present in the irony of the Jews' response to Jesus' saying he would go and they would not find him, where they speculate whether he would go to the Greeks (7:33-36). This clearly foreshadows the Gentile mission. The same is true in 10:16 when Jesus speaks of other sheep not of this fold and in 11:51-52 when Caiaphas predicts that Jesus' death will benefit not only the Jewish people but all God's scattered children.

The Gentile mission theme also lies behind the approach of the Greeks to Jesus in 12:20. The verse before has the Pharisees bemoaning that 'the world has gone after him.' The irony is obvious when immediately the author tells of the Greeks requesting to see Jesus. Between them and Jesus are Philip and Andrew, perhaps symbolic of the role the disciples will have in carrying the gospel to the Gentiles. Jesus' acclamation that the hour of glorification had come refers primarily to his death and return, but also to what would flow from it, namely the mission of the disciples to the world. 12:24 makes the link specific: 'Truly, truly I tell you, unless a grain of wheat falls into the ground and dies, it remains alone; if it dies, it bears much fruit.' The same theme appears a few verses later where Jesus exclaims: 'And I, if I be lifted up, will draw all people to me' (12:32).

Jesus' going away (7:33f), his death (10:15f; 11:51f; 12:24,32f), his exaltation (12:32) and glorification (12:23), will result in the sending of the disciples, equipped by the Spirit, for mission to the world. This is doubtless the background for the promise of Jesus that the disciples will do the works he does and 'greater works than these' (14:12). In such work Jesus promises them answered prayer (14:13f), adding that this is so in order that the Father may be glorified in the Son. Mission brings glory to the Father and the Son. The same thought reappears in 15:7f: 'If you remain in me and my words remain in you, ask what you will and it shall be done for you. In this is my Father glorified that you bear much fruit and become my disciples.' Similarly fruit bearing and prayer is linked in 15:16. In 15:1-17 fruit bearing is related to the vine image. In both contexts Jesus speaks of the commandments he gives the disciples (14:15,21,24; 15:10,12,14,16,17). These include the commandment to mission, as 15:16 illustrates: 'I have appointed you that you go and bear fruit and that your fruit remain.' We shall see under 14. '...to build up the community in faith.', below, that the same context links the love commandment closely with the command to mission (15:12; cf. 13:34f).

14:16 directly relates this commission (14:15) to the promise of the Paraclete. The promise of the Paraclete is here the promise of indwelling presence (14:16f). Beside it (and mediated through it) is the promise of the indwelling presence of Jesus and the knowledge which that brings (14:18-20). Then the author returns to the commission theme (14:21). The structure confirms the importance of the promises of presence for the mission theme. The promise is repeated in 14:23f in the same connection, this time speaking of both Father and Son indwelling. The words promising the teaching ministry of the paraclete (14:26) should also be seen as connected to the mission theme.

The Paraclete is promised in 15:26f amid ominous predictions of violent opposition to the disciples' mission (reflected also in 17:14). In 16:5-15 the Paraclete's work is also to be seen in relation to the mission. In particular the Paraclete's case about sin, righteousness and judgement in expounding Jesus' death represents central preaching themes of the mission.

Mission is probably reflected symbolically in the miracle of the fish catch in ch. 21, perhaps its universality in the number 153. It is also likely that the accounts of healed people telling others of their healings have situations of missionary witness and opposition in mind (eg: the lame man in ch. 5 and the blind in ch. 9).

Mission is above all the fruit of Jesus' death and return, because through this event the Spirit is given and the disciples are commissioned.

14. '...and to build up the community of faith.'

A particularly strong feature of the last discourses is the exhortation to unity and, as we have seen, it is frequently related to the impact this has on the world. The most celebrated examples are: 'A new commandment I give to you that you love one another as I have loved you, that you love one another. By this shall all people know that you are my disciples, if you have love one for another' (13:34f) and the prayer of Jesus for his disciples and those to follow them: 'that they may all be one, as you Father are in me and I in you, that they also may be in us, that the world may believe that you sent me. The glory you have given me I have given to them, that they may be one as we are one, I in them and you in me, that they may be completely one, so that the world may know that you sent me and that you loved them as you loved me' (17:21-23).

Recognition that they are Jesus' disciples and recognition that the Father sent the Son are connected, the one being a witness of the other. The connection between mission and community is also present in 15:1-18. Here, too, we find through the image of the vine the theme of indwelling. The unity derives from the unity which already exists between Father and Son and from the life that flows from the Son. We saw that 15:1-18 stands as a timeless statement of the continuing basis of unity with the Son and of disciples with one another for mission. The commandments Jesus gives include the fruit bearing of mission and loving one another and both are possible because of the life in the vine, the love shown in Jesus' giving himself for them. This love-unity-mission theme is most strongly represented in 13:34f; 15:1-18; and ch. 17.

A similar concern for unity in relation to mission is found in 10:16f and 11:51-52, though here the gathering of the one flock and the benefit for all the scattered children of God seems rather to come at the other end of the perspective, ie: unity is the goal of the mission as well as its means.

In ch. 14 the focus of community is that between Father and Son and, through the Paraclete, that between the disciples and the Son. After Easter the Spirit, once present to the disciples through the person of Jesus in his earthly ministry, will come to dwell in the disciples (14:17). They will also see the Son, know that he is in the Father (as already affirmed as mutual indwelling between the two in 14:11), and know that he dwells in them and they in him (14:19f). Similarly the Father and Son will dwell in the disciples, according to 14:23. The focus here is communion with Father and Son.

The footwashing narrative emphasises community as mutual serving, especially through the second interpretation. As it stands, the juxtaposition of this interpretation with that of the washing as Jesus' cleansing his disciples connects the community of disciples with Jesus and the community of disciples with one another. The second flows from the love shown in the first. The emphasis on community of disciples, not articulated in ch. 14, becomes a major focus in ch. 15 and in Jesus' final prayer in ch. 17, perhaps reflecting changing situations in the Johannine community, but it is always connected to the theme of communion first with the Son and the Father.

This community or communion with the Son and the Father through the Son is important in the light of Jesus' going away. Apart from 14:16f, the promise of the Paraclete relates to knowledge rather than presence, but presence, particularly empowering presence, is also presupposed in the account of the giving of the Spirit in 20:22.

Communion with the Father and the Son is already possible through the ministry of the earthly Jesus. He is light and life and bread. To follow him and to believe in him is to receive the gift he is. The issue, therefore, of mediating his presence after Easter is of great importance. We have seen that the Spirit does this both by presence and also by mediating his word. In ch. 6 we find reference to the future gift of life through the Son of Man, a term used of Jesus predominantly in association with his death and return: 'Do not labour for the food which perishes but for the food which endures to eternal life, which the Son of Man will give you' (6:27). The future tense is to be taken seriously and refers to the nourishment as it will be given in the post Easter period by the ascended Son of Man (cf. 6:62). In 6:53 this is identified more closely as eating the flesh and drinking the blood of the Son of Man in what is doubtless a reference to the eucharist. The eucharist is then a way in which the communion is established and maintained. A similar reference to the future mediation of life through Jesus as Son of Man is found in 3:14f: 'As Moses lifted up the serpent in the wilderness, so it is necessary that the Son of Man be lifted up, so that all who believe might have life in him.'

It may be that the wine imagery in the Cana wedding feast contains a eucharistic allusion as well as reflecting on the wine which has come with the Son's coming. We have also noted the promise of a new temple in Jesus' resurrection (2:21), probably carrying with it an allusion to the new communion in him. The irrelevance of Jerusalem and Samaritan temples according to 4:19-26 similarly points to the new worshipping community of the Spirit. The narratives of the wedding feast, the temple expulsion, the exchange with Nicodemus and the meeting with the Samaritan woman seem to have been written with a particularly strong constant dual reference to the situation before and after Easter leading to a much higher degree of anachronism than elsewhere in the gospel (see especially 3:3-13 and 4:35-38).

We have also noted the possibility that the issuing of water and blood from Jesus' side may allude to the eucharist and baptism (also in 3:5). The eucharist may also be suggested in the meal in 21:9-13, as it seems to be already in the narrative of the feeding of the 5000. Possibly the mention of Jesus' seamless robe is meant as a symbol of unity, but this is uncertain.

We began by noting how in many passages unity is related to mission. We saw how community is frequently portrayed as derived from the communion with the Son (and the Father) through the Spirit, through Jesus' word and through eucharist. The final chapter, in specifying Peter's pastoral role and the distinctive position of the beloved disciple (and by implication his community), represents a concrete working out of the community issue in history. The author is concerned for the unity of the Church.

The ultimate community to which all this leads is, for the author, the fulfilment of Jesus' prayer that his disciples follow him right through to the goal of the Father's presence: 'I wish that where I am they may also be, so that they may see the glory which you have given me because you loved me before the foundation of the world' (17:24). This is the place Jesus goes to prepare for them (14:2) and to which he shall come to take them (14:3). The same promise expressed in other words appears in 12:26 'If anyone serves me, let him follow me, and where I am there will my servant also be. If anyone serves me, him will my Father honour.' Thus the story ends where it began: the Son with the Father, but now the disciples will share this glory. This is the implicit focus of the author's eschatology. Explicit references to a future parousia of the Son are few (14:3; 21:22f). References to a future judgement day (5:28f; 12:48; cf. 5:45) and to a future resurrection of the dead (5:28f; 6:39f,44,54) also appear, but are incidental to the primary concern: the relationship with Father and Son now and ultimately being with them in glory in heaven.

15. Conclusion

We have reached the conclusion of the outline of the structure of the author's christology. The central event is the Son's making the Father known, bringing light and life and truth, and completing the Father's work. All else focusses on this. His having been with the Father, being sent and coming from the Father, is what makes this possible. His return to the Father, exalted, glorified, ascended and his sending the disciples and the Spirit is what makes it possible for this to be understood, announced to the world in mission and lived out in the community of faith. The sending of the disciples and the Spirit is parallel to the sending of the Son, but not independent of it. There are not two revelatory events, the Son's and that of the disciples and the Spirit. There is one single revelatory event, the work of the disciples and the Spirit is revelatory only in the sense that it reveals the revelation of the Son.

The Father sends and authorises the Son, who knows the Father, comes from the Father, makes the Father known, brings light and life and truth, completes his Father's work, returns to the Father, exalted, glorified, ascended, sends the disciples, and sends the Spirit, to enable greater understanding, to equip for mission, and to build up the community of faith.

PART III

ISSUES OF JOHANNINE CHRISTOLOGY

In Part I we examined Bultmann's christology of John and briefly reviewed research since Bultmann, which, partly in response to Bultmann and partly independently, has raised and revived major issues for any new attempt to understand Johannine christology. Renewed attention has been given to questions concerning the meaning of Jesus' death. Was it a real death, preceded by real suffering? Was it a work of salvific significance, the achievement of atonement, a moment of change in world power, or primarily a portal for a triumphant Son of God? What is the meaning of exaltation and glorification in relation to Jesus' death and return to the Father? How significant is the notion of his return to the Father and the giving of the Paraclete? What is the saving event in John? His death, his incarnation, his returning? Some of the major issues concern the nature of Jesus himself. What role does pre-existence play? What is the character of his oneness with the Father? Is it subordination? Is it such that the glory submerges Jesus' humanity? Is he a god striding the earth? Do miracles play a central role in Johannine thought? Has the earthly historical Jesus still a place? These raise, in turn, questions about the nature of the gospel portrait itself, its setting, and its use in our own world.

In Part II we examined the text of the gospel, following Bultmann's agenda of first seeking to identify the central structure of the christological story. In the light of this we shall now turn to the particular issues raised at the conclusion of Part I and examine them one by one.

A. THE DEATH OF JESUS IN JOHN

1. The Return of the Son to the Father

The pattern of the author's christology puts as the central act the Son's making the Father known bringing light and life and truth, and completing the works of the Father. For this the Son came from the Father. After this the Son returns to the Father. The cycle is complete. The Son returns where he was with the Father before the world began. Therefore at its simplest Jesus' death is the mode of his return to the Father.

To know the Son comes from and returns to the Father, his whence and his whither, is to know who he is, for it is to know him as the sent one. His return to the Father, like his coming from the Father, authenticates his claim. The Paraclete declares his righteousness on the grounds that he returned to the Father (16:10).

Seen in this perspective, Jesus' death is his exit. This is primarily how Käsemann and Schulz see the meaning of Jesus' death in John and they are followed by many others. It is the triumphant exit of the revealer.[1] The following sections will show that this too quickly ignores others aspects.

2. Completion of the Task - by an Act of Atonement?

Jesus' death is more than simply the exit route of the revealer. The suffering and death is itself part of the Father's commission. It is the cup the Father has given for him to drink (18:11) and the hour before which he was distressed, but to which he had come to face suffering and death (12:27). The Father commanded the Son to lay down his life (10:18) and Jesus concludes the first discourse with the words: 'That the world may know that I love the Father and that as the Father has commanded, so I act, arise let us go hence!' (14:31). The Son has come to do the Father's will and complete fully the task set before him (4:34; 5:36). In 17:4 he declares he has done so; his last words, 'It is finished' (19:30), set the seal on his ministry.

Facing suffering and death belongs to the commission of the Son. But why? A number of scholars see the final task of this commission as an act of vicarious atonement.[2] Accordingly by adding after 'to do the will of him who sent me', the words, 'and to complete his work' in 4:34, Jesus would be singling out vicarious atonement as a second task.[3] The grounds for seeing atonement as the completion of the task are basically threefold: the alleged presence of allusions to Jesus' death as vicarious sacrifice in the gospel, the presence of other texts which suggest that the gift of life becomes available only after Easter and so imply that it is available only as a result of the work of Jesus' death, and the singling out of the passion as a distinctive task in the passages mentioned above. We shall consider these three arguments in turn.

In Part II we noted a number of passages which, with varying degrees of certainty and uncertainty, might refer to Jesus' death as an act of vicarious atonement. We postponed assessing that degree of probability in each case because the extent to which one reference might carry that meaning depends on the extent to which it is present elsewhere. In other words, they need to be considered as a whole. It is also easier, having considered them as a whole, to examine their overall role and function, their weight and valency, within the gospel's christology.

John 1:29 (36) Its Role and Status in the Gospel

The clearest reference is the first, 1:29, 'Behold the lamb of God who takes away the sin of the world.' It stands without further interpretation in the immediate context. On the other hand, at least its opening statement, 'Behold the lamb of God', is repeated in 1:36. It represents the first words of the first witness, John the Baptist, on seeing Jesus, and on the second occasion in 1:36 it is his first word to the first potential disciples of Jesus. In addition it may form an inclusio with the Passover allusions of the passion narrative, but to that we shall return below. The statement is in itself therefore something of a paradox. It holds a position of significant prominence in the gospel, yet with the possible exception of uncertain indirect references in the passion, its imagery is completely absent in the rest of the gospel.

Some have therefore suggested that the author makes use of a traditional statement whose meaning would be known to his readers.[4] Becker accounts for it as tradition added by the Johannine redactor.[5] At whatever stage such tradition entered the gospel, the case for it as tradition is strong. It is another question to ask what role it now plays in the gospel. Painter, for instance, suggests that it carries little weight and should not be taken as evidence of vicarious atonement in the author's christology.[6] It could represent the use of traditional formulations and for the author and his readers function simply as another way of identifying Jesus as the revealer, without carrying with it the specific thought that he is such because of a particular task of atonement to which he will proceed. This would then account already for the dropping of second half of the saying in 1:36.

Equally, one could argue, that it could be identifying the specific act of sacrificial atonement from the beginning in carefully chosen words, whether taken from tradition or not, as an important theme of the gospel.[7] 1:36, for its part, would simply be a shorthand way of referring to the total concept. Many who acknowledge the presence of expiatory sacrificial imagery here, see it as subordinate. Thus Riedl sees it as subordinate in importance in the gospel to the resurrection.[8] Similarly Ibuki sees it as subordinate to the overall theme of the truth of the love relationship between Father and Son,[9] and Onuki, as subordinate to the task of revelation as a whole.[10] Schnackenburg speaks of the atonement motif being melted into the Johannine conception.[11] The extent to which 1:29 bears weight in the christology of the gospel depends upon the way it functions in the gospel as a whole and upon evidence that elsewhere in the gospel death as vicarious atonement has central importance.

John 1:29   Its Imagery

Investigations of what the statement says in itself have been extensive and I refer to commentaries for fuller discussion. 'Taking away' (*airōn*) sin can have various meanings: destroying sin, removing sin, or bearing it. Forestell shows that it can mean simply 'forgive', like *aphiēmi*[12]. This would accord with the usual Johannine way of dealing with sin, either by the word of the Son (cf. 15:3) or by overpowering the prince of the world (12:31, 16:9).[13] Hegermann suggests that it means take away sin by exposing it for what it is.[14] For Boismard taking away sin means enabling people to stop sinning through giving them the revelation of God.[15]

The motif, 'lamb', may be messianic, as Dodd suggested.[16] This would be in keeping with the strong messianic emphasis of the immediate context. A non vicarious interpretation of 1:29b would then be possible: Jesus would be the messianic lamb sent by God to deal victoriously with the world's sin. Lamb might suggest either the ram symbol or the paradox of weakness through which the victory is won and so reflect traditions present elsewhere in Revelation (Rev 5:6,12; 14:1). Brown holds open the possibility that John the Baptist may have intended a messianic sense, but argues that this is no longer determinative in the context.[17]

Most see a sacrificial motif in the use of 'lamb' and therefore interpret *airōn* ('takes away') accordingly. Even Forestell, who vigorously denies a cultic interpretation of Jesus' death elsewhere in the gospel, acknowledges its presence here.[18] A number of possible explanations of the sacrificial meaning have been offered: Jesus as the passover lamb,[19] the lamb in terms of Isa 53,[20] or of Isa 53:7 (the lamb for the slaughter),[21] the lamb as servant of Yahweh (usually in combination with Isa 53 and 42),[22] the lamb of the story of Abraham's willingness to sacrifice Isaac,[23] the tradition of Moses as a lamb,[24] and the lamb of the daily sacrifice.[25]

John 1:29 and Passover typology

The killing of the passover lambs, though not originally a sin sacrifice, had come to assume vicarious significance in Judaism in the time of the gospel[26] and so had come to be used in this way of the death of Jesus (cf. 1 Cor 5:7; 1 Pet 1:19). It was enhanced by the use of passover typology. In the fourth gospel the period of Jesus' ministry includes three passovers. Before the third Passover day, a sabbath in that year, Jesus is crucified and must have died about the time when the passover lambs were slaughtered. A Passover interpretation of 1:29 would cohere well with the chronology of the passion. Is there evidence of the author interpreting the chronology typologically? At most it may be present when the author notes that Pilate handed over Jesus to be crucified on the day of preparation of the passover at the sixth hour (19:14). But there is no precise dating of his death linked with passover so as to suggest a link with the time of the slaughtering of the lambs. Even more significant, in the one place where a passover allusion is a possible option, namely when the soldiers leave Jesus' bones unbroken, the author has made a time reference, but omitted any reference to the Passover. Other motifs adduced in favour of a passover typology include passover references and possible passover lectionary background in ch. 6 and the use of hyssop at 19:29.[27] The evidence for an intended passover typology in the chronology of the passion and also in the account of Jesus' unbroken bones is not strong and therefore arguments that 1:29 and this event function as an inclusio are at most very uncertain.[28]

John 1:29 Isaiah 53 and 42

The case for seeing in 1:29 the announcement of a passover theme of importance for the gospel as a whole is weak and unconvincing. This does not rule out the possibility that it is still the background for the formulations we have before us in 1:29. The same is equally true for the Isa 53, servant of Yahweh, and Isa 42 interpretation. Dodd has shown that the 'talya' theory, according to which this same Aramaic word, meaning either lamb or servant, appears behind the 'Son' of the Synoptics and the 'lamb' of John has insufficient basis.[29] There seems more ground for arguing a connection between 'lamb' and 'servant' through an allusion to Isa 53, perhaps also through Isa 42:1. If we were to read *eklektos* ('chosen one') instead of *huios* ('Son') in 1:34, we could read it as an allusion to the baptismal tradition of the synoptic tradition where Jesus is addressed by God in the words, 'You are my beloved Son. In you I am well pleased' (Mark 1:11), probably a combination of Ps 2:7 and Isa 42:1. 'Lamb' and 'chosen one' would then form an inclusio in John 1:29-34.[30] The reading, 'Son', could equally allude to the same tradition. But the motif of vicarious suffering would connect better with Isa 53 than with Isa 42. Yet, while Isa 53:1 is applied in 12:38 to Jesur in probable allusion to the revelation he has manifested on earth, there is no indication elsewhere of Isa 53 and its vicarious suffering servant motif playing a role in the gospel. As with the passover imagery, so, too, this does not rule out the possibility that it lies behind the formulation of 1:29 as an individual saying.

Akedah Typology

The Akedah motif, the binding of Isaac, could lie behind the formulation, here. Other evidence for it could be found, perhaps, in the references to 'the only Son' (1:14; 3:16,18) and some would see it also behind 3:16 ('God..gave his only Son'; cf. Rom 8:32), in 1:34 ('the chosen one', cloredy related to 'beloved' and 'only/unique' as epithets of the Son) and in the fact that Jesus carries his own cross in John. But none of these is more than a possibility and together they hardly allow us to speak of Isaac typology playing a significant part in the gospel.

Neither the imagery system which has led to the formulation of 1:29 (whether messianic, passover typology, Isa 53, or Akedah typology, or any combination of these) nor the imagery of the verse itself plays a significant part in the gospel. Among the various possibilities I think it likely that it referred to Jesus' death as vicarious sacrifice and is probably taken from the common tradition of the author and the community. The question remains whether the general idea of vicarious sacrifice assumes greater significance in the gospel than this or whether in the present context it asserts primarily no more than that here is the saviour of the world.[31]

Other alleged allusions to vicarious atonement - John 6:51c

In IIB2 we considered the way the present form of ch. 6 makes allusions to the eucharist in 6:51c-58 and probably already if thd account of the feeding of the 4000. It is likely that the Johannine community knew a form of the eucharistic tradition which contained elements interpreting Jesus' death as vicarious. The words, 'the bread which I give is my flesh for the life of the!wormd' (6:51c), may refer directly to the nourishment the Son will give in the flesh (and blood) of the eucharist, about tn be described in the following verses.[32] They may, however (perhaps, also) refer to Jesus' offering himself vicariously, sacrificially or otherwise, by his death on the cross.[33] But the response of the Jews in 6:52 focusses upon the giving of flesh to eat, not on vicarious dying. This may reflect Johannine irony, though it would be more usual to see the irony work in the way that the focus is the same action, giving to eat, with the Jews then failing to comprehend the spiritual nourishment. This is confirmed by what follows, so that the primary reference of 6:51c is most likely not Jesus' vicarious death, but the gift of his flesh (and blood) in the eucharist. In the light of this connection it is also improbable that it refers simply to Jesus' giving himself (non vicariously) for the benefit of others, as Forestell suggests.[34] We have seen that 6:51c-58 belongs closely with 6:27 which speaks of a future gift of food given by the 'Son of Man'(!), who, as the ascended 'Son of Man'(! 6:62), will give his flesh and blood (as 'Son of Man!' 6:53) to his own. Undoubtedly vicarious atonement belongs within this eucharistic tradition, but it is not the major focus of the context nor of 6:51c.

John 10:11,15

The issue of vicarious atonement in 10:11-18 is strangely similar. Here it is probably reflected in the statements, 'The good shepherd lays down his life for the sheep' (10:11) and 'I lay down my life for the sheep' (10:15).[35] The use of *hyper* ('for') suggests this, probably reflecting its use in community tradition to speak of Jesus' death as vicarious. The statements need not, of themselves, imply vicarious death. They could be read as indicating that Jesus will lay down his life in order to benefit his own,[36] for instance, in order to return to the Father and send the blessings of the Spirit. The image itself suggests a shepherd going so far in defending his sheep that he loses his life. I think it likely that a motif of vicarious death does lie behind the formulations, but once again it is not this which is the focus of attention.[37] In 10:11-13 the focus is on real caring for the sheep as opposed to those who do not care. In 10:14-18 the attention moves to the Son fulfilling the Father's mission and the special relationship between the two. In this context we find the statements about laying down his life completely integrated within a different perspective: Jesus must undergo death to return to the Father. 'For this the Father loves me, because I lay down my life in order that I might take it up again. No one takes it from me, but I lay it down of myself. I have authority to lay it down and I have authority to take it up again. This command I received from my Father' (10:17f). Vicarious atonement is, at most, incidental here.

John 11:50-52; 18:14

The unwitting prophecy of Caiaphas, 'that one should die for the people and the whole nation not perish' (11:50) or in its expanded version, 'that Jesus was going to die for the nation, and not for the nation only, but so that also all the children of God who are scattered may be gathered into one' (11:51f), probably entails a reference to vicarious atonement.[38] It is similar to 10:16, where after repeating that he would lay down his life, Jesus announces that there are other sheep not of that fold and he must gather them, that they would heed his voice and they would become one flock with one shepherd. Both passages emphasise unity. Both may relate this achievement entirely to the vicarious atonement. Our consideration of the mission theme suggests, however, that a lot more is invnlved. The mission is also made possible through the Son's going to the Father through death, his giving of the Spirit and his empowering of the disciples to bear fruit. The notion of vicariour atonement seems present, but equally subordinate here as it is in 10:11-18.[39] The reference in 18:14 back to Caiaphas' prophecy, a few verses after Jesus' words about drinking the cup (18:11), need not imply the two are directly linked, the cup as the task of atonement.[40]

John 12:24, 32; Isa 52:13

The same notion of Jesus' death bearing the fruit of mission is evident in 12:24, the saying about the dying seed, and in 12:22 about the lifting up of the Son of Man from the earth wh'ch vill draw all people to him. It is not primarily vicarious atonement which achieves this, either in 12:24[41] or in 12:32,[42] but the Son's death and return in exaltation to the Father and what this makes possible: revelation, the sending of the Spirit and of the disciples, and, above all, mission. Nor should a possible background of exaltation and glorification in Isa 52:13 LXX imply that where these terms are used the notion of vicarious atonement present in Isa 53 is in view.[43]

John 15:13

The saying in 15:13, 'Greater love has no one more than this than someone lays down his life for his friends', reflects the common motif of dying in the interests of others as evidence of friendship and need carry here no allusion to vicarious atonement.[44] I think, however, it probably does, especially in the light of the evidence for such traditions elsewhere in the gospel.[45] Its use of *tithēmi hyper* ('to lay down one's life for') may reflect a common formulation for Christ's vicarious stffering in the author's community (cf. also 10:11,15; 1 Jn 3:16), though the same expression is also used in Peter's enthusiasm for self sacrifice for his master (13:37f . But the saying is only illustrative in its present context, and not itself the focus of attention or the major theme.

John 3:16, 14f

Other alleged references to vicarious atonement are uncertain. 3:16 speaks of God so loving the world that he gave his only Son. The author probably dravs here upon a traditional formulation found elsewhere in the New Testament (cf. Gal 4:4; Rom 8:3; Eph 5:1), sometimes as an expression of vicarious atonement. It is clearly used in this way in 1 Jn 3:9f. It may be present in 3:16.[46] And some see Isaac typology here.[47] But the verses which follow and repeat the formulation negatively expound it in terms of the coming of light into the world and not in relation to Jesus' death as vicarious at all (3:17-21). This strongly suggests we should read 3:16 in this way, too, as another way of saying that the Father sent the Son to save the world by bringing the gift of light and life.[48]

3:16 is also linked, however, with 3:13 and 14f which clearly do relate to Jesus' death and return to the Father. 3:15 and 3:16 contain similar statements about faith and the promise of eternal life. Some interpret the lifting up of the serpent as a symbol of vicarious atonement.[49] As we shall see in IIIA4 below when we consider the exaltation sayings, this is most unlikely here.[50] Lifting up does refer to Jesus' crucifixion here and elsewhere in John (12:32f), but only as what is seen outwardly. The eyes of faith see the path to exaltation in heaven. 3:16 is, therefore, best taken closely with the similar formulations which follow and not as a reference specifically to Jesus' vicarious death. If it were to be taken as referring to Jesus' vicarious death, we would have to reckon with the significance of the author's not developing it further in what follows, but reverting immediately to statements about the Son's coming into the world as revealer.

John 17

Jesus' final prayer contains cultic imagery relating to the completion of his task through death. He prays: 'For their sake I sanctify myself, so that they also may be sanctified in truth' (17:19). But this no more implies for Jesus that his death is an expiatory sacrifice,[51] than it does for the disciples, for whom Jesus has just prayed: 'Sanctify them in the truth. As you sent me into the world, I, too, have sent them into the world' (17:17f). Hebrews portrays Jesus as high priest and victim[52] and some have sought indications of this motif, beside 17:19 and its parallel in 10:36, also in: the confession, 'holy one of God' (6:69); Jesus' seamless garment (19:23); and his being placed between two thieves (19:18b) as between the two cherubim. But this is little more than speculation.[53] In 10:36 Jesus refers to himself as 'the one whom the Father sanctified and sent into the world.' Sanctification is setting apart for a holy commission. It does not imply that the nature of the commission itself is cultic or has to do with sacrifice[54] or with Jesus' death as sacrifical atonement.[55]

Other Cultic Imagery

Cultic imagery also appears in the motif of cleansing, which is probably implied in the reference to jars of purification in 2:6 and in the baptismal imagery of ch. 3, and is certainly present in the narrative of the footwashing in ch. 13. Lindars links 1:29 with the promise that Jesus would baptise with the Spirit (1:33), suggesting this entails the element of cleansing, and so finds cleansing linked with vicarious sacrificial atonement in the reference to the jars and to Jesus' hour in 2:5f, and especially also in the footwashing episode and in the *hyper* sayings, even though he sees it not as central to the author's concerns.[56] The link however is tenuous and cleansing need not imply vicarious sacrifice. Purification rites were often quite independent of sacrifice. The most that could be said for taking the footwashing episode in this way would be if Jesus' laying aside his garments were meant to symbolise his death. But this is far from certain.[57] Dunn sees an allusion to washing by the Spirit which as water will flow grom tie side of Jesus.[58] Segovia sees the washing as rather an indication of the fruit which flows from Jesus' glorification[59] and Schnackenburg, of the life and love given the disciples.[60] Bultmann rightly connects the footwashing with 15:3, cleansing through Jesus' word.[61]

John 19:33,36; 20:20,22

In IIB5 we have already considered the possibility of a reference to Jesus as passover lamb in 19:33,36 as very slight. Even more uncertain is a possible reference to the vicarious benefits of Jesus' death in the flow of water and blood from his side (19:34f). It is certainly implied, if the eucharist is in mind, otherwise, probably not. De la Potterie suggests that authority to forgive sins (20:23) and Jesus' showing the disciples his hands and side (20:20) are linked through the notion of Jesus' death as vicarious sacrifice, but this is far from certain.[62]

Life available only after the cross? John 3:14f; 6:27, 53; 7:38f

Before drawing this to a conclusion I want to note three other texts which, together, form the second argument for vicarious atonement in the gospel, namely those which imply that the gift of life comes only after Easter and therefore must assume the work of atonement. Two of these are Son of Man texts (3:14f; 6:27) and both imply the gift lies in the future, viewed from the perspective of Jesus' ministry. In IIB2 we have already linked 6:27 with 6:51c-58, verses which do indeed presuppose Jesus' vicarious death, inasmuch as they speak of the future gift of the eucharistic flesh and blood. 3:14f relates the gift of life to Jesus' being lifted up, primarily a reference to Jesus' exaltation, but because of the connection with

6:27, 51c-58, it possibly also presuppose that this gift of life will result from Jesus' death as a sacrifice, though this need not be so, since it is through the exaltation that the gift of life becomes widely available through the Spirit. 3:16, and especially 3:17-21, return immediately to the notion that the life is already available in the person of the sent one. A similar dual reference is to be found in 7:37-39.

7:37-39 has Jesus offer water, much as he had to the woman of Samaria and much as he had offered bread (7:37). But then Jesus adds a promise relating to the future about flowing rivers (7:38) and the author identifies these abundant rivers as the Spirit to be given after Jesus was glorified (7:39). As Jesus in ch. 6 offers bread in his person then and there and also promises food to come, so here there is a twofold focus; but, unlike ch. 6, here it is not related directly to the eucharist and vicarious atonement, but to the coming of the Spirit. This passage cannot be used as evidence for the importance of vicarious atonement in the gospel's christology, nor to argue that all references to the gift of life in Jesus' ministry the gospel are proleptic.[63]

Finishing his work - by Atonement?

17:4, which refers to Jesus' having completed his work, has been interpreted as a reference to Jesus' achievement of vicarious atonement.[64] This assumes that the reference in 2a to Jesus' being given authority over all flesh refers to his death and exaltation, so that the life which 2b describes as being given by the Son is the result of this achievement. It is much more convincing to see 2 referring to Jesus' authorisation and sending into the world to make the Father known.[65] 17:3, therefore, relates the gift of life not to an achievement of atonement, but to the possibility of knowing God in Jesus Christ. Nor need the promise of the truth that sets one free (8:32) be an allusion to vicarious atonement, as T.E. Müller suggests.[66]

The statements about Jesus' death as a task yet to be fulfilled or as a task completed say nothing about vicarious atonement. Whether this should even be taken into account depends on our assessment of the evidence considered thus far about the place of the notion of vicarious or sacrificial atonement in the gospel. Our survey shows that traditions about vicarious and sacrificial atonement were both known and used by the author. But significantly, while known and doubtless accepted by the author, they occur largely in an incidental manner. Our survey in Part II delineated the basic structure of the author's christology and found that vicarious or sacrificial atonement did not play a significant part. In a gospel full of christological reflection and summaries, vicarious atonement is conspicuously absent where we should most expect it. It does not occur in summaries, is never the focus of particular development or discussion as a theme in itself, and is absent as a major theme in the last discourses of Jesus with his disciples.

Conclusions

Wrede was right when he identified the presence of vicarious atonement in the gospel and in saying that, in contrast to the idea of life through the revelation of the word, it was a concept which had sprouted on a different field.[67] And as

Holtzmann also pointed out, the concern of the evangelist is with healing and forgiveness through revelation, a revelation so complete that it already offers what is traditionally attributed to vicarious atonement.[68] On the other hand, Bultmann's suggestion that for the author the whole life of Jesus from beginning to end is a sacrifice is an interpretation he brings to the text not that of the evangelist.[69]

This does not mean the author rejects the idea of vicarious atonement or has no place for it.[70] That is clearly not the case. He presupposes it, but uses it incidentally, illustratively and confessionally.[71] It was known to him at least in the context of eucharistic tradition. But it does mean that it is not central to his christology as presented in the gospel and should not, therefore, be read into christological or soteriological statements which do not otherwise indicate its presence. It is thus unlikely that in having Jesus say he has completed his work, the author means that he saw himself having a twofold commission, to make the Father known and to achieve atonement by his death. Nowhere in such contexts is there the slightest suggestion of this. It is an exaggeration to say, with Beasley Murray, that Jesus' death as exaltation means no lessening of the place of vicarious atonement.[72]

A number of scholars note the comparative change in emphasis on sacrificial atonement in the Johannine epistles[73] and suggest that this is to be accounted for as a counterbalance to the gospel's lack of emphasis on this aspect[74] or that it has led to redactional additions of the motif within the gospel itself.[75] Schnelle's suggestion that the statements about vicarious atonement carry significant weight for the author in countering the docetism already evident behind the epistles is unconvincing.[76]

Accordingly we must see the author focussing his christology on the revelation envoy model, the structure outlined in II above, and understand Jesus' task and commission in these terms. Within this pattern vicarious atonement, sacrificial or otherwise, has no direct role, but it does form part of the wider tradition the author inherits and which he may occasionally use in expounding his overall theme. Its presence should not be denied, but its subordinate place recognised, both in the perspective of the structure as a whole and in the manner in which it is used in the passages considered.

3. Completion of the Task - Revelation and Judgement

If the task to be completed through Jesus' suffering and death is not seen primarily as vicarious atonement, how is it understood? The answer must at first be related to the Son's commission overall. The Son came to make the Father known. This task did not cease before the passion, but remains the Son's task until the end. This is precisely the kind of understanding we find in ch. 17 where completion of the task stands within a context which speaks of Jesus' having given the disciples his Father's words, name, and glory in obedience to the Father's command. It also makes good sense of 19:30 ('It is finished') and of 4:34 'My food is to do the will of him who sent me and to finish his work.' In the latter verse there is no suggestion of difference between the will to be done and the work to be completed.

The Cross the Climax of the Revelatory Task

To the end of his life the Son continued to make the Father known. As he says to Pilate: for this he came into the world, to bear witness to the truth (18:37). The passion is therefore part of the revelatory life on earth of the Son. As Bornkamm has emphasised, it looms on the horizon throughout the gospel.[77] It is the ultimate end of the Son's faithful obedience to this task, the ultimate expression of love for his own and the love he has for the Father.[78] In this sense it reveals the character of the relationship between Father and Son which has been there throughout the ministry. The passion and death belong to the total life and ministry of revelation and therefore, of necessity, to the completion of the commission.

Forestell goes beyond this in claiming that the cross completes the revelation of love and the destruction of sin, so that it is not until this event that the benefits of divine salvation are available to believers.[79] But this runs in the face of the evidence of the gospel according to which the life is available already in the presence and the promise of the revealer.[80] The climax of revelation comes to expression particularly in the drama of the passion narrative, where Jesus is mockingly set forth as royal messiah and crucified under the accusation 'King of the Jews'. This is a powerfully ironic presentation of Jesus as, in truth to the eyes of faith, the one who has been the Christ, the Son of God, the King throughout his ministry.[81] It is not that Jesus becomes these by enthronement or exaltation on the cross[82] or that the events foreshadow or represent a heavenly enthronement, as our treatment of exaltation and glorification, below in IIIA4, will demonstrate.[83] The language of royal messianism is not used of Jesus' heavenly exaltation and glorification. Rather the passion narrative presents him as what he was and had been throughout his ministry, the Son of God and King of Israel, understood within the framework of the author's christology: the Son who make the Father known.

Paradox of Revelation in Wretchedness?

Bultmann emphasises that the cross is the necessary completion of what had begun in 1:14, the truth and paradox of the incarnation, and as not going beyond this.[84] This belongs to his strong emphasis on the divine glory of the ordinariness of Jesus. 'Behold the man' (19:6) is a call to see this revelation in wretchedness. Without question Jesus is presented as facing suffering and humiliation in the passion narrative. This belongs to his obedience. It is the cup he must drink (18:11). It is another thing to suggest that it is precisely the paradox of suffering and divinity which constitutes the revelation, his wretchedness and ordinariness as human being, or even as servant of God. Real wretchedness is portrayed and motifs of servanthood are present, but they serve to reveal not Jesus as the 'real' man or the predicted 'suffering servant'; rather they portray the obedient Son, Israel's Messiah, sent from the Father to make him known and the lengths to which people went to reject him. And even the abuse and rejection serves ironically to expound who he truly is, to the eyes of faith. Baum Bodenbender argues for an emphasis on humiliation on the part of the author in the passion narrative and we shall argue in IIIB4 below that this motif is present. But it must not be stressed at the expense of elements emphasising Jesus as king, which, despite Baum Bodenbender's claims, continue to play a dominant role in the narrative.[85]

Completion of the Commission

Jesus' death is therefore not only his return as Son to the Father. It also brings to a climax the Son's claim and brings his commission and work to its completion. Because this work is seen as a whole, the earthly ministry up to and including death, the evangelist can speak of God's sending the Son with all this in mind. This is the sense in which 3:16 is to be understood. The following verses continue with the obverse side of the sending: judgement in response to the light come into the world. The author does not isolate the death of Jesus as a work of revelation, though it brings that work to the climax and in it we see manifested the Son's complete obedience and love (14:31). It manifests the extent of the Son's love also for his friends (15:13). It brings the Son's work of glorification of God to a climax, but it is not considered a separate work, either as a work of atonement or as a work of revelation or as a work of glorification of the Father. It is completion of the ministry in which both the latter are already present. In that sense Bultmann is right in saying that it does not add to what has already been there.[86] But this is far from saying that the passion is lost sight of in the gospel and tags along somewhat irrelevantly at the end as Käsemann's analysis suggests.[87] Martyn characterises rather the 'Grundschrift' of the gospel in this way.[88]

The Moment of Truth: the Judgement of Jesus and of the World

There is a sense in which the passion is different in revelatory character from the rest of Jesus' earthly ministry. For by its very nature as a climax of the conflict which Jesus' coming brought, the death of Jesus has a special quality and brings an intensity to the encounter. It is the moment of truth. Jesus' claim to be the Son sent from the Father has been meeting rejection. The trial begins long before Jesus' appearance before Pilate. This is the strength of Harvey's portrayal of the gospel as the trial of Jesus from beginning to end.[89] And Appold notes that the cross brings to a climax the note of rejection already announced in the prologue: 'He came to his own and his own did not receive him' (1:10f).[90] At the conclusion of his ministry Jesus faces the final hour. It will be an hour of suffering and pain, because the threats of rejection will now fulfil themselves in crucifixion. For here the world finally passes its verdict of rejection on Jesus; and Jesus, facing suffering and death, maintains his obedience to the end and is vindicated. But the verdict passed against him is also a verdict passed against the world and its ruler. The world is revealed in all its lostness and sin.[91]

Thus the Paraclete, according to 16:7-11, takes the event and expounds it as revelation of sin, righteousness and judgement. The climax of the conflict and its sequel reveals what is at a stake. It unmasks sin as rejection of the revealer. It reveals righteousness as belonging to the Son, because it is he who comes out of the conflict vindicated, shown by his return to the Father. And the event is also revealed as judgement, because through its revelation the ruler of the world is disempowered. This passage is crucial for revealing how the gospel understands Jesus' death. The conflict of light and darkness had been introduced already in the prologue. It continues as a theme linked with judgement throughout the gospel. Judgement to life or death is determined by one's response to Jesus. Jesus does not come to judge, yet by implication his coming brings judgement and his death drives it to its climax.

The Turning Point in Revelation

Yet the death is more than a negative revelation, ie: a revelation of the world's sin in rejecting Jesus. The death also belongs to the total event which includes Jesus' death, return to the Father, exaltation, glorification, ascension and the sending of the Spirit. The result of this total event is greater understanding both of who the Son is and of the scriptures. The death is therefore not only the 'Ende', but also the 'Wende' (turning point).[92] This 'greater thing' resulting in greater understanding began with the passion and death of Jesus. The structure of the gospel's christology is such that the greater knowledge and revelation comes as a result of the work of the Paraclete, which comes, in turn, as a result of the total event, Jesus' death and return to the Father's glory. We see this connection in 7:39 ('The Spirit was not yet, because Jesus was not yet glorified') and 12:16 ('When Jesus was glorified, then they remembered that these things were written about him and that they had done these things to him'). The death of Jesus must not be isolated from the total event, in which there is also the positive revelation through the return of the Son to the Father in vindication and the dynamic activity of revealing and bringing greater understanding about Jesus made possible by the gift of the Paraclete.

14:30f illustrates this emphasis: Jesus says, 'No longer shall I speak much with you, for the ruler of this world comes; and he has no part in me, but that the world may know that I love the Father, and as the Father commanded me, so I act, arise, let us go hence.' The relationship between the Son and the Father, the Son's having been sent to do the Father's will, remains the central revelatory concern. The cross is the climax of the encounter which the Son's revelation has brought. But the climax makes possible a deeper understanding of what that revelation is about, for it exposes for the eyes of faith who the players are. 14:30f belongs with 16:7-11 and 8:28, where we have the same promise in other words, 'When you have lifted up the Son of Man, then you shall know that I am the one.' Jesus' death, exaltation and return to the Father are a revelation about revelation. They unfold to the eyes of faith that Jesus truly is the revealer and that those who have rejected him have committed sin and are condemned. To reveal this will be the work of the Spirit. When 10:17 says that the Son lays down his life that he may take it up again, it throws the emphasis forward from the death to what will come as a result of his return to the Father. While the previous verse sets this in the context of mission, the wider context also relates it to Jesus' return to the Father and the giving of the Spirit, which enables knowledge and therefore mission.

Casting out the Ruler of this World

The motif of the casting out of the world's ruler appears twice in John (12:31; 17:11; cf. also 16:33) and 'the ruler of this world' appears also in 14:31. The author uses this traditionally apocalyptic motif in relation to the event of Jesus' death and return to the Father. It cannot mean that all evil has been banished from the world, since the disciples are to face rejection as had their master. But Jesus promises, 'In this world you shall have trouble; but be of good cheer I have overcome the world' (16:33) and elsewhere guarantees that no one will pluck his own from his hand (10:29). In this light the power of the ruler of this world, the devil, is limited, but still active. The casting out (12:31; 16:11) seems then to be understood as exposure. The devil is exposed for who he is and therefore, for believers, disempowered to the extent that they can recognise his works and not serve him.[93]

The motif should not be thrust into the centre of Johannine soteriology as though here in this act salvation is achieved, any more than should notions of vicarious atonement. Both should be seen within the perspective of the christological structure as a whole. I think it unlikely that the author meant by casting out the ruler of the world some actual change in the power structure of the universe crucial to salvation,[94] or a disempowerment of the devil and thus achievement of access to transmortal salvation[95] or a casting out of Satan from heaven replaced now by the Son of Man.[96] Nor is it likely that the author means the casting out to be understood proleptically of the climax of history, as van Hartingsveld proposes.[97] 16:11 links it too closely with the event of Jesus' death and return. Nor is it clear that we have here, as Strathmann suggests,[98] the idea of overcoming the devil who had prevented people being drawn to Christ, or the notion that like a gnostic redeemer Jesus pioneers the way to the Father by overcoming the barrier through death, as Bultmann suggests.[99] The way motif is used in John, but relates to Jesus himself as the way inasmuch as he is also the truth and the life who by the gift of his person opens the way to the Father (14:1-11).

Conclusion

Jesus' death and return represents both a positive and a negative revelation, a judgement of vindication and of condemnation. It brings to sharp focuss what is already at stake in each encounter with Jesus in his ministry. The one who believes has eternal life; the who does not, stands condemned (3:16-18,36). Aside from the revelatory nature of the encounter, the 'Entscheidungsdualismus', and the promise of life now as the gift to those who believe, the author shows little interest in either future aspects of judgement or present aspects of condemnation. There will be future resurrection and judgement and the criterion is response to the Son's revelation. But whereas believers presently enjoy life, unbelievers receive no sentence beyond being condemned not to have life and light, to remain in darkness and death. It is not that the positive rewards of traditional eschatology are available to believers, whereas the negative rewards or punishments are not available until later for unbelievers. For the focus of John is not rewards and punishments, but life in relationship. The author may well have had something to say about future rewards or punishments, but these are peripheral to the concerns of the gospel.

Jesus' death is interpreted, then, consistently within the framework of the revelation structure of the author's christology and as such it represents the climax of the Son's fulfilment of his task. As an event pitting claim against claim, it brings to a climax the issues of Jesus' life: the world rejects the Son and thereby exposes itself as sinful and its ruler for what he is. At the same time Jesus' rejection and subsequent vindication by his return to the Father reveals, for all who want to see, that he is the one he claimed to be. The climax of the ministry of the revealer becomes in itself a revelation about revelation, mediated by the Paraclete.

4. Glorification and Exaltation

In the fourth gospel Jesus' death is both the climax of his work on earth and the event of his return to the Father. Two of the motifs used by the author to describe this are glorification and exaltation. In this section we shall consider these motifs more closely, their precise reference, and the motifs associated with them.

Bringing glory to God by obedience to his will

The gospel sometimes uses the word, 'glorify', *doxazō*, to describe what happens when the Son fulfils the Father's commission. Thus in the Johannine version of the Gethsemane prayer (12:28), Jesus, facing the challenge of the hour which awaits him, prays, 'Father, glorify your name.' The Father promises in response that he will make this possible, having done so already during Jesus' earthly ministry to that point: 'I both have glorified it and will glorify it again.' There is no need, with Thüsing, to read the words, 'have glorified', against their natural sense as an allusion to Jesus' death as well as his ministry and to read 'will glorify' as a reference only to the future mission of the disciples.[100] The latter may include the work of the disciples indirectly, but primarily it refers to the immediate events by which Jesus will glorify God by his obedience, just as he has done in his ministry to this point.[101] In the hour of his passion and death Jesus, the Son of Man, will glorify God by his faithful obedience: 'Now is the Son of Man glorified and God is glorified in him' (13:31). Peter, too, will glorify God by his death (21:15).

To glorify God is also the task of the disciples as they fulfil the commission given them. 'In this is my Father glorified that you bear much fruit and become my disciples' (15:8). Their witness and work is made possible by the Paraclete and by answer to prayer: 'Whatever you ask in my name I will do it, that the Father may be glorified in the Son' (14:13). Similarly Jesus prays that he may continue to glorify God in the future beyond his death and return: 'Father, the hour has come; glorify your Son, that your Son may glorify you' (17:1). This future work of glorification is doubtless perceived as the same work of the Son's, but now carried out through the Paraclete in the disciples as they fulfil their commission. At the same time, therefore, Jesus can say of the Paraclete: 'he shall glorify me, because he shall take what is mine and declare it to you' (16:14). And already during his earthly ministry Jesus was glorified by the disciples' response (17:10).

In all the passages considered thus far, 'glorify' means 'to bring honour or praise to someone'. On occasion the noun, 'glory', *doxa*, is used similarly in the expressions, 'give glory to' or 'receive glory from'. Jesus 'seeks the glory of him who sent him' (7:18), not his own. The focus here is on Jesus' glorifying God. In 8:49b-50 the movement is reciprocal: 'I honour (*timaō*) my Father and you do not honour (*atimazete*) me. I do not seek my own glory. There is one who seeks it and judges'; cf. also 8:54, 'If I glorify myself, my glory is nothing; my Father is the one who glorifies me.' In 5:44 Jesus confronts the Jews, 'How is it you cannot believe, you who receive glory from one another, and you do not seek the glory which comes from God alone?' (cf. also 5:41). This may refer simply to praise from God; it may possibly refer directly to Jesus as the embodiment of glory (cf. 1:14); and we shall return to this possibility below. Finally the meaning, 'honour, praise' is represented also in the comment about secret believers who 'loved the glory of people more than the glory of God' (12:43) and in the Jews' exhortation to the blind man, 'Give glory to God' (9:24).

God glorifies the Son of Man with his heavenly glory

To glorify God means to honour him, not to add anything to him, such as light or power. But when God glorifies a person there is often some way in which he does give something which that person did not previously have. This may not be the case where the meaning is simply, 'praise', as in many of the texts above; but there are other texts where this fuller meaning is present. They usually relate in some way to God's glory as belonging to his divine presence and more closely reflect the meaning of use of kabodh ('glory') in the Old Testament and Jewish literature. This is particularly so in texts relating to Jesus' death and return to the Father in heaven.

Jesus' glorification with pre-existent glory: 17:1,5; 12:41

This is most evident in 17:5 where Jesus prays: 'And now, Father, glorify me with yourself with the glory which I had with you before the world existed'; similarly the opening words of the prayer: 'Father, the hour has come; glorify your Son, that your son may glorify you' (17:1). It is also Jesus' prayer that the disciples may share this: 'Father I wish that where I am they may be with me, that they may see my glory, which you have given me, because you loved me before the foundation of the world' (17:24). The closest parallel to these texts lies in the prologue which speaks of the Word being with God in the beginning (1:1f) and of the Son being in the bosom of the Father (1:18). On earth, facing his death, the Son looks forward to returning to this glory he once shared and will share again as the gift of the Father. It is probably also this pre-existent glory to which 12:41 refers: 'Isaiah said these things, because he saw his glory and spoke concerning him,'[102] though some take Isaiah's vision as one also of the future glory of the incarnation[103] or of its reward.[104]

God glorifies the Son of Man in himself (God): 13:31f

13:31f must also be understood in this context. 'Now is the Son of Man glorified and God is glorified in him. If God is glorified in him, God will also glorify him in himself and will glorify him immediately.' Our discussion above showed that these verses are best understood as referring to one single event, seen under two aspects.[105] It does not refer to two events, either the hour and the mission to follow,[106] or the ministry to this point and beyond it,[107] or earthly and heavenly glorification,[108] or to the footwashing and then to what is to follow.[109] Nor is it a statement about the revelation of glory, as Caird suggests in reading the passives of *doxazō* in a reflexive or causative sense when referring to God, so that God causes himself to be revealed in the Son of Man.[110] It is one event, which has virtually happened, now that Judas has set it in motion (13:30) and could be spoken of as having happened (13:31,32a); yet Jesus still faced its reality ahead of him with its consequences as a future event (13:32bc).

The formulation, 'God will glorify him in himself, *en autō*, is remarkably similar to 17:5, 'Father, glorify me with yourself, *seautō*. To deny this connection, as does

Moloney, on the grounds that here 'Son of Man' appears and there, 'Father', and by implication, 'Son', is to drive an artificial distinction into the text.[111] In 13:31f there is a mutuality: the Son of Man will glorify God through his obedience in fulfilling his commission by facing suffering and death. This is the meaning 'honour' noted above. In response, the Father will 'glorify the Son of Man', God's glorifying adding weight as it were to the honouring, for it is restoration to the gift of glory in the divine heavenly presence. There is a similar mutuality in 17:4f, where Jesus' prayer for glorification follows his affirmation: 'I have glorified you on earth, having completed the work you have given me to do.'

The hour of glorification of the Son of Man: 12:23

12:23 is similar: 'The hour has come for the Son of Man to be glorified.' Here Jesus' glorification is associated in the context with the mission theme, the coming of 'the world', specifically, the Greeks (12:19-22), the seed bearing fruit (12:24), and the Son of Man drawing all to him through his exaltation (12:32). 12:23 does not mean by glorification, primarily the glory which will come to the Son through mission, as Thüsing suggests.[112] Rather the Son of Man's glorification by the Father will lead to mission, through the gift of the Spirit, the sending of the disciples and their bearing fruit. 17:1 preserves this connection when Jesus prays: 'Father, the hour has come; glorify your Son that the Son may glorify you.' We saw above how mission is associated with glorifying God. So also here in 12:23 the primary reference of glorification is to returning to the glory of the Father,[113] not the mission itself. Nor is it primarily a reference to the cross on the grounds that 12:16 and 7:39 promise the Spirit after Jesus' glorification and that 19:30 be read as fulfilment of this promise, as Moloney suggests.[114] Apart from the doubtful exegesis of 19:30, this interpretation also flounders on the understanding of the giving of the Spirit in the last discourses and in ch 20 and on its assumption that the glorification of the Son of Man must mean something entirely different from 17:5.

'Jesus was not yet glorified' 7:39; 12:16

The connection between the glorification of the Son and the sending of the Spirit is made explicit in 7:39, 'The Spirit was not yet, for Jesus was not yet glorified.' It was when he returned to the Father that Jesus would send the promised Spirit Paraclete. Similarly 12:16 notes Jesus' glorification as the turning point in the disciples' perception of Jesus' ministry and of the scripture: 'The disciples did not understand these things at first, but when Jesus was glorified, then they remembered that these things were written concerning him and that they had done these things to him.' 2:22 stands as a parallel: 'When therefore he was raised from the dead, his disciples remembered that he said this' and confirms that glorification has not just Jesus' death, but the total event of resurrection and return to the glory of the Father in mind.

'...that the Son may be glorified through it' 11:4,40

This glorification of Jesus as he returns through his death to the Father is also alluded to in the Lazarus story, where Jesus declares: 'This sickness is not to death but for the glory of God, that the Son of God may be glorified through it' (11:4), a saying which Jesus recalls again in 11:40.[115] Beyond its immediate reference to the glory in the miracle, this is doubtless a prediction of what the miracle would ultimately lead to according to John's account: Jesus' death and so his departure to the Father.

Other possible glorification texts: 5:44; 8:50, 54

Earlier we noted some passages where already during his ministry Jesus speaks of glorifying God and receiving glory from him. Most likely these refer primarily to praise and honour to God and from God, as the contexts suggest. In some texts however it is also possible that the hour of glorification may also be in view. This might be the case in the following: 'you do not seek the glory which comes from God alone' (5:44); 'I do not seek my own glory. There is one who seeks it and judges' (8:50); 'If I glorify myself my glory is nothing; my Father is the one who glorifies me' (8:54); but this is far from certain.

Glorification - Conclusion

The major passages considered represent a consistent pattern, even to some degree a consistent terminology (as well as 'glorify', note the title, 'the Son of Man' in 13:31f; 12:23). Glorification means primarily God's restoration of Jesus to glory in heaven, the glory which belongs to God himself and which he shared with the Father before the world began.[116] Jesus' glorification, his return to the Father, is also associated with the fruits which flow from his presence in heaven: the giving of the Spirit, greater knowledge, and mission. The Father's glorification of the Son is also a response to the Son's glorification of the Father by carrying out his commission even to death.

Glorification: the cross, paradox of suffering and glory?

The consistent pattern of passages referring to Jesus' return to the Father as glorification counts, in turn, against a number of common interpretations of glorification for which there is inadequate foundation in the text. These include seeing glorification in the sense of Jesus' passion being 'his finest hour', the moment of heroic suffering,[117] and Bultmann's interpretation, followed by many,[118] which reads John in the Pauline sense of the cross as the paradox of glory in suffering. This depends both on Bultmann's understanding of the revelatory paradox of glory in human flesh as he sees it already in 1:14 and on his demythologising of Jesus' return to the Father. We shall see below that the relationship between the glory of the only Son on earth and the glorification by the Father with pre-existent glory is to be perceived differently. There is glory in the ministry of revelation and this continues to the end, to the cross, but the glorification texts are not referring to glorification with this glory on the cross. They speak of glorification with heavenly glory awaiting the Son who completes his commission by revealing the glory of revelation up to and through his passion and death.

The Cross: glorification, exaltation, enthronement?

Many interpret the cross as both glorification and exaltation, usually in association with the royal motifs of the passion either as enthronement[119] or symbolising Jesus' continuing kingship.[120] The resultant picture which emerges from both alternatives is one of Jesus the enthroned glorified one who rules from the cross of shame. There is no denying the theological and devotional power of such an image, but it is not the gospel's. Nor is it supported by the conjunction of *doxazō* and *hypsoō* in Isa 52:13, since there it refers to the response to the servant's suffering, not to the suffering of death itself. The interpretation of the cross as exaltation and glorification misreads the clear meaning of the glorification passages; and in the case of one alternative it reads in the enthronement idea. We have noted in IIB5 and IIIA3 that the royal messianic motifs of the passion probably do not indicate enthronement and should not be merged with exaltation, glorification concepts. Messianic motifs are consistently related in John to the status of the Son as the revealer, not to any notion of his return to the Father as enthronement. Return to the Father and what it entails is never interpreted using messianic or royal enthronement motifs.

Glorious triumphant exit?

By contrast Käsemann emphasises Jesus' supreme confidence and might in his triumphant exit from the world and see this as his glory and glorification.[121] But this fails to take into account the passive voice in so many of the glorification sayings and the fact that they speak of something not available for the Son on earth. It is the Father who glorifies the Son and he does so with the glory once shared with himself before the world was made, to which the Son returns and which the disciples will see only when they join him in the heavenly presence of the Father.

Glorious Love Revealed? Glory Reflected?

Others speak of the glory manifest on the cross as the glory of the oneness shared by Father and Son.[122] This is doubtless consistent with Johannine christology elsewhere, for the Son continues as the revealer to the end and as the revealer he manifests God's glory to the world. But it is a misinterpretation of the glorification passages to read them as speaking of God's glorification of Jesus by revealing the glory of the divine relationship they share. This harmonises and distorts the text and seems influenced by the concern to avoid saying that the Son on earth lacked glory in any way. This depends in turn on a mistaken view of the relationship between 1:14 and the glorification sayings, as we shall presently see. It is better to speak with Blank and others of Jesus' subsequent glorification casting its light upon the Jesus of the cross.[123] This may be allowed in the sense that Jesus faced death confidently, assured of the glorification to follow (cf. 12:28); the gospel portrays his bearing as a reflection of such confidence, much as it is also true of believers facing martyrdom.[124] For the evangelist, this perspective is by no means limited to the passion, but belongs rather to the Son's confidence in the Father throughout his ministry.

Glorification in heaven and glory manifest on earth

Having noted the consistent pattern of meaning in the glorification texts and the many interpretations which have led scholars to deny it, we turn to another group of sayings which have lain in part behind these attempts at harmonisation. By allowing the glorification texts to say what they say, these other passages may also be seen to have a consistent meaning and not to conflict with the former.

The glory of the sent one: 11:4,40-42

We have already noted that at one level Jesus' words in 11:4 refer to the glory to be manifest through his raising Lazarus from the dead: 'This sickness is not to death but for the glory of God, that the Son of God may be glorified through it' (11:4), a saying which Jesus recalls again in 11:40, 'Did I not say to you that if you believe you will see the glory of God?' What is this glory? At the level of the event an important clue is to be found in Jesus' prayer which follows: 'Father, I thank you that you have heard me. I know that you always hear me, but I spoke for the sake of the crowd standing around, so that they may come to believe that you have sent me' (11:41f). Beyond the fact that Jesus has the power to perform the miracle is its central significance as a sign that he is the sent one, or, as he puts it in response to Martha, 'I am the resurrection and the life' (11:25). The glory is the

glory of the sent one, the revealer, who brings life, and, through the manifestation
of the glory of God, the Son also is glorified.

Manifesting the glory: 2:11

A similar idea lies in 2:11, where the author writes: 'This was the first of the signs
which Jesus did in Cana of Galilee and manifested his glory, and his disciples
believed in him.' We have noted in IIB1 above that this miracle conveys much
more than Jesus' power to change water to wine. A level of symbolism is present
at least to the extent that Jesus is portrayed as the giver of new wine.

'We beheld his glory, glory as of the only Son of the Father' 1:14

The clearest statement about the Son's glory, and the one which forms the
background for both passages we have considered, is found in the prologue. 'The
Word became flesh and tented among us and we beheld his glory, glory as of the
only Son of the Father, full of grace and truth' (1:14). This is revelatory glory as
the context confirms: it is explicated as grace and truth, set in contrast with the
Sinai revelation, and expanded in 1:18: 'No one has ever seen God; God the only
Son, who is in the bosom of the Father, he has made him known.' The revelatory
glory derives from the being of the Son in relationship to the Father: he is the
unique Son, bears the 'theos' designation, and was in the bosom of the Father. It
was in the flesh, as he tented among us, that the glory became visible. In the
exposition which follows of the days of Jesus' flesh, the author shows how the
Son's glory was there to see in word and deed, right up to and including suffering
on the cross. Finally, mention should be made of the judgement passed on the
secret believers in 12:43, who 'loved the glory of people more than the glory of
God'. It possible that here, too, there is a hint of Jesus as the bearer of divine
glory.[125]

Relating the two uses of glory

How then does this glory relate to the glory which Jesus enjoyed in his pre-
existence and to which he returned. Both are related. Both derive from God. Both
are different. The heavenly glory is not on earth, but belongs to the being of the
Father in his heavenly state and to the relationship of Father and Son in that state.
It is a glory not seen on this earth. Seeing it is Jesus' prayer for believers when
they follow the path Jesus trod at his death and join him with the Father (17:24).

It is not inconsistent that the author also uses 'glory' of the Son on earth. 'The
glory which you have given me I have given them' (17:22). Here 'glory' stands
parallel to 'word', 'words', 'name' and, like 1:14, is the glory of revelation. The
revelatory glory derives from the Father and belongs to Jesus' being as Son. To
see this glory is to know that he is the Son of the Father, the sent one, the life and
the light. In his coming he does not cease to be that Son and, therefore, does not
cease to have that glory. It adheres to the status and being which is his. And to see
him is to see the Father and to see in him the glory of God.

Yet the author has not collapsed eschatology into a timeless christology or
abandoned spatial dimensions.[126] There remains a not yet and a not here in the

author's theology and this applies equally to his portrait of the earthly Jesus during his ministry. It relates to much more than the motif, 'glory'. The author consistently maintains a distinction between the event of Jesus' ministry and the greater event of his return to the Father. The difference between the revelatory glory and the glory with which he will be glorified corresponds to the difference between his being on earth and his return to the Father. It is not that the Son manifests only a certain proportion of the divine glory. He manifests divine glory. But the author reserves a spatial and temporal distinction between the fullness of divine glory possible on earth and the fullness of divine glory possible in heaven, just as he retains and does not demythologise the notion of the Son's coming and going. This constitutes the difference between the two uses of glory.

The two uses of glory: interpretations in research

The two uses have long been recognised. Holtzmann spoke of two uses.[127] Schnackenburg acknowledges the tension which exists,[128] and similarly, Käsemann.[129] Schnelle speaks of the paradox of the one unchanged glory manifest in different ways to which the Son also returns.[130] This does little more than restate the problem. Appold comes closer to defining the Johannine use when he explains the two uses along the lines that only the place changes, not the glory itself.[131] But this fails to take into account the return of the Son to a glory awaiting him. Better is Bühner's use of the envoy model to relate the two uses. The envoy bears the glory that belongs to his commission and to his being the sent one; but he returns to the source of this glory.[132] B. Weiss spoke of the earthly as a Platonic reflection of the heavenly glory.[133]

Proleptic glory?

Thüsing speaks of the manifestation on earth of the love which belongs to this glory, but not the full power of its light. From this the Son departs and to it he returns.[134] He distinguishes the two as the glory of the relationship of oneness and love[135] and the pre-existent and post-existent glory,[136] but also speaks of the former as a proleptic use of glory of the earthly Jesus in the light of the post Easter glory.[137] Bultmann and Nicol consider texts like 2:11 to relate both to Jesus' earthly ministry and, proleptically, to Jesus' post Easter glory.[138] This may be so, given the levels of meaning in the Cana wedding narrative and the continuity of glory in the person of Jesus, pre- and post-Easter. But it will not do to interpret 1:14 and 2:11 proleptically as referring not to earthly, but post Easter heavenly glory as a way of relaxing the tension, as does Johnston.[139] It is misleading to relate 1:14 primarily to the events from John 13 onwards, on the basis of a division of the prologue into two parts matching two halves of the gospel, as does Theobald.[140]

One unchanging glory?

It is also harmonising when Bruce and Onuki assert that Jesus' glorification means no addition of glory after Easter, but only greater ability on the part of the disciples to behold it,[141] or when Schillebeeckx, not unlike Käsemann and Appold who stress the constant glory of divine oneness, argues that the whole life of Jesus from 1:14 onwards is glory so that no glorification is needed,[142] or when Hegermann claims that the glory remains constant because it represents the presence of God who is always with the Son.[143] Nor is it likely that the glory for which the Son of Man prays is corporate glory for his own, as Caird suggests.[144] Any discussion must take into account that the incarnation implies both manifestation of glory and departure from glory to which the Son will return.[145]

Those who dispute that Jesus could have received more glory than he already had must deny the clear statements such as 17:5. They speak of the crucifixion as an unveiling of the glory that had always been there. This is true of Bultmann, who demythologises the concept of glorification, so that it means, in effect, that Jesus remains the revealer.[146] At most, like Cadman, he uses glorification in a future sense in relationship to fruit being born in mission and the gathering of Jesus' own, one of the uses evident in the gospel (16:14), but not the major one.[147]

Glory, veiled and unveiled?

The idea of the cross as revelation or unveiling has often been used to suggest that that during Jesus' ministry his glory was veiled, either in humility or in ambiguity.[148] Those who posit a Semeia source usually see it treating Jesus' miracles as an unveiling of his glory.[149] For the gospel both Thüsing and Nicol argue that this glory is seen only after the gift of the Spirit.[150] Hofbeck counters, that this is not so, for the life promised in the signs is more than proleptic. It is a present reality in the person of Jesus. The glory of the signs is veiled to unbelievers, but not to the eyes of faith.[151] Schottroff argues that the manifestation takes place through the flesh and the signs in a way that leaves them untouched and in themselves irrelevant.[152] By contrast, Käsemann sees the humanity of Jesus seriously called into question by the manifestation of glory. The miracles are not irrelevant; they are demonstrations of the divine glory. Thus he denies a future glorification adds anything to what is already there.[153] Ibuki also points to the glory as manifest not only in the signs, but reinterprets glory to mean the glory of the relationship of love between Father and Son.[154] Forestell emphasises that the glory is manifest throughout the earthly life up to and including the cross and Easter event.[155]

The latter are surely correct in seeing 1:14 and 17:22 referring to a glory present in the ministry and veiled only to the eyes that will not see. There is, therefore, no need to harmonise the two uses of glory along the lines that the one glory is veiled, then unveiled. Jesus' glorification is not an unveiling, but a return to the glory he had with the Father in the beginning. The same must be said of those attempts which define glory as the oneness and love shared by Father and Son, always present but fully visible at Easter.[156] Without question the cross as the climax of the obedient life reveals in a unique way the relation of Father and Son, the love which constitutes it and the glory, the grace and truth, manifest through it.[157] But this should not be confused with the glorification of Jesus which his death inaugurates as the first step in his return to the glory he had with the Father before the world was and for which he prays.[158]

Glory: Tradition and Redaction

Some have explained the two uses as coming from different sources or levels of composition. Wilkens attributes to the narrative source and the heavenly use to the sayings source.[159] For Richter 2:11 and 11:40 come from the Semeia source, pre- and post-existent glory sayings from the evangelist, and 1:14 from the redactor.[160] Becker sees glory linked with sending as the view of the evangelist, the idea of postexistent glory, as in ch. 17, coming from the redactor.[161] U.B. Müller sees 1:14,16 as belonging originally in a miracle christology and referring only to Jesus' ministry, then taken up and linked by a redactor with the cross as glorification.[162]

Glorification of Jesus' human nature?

Riedl develops a detailed theory taken from Thomas Aquinas according to which the tension between Jesus having glory on earth and his receiving glory at Easter is to be solved by the suggestion that it is the human nature which is glorified at Easter. This suggestion goes back to Cyril of Alexandria. It means taking *autō* ('in him' or 'in himself') in the phrase, 'God will glorify him in himself' (13:32), to refer not to God but to Christ. Accordingly God glorifies the man Jesus in the Son.[163] The glorification includes the filling of Jesus' humanity to the full with divine glory as he reaches the highest level of knowledge of God. Thus the human Jesus asks in 17:1,5 what he has already as a Son. Riedl develops this into a three stage theory: pre-existence, filling the human Jesus, flowing out into the world. There is no addition of glory at any point.[164] But the theory depends heavily upon the assumption that the author operated with a two nature theory. There is no trace of this in the gospel. It does not make sense on this theory that the same Jesus in ch. 17 prays as a human being for glory and refers at the same time to glory he received as a gift in pre-existence.

Equally inappropriate is the view according to which glorification attaches primarily to leaving the flesh for the spiritual form of existence[165] or the suggestion that Jesus' reference to former heavenly glory (17:5) and to Isaiah's seeing it (12:41) are merely an apocalyptic way of talking about what is destined for the Son in the task of revelation he is to bear on earth, for both fail to take the context of the glorification sayings seriously.[166]

Glorification and Glory: Conclusion

There is therefore a glory which Jesus bears as God's Son and which he manifests in the world to the eyes of faith. This is his revelation of the Father and may be seen in his work and words. It is a glory which enables him to perform miracles. These should not be denied, as did Bultmann,[167] or denied any relevance with Schottroff.[168] Faith in the signs as miracles entails not ignoring the miracles altogether, but seeing in them a pointer to who Jesus is, both as the Son able to perform the miracle itself and as the bearer of life often symbolised in the miracle narrative. Many assume that it was only the glory of miracle power which had been emphasised in the author's sources. In taking up such sources the author has not denied the miracles as manifestations of power, but has been critical of faith which stopped there.

In the deeds and words which his unique origins enabled him to perform and speak, the Son gives glory, as he gives himself, the revelation, to his disciples. But there is also a heavenly glory which belongs to the presence of the Son with the Father in heaven. This lies behind statements which speak of Jesus' glorification through the event of his death and return to the Father. Beside these is the less specific use of glory in the sense of honour, mostly used of the Son's glorifying the Father through the fulfilment of his will, especially through his obedience to the end, to death, but also used of his disciples and of the Paraclete, who through their work glorify both the Father and the Son. Of the two primary uses, both interpret the death of Jesus, one, more by implication, as the completion of the work of revelation, the other quite specifically by portraying the death as the means whereby the Son returns to be glorified in heaven by his Father.

Lifting up and Exaltation: text, language and tradition

Closely associated with the concept of glorification is the author's use of the exaltation motif. The word *hypsoō* ('to lift up, to exalt') occurs in the gospel in three passages:

'And as Moses lifted up the serpent in the wilderness, so must the Son of Man be
    lifted up, that all believing may have life in him' (3:14f)
'When you have lifted up the Son of Man, then you will know that I am the one,
    and I do nothing of myself, but as the Father taught me, so I speak' (8:28)
'And I, if I am lifted up from the earth, will draw all to myself. This he said
    indicating by what death he was going to die. The crowd therefore replied
    to him, "We have heard from the Law that the Christ remains forever, and
    how do you say the Son of Man must be lifted up?"' (12:32-34)

The word *hypsoō*, like its equivalents in Aramaic and Hebrew, can mean a literal lifting up as well as a metaphorical lifting up, an exaltation.[169] It could and did function therefore as a base for puns both in the semitic languages of Hebrew and Aramaic and also in Greek.[170] It is used to describe exaltation in New Testament christological tradition of Jesus' exaltation to God's right hand or to heavenly lordship (Acts 2:33; 5:31; cf. Phil 2:9).

Lifting up: crucifixion only?

In John it certainly refers to Jesus' crucifixion as a lifting up. This is made clear by the author in 12:33, where he treats the saying as a prediction of the manner of Jesus' death. In 18:32 he refers back to this after noting that Jesus was handed over to Pilate for trial: 'so that the word of Jesus might be fulfilled which he spoke indicating by what death he was going to die.' This may reflect a concern to deal with the offence created by the crucifixion for belief in his messiahship (cf. 12:34).[171] Crucifixion also matches the image of the lifting up of the serpent in 3:14 and the Jews' initiative in Jesus' crucifixion is reflected in 8:28, 'When you have lifted up the Son of Man.'

It is possible to let matters rest there. *hypsoō* would mean nothing more than the lifting up of Jesus onto the cross and is simply a synonym for 'crucify' in each of these verses. In 3:14 this would give the meaning either that the actual death, itself, is the basis for the promise of the healing of eternal life, namely death understood as a vicarious sacrifice, on which see IIIA2 above, or that crucifixion began an event which through the giving of the Spirit would lead to the gift of life becoming more freely available. 8:28, with its promise of knowledge, would cohere well with the idea of the promised Spirit, bringing knowledge, especially by interpreting the meaning of Jesus' crucifixion and death as is done in 16:8-11. In this case the knowledge would also bring judgement.[172] 12:32 could contain a reference to vicarious atonement as the basis for the salvation offered to all and so the basis of drawing all, as considered above in IIIA2. Thüsing argues this unconvincingly on the basis of *poiō* in 12:33, which he takes to refer to Jesus' death as salvific, whereas 18:32 makes it clear that the mode of execution is intended;[173] or it, too, could refer to the crucifixion as the beginning of the event which would lead to the Spirit and to world mission.

Lifting up/ Exaltation and Isaiah 53?

We have already seen how vicarious atonement does not play a major part in the author's christology. This counts against it doing so here in two of the three passages. The same must be said of attempts to make a link between the language of exaltation and glorification and the suffering servant of Isa 53. This is not the meaning of glorification in John, as we have already seen, and, where both *hypsoo* and *doxazo* are used in the context of Is 53, namely in Isa 52:13, they refer rather to the vindication of the servant, not his suffering. Their conjunction in describing Jesus' final 'hour' of vindication may well be influenced by Isa 52:13,[174] though a similar conjunction, together with the idea of vindication, is found also in Isa 5:16; 33:10; 45:25, as Caird and Klaiber point out.[175] The use of *hypsoō* and *doxazō* in these contexts supports the idea that in John they are being used to describe the same event: Jesus' path of exaltation and glorification through the cross to heaven. Accordingly the author has also made use of the potential dual reference in *hypsoō*.

Lifting to the cross, exaltation to glory: two ways of seeing

The world sees a crucifixion; believers see it as the path to exaltation. The word, *hypsoō*, enabled the author to describe two realities, the reality of crucifixion and the reality of Jesus' return through this event to exalted glory.[176] Unfaith sees only one reality; faith sees both. We have, therefore, a typical word play of the evangelist which functions powerfully as irony at the heart of the author's christology. It also accords with the use of *hypsoō* in Christian tradition, such as in Acts 2:33; 5:31 and Phil 2:9, to express exaltation. The author's use of *hypsoō* to refer both to crucifixion and to the exaltation of Jesus to God in heaven receives further confirmation when we recall how it belongs within a particular cluster of vocabulary associated with the Son of Man title: glorification, exaltation, ascent, judgement, the 'hour', and the greater event motif, as we noted in IIC above.

The context of the exaltation sayings illustrates this connection. 3:13 has just referred to the ascent of the Son of Man. 8:28 belongs in the broader context of the Jews' perplexity about where Jesus is going (8:21-24), his return to the Father. 12:32 follows a statement about the hour of the world's judgement having come when the ruler of the world would be cast out. In the next allusion to the same theme, 16,8-11, the judgement of the world and the vindication of Jesus is related to his death and return to the Father. The wider context of 12:32, stretching back to 12:19, is embraced by the theme of mission and of Jesus' death and return as the event which makes it possible. In this sense the parallels to 12:32 are 12:23 and 24, where, at the coming of the Greeks, Jesus declares, 'The hour has come for the Son of Man to be glorified. Truly, truly I tell you unless a grain of wheat falls into the ground and dies, it remains alone; but if it dies it bears much fruit.' We have already seen that glorification refers here to Jesus' being brought through death to the glory he once shared in the beginning with the Father. Seen in this light, all three passages cohere impressively and take their place within a cluster of motifs by which the author explicates the significance of Jesus' death and return. Exaltation, with glorification, explicates the significance of Jesus' death and return.

Crucifixion: paradox of exaltation and glorification?

Exaltation in John is, then, another way of the author's saying that, through the event of his death and return, the Son of Man has been glorified with the glory he shared with God before the foundation of the world. This is far more likely than the suggestion that exaltation and glorification have been transferred by the author to the crucifixion itself,[177] let alone, that, by association with Isa 53, they also include the notion of the vicarious sacrifice of Jesus for his own.[178] An explanation of *hypsoō* which would see it as having a single meaning, namely execution on a cross, and would see crucifixion as the beginning the total event through which life, the Spirit, mission are made available, would be more coherent with the main structure of the author's theology, but it, too, fails to grasp the full import of the passages by limiting *hypsoō* to the crucifixion. For the ascent onto the cross is the ascent ultimately to heaven itself. When the world lifts Jesus to the cross and to death, it unwittingly sets in motion an event of far greater significance. For through death he returns exalted and glorified to the Father.

The common misinterpretation which applies exaltation and glorification to the cross arises, in part, from the persistence of the Bultmann model of Johannine christology which sees exaltation demythologised by the author, so that the crucifixion itself is interpreted as a great Pauline paradox of glorification and exaltation. The result is startling, provocative and immensely challenging: glory in shame, exaltation in humiliation.[179] But, once we concede, that glorification cannot be understood like this in John, then the case for taking exaltation as referring to anything other than exaltation to God in heaven is seriously weakened. Here we tread the same ground again in noting that royal messianic imagery in the passion narrative cannot be used to support this kind of interpretation of the cross in John in relation to the exaltation motif, any more than it can, in relation to glorification. Nor is there sufficient evidence in it of enthronement christology, and, even if there were, it is not linked with the exaltation theme.

There is also no evidence in the gospel for Bittner's contention that 'lifting up' is primarily a messianic image based on the lifted ensign of Isa 11:11.[180] Similarly Bühner's theory of an action taking place on two levels (lifting up on the cross, at one level, heavenly enthronement, on the other) imposes a foreign framework onto the text.[181] This is not to deny we see in John the true king of Israel on the cross nor to ignore the powerful irony expressed in the fact that the mockery of the trial, transposed into the key of faith, plays the melody of faith's affirmation: Jesus is the Christ, the Son of God. But neither the exaltation nor the glorification motifs are made to say this in John, however well they have been so used in theology and edification.

Exaltation is not, therefore, exaltation onto the cross without being exaltation through this to heaven.[182] Neither do exaltation and glorification refer only to Jesus' death on the cross.[183] Pamment's argument to the contrary, that this language does not occur in 20:17 where Jesus speaks of return or ascent to the Father and that allusion to Jesus' death in 12:24 means we must take 12:23 as referring to Jesus' death, are not convincing as passages like 3:13f and our review (IIB2) of ch. 12 has shown.[184]

There remains, however, a distinctively Johannine paradox in the fourth gospel the use of *hypsoō*: faith sees the cross, the pathway of suffering, as the pathway to glory. We shall return in IIIA7 to this paradox and its implications for understanding discipleship in John.

Exaltation on the Cross: Glorification in heaven?

A different approach is taken by Thüsing, who distinguishes glorification and exaltation. Jesus is exalted on the cross, so that he continues to rule from the cross. Glorification includes the cross, but refers primarily to his subsequent return to glory.[185] In this way he holds exaltation and glorification apart and yet does so in a way that confuses. He speaks of exaltation, for instance, as a 'Bild', a picture or image,[186] and sometimes speaks of it as exaltation to the throne of glory.[187] His diagrammatic representation of exaltation and glorification does in fact equate exaltation and glorification as return to heavenly glory;[188] yet he continues to use the idea of exaltation upon the cross as a 'Bild' in such a way that he can say that the Son rules from here and draws people first to the cross and only then into glory.[189]

Glorification, exaltation, and ascension

Both glorification and exaltation interpret Jesus' death in John as his return to the Father, to glory on high. Both are associated with the title Son of Man. They belong together within a cluster of motifs. The review in IIC showed that to this close association of ideas also belongs ascension.

The attempts of Moloney and others to deny its presence in 3:13 and 6:62 are unconvincing. Moloney first notes that the words, 'No one has ascended to heaven', might well be reflecting a common tradition (reflected in Deut 30:12; Prov 30:4, Bar 3:29; Wisd 9:16-18) which the author is using to counter alternate claims to revelation.[190] Such claims were widespread and diverse and might include mystical ascents,[191] ascents of Moses or of prophets,[192] apocalyptic visions and visionaries,[193] Philonic ascent,[194] and gnostic revealers.[195] Moloney goes on to argue for a translation which would continue the verse: 'but there is one who has descended, the Son of Man.' In this way he rules out any allusion in 3:13 to the ascent of the Son of Man.[196]

This runs counter to the natural reading of *ei mē* in 3:13 to mean 'except' and is widely rejected.[197] The fact that the usual translation would have Jesus speaking anachronistically here should not, in itself, be a problem, since already 3:11 does so. Furthermore the allusion to Jesus' death and exaltation in 3:14f makes the translation most unlikely, even more so, if, unlike Moloney, we understand exaltation to include exaltation to heavenly glory. Attempts to see in 3:13 a pre-existent ascension as part of the process of authorisation, as Bühner and others suggest,[198] or an earthly ecstatic one after the model of Paul's being caught up into the third heaven,[199] or an allusion to Jesus' ascent from the waters of baptism,[200] or the idea of constant traffic of Jesus between earth and heaven,[201] are also unconvincing for this reason. The manuscript tradition which added, 'who is in heaven' understood the anachronism perfectly.[202] Jesus is represented here as speaking from a post Easter perspective.[203]

The ascension of the Son of Man is alluded to in 3:13. This is not to deny the difficulty in the flow of thought within the passage. After 3:12, with its contrast between earthly and heavenly revelation, we might expect 3:13 to be countering the claims of rival revealers, and so it does. But if it were as simple as that, then we might well wonder why the author has not formulated 3:13 more clearly and used a simple adversative. The credentials Jesus pits against the rivals are not only his descent. They also include his ascent, but not a preceding ascent. It is the one who descended and also ascended again who is qualified to be the revealer par excellence. In his coming he brings revelation to earth ('earthly things' including birth from above, 3:12); in his going he makes possible knowledge of 'heavenly things' (3:12). Both events, the revelation through descent and, above all, its abundant availability and greater understanding achieved through ascent, make Jesus the superior revealer. Accordingly the author goes on in 3:14f to refer to the latter and how it will be achieved: through exaltation.[204]

Moloney offers an unusual interpretation of 6:62 through which he again seeks to deny the presence of the ascension motif. 'Then what if you were to see the Son of Man ascending where he was before?' is, according to Moloney, a taunt aimed at popular expectations of ascending revealers. 'There will be no ascension to where he was before.'[205] But once we allow ascension in 3:13 (it is also present in 20:17), there is no reason to dismiss it here. 6:62 and 3:13 both point to something greater still to come and, like 3:14, which also refers to that coming event, do so using the title Son of Man.

The Son of Man's glorification, exaltation, ascension and 1:51

The first occurrence of the title, Son of Man, in the gospel, 1:51, must also be considered in this context. Nathanael has confessed Jesus king of Israel and Son of God, a confession substantially the same as that which the gospel as a whole seeks to elicit (20:31). Jesus responds: '"Because I said I saw you under the fig tree do you believe? You shall see greater things than these." And he said to him, "Truly I tell you, you shall see the heaven opened and the angels of God ascending and descending on the Son of Man."' Some see here a saying which related perhaps at one time to the parousia.[206] Many see it in its present form and context as a reference to the glory to be revealed during Jesus' ministry.[207] Most point to a first fulfilment in the miracle at Cana where the evangelist notes that through this sign the disciples saw Jesus' glory. Most also relate the imagery in some way to the story of Jacob's ladder in Gen 28 and its exegetical tradition, interpreting Jesus either as the ladder (a bridge of revelation between heaven and earth) or as represented in the Jacob figure. The theme of the saying is Jesus as the revealer.

In itself this interpretation seems compatible with what follows, but it is less so
with what precedes, for it fails to explain adequately the 'greater' motif. This
could mean no more than the promise of greater or more miracles than those
already seen by Nathanael. But this seems hardly an adequate explanation. Had not
Nathanael made an adequate confession? The 'greater' seems rather to be
qualitative than quantitative. There is no indication that this is poor, miracle based,
faith of the kind the evangelist shuns in 2:23-25. It is likely therefore that we have
here the kind of contrast found elsewhere in the gospel and explicitly in relation to
the Son of Man title (3:12-14 and 6:62), namely, a contrast between the events of
Jesus' earthly ministry and its revelation, on the one hand, and the events of Jesus'
death and ascent to the Father, on the other. The saying, itself, lends this support.
The heavens are not opened for the descent of a dove or for a manifestation to be
seen on earth. The promise is of a vision of the Son of Man in glory. We shall look
into heaven and see the angels centering their service on the Son of Man. This
makes it more probable that 1:51 refers not to the ensuing earthly ministry, but to
the exaltation and glorification of the Son of Man.[208]

Some have seen in the ladder an allusion to the cross.[209] That is somewhat
speculative. A number of scholars who espouse the view that 1:51 refers to Jesus'
ministry also go on to include the cross as the climax of revelation,[210] confirming
that 'greater' demands more than the miracles to follow in the ministry. A number
note the close link between 1:51 and 3:13.[211] It is more satisfactory to see it as
primarily a reference to the exaltation and glorification of the Son of Man. The
Jacob imagery is no more difficult for this interpretation than it is for others. Is
Jesus pictured as the heavenly Jacob? Is he in some sense the ladder? An
exegetical tradition related to the former is more likely.

Glorification, exaltation, ascension and 'the Son of Man'

Closely associated with glorification, exaltation and ascension motifs in John is the
Son of Man title. In his 1964 article on the Son of Man Schnackenburg has noted
this circle of themes.[212] He notes also its traditionally judicial character, reflected in
the judgement saying of 5:27,[213] and probably also in the use of the title in 9:35 (cf.
9:39). Schnackenburg argues against seeing the presence of the title behind use of
ho anthrōpos, the ecce homo saying (19:5), the image of the vine (in the light of Ps
80:8,17),[214] and the 'I am' saying of 8:28.215 He suggests a possible link with Son
of Man tradition in the use of Zechariah in 19:37,[216] but, beside this, rightly in my
assessment, limits the influence of Son of Man tradition to passages where the title
occurs. Cullmann suggests that 'Son of Man' lies originally behind 'flesh' in 1:14
and was avoided by the author because of anthropos speculation,[217] but of this there
is no evidence. Some have suggested that the sealing of the Son of Man in 6:27
refers to his exaltation,[218] but more likely it refers to the Son of Man's authorisation
and sending[219] or perhaps his baptism.[220]

According to Schnackenburg the author's contribution lies in having expanded the
use of Son of Man in Johannine tradition where it had related primarily to parousia
and exaltation. In doing so, he has included the cross as part of the process of
exaltation and glorification and has introduced the idea of the descending and
ascending Son of Man.[221] Whereas in Paul we see the cross as the paradox of glory
in suffering, in John we see the paradox in different form. As noted above, the

cross is a path of suffering, but to the eyes of faith it is also the ascent to the glory of the Father.[222] Schnackenburg still sees no real distinction in John between the use of 'Son' and 'Son of Man'.[223]

Maddox notes the virtual absence of 'Son of Man' in the last discourses (cf. only 13:31f),[224] but points out a similar infrequency of other titles and notes that its themes continue.[225] He argues, however, rightly, that this also reflects an incomplete assimilation of 'Son of Man' and 'Son'.[226] Moloney emphasises this difference, setting out the differences in parallel columns, but the distinctive character which he attributes to the Son of Man rests heavily on his unconvincing exegesis of ascension in 3:13 and 6:62 and of the concepts of exaltation and glorification. Accordingly, for him Son of Man is primarily the title for Jesus as the revealer on earth, the man, announced in 1:51 and fulfilled in the 'ecce homo' scene of 19:5, which he takes as a Son of Man reference.[227] In this way he virtually eliminates what is the dominant motif associated with Son of Man, namely the event complex which begins on the cross and ends in glory, and reduces all Son of Man sayings to statements about revealing. He also argues that this is the primary focus of the judicial uses in 5:27 and 9:35. Moloney acknowledges glorification (17:1,5; 11:4) and ascension (20:17), but argues that they mean something different because of the absence of the Son of Man title, though the same concepts also occur with the title earlier in the gospel.[228] Somewhat in tension with this claim is his acknowledgement of this fuller use of glorification in the Son of Man saying in 13:32.[229] Moloney also emphasises humanness as an aspect of the title, a claim for which I see no justification in the gospel once one abandons Moloney's denial of the role of ascension, glorification and exaltation in the gospel.[230] Even less can I find an antidocetic orientation in its use as Schnelle suggests.[231]

There can be no denial that revelation in the sense of bringing life is present in John's use of Son of Man and this is especially evident in the image of the bread which descends from heaven in ch. 6. It must also be present in the notion of descent in 3:13 and belongs to the descent ascent pattern of *katabainō/anabainō*, which, apart from 20:17, is used consistently in Son of Man contexts. At this point the Son of Man and the Son - Father patterns overlap, though the language of coming and returning is different and much more frequent with the latter. But our analysis in II showed that the revealer motif is predominantly associated not with Son of Man but with Son - Father. Leaving aside the overlap which exists, the Son of Man designation and its associated imagery (exaltation, glorification, ascension, the hour, judgement, the greater things) is used in interpreting the climax of Jesus' ministry, his death and return to the Father and this is its predominant use in the gospel.

5. Death and Resurrection

The most common way the author has Jesus speak of the events following his death are in terms of return to the Father, glorification, exaltation, and ascension. These four encompass a single event. By contrast, in the author's narrative, passion is followed by burial, empty tomb and resurrection appearances. How do the two relate?

Mary and Jesus, risen, but not ascended: 20:17

The point at which the two most clearly come together is in the words of Jesus to Mary Magdalene: 'Do not hold onto me, for I have not yet ascended to the Father. But go to my brothers and say to them, "I am ascending to my Father and your Father and my God and your God"' (20:17) Here the promises of the last discourses are echoed, in particular 14:12,28, 'He who believes in me, the works which I do he will do and greater works than these will he do, because I go to my Father'; 'I go away and return to you. If you loved me, you would rejoice, that I go to the Father, because the Father is greater than me.' This relates in turn to the gift of the Spirit and the relationship of oneness which it will bring (cf. 14:16-20). The narrative to follow in 20:19-23 will tell of the giving of the Spirit to the disciples.

As we have seen above, the most natural reading of 20:17 is to see expressed in it the assumption that, at the point of her contact with Jesus, he had not yet completed the ascent to the Father and that, by the evening when he appeared to the disciples, he had.[232] There is no need to deny this[233] or to assume ascension must follow later.[234] This reading does not depend on the argument that here touching is not possible and in the evening or with Thomas it is.[235] It depends on what is actually said: 'I am ascending', and on what has been said about its implications for the giving of the Spirit. The difficulty of Jesus' enigmatic words that he has not yet ascended to the Father and that he is about to ascend should not be harmonised away by a spiritualising or metaphorical interpretation which understands ascent to mean the process of coming and bringing life to the disciples[236] or in some way to mean both return to the Father and return to the disciples simultaneously.[237]

It is much more fruitful to acknowledge the tension which exists and to understand it as arising from the author's use of different traditional ideas.[238] The author does not appear to espouse the view that Jesus ascended directly into heaven from the cross or was exalted or glorified directly at, or from, the point of death, though much of his language could be read in this way.[239] Dodd approaches this view in maintaining that the resurrection is merely an event on the earthly plane corresponding, on his Platonic model of interpretation, to the real heavenly event in the glory of the cross.[240] The language of return, glorification, exaltation and ascent might easily lead to this, but the author remains within the traditional pattern attested by his narrative of death and resurrection on the third day. Wilkens argues that the tradition of the appearances belongs to the narrative source which he posits, and ascension from the cross, to the sayings source.[241] Lindars suggests the appearance stories are a concession on the part of the author to faith not fully fledged, pointing to the Thomas episode,[242] but this cannot be said of the other appearances, nor to my mind of the Thomas story. The author integrates the two sets of concepts within a narrative which portrays Jesus passing through the following stages. He dies, is buried, is raised, is seen by Mary Magdalene, then ascends to the Father (here we must include glorification and exaltation), and appears to the disciples. There is no bodiless glorification.[243] The appearances are made after his ascent and return and, consistent with the promises of the last discourses, his return makes possible the giving of the Spirit and the equipping of the disciples for mission.

This is not the pattern of Luke-Acts where an appearance, including assumption into heaven through clouds, commonly referred to as an ascension, completes a series of appearances over a 40 day period, though even Luke's writings may reflect an alternative view according to which Jesus makes his appearances from heaven, as in the case of Paul's encounter with Jesus on the Damascus Road. The Johannine pattern of revelation of the risen one to his own from heaven may well reflect tradition. The peculiarity of John's account becomes then the pre-ascension encounter with Mary.

The somewhat awkward appearance to Mary does reflects a tension between two systems of thought: exaltation, glorification, ascent and return, on the one hand, and resurrection on the third day, on the other. In the author's hand it functions primarily to make a statement about an appropriate and an inappropriate response of faith. In its present setting it serves to direct attention away from a faith which clings to the earthly form of Jesus and towards life in relation to the exalted and glorified Lord who gives the Spirit. Thereby the author makes the encounter with the disciples the event of paramount importance. The traditional encounter with the woman (or women) becomes its incomplete forerunner. It is at this cost that the author has embellished the tradition, producing the present remarkable and powerfully dramatic episode.

Jesus' resurrection elsewhere in the Gospel

The fourth gospel also refers to Jesus' resurrection within the main body of the gospel. If there are not hints of it in the 'three days' of 2:1, there is the explicit prediction of 2:19, 'Destroy this temple and in three days I shall raise it.' Typically the author has the Jews interpret the words literally, then adds his own footnote: 'He was speaking about the temple of his body.' The resurrection becomes, then, the answer to the Jews' quest for a sign of authentication for Jesus' activity (2:18). Consequently the author adds, 'When therefore he was raised from the dead, his disciples remembered that he had said this and believed the scripture and the word which Jesus spoke' (2:22). From this three things are clear: firstly, Jesus' resurrection is the sign of his vindication and will enable Thomas to proclaim, 'my Lord and my God' (20:28). Secondly, Jesus' resurrection functions for the author in the same way as his exaltation, glorification, ascension and return to the Father. It belongs to this single complex event. This is evident from the way similar understanding on the part of the disciples is said to have come 'when Jesus had been glorified' (12:16). When Jesus was raised and when he was glorified are functionally equivalent in the two passages (2:22; 12:16). And thirdly, what comes into being as the result of Jesus' resurrection will replace the temple. In Jesus there is now the possibility of worship in spirit and in truth (4:23) and, more specifically, the promise that because of resurrection, the Son and the Father will come through the Spirit and make their dwelling in the disciples (14:19-23).

Resurrection and the 'greater event'

The integration of resurrection, along with the exaltation, glorification, ascent and return to the Father, within the total concept of the single event complex is apparent also in 14:19, 'Yet a little while and the world will see me no more, but you will see me, because I live, you also will live.' Here the fact of Jesus' being alive is singled out, but done so in a context which assumes his return to the Father and, by the Spirit, his coming with the Father to dwell in the disciples. Similarly 10:17f focusses on Jesus' authority to lay down his life and take it up again. This, in turn, is related to the work of mission by which he will gather his sheep into one (10:16).

In both cases taking up life again could be understood without a story of resurrection from an empty tomb on the third day. But the total context of the gospel demands that this is not the case. Resurrection is how the author portrays Jesus' taking up his life to have occurred. This is the Jesus tradition he has received. Nevertheless, as an event, it is so integrated within the wider event and its significance, that characteristically the risen Jesus tells Mary to tell the disciples only that he ascends to his Father and theirs (20:17). For not the resurrection in itself, but the total event, resurrection, exaltation, glorification, ascension, and return to the Father, is the 'greater' event to which the ministry looks forward and through which the full impact of the revelation that took place in that ministry will be made known. For through that 'greater' event 'greater things' become possible through the sending of the Spirit and of the disciples, who are able to confront the world with the truth that Jesus is the Son come from the Father to make him known. At one level therefore the resurrection adds nothing to the revelation, as Bultmann points out;[244] at another, as part of the 'greater' event it is resurrection that makes the story of revelation possible.

6. The 'Greater Event' and the Spirit

In the discussion of Jesus as 'exalted, glorified, ascended' in IIC9 I drew together texts which showed a pattern within the gospel according to which, from the standpoint of the earthly ministry of Jesus, something greater would be inaugurated by the event of Jesus' death and return. These were, in particular, 1:50f, which points to the Son of Man in exaltation; 3:12, promising heavenly things, explicated in the following verses as the ascension and exaltation of the Son of Man (3:13f); 6:61f, contrasting the descent with the even greater event of the ascent of the Son of Man to where he was before; and 14:12, promising greater works which the disciples would do because Jesus goes to the Father (echoed in 14:28). The 'greater event' describes the Son's return and his exaltation, glorification and ascent as Son of Man. Whereas these describe what the event entails, the contrast expressed in each of these texts, which I describe here as the 'greater event' motif, gives this total event a special status in relationship to the event of the Son's coming and his work of making known the Father on earth. In this section I want to explore further the nature of this relationship.

Implications of the 'Greater Event'

The review of texts relating to Jesus' death and return also showed that references to exaltation, glorification, ascension and return rarely stand alone without some explanation of their implications. The review set this out simply as the sending of the disciples and the sending of the Spirit to make possible greater understanding, to equip the disciples for mission, and to build up the community of faith. Each of these fruits of the event relates to each other and together they explain why the event is 'greater'. The Son goes away and sends the Spirit Paraclete; the risen Christ also sends the disciples. Both are sent to be bearers of revelation, as the Son was, but it is no independent revelation. It remains the revelation of the Son. Both belong together. The Spirit enables the disciples' recall and leads them to fuller understanding of the Son's words and deeds and of their meaning in the light of scripture. The Spirit, therefore, makes the mission of the disciples possible. Through them it confronts the world with the meaning of the Son's coming, his death and vindication. The mission of the disciples will bear fruit and lead to the gathering of the Son's community from throughout the world, bringing glory to him and to the Father. The Spirit also makes possible the presence of the Father and the risen Son dwelling in the disciples and the communion in unity among them. They enjoy the life which flows from that and feed on it through the sacrament of the Son of Man's flesh and blood.

The 'greater' event is 'greater', not because it adds to the life and light present in the person of the Son, the revealer. For this revelation is complete in the person of the Son and remains so throughout his ministry up to and including his death on the cross where the crisis it engenders is brought to a head. It is not 'greater' because it entails the fruits of one further task, the work of atonement, a benefit not present in the Son's revelation thus far, for the author, while using vicarious atonement tradition, does not give it that kind of status and it is absent where the 'greater' theme and associated concepts are being used. The 'greater' event is 'greater' because it makes available for all the true significance of the event of revelation. It represents the Son's vindication and makes possible and accessible in a new way the encounter with the Son who came as the sent one from the Father and made him known in word and deed. The 'greater' event has accordingly a hermeneutical function. But it is not just a hermeneutical function for the author. It is an event. The Son has returned to the Father, risen, exalted, glorified, ascended and this is also promise of future heavenly dwelling for the disciples. For the Son it is 'greater' because it means his return to glory after the completed task. And it is precisely because of this return that it is 'greater' for the disciples, for it enables the story of Jesus to be understood and made known. Thus, return to the Father who is 'greater', makes the 'greater works' of the disciples possible (14:28,12; cf. also 20:17).

Life only after the 'Greater Event'?

Frequently the promise of the greater event is interpreted in an exclusive manner, which suggests that the life which the Son has and is, became available only through the Spirit's coming, and was not really available during his ministry.

Haenchen, for instance, argues that there is no true faith, no birth from above, before the giving of the Spirit.[245] Thüsing argues similarly, linking 7:38f with 19:34, the flow of water and blood from the side of Jesus.[246] Scholars who, like Thüsing, stress the importance of the death of Jesus as a saving act logically lean towards this position. Dauer even sees an allusion to atonement implicit in 7:37-39,[247] and Schnackenburg says its promise of salvation is accessible only after Easter.[248] Haacker acknowledges the problem in denying that salvation is present in the person of the revealer, but finally argues the necessity of both the Spirit and the work of atonement for salvation.[249] Forestell who denies atonement plays such a role, nevertheless claims that it is not until the work of revelation is completed by Jesus' death that the benefits of salvation are available.[250] Similarly Becker points to the necessity of victory over the power of death as first needing to be achieved.[251] Dodd argues that the real gift of life is available only after the cross and resurrection.[252] Painter, too, speaks only of a proleptic faith before Easter in John.[253] Nicholson believes that such lack of knowledge continues even in ch. 20 until 20:22 and the giving of the Spirit[254] and for Schillebeeckx any pre-Easter offer of life is but a pledge or preliminary sign of what will become available after Easter.[255] Similarly Johnston argues that the glory of 1:14 and 2:11 can only be understood proleptically of the post Easter period,[256] Hamerton-Kelly says that only after this event can what was eternally present be known.[257] This is closer to what I take to be the Johannine understanding, inasmuch as it does not interpose an additional achievement such as atonement or victory and acknowledges that the revelation was present in the ministry of Jesus, but it is still hard to reconcile such statements with the gospel narrative which assumes that some did in fact receive the sent one and his revelation. Onuki speaks of a paradox that saving knowledge of Christ's divinity is possible only after his resurrection and yet is mediated by his earthly ministry,[258] but this, like many of the approaches mentioned, confuses the process of growth of awareness in history with the evangelist's understanding that in the person of the earthly Jesus life was already offered.

'Greater Event' - Deeper Understanding

Here Bultmann is nearer the mark in arguing that nothing is added to the revelation by the coming of the Spirit but deeper understanding.[259] More precisely Segovia argues that the disciples do not misunderstand the meaning of Jesus' coming, but only the meaning of his departure.[260] Bultmann promptly demythologises this along the lines of distance producing better perspective,[261] but his basic observation is correct: it is a matter of greater understanding. Already Baur emphasised this.[262] But the issue is less whether there is growth in understanding through the coming of the Spirit, which no one denies, and more whether this implies that no salvation or life, no knowledge that saves, was possible before Easter and therefore that the 'greater' event was 'greater' because before it no salvation was available. Porsch vigorously denies such an implication[263] as does Ibuki, who speaks of development of the truth already there through the activity of the Spirit in the word of Jesus.[264] Hofbeck distinguishes similarly between the promise of life within through the Spirit as the gift of the exalted one and the life and resurrection already present in the work and words of the earthly Jesus.[265] T.E. Müller offers an interesting variant explanation. Acknowledging the problem and emphasising, as he does, the importance of the atoning death, he speaks of a unique and unrepeatable situation existing before Easter where life was given through friendship with the earthly Jesus.[266]

7:37-39 Life only after Easter?

The passage 7:37-39 has been one of the main arguments for those denying salvation until after the giving of the Spirit. Jesus calls the thirsty to drink and promises rivers of living water (7:37f) and the evangelist adds: 'This he said of the Spirit which those who believe in him were about to receive; for the Spirit was not yet, because Jesus was not yet glorified.' On the basis of this statement Thüsing interprets all the images of life and salvation, such as water, bread, light, resurrection, as referring to a reality not available until after the coming of the Spirit.[267] These, he argues, reflect the author's post Easter perspective, particularly the image 'resurrection' which derives from the Easter event.[268] The author had no interest in what might have been available before Easter. He acknowledges that the author would have believed there was life in the earthly ministry, but that how it might have been available to the disciples was as of little interest to him as the issue of how Old Testament saints might have received life.[269] Blank writes in similar terms that the evangelist knew of no proclamation or message of Jesus independent of what the church proclaimed.[270]

But it is precisely this insight which calls Thüsing's interpretation into question. For then the author would have perceived the proclamation of Jesus as being substantially no different from that of the post Easter community. Our perception that post Easter perspectives govern the presentation of Jesus in John should not be confused with the issue of how the author portrays, and to that degree, believes, the earthly ministry to have been. Besides, it is not so that the author is unaware of difference in understanding between the earthly ministry and the post Easter church. That is what is at issue. The evidence points in the direction of the author being very interested in what the incarnate Word said and did and being convinced that the word of the Son brought life, while at the same time being aware that fuller understanding was possible only through the gift of the Spirit after Easter. Ultimately the gift of life is centred not in events, but in the person. Soteriology which is essentially christology renders such distinctions of time irrelevant.

The Promise of the Indwelling Spirit

Porsch, rightly, draws attention to 14:16-17, 'And I shall ask the Father and he will give you another Paraclete, that he may be with you forever, the Spirit of Truth, whom the world cannot receive, because it neither sees nor knows him; but you know him, because he remains with you and shall be in you.'[271] Beutler notes here the fulfilment of the promise of the new covenant of Jer 31.[272] The Greek for 'remains' *menei* can be accented to read either as a present, the most common reading, or as a future. Some manuscripts have 'is' as an alternative to 'shall be'. The text as quoted has strong external support and also makes best sense on internal grounds, since the Spirit is spoken of as a future gift in 14:16 and the text implies a contrast between two modes of the Spirit's presence: the disciples know him (present) and he will be given (future). Accordingly, 14:17 speaks of two modes of the Spirit's presence with the disciples: he remains *with* them and shall be *in* them.[273]

The Spirit in Jesus' ministry

The Spirit was not absent during the ministry, but present and effective through Jesus, upon whom the Spirit remained (*menon*, 1:34, cf. 1:33; 3:34). The promise of baptism with the Spirit and the indwelling of the Spirit came to fulfilment only after Easter.[274] The presence of the Spirit in Jesus' ministry is attested not only through his baptism, but also in 6:63, where Jesus says of his words: 'The Spirit makes alive; the flesh is of no use; the words which I have spoken (sic!) to you are spirit and are life.' The juxtaposition of this statement with Jesus' prediction of his ascent does, it is true, allow the inference that the author may also have in mind the work of the Spirit after Easter, but primarily he is referring to the words that Jesus has spoken during his ministry, and, shortly after, it is to these words that Peter responds with his confession: 'You have the words of eternal life and we have believed and come to know that you are the holy one of God' (6:68f).

Merging Horizons in John 3

A similar reference to the Spirit in the ministry of Jesus is present in 3:1-11, though here the situation is reversed. The passage speaks of birth of the Spirit, from above, and continues in a way which clearly has the post Easter situation in mind: 'We bear witness to what we have seen and heard and no one receives our testimony'(3:11). Jesus gathers into the 'we' both himself, as the one and only Son who has come from above, from the Father, and those who will be given authority to become children. Here two sets of ideas are merged, the Son and the children; and also the pre Easter and post Easter horizons. Statements about birth by water and by Spirit and about witness fit best the post Easter horizon, but this should not lead us to conclude that therefore the author would have meant that no rebirth and no seeing of the kingdom had been possible during the earthly ministry. The context portrays Jesus in the midst of the disciples as the Spirit bearing Son of God par excellence.

7:37-39   Life and its abundance

7:39 neither means the Spirit was not in existent before Jesus' glorification nor can it mean it was not active in Jesus' ministry in a way that benefitted the disciples. Nor is this the implication of 7:37-39 as a whole. It reads: 'On the last great day of the feast Jesus stood and cried out saying, "If anyone thirsts let him come to me and drink. He who believes in me, as the scripture said, out of his belly shall flow rivers of living water." This Jesus said about the Spirit which those who believed on him were going to receive; for the Spirit was not yet (given), because Jesus was not yet glorified.' I have supplied in brackets the words, 'given', because the sense of the Greek requires it. I have followed the punctuation of Aland's printed text in taking 'he who believes in me' with what follows, rather than with what precedes.[275] To do the latter would mean the one who believes in Jesus should come and drink and allows then the interpretation of 7:38 that it is out of Jesus' belly that the rivers of living water will flow, which would refer to the gift of the Spirit by Jesus,[276] and some also take it in addition as an allusion to 19:34, where water and blood flowed from the side of the crucified one.[277] Reading it in this way raises the acute difficulty that Jesus is portrayed as standing before people, inviting them to come to him and drink, but in fact offering them something which the author would be fully aware could not be theirs until after Easter. He would be offering them nothing but promise. Is this tenable?

It is better to read 7:38 as a promise of abundance and relate it to 4:14, 'Whoever drinks the water I shall give him will never thirst, but the water which I shall give him shall become in him a spring of water welling up to eternal life'[278] and to 6:35, 'I am the bread of life. He who comes to me shall never hunger; he who believes in me shall never thirst.' Accordingly 7:37 is not an invitation to drink which cannot be fulfilled until much later. That presses anachronism far beyond what is usual in the gospel. Rather in this verse Jesus, speaking like Yahweh and Torah/Wisdom of old, offers drink and nourishment now, just as he had offered bread from heaven in ch. 6. As water was poured out on the last day of the feast, so Jesus offers the water of life. Yet characteristically 7:38 expands this promise in view of its future abundance made possible through the future coming of the Spirit. It is the equivalent of the shift from 'with you' to 'in you' in 14:17,[279] and from bread to eucharist in ch. 6.

The presence of an allusion in 7:38 to the vision of the temple in Ezek 47, which many see here, is possible.[280] The parallel with 4:14 may indicate that we may have here an echo of the Jewish tradition which saw Torah like a wellspring in the faithful. The punctuation present in Aland favours the interpretation I offer here. The one who responds and drinks is promised abundance. But even should we read 7:38 christologically, we are not bound necessarily to deny any relevance in 7:37 for the ministry of Jesus. One could see the promise of 7:37 as a real offering during Jesus' ministry and 7:38f as the prediction of the 'greater event' and its promised abundance. Therefore the use of 7:37-39 to support the argument that faith and life before Easter can only be proleptic stands on weak ground.

Life before and abundance after the 'Greater Event': Conclusions

The concern of this section so far has been to clarify the extent to which the 'greater' event is 'greater' and, in particular, to guard against those interpretations which do so at the expense of denying salvific significance to the earthly ministry of the revealer, or, at least, of denying access to its salvific significance at the time of its occurring. We have considered this especially in relationship to the promise of the Spirit. The strongest argument against such an interpretation lies less in passages which promise what the Spirit will do and more in the portrayal of the ministry of the Son in itself as the salvific act. IIIC1 will demonstrate the centrality of this as the salvation event. But in the light of it and of the considerations thus far, we can see that the primary significance of the 'greater event' for faith is that it gives greater understanding of and access to the revelation event itself, the coming into the world of light, life and truth in the person of the Son, in his words and his deeds from his baptism to his passion.

The Spirit in sayings, discourse and narrative

Finally I want to comment on the relationship between sayings material and narrative in the way the Spirit is portrayed. The difference is similar to the one we noted between the narrative of resurrection appearances and the statements about Jesus' death and return. In the last discourses the Paraclete is portrayed as personal and personally active in the promises given the disciples. The only exception is 14:16f where the neuter pronoun, corresponding to the neuter noun, *pneuma*, is retained, but in the same discourse the personal 'he' appears when the Spirit is referred to a second time in 14:26. Elsewhere in John *pneuma* is not more closely defined in this regard. The Spirit descends and remains on Jesus (1:32f); Jesus will baptise with the Spirit (1:33); himself receives the Spirit without measure (3:34); the Spirit is what makes alive (neuter, 6:63) and is related to Jesus' words being 'spirit and life' and also to worship of God as 'spirit' (4:24) in 'spirit and in truth' (4:23f); disciples are born of the Spirit (3:5f,8), and are compared to the wind, the spirit, which blows where it wants to and no one know where it comes from or where it is going (3:8). None of these references makes the Spirit directly personal and this is true also of the author's note in 7:39 about the Spirit being given after Jesus was glorified, though we should assume so in the light of the promise expressed in the last discourses. Yet, after the very personal portrait of the Paraclete, Spirit of Truth, in the promises of the last discourses, the event which demands to be seen as its fulfilment in the gospel, 20:22, again uses very impersonal language: 'And saying this he breathed on them and said, "Receive the Holy Spirit".'

Both Thüsing and Porsch note the difficulties in seeing 20:22 as fulfilment of the promises of the Paraclete.[281] On the one hand, they argue, the narrative speaks of the Spirit as breath, has Jesus give the Spirit while on earth during the time of his resurrection appearances, and sets the Spirit in close association with authorisation to bind and loose sins; and on the other hand, in the last discourses the Paraclete is personal, comes in Jesus' absence from the earth, is in fact the mediation of his presence, brings thus the joy which endures in Jesus' absence (16:22), and relates to much more than the authority to bind and loose. While not merely symbolic event, it functions primarily as a symbol of what now begins and continues in the life of the community.[282] The differences are not to be denied, though some must be qualified. For it is, as we have seen, compatible with the author's christology that the Spirit be given during the appearances, because he has ascended first to the Father (20:17). We should note also the words of commission which precede, which could not be more characteristic of Johannine sayings material and indicate that the giving of the Spirit equips for mission.

Yet the differences are significant. The uncharacteristic elements continue with 20:23, the promise about binding and loosing sins, a motif not present elsewhere in the gospel. The differences probably reflect the author's use of traditional sources,[283] so that he takes an account of Jesus' giving the Spirit by breath, and works it into his narrative as a whole in such a way as to enable the reader to find here the fulfilment of the promised Paraclete.[284] It is not 'so foreign' as to need to be attributed to a redactor, as Forestell suggests.[285] Nor should the reference to Jesus' giving up his spirit at death be seen as the original gift of the Spirit or its foreshadowing, as we saw in IIB5 above.

The evangelist portrays the gift of the Spirit as something given by Jesus to the disciples on the evening of resurrection day after he had risen and ascended to the Father, as he had promised them. In the sense that the promise of the Spirit is here fulfilled, this is the Johannine 'Pentecost'.[286] It is not the point of revelation for them, as though they only now understood who he was. It brings, however, the promise of better understanding. They had already welcomed him and seen the resurrection evidence which confirmed the claims they had believed already during his ministry. The Spirit is given in the context of their commission, for their greater works, and with it they carry the authority of their task. If we should also see echoes of the creative breath of life of Genesis here, we witness here a new creative beginning. The primary function of the narrative is to announce the promise fulfilled. The 'greater' event has taken place and its 'greater' blessings are now present for all. The Spirit will bring greater understanding, bring forth the fruit of mission and mediate the presence of the Son and the Father to the believer in the community of faith and sacrament.

7. Pattern and Paradox

The author writes in a community which faces persecution and has faced it in the past. The last discourses promise that, as the Son faced hatred, so the disciples would face rejection in the world. This theme is particularly strong in 15:18-16:4. Probably 16:19-22, which addresses primarily the gap between Jesus' death and his resurrection appearance, is also intended to bring comfort for disciples facing situations of suffering. Similarly the comfort to the troubled disciples who face the Son's departure in ch. 14 also brings comfort to the troubled lives of disciples in later generations. To them the second Paraclete will come. In the same way Jesus prays for the care of future disciples in ch. 17.

The Pattern

Underlying all these comments is the assumption that the disciples will also suffer and that they also have the promise of following Jesus through suffering to be with him in the end in glory. 12:25f already underlines the parallel between the path of the disciples and that of Jesus. Jesus had just spoken of the necessity of his own death as a seed falling into the ground (12:24). He continues: 'He who loves his life will lose it and he who hates his life in this world will keep it to eternal life. If anyone serves me, let him follow me, and where I am, there will my servant be also; if anyone serves me, him will my Father honour.' 13:33,36 suggest also that the following will lead ultimately to the presence of Jesus with the Father in heaven: the disciples cannot at that time go where Jesus goes, but, unlike the Jews, they will follow him later (as in 17:24).

Coming before the passion narrative, these promises and warnings suggest that the passion narrative must also be seen as, in some sense, a pattern for the disciples.

They do not have the same power and knowledge, but they have the same confidence that their end is with God. Wengst suggests that the author develops as a major theme the presence of God in the suffering of Jesus in order to offer comfort and strength to his church facing the prospect of suffering.[287] U.B. Müller also sees an aim of the passion narrative as comfort for believers, but takes the author to task for its illusory nature.[288] Hegermann stresses the importance of such suffering in the light of the missionary situation where the disciples can look to the passion and be reassured that fruit comes through suffering.[289] Martyn notes that by transferring the temple expulsion to the beginning of the gospel the author effectively has Jesus face the same issues as those confronting the Johannine church: the charge of ditheism and the prospect of martyrdom.[290]

There is no indication within the narrative itself that it should function in this way, though texts like 12:25f make it probable. This at least implies that the author would understand Jesus' suffering as real suffering and not illusory, as U.B. Müller suggests, and the following verse, 12:27, which speaks of Jesus being deeply troubled, would confirm this. We shall return to the theme of the reality of Jesus' suffering in discussing the reality of his humanity in IIIB4 below. The understanding of Jesus' death as a pattern for the disciples may also be present in the narrative of the footwashing. The disciples are to serve one another as Jesus serves them (13:12-17). A more explicit link is made in 15:13 where Jesus uses his death as an illustration of love to be shown among disciples. There is also evidence that the author expands the use of Old Testament passages in order to show God's hand through scripture fulfilment and thus deal with the offensiveness of a suffering, crucified Messiah.[291]

The Paradox

The Son is therefore the pattern in his suffering, just as he is in his sending (20:21). Jesus' suffering also represents a paradox, at least, to the world. For here is the unique Son of the Father, he who was in the beginning with God, facing suffering and death. For all the statements about return, exaltation, glorification, ascension, to which his death leads, and for all the supremely confident self awareness of the Son before his accusers and Pilate, the narrative still reads as an account of genuine suffering. Nowhere does the evangelist hint that the scourging had no impact, the thorns no sting, his appearance, when Pilate presents him with the words, 'Behold the man' (19:5), a mere disguise; nor should his cry of thirst be read simply as an attempt to fulfil scripture. There was a cup of suffering to be drunk (18:11), an hour of pain to be faced (12:27), however triumphantly. From this dead body issued the same water and blood one would expect from any other, for he was human flesh (19:34). The author especially emphasises this (19:35).

This emphasis on real suffering and death is there. It is there beside a much more dominant one, which overlays the narrative with constant allusion to Jesus as the one sent from the Father. Yet this has not been done to the degree that the passion narrative ceases to be a passion narrative, his suffering, real suffering, and his death, a real death. It is, on the one hand, by no means the central theme that Bultmann makes it, where he sees in it the paradox of the glory in the flesh present throughout the whole ministry and in particular in the pathetic figure presented by Pilate with the words, 'Behold the man!' Yet, on the other, it remains part of the

story and for the disciples qualifies the nature of the pattern. For they, too, who
have found in him the way to the Father, the light and the life, must face darkness
and death in this world if they are to follow him. The Johannine paradox lies less
in the juxtaposition of glory and suffering which confronts human confidence and
challenges human self sufficiency and more in the notion that the pathway to glory
for the Son as for the believers is the pathway of obedience that leads through
suffering.

8. Conclusion

As the Son came from the Father, so the Son returns to the Father through death.
Our analysis shows that his death is much more than a point of exit. The
commission is not completed until death. We explored the suggestion that this
means that the author sees the act of vicarious atonement as the final task of the
commission, but found this not to be the case, even though the author knows of
and makes use of traditions of vicarious atonement. The passion rather brings to a
climax the work of revelation inasmuch as the conflict of claim and counter claim
reaches the point where through the Jews and Pilate the world rejects the Son,
putting him to death. The judgement on the Son becomes at the same time a
judgement on the world for its sin and its ruler, for the Son's return to the Father is
his vindication.

We also considered the motifs glorification and exaltation and found that they
describe the action whereby God raises the Son to his glory in heaven. They are
not paradoxical assertions about glory or exaltation in suffering. These terms,
together with ascension, the title Son of Man, and the motif of 'something greater',
form an association of ideas whereby the author describes the event faith perceives
to have occurred at the death of Jesus. The author also integrates this association
of ideas with the tradition of resurrection and resurrection appearances. The
'greater event' thus described becomes the basis for 'greater blessings' which
follow. These are made possible through the sending of the Spirit and the sending
of the disciples. The Spirit makes greater understanding possible of the fact that
the Son came from the Father to make him known. The mission of the disciples,
equipped for their witness by the Spirit, bears fruit to the glory of God. Altogether
this produces a growing community of believers, who, like the first disciples,
enjoy the indwelling of the Father and the Son through the Spirit, are nourished by

the sacrament of flesh and blood, and are called to live in communion with one another, with the Son and the Father.

We saw that the 'greater event' does not add to the revelation of the Son as if it was incomplete or inaccessible until it had happened. But it takes the knowledge of faith already in existence and deepens it, enabling greater knowledge and scriptural understanding of who Jesus was and is and of what he said and did. The 'greater event' serves then also a hermeneutical function and ultimately explains how it is that the author could write the gospel he did. The centre remains the primary event, the Son's making the Father known, and all else serves this. The Spirit is the primary agent in this hermeneutical function and the author integrates the Paraclete sayings of the last discourses with a traditional account of Jesus' giving the Spirit by breathing on the disciple on the evening of resurrection day.

We also noted how the passion serves as a pattern for the disciples as they follow their Lord. They, too, face suffering and they, too, will find the goal of their journey where he is in the glory of the Father. Despite the heavy emphasis throughout the passion on the Son as the revealer, the true meaning of his messiahship, there is nevertheless sufficient evidence that the author considered the passion a real passion. For the world this is a paradox: the Son of God faces humiliation and death. For faith it is the Son fulfilling the Father's commission in obedience faithfully to the end, and then returning to glory.

We have seen that the centre of Johannine christology remains the Son's coming to make the Father known. This is the saving event to which all else points. In our next chapter we examine the nature of this saving event.

IIIB. THE SALVATION EVENT IN JOHN

1. The Salvation Event - Revelation?

According to the basic structure of the author's christology the salvation event consists in the coming of the Son, sent by the Father to make him known in word and deed. The response to this event determines salvation or condemnation. The glorification, exaltation, ascension, and return of the Son to the Father vindicate the Son and judge the world, and confirm that his coming was the salvation event, as the gift of the Spirit makes it possible to understand more fully what this event means. This event is the subject of the disciples' proclamation as they fulfil the commission given them by the Son in all the world. It is the salvation event. But in what does this event consist?

In Part II we noted the wide variety of expressions used to describe the Son's fulfilment of his divine commission. The Son who has come from the Father witnesses to, tells of, what he has seen, heard, been taught, commanded, told. He does the works of the Father, including the signs which both manifest his being as Son and point to his role as the bearer of life and salvation (water, bread, light, resurrection and more). The Son is the Word, as the prologue states in the beginning, and he makes the Father known (1:18). Because he speaks the words of God, to see him is to see the Father. In short the Son reveals the Father.

This pattern is one of revelation and it assumes that salvation comes in response to this revelation. On the surface this is straightforward and clear. But when we begin to examine the words and deeds of Jesus, problems emerge. How did the author understand this pattern of revelation? What did the Son reveal?

What does the revealer reveal?

If we look for content in the words and deeds of Jesus, we do not find detailed secrets of the heavenly world. We find some predictions about the future, especially about the future of the Son, the disciples and the Spirit, but these are ancillary to the main work of revelation. For they refer to the 'greater event' and its effects through which the revelation in Jesus' ministry is more fully understood and made accessible, not to the revelation itself. We also find claims about the Father, especially about his love, but beyond this there is no passing on of information such as we might expect after a statement like 3:32, 'What he has seen and heard, to this he bears witness.' Most of the discourses concentrate on Jesus' claims about himself. Jesus proclaims and argues for the truth about himself as the revealer, the Son sent from the Father to make him known. One could speak of a self revelation, but the content of that self revelation is that he is the revealer of the Father and only in that sense that he and the Father are one and to have seen him is to have seen the Father.

Already Baur noted that the revelation in the fourth gospel is a self presentation.[1] Wetter and Büchsel both stress that the evangelist offers only the fact of the Son's coming from God, not the contentsof a revelation.[2] But it was above all Bultmann who repeatedly drew attention to this fact and made it the mainstay of his interpretation of Johannine christology.[3]

The revealer reveals he is the revealer

The many statements, formulated in the language of communication of information from the Father, are claims which have no literal fulfilment in the gospel. Jesus offers no such body of information of what he has seen and heard. There is no detailed programme of ethics, no set of teachings about God, no prophecy of the end time. There is nothing which equates to the Sermon on the Mount except in the most general terms. There is no preaching of the kingdom of God or teaching in parables, except as part of a wide range of sayings about himself as the revealer Son.

Jesus presents himself with the claim that he is the Son who speaks the Father's words and does his works and that to respond to him is life. If the author uses this revelation pattern without intending that we should understand Jesus as an information bearer, what is really happening? What is salvific here, if it is not revelation or knowledge as we are first led to assume? How should the revelation pattern be understood if not primarily in terms of revelation?

How is the revealer model being employed? Confronting paradox?

Bultmann's answer was that the language of revelation is used in the fourth gospel as a way of talking about the self presentation of the Son in encounter. He specifies this even further in the claim that what is presented, using the revelation pattern, is the sheer fact of the human flesh as the place of divine glory, sometimes formulated by him as the mere fact of his coming, the 'Dass', not the 'Was' (the fact that he came, not what actually happened), though with this formulation we should also note that, according to Bultmann, for the author, statements about coming and going were also only symbols of the paradox, the human and divine glory.[4] It is this offence or paradox which is salvific inasmuch as it calls into question human self understanding and self sufficiency.[5]

The quest for revelation content

Dissatisfaction with the description of Jesus' message as merely the fact of his coming had already been expressed long before Bultmann by Lütgert, who argued that, as well as the fact of his coming, also the fact of his sonship was the content of Jesus' revelation and this was manifest particularly through his miracles as acts of revelation.[6] But it was above all in reaction to Bultmann that the strongest criticisms have been voiced.

Haenchen argues that the content includes words about God and the fact of God's love.[7] He makes the important observation that the question of who God is becomes central for the Johannine understanding of revelation and rightly calls into question the sheer arbitrariness of the claim as formulated by Bultmann.[8]

Like Lütgert, Käsemann points to sonship and to the nature of the relationship of Father and Son as the content of revelation, and those scholars who attribute a major role to atonement

motifs in the gospel usually claim that revelation must include a reference to it.[10] The first
suggestion is surely true, but does not take us far, especially not concerning the revelation
itself; for it merely tells of the unique relationship which makes it possible, not about the
revelation itself. The connection with atonement is forced and not justified by the actual texts
which speak of revelation. This is not to deny that the revealer is also the one who would
suffer and that that in itself conveys something of a revelation, much in the sense of
Bultmann's paradox. Brown argues that revelation includes teaching about the creator giving
light and life, God's love, the love commandments, the Holy Spirit, baptism and the eucharist,[11]
and even claims that much of the teaching of the Sermon on the Mount is to be found in John.
The latter is surely an exaggeration, the sacraments incidental, the Holy Spirit functional, and,
beyond that, we have the light and love which Haenchen affirms. We can scarcely speak of
quantitative revelatory data as the envoy revealer model would suggest.

Schnackenburg points to the Son's role[12] in making access possible to the world of God and his
uniting two worlds by his incarnation and in similar vein Becker points to the Son's making
known to us our cosmic situation and overcoming the devil.[13] A dualism is indeed presupposed
in the gospel, but is not itself the revelation and overcoming the ruler of the world is not a
major theme. Weder emphasises that the 'how' is as important as the 'that', namely that the
Son came in flesh and blood;[14] for, he argues, the gospel is concerned with Jesus' ministry as
much as with his death and return, and does not reflect the Pauline focus which is mainly on
the single event of the cross and resurrection.[15] This is not to be denied, but none of these
suggestions can explain away Bultmann's central observation that in the gospel the Son speaks
like an envoy bearing a communication of what he has seen and heard and been told, but fails
to deliver any communication of this kind.

Can the 'How' replace the 'What' of revelation?

Meeks notes Bultmann's puzzle and offers a pertinent sociological observation that this model
of christology arises out of a situation where the community is experiencing alienation and so
looks to Jesus as its 'stranger',[16] a term taken up, in turn by de Jonge into the title of his
collected essays. But beyond its sociological function, how was the myth understood in the
Johannine community?

O'Day has recently challenged Bultmann's 'Dass' (that) of revelation and the attempts of
Käsemann and others to fill out the content of the 'Was' (what) of revelation, with
christological dogma and suggested we look again as the 'Wie' (How) of revelation.[17] Her
study belongs to a rich developing tradition of literary studies of the gospel concerned to
examine how the text works and the importance of narrative in communication of the gospel.
A one-sided emphasis on the literary would easily come to mean: the Word became text and
dwells among us! But it is a false and unnecessary antithesis to pit 'How' against 'What' in
this way. The 'How' evokes all the more strongly the question: 'What?' and shifts the focus in
a useful way from 'What?' as information data to 'What?' in the sense of 'What person?' or
'Who?' The centre becomes then less the 'Dass', the 'Was' or the 'Wie' and becomes the
'Wer?' (Who?).

Revealer envoy language serving to express encounter and invitation

The word, revelation, does not occur in the gospel, as Haenchen points out.[18] What we do find
is language of communication and language of epiphany (eg. 'I am' sayings) combined in the
pattern of the coming and going of an envoy. Schweizer used the gospel's own forensic term,
'witness', rather than revealer to characterise the centre of Johannine christology and thereby
was able to highlight the confrontative component of the gospel.[19] This is hardly the central
motif, but its use instead of the language of revelation does enable us to see more clearly in the
gospel the quality of personal encounter and confrontation. This was already implicit in
Bultmann's understanding, even the use of witness,[20] since he characterised the Son's action as
a call or invitation, doubtless with gnostic parallels in mind, but nevertheless accurately
representing what the Son in fact does.[21]

Others, too, have picked up the language of encounter and confrontation.[22] Forestell
understands the revelation as a communication of that life which the Son receives from the

Father[23] and speaks of a dynamic intercommunion as the character of salvation.[24] Similarly Ibuki stresses that the revelation of the relationship of the Father and the Son is not a communication but an event.[25] Haacker also tries to get away from the communicative or noetic aspect of revelation. He lays emphasis on the role of the Spirit in association with the word and on personal encounter rather than revelation as information.[26] His use of the founder motif as an alternative to revealer, partly in order to rehabilitate the place of atonement in John, is not, however, convincing; the motif is foreign to the gospel and it does not do justice to the presentness which the element of encounter and confrontation demands. T.E. Müller makes a distinction between the time after Easter when salvation comes through encounter with Christ on the basis of his work of atonement and the time before Easter when salvation comes directly through the encounter with his person.[27]

The authors we have considered above rightly emphasise, in one way or other, the importance of confrontation or encounter in John's christology, an emphasis already highlighted by Bultmann.[28] In what follows I want to explore the issue further by examining first how it is that Jesus presents himself, if not as bearer of revelations; and secondly, what happens to people when they respond to the Son, in order to perceive from the perspective of the receivers the nature of the salvation brought by the Son in his making the Father known.

Encounter with what, with whom?

Jesus presents himself with a claim to the people of his day: he is the one who has come from the Father and calls for faith in himself. The claim for allegiance presented in this manner could appear quite arbitrary. Others, too, might present themselves with such absolute claims. This raises the question of their validity. The author does not simply present Jesus with his claims. He begins with the prologue which relates Jesus to God and to creation. The one who is to make such claims is not some arbitrary fanatic, but draws his being from God and has been involved in the creation of all things. He has also been involved in the history of God's people, or, at least, been the light and life from the beginning of time. The validity is supported also by the witness of John the Baptist, by the witness of scripture, directly as witness to Israel's Messiah and indirectly through typology and symbol, and by the use of language elsewhere associated with claims of divine representation (life, light, truth, etc).

These are in part the interpretations of the author and in part Jesus' words about himself, as portrayed by the evangelist, so that there is a certain circularity of argument. We are being asked to believe both Jesus' self claims (mediated by the evangelist) and the claims the evangelist, himself, makes about him directly. Retrospectively, the evangelist can appeal to the resurrection and return of the Son to the Father as vindication of these claims. Nevertheless the evangelist does present Jesus as making absolute claims about himself, being in that sense his own chief witness, and thematises this in conflict with the Jews.

The apparent arbitrariness of these claims is somewhat modified when we examine their nature. The claims are designed primarily to elevate not Jesus himself but God. Haenchen pointed to the importance of theology in the strictest sense for understanding the nature of the Son's revelation and the theocentricity of the gospel is widely recognised.[29] The evangelist builds thus upon the presupposition that God is in some sense known. For all his claims, Jesus does not impart detailed information about God, but speaks on the assumption that God is a word that makes good sense to his hearers. Since this is so, it is equally important to examine the unexpressed assumptions about God present in the gospel, for Jesus' claim and significance is inseparably connected with them.

Direct teaching about God is sparse in the gospel, largely because Jesus is not presented as offering teaching about God. Some important presuppositions are evident. God is creator. There is no absolute dualism here. 'God is Spirit and they who worship him must worship him in spirit and in truth' (4:24) - a rare example of direct teaching about God on the lips of Jesus in the fourth gospel. It is important because he uses it to relativise the cultic centres of both Samaritans and Jews. God transcends space in such a way that he is to be worshipped as a spiritual being. Porsch shows that, as Spirit, God himself is the active ground, making a relationship with himself possible.[30] The author assumes God's involvement in history in the past and that he continues to speak to people, teach and draw them to himself in the present. The Father is said to give people right to become his children. He is also linked with judgement. But by far the most dominant impression is that the Father is concerned and involved in the world of people, giving gifts, and sending people for specific tasks. God's attitude to the world of people is one of love and this motivated the sending of the Son.

The attempts of Käsemann, Schottroff and Lattke to deny that the statement of 3:16, God loved the world, has weight for the evangelist are unconvincing,[31] and rest on the assumption that such a statement stands in tension with the author's dualism. But 'world' here is the world of people viewed in their potential for transformation and in the gospel as a whole the potential for such transformation is assumed by the act of sending the Son and of his sending the disciples.[32] Ibuki is right in noting that the love between Father and Son is one which reaches dynamically out into the world.[33]

The God we recognise here is largely the God known to us in much of the Old Testament and the writings of the New. God is not uninterested, aloof, divided, distracted, but has involved himself and seeks a relationship between himself and people. God is involved, yet above; engages himself, yet also transcends. It is doubtful whether any of this is distinctively Johannine. What is distinctively Christian is that God is related to Jesus in a special way and what is distinctively Johannine is the particular way this is expressed in the fourth gospel.

When, therefore, in the fourth gospel, Jesus claims to be the Son sent from God the Father, already a lot on information is implied through the use of the word, 'God'. When, therefore, beyond the claim to be the sent one and to enjoy a special relationship with him, Jesus offers not primarily information, but a claim for allegiance, a call to faith, we are not left in a knowledge vacuum. For the Son offers not a new theology, but, as God's representative and envoy, offers God and to offer God is not to offer an abstraction according to the presuppositions of the author, but someone known. The Son's claim for allegiance to himself is a claim for allegiance to God. His mission is not one of revelation, as the revealer-envoy pattern at first suggests, but of encounter and invitation. He offers a relationship with himself and thus with God. The offer is absolute in its claim and at the same time totally without preconditions, in the sense of people needing to establish a level of worthiness or deserving before the offer applies to them.

The 'What?' and the 'Who?' in the mirror of response

In the light of these observations the distinctive imagery of the Son's claims makes sense and the nature of salvation may be read from the nature of the response demanded. In ch. 1 the relationship between Jesus and his disciples has two elements. The first is John the Baptist's witness in the presence of the disciples concerning who Jesus is. It is a claim to be believed. The second is the personal following, sometimes at the level of enquiry in response to John, sometimes in response to Jesus' direct command. In the relationship of following there is room for growth and promise of new understanding, as Jesus tells Nathanael. Elsewhere it is clear that following Jesus in the literal sense and acclamation of him as Messiah or prophet on the basis of his miracles may not indicate that a saving relationship has been established. The saving relationship includes right understanding of who Jesus is, including right understanding of his miracles as signs, and response to him on that basis.

The miracles or signs may evoke the response of wonder and at this level miracle based faith may go no further than asserting with Nicodemus that Jesus is a teacher from God, with the Samaritan woman and the healed people that he is a prophet, or with the 5000 and the crowd at his entry that he is the prophet or the messianic king. That may be a first step,[34] but it remains an inadequate response and the author has Jesus attack it accordingly.[35] Bittner's attempt to turn 4:48 into a positive statement about the need for signs and wonders is unconvincing, especially after 2:23-25 and similar statements in the gospel.[36] Neither does the evangelist deny the reality of miracles[37] or their relevance.[38] Miracles matter and are not mere symbols.[39] But the boundary to true faith is crossed where faith sees in the performance of the miracle the glory of the revealer and then faith, primarily at the level of the reader, can also see the miracle itself as symbolic of the life and light and truth which he brings and which he is.[40] Kee has noted a similar symbolic use of miracles in the Isis cult,41 but the parallels which exist fall short of convincing evidence that they have a direct relationship with the Johannine use of miracle stories.

If you believe the works, you must eventually come to believe the words. A progression to full faith is occasionally traceable in narratives. The Samaritan woman (ch. 4) progresses from seeing Jesus as a mere man, to belief he may be a prophet because of the miracle of supernatural knowledge, to belief he is probably the Messiah (on the same basis), to belief with her fellow Samaritans that he is saviour of the world. The blind man (ch. 9) makes a similar journey. One may also note the development of the faith theme in ch. 20, from grief and astonishment to belief in the miracle of resurrection, to letting go of the human appearance of Jesus or foregoing the direct physical contact, to trusting the witness and believing the Son to have returned to the Father and to have given the Spirit.[42]

In itself right understanding is not perceived as an intellectual hurdle, as if it should entail a complete understanding of christology. For the truth is there for eyes that want to see and ears that want to hear. Essentially right understanding is belief in what constitutes the basic structure of the author's christology, namely that the Son has come as the sent one from the Father to make him known, to do his works and to offer life and light and truth. The disciples grasp this truth and after Easter the Paraclete will lead them to greater understanding.

Beside right understanding the saving relationship also includes faithful allegiance, remaining in the relationship, abiding in the vine, obedience to the Son's commandments, above all, mutual indwelling, loving and being loved by the Son and the Father. These are relationship terms. Coming to faith, being born from above, receiving the right to become a child of God, is the beginning of an ongoing faith relationship in this sense. The author does not address directly the problem of what happens when a believers sins, though indirectly Peter's experience shows that repentance is possible. Ideas of perfectionism, as present in the context of the epistle, are not evident in the gospel. The assumption is that the saving relationship is one which continues and grows. But it is also one which may be terminated, as disciples opt to cease the allegiance, perhaps because of the extent of Jesus' claims, perhaps as an act of apostasy and betrayal.

Predestination and Dualism

Beside these statements about the response of faith must stand others which speak of the Father drawing particular people who are his own to faith and destining others not to believe, or, in the case of Judas, to betray. Bultmann argues that the language of predestination never obviates the basic intention of universality of the offer of salvation in John.[43] Response to this offer determines whether people are in darkness or light and are so described as predestined to faith or unfaith, not deterministic dualism. It is not difficult to find statements which speak in determinist categories from which to argue that the evangelist's thought is primarily deterministic. This is argued most recently by Bergmeier, who traces this to Jewish attitudes of the kind found in Qumran and argues that such dualism is found in gnosticism only through secondary Christian influence, whereas gnostic dualism is not deterministic.[44] Langbrandtner, following earlier observations by Haenchen and Schottroff, succeeds in showing that gnostic soteriology is based upon 'Entscheidungsdualismus' ('dualism of decision'),[45] much as that argued for the fourth gospel by Bultmann and many others,[46] but denied by him to gnosticism. While there is evidence for this, gnosticism is also very diverse and it should not be denied that cosmic anthropological dualism plays a much larger role in gnostic writings generally than in John[47] and should not be overplayed in John to the degree that protology becomes central.[48] Becker traces various stages of development in Johannine dualism from the Qumran type to a gnostic-like dualism of decision supported by an ontological dualism, through to a deterministic dualism evident in relationships with the Jews in John 8 and in relationship with other Christians of different beliefs in the first epistle.[49] In particular, renewed interest in reconstructing the history of the Johannine community offers an important resource for understanding Johannine dualism.[50] Fundamentally, despite its cosmic dualistic presuppositions to which we shall return below, the gospel has at its centre the importance and possibility of a continuing faith response to the Son.

Salvation offered and received

In returning then to the response required and given as an approach to understanding the nature of the salvation which the Son brings, we can note that the benefit of salvation consists primarily in the relationship offered. This includes a cognitive element, namely, belief that the Son is the sent one. In that sense it is right to say that there is revelation content involved, the revelation that the Son has a unique relationship of oneness with the Father and speaks and acts for him. Responding to him means believing this; it also means entering the relationship he offers. The joy of the believers is oneness with the Son. The believers enjoy eternal life now though there is a future element inasmuch as one day they will join the Son in the heavenly presence of the Father and see his glory. The gift of salvation is mostly described using images such as water, bread, light, life, resurrection. The giver is, however, also described as the gift. He is the bread, light, life, resurrection, way, door, truth. The double reference of these images for both the gift and the giver is possible because it is primarily the person and the personal relationship which is at the centre of salvation, not a place, a possession, a body of knowledge, or a set of charismatic powers.

This is widely recognised as a major characteristic of Johannine christology.[51] Becker, however, disputes it as characteristic of the author of John 17, which speaks of the Son only as giver (of words, name, glory).[52] But it is doubtful whether absence of a specific identification of gift and giver in John 17 justifies this conclusion, especially because statements about Jesus as bearer of the word are common elsewhere in the gospel as part of the revelation envoy pattern. This is not to deny the elements peculiar to John 17, especially the giving of the name and of glory. At the same time these motifs, especially, are ways of talking about God himself, and the promise of indwelling also coheres well with the notion of the giver as himself the gift.

Existential Imagery for Salvation

The images used of Jesus as both gift and giver reflect fundamental human need: light, life, water, bread, way. This is emphasised rightly by Bultmann.[53] This was the strength of his existentialist approach to John. For, whatever the religio-historical background of these motifs (Torah, Sophia, gnostic symbolism), they imply that what Jesus brings belongs to the essence of what a human being needs and, conversely, what a human being needs is to be found in Jesus. Bultmann emphasises that the prologue enables us to identify a connection between the Word as agent of creation and the Word as bearer of basic human needs.[54] Human beings do not have revelation through creation; but they do have a certain questioning, a negative knowledge, a sense of dependency which comes to fulfilment in response to the Word and, beyond that, the creation may, as Painter suggests, function as symbol bearer of the Word.[55] Bultmann writes that creation and redemption stand in continuity because of the prologue.[56] This is a correct observation about consistency within the gospel, though at no point does the author make it explicit, as he might have. Painter points particularly to the frequency in the gospel of Torah imagery used christologically as a reflection of conflict with the synagogue. This is probably the most likely medium of many of the existential creation images into Johannine christology.

The gift of salvation in John does not represent an addition to the created human being or a distraction from it, but rather something which belongs to it. This is true, notwithstanding the fact that the existential images are used symbolically of spiritual truth. The relationship offered is with the Son and the Father who is also the Creator. But while the focus is entirely upon the gift of this relationship, it is appropriate to ask to what degree the way in which this gift is expounded in the gospel implies nevertheless a tension with the notion of creation of all things, presupposed elsewhere in the gospel. It is legitimate to ask this question because the theme of creation is not developed at any point in the gospel and because it has a bearing on our understanding of Johannine soteriology.

We have noted that the gift is of a growing and living relationship and that at least two stages may be detected: oneness with the Son and Father on earth and oneness with the Son and Father in heaven. The contrast between heaven and earth is present throughout the gospel. To be 'of the earth' is not to be saved. But this does not imply an ontology according to which sheer physicality is evil. It does however imply a hierarchy of order in God's creation between heaven and earth. To be 'of the earth' means limiting oneself to seeing only at an earthly level and failing to see the kingdom of God. Here we meet the complicating factor of election and choice. But both statements are juxtaposed in expressing the belief that some see and some do not and those who do not carry responsibility for their continuing blindness. The assumption is not, however, that a superhuman capacity is added to people when they are enabled to see, but rather that seeing and hearing is the true state of the human being. In other words, the gift of salvation is primarily to be seen as a relationship within which human beings have life and have it in abundance as they open themselves to the Son and the Father. In this they do not cease to be human beings in order to become superhuman beings, by addition of the divine or subtraction of the human; they become human beings as they were created to be.

The images of salvation express the gift in various ways. Light gives security by showing the way and exposes the wayward; it brings salvation and judgement. Life contrasts with death and almost ceases to be an image since life in its fullness is found only in unity with the Father and the Son. Water quenches thirst and makes life possible; bread nourishes and so also mediates life. Resurrection symbolises transformation from death to life through faith, an image borrowed from literal eschatological hope also present in the gospel. Door speaks of Jesus as the means of access to relationship with the Father and way is used similarly, though also having in mind the ultimate heavenly destination. Vine brings together emphasis on ongoing relationship with the Son, the notion of bearing fruit in mission, and also unity among the disciples as branches in the vine. Shepherd expresses both leadership and a contrast with false leadership claims; it also entails the themes of mission and unity.

Salvation an ongoing, expansive relationship

The saving relationship is not static and unchanging, as though salvation were thought of as passively receiving a gift. It is dynamic and developing, a relationship which reproduces itself, in much the same way as the relationship between Father and Son led to the offering of a relationship to the world. The saving relationship is therefore one of being commissioned. The mission of the disciples is likewise not primarily one of information giving, though it includes information about who the Son is, his coming, ministry, death and return, glorified, exalted, and ascended, to the Father. It is a mission which offers relationship. In one sense it is unlike the Son's mission who offered relationship with himself as relationship with the Father. On the other hand, the relationship focus of the salvific gift gives to community in relationship a central significance in the fourth gospel. This is both what we might deduce, given the author's starting point, and what we find expressed in the gospel itself. Being Christian means being in relationship with the community and in the community being in relationship with the Father and the Son, being in a communion of love that is forever expansive. Appold rightly shows how the oneness motif expands to include the notion of gathering the children of God, expressed in 11:52. Less convincing is his attribution of this motif to the pattern of the gnostic redeemer gathering his own.[57]

Accordingly, the gift of salvation in John is primarily a person and a relationship with a person, the Son, and through the Son, a relationship with the Father. In this relationship human beings find their deepest needs to be met. It is a relationship ultimately with God who is creator and with the Son, the Logos active in creation. It is ongoing and finds its ultimate end in the heavenly presence of the Father. Its primary focus is the present, where it is lived out in a community of love and witness, where the spirit gives knowledge and equips for mission.
Salvation, eschatology and cosmic dualism

It is this primary focus on relationship which forms the basis for the author's eschatology. At its centre is the relationship of life and its ultimate future is the shared presence with the Son and the Father in heaven (17:24). It is therefore not a relationship which reaches its ultimate potential already on earth,[58] though it is a life giving relationship already on earth. This should not, however, be used as a criterion for denying the presence of elements of traditional collective eschatology in the gospel. The gospel still has a place for parousia, resurrection, and judgement day. The individualising application of the parousia tradition of 14:3 in 14:18-22 need not imply denial of the former altogether.[59] But these are no longer central.

The dualism of heaven and earth, both created spheres, but from one of which it is desirable to escape, lurks beneath the gospel in a way that could have led potentially to an absolute dualism of a gnostic kind.[60] It has not gone that far in John. There is ontological dualism, but the two parts are not unconnected.[61] They remain God's creation, though the author shows little interest in creation (outside the prologue).[62] There is still some sense of belonging within a history of a God who has acted in relation to figures of the past like Abraham, Moses, Isaiah, even if this past is now seen totally from a christological perspective. It is this God who has sent his Son. Unlike gnosticism, therefore, the centre of focus is not place and therefore change of place, but a person.[63] Christology or better, theology, not cosmology or anthropology, determines soteriology. There is no room or licence here for multiple redeemers and redeeming acts, because at the centre is not soteriology, but the claim of the person God in his Son.

Nor is it correct simply to say that protology has usurped eschatology.[64] Future hope remains important, but the focus of this future is no longer a great cosmic event, but joining the Son where he is with the Father. This is the outworking of the underlying dualism. The dualistic framework determines to that degree the nature of eschatology and soteriology. It may be reflected in the author's use of the tradition about casting out the ruler of the world, as Becker suggests.[65] I doubt if it should be seen as contributing to an understanding of the incarnation as somehow bridging the two realms as Schnackenburg suggests.[66] It remains rather in the background, providing the stage on which the drama is set; at the centre of that stage is the personal claim and declaration of God in his Son. Whereas soteriology, anthropology and cosmology are central for gnosticism, and saviour figures or saving initiatives may vary and need not even be consistent within a single document, this is not so in John. In John, by contrast, christology and the soteriology of relationship with the person of God through his Son is the constant; beside this it can tolerate side by side both its underlying dualism and traditional elements of eschatology of a very much more diverse nature.

Salvation: Conclusion

Salvation is therefore not primarily a place, a reward, a body of knowledge, a gift of powers. Nor is it perceived contractually as a covenant inaugurated or a status restored. Nor is it perceived primarily as the achievement of a sacrifice, or the fruit of the cross and resurrection as in Paul.[67] Nor is it primarily presented on the model of rescue or deliverance. It is presented as the gift of the Son from the Father. By far the most dominant model is that of the Son as envoy of the Father bearing revelatary information. But it is evident that the author is making use of the envoy not to make claims about information, but to present the Son as one who encounters and confronts the world with the offer of a relationship through himself with the Father. He does not make the Father known by imparting information. The author assumes basic knowledge about God. The Son claims an intimacy with the Father, in that sense, knowledge of the Father, on the basis of which he calls people to believe his claim and so enter a saving relationship with himself and the Father.

Salvation and the 'Greater Event'

Accordingly, salvation is present in the person of the Son, the gift of relationship he brings. The Paraclete leads the disciples to greater understanding of the event of the Son's coming. It does not first make the salvation accessible, as though it was present only proleptically in the presence of the Son or as though no one received it during his ministry. Nor is the life first made accessible through Jesus' atoning death.[68] This way of speaking of the work of salvation was known to the author and he uses its imagery from time to time by way of illustration. But it is not dominant and should be used to deny the saving impact of the Son during his ministry. Nor should those few passages where Jesus speaks of the gift of life in a future sense (3:14f; 6:27,51-58) be made the basis for denying life in the presence and person of the Son in his ministry. For they predict the availability of life after Easter, particularly in the context of the eucharist and Son of Man traditions. The manner in which the author perceives the salvation events demands that the life is offered through relationship and this relationship is freely offered in the coming of the Son.

This does not mean that from the standpoint of the post Easter community the death of Jesus is superfluous. The reality which faced the post Easter situation was that Jesus' life had come to an end on earth. Had that been anything other than the faithful fulfilment of the divine commission of bearing the revelation of God even to death, then the issue of Jesus' salvific significance would have been called into question. In that sense Jesus' obedience to the end belongs necessarily to the post Easter proclamation of the message of salvation. In addition the death of Jesus brings this ministry to its climax and becomes the ultimate exposure of the world's sin, Jesus' vindication and the judgement of the world and its ruler. But the centre remains the Son and life through faith in him.

In the light of this centre we can also see how the author understands the traditional notion of forgiveness of sins. Forgiveness is primarily the gift of the word and implied in the relationship he offers.[69] Similarly the footwashing episode symbolises this gift, linking it to the Son's obedience and love from the beginning to the end, not in the sense of foreshadowing a forgiveness not yet available until an act of atonement, but expressing now the gift of cleansing, so that Jesus, then and there, can proclaim them clean.

The central structure of the author's christology is the pattern of the revealer envoy. The author employs this to set forth Jesus as the one who calls people to believe his claim and to join in relationship to him and the Father and so find life. This is the event of salvation which reaches its climax in Jesus' death, its vindication in his return to the Father; to this the disciples and the Paraclete bear witness and the Paraclete leads them to greater understanding of its truth. In the following sections we shall explore more fully the nature of this event, particularly what it implies concerning the nature of the Son.

2. The Salvation Event and Pre-existence.

A careful examination of the way the author understands the pattern of statements which form the central structure of his christology has shown that the author has reinterpreted the language of revelation and communication. The salvation event is not literally the telling what the Son has seen and heard, but the presenting of the Father's claim, his personal challenge in the Son, an encounter aimed at the response of faith which enters a relationship with the Father through the Son. Similarly we must ask what role pre-existence plays for the author as he interprets the pattern.

The patterns tells of the Son having seen and heard from the Father in his pre-existence what he has made known on earth. But the fact that in reality the author does not have the Son tell what he has seen and heard, raises the question whether he also means us to take literally the statements about seeing and hearing the Father or in what sense he understood them. And if it is not a passing on of information to which he was privy in pre-existence, how does pre-existence function in relationship to the work of salvation as the author understands it?

Pre-existence - Significant for Johannine Christology?

The question becomes more acute when we note that sometimes the pattern of hearing and seeing the Father is not related to Jesus' pre-existence at all, but is something happening in the present and also in the future. Bultmann made much of this observation in his claim that ultimately the author has demythologised pre-existence, so that it plays no part as such within his christology at all.[70] Others, like Lütgert, Brun and, more recently, Robinson, make a strong case for taking a large number of those texts which speak of Jesus' hearing or seeing the Father as references not to pre-existence at all, but to earlier experiences of Jesus on earth.[71] In the following I shall review the relevant texts in the light of our findings thus far, and, in particular, of the insight that not information but encounter forms the central salvation event in John.

Pre-existence and 5:19f

A key text is 5:19f, 'The Son can do nothing of himself, but only what he sees the Father doing; what he does, the Son does these things likewise. For the Father loves the Son and shows him all that he himself is doing, and greater things than these will he show him that you may marvel.' 5:30 reads similarly, 'I can do nothing of myself; as I hear, I judge, and my judgement is just, because I seek not my will, but the will of him who sent me.' The Son sees, and the Father shows him in the present, what the Father is doing; and he will do so in the future. The Son hears the Father, and this is the authority of his judgement. Judgement belongs to the 'greater things' to be shown the Son according to 5:20. These texts assume a present seeing and hearing during the earthly ministry and apparently also a future seeing and hearing on earth.[72] Nothing in the context suggests that they refer only to the post Easter Jesus, as Blank and Thüsing suggest.[73]

Past seeing, hearing, and knowing - pre-existence?

Since this is so, it is possible to argue that passages which refer to such seeing and hearing in the past are also perceived as having taken place on earth, and not during pre-existence at all. These include, it is claimed: 8:26, 'What I have heard from the Father I speak to the world'; 8:28, 'As my Father taught me, so I speak'; 8:40, 'I have spoken to you what I have heard from the Father'; 12:49, 'I have not spoken of myself, but the Father who sent me gave me instruction, what I was to say and speak'; 15:15, 'All that I have heard from the Father I have made known to you'; 3:11, 'What we know, we speak, and what we have seen, to that we bear witness'[74].

A further argument cited in support of the texts in ch. 8 is the parallel made in 8:38 between Jesus and the Jews: 'What I have seen from the Father I speak; and what you have heard from (your) father you do.' Clearly the Jews have heard from their father not in any pre-existence, but as human beings on earth and their father is the devil. Accordingly, it is argued, Jesus will have heard from his Father while on earth, if the analogy is to be effective.[75]

Similarly 3:11 includes knowing and seeing of human beings together with the knowing and seeing of the Son himself. It would be strange, it is argued, for the reference in the one case to be to an earthly experience and in the other to a heavenly one.[76] 16:13-15 promises revelation to the disciples through the Spirit while they continue their work. Why, it is argued, should such revelation not have been available to the Son during his earthly ministry?[77]

Some also argue that 3:34f should be understood similarly of Jesus' equipping with the Spirit to speak God's word on earth, 'Whom God has sent speaks the words of God, for he does not give the Spirit to him by measure. For the Father loves the Son and has given all things into his hands.'[78] Accordingly Brun, reading the longer text, takes 3:32 to refer to an experience on earth: 'What he has seen and heard to that he bears witness.' Holtzmann had denied this, finding a conflict between the pre-existence tradition found in 3:32 and the tradition of prophetic inspiration in 3:34.[79] But Brun argues, to the contrary, that in the words, 'of the earth' and 'of heaven' (3:31), only a contrast in quality, not one of origin, is expressed, and points to 1:33, where John the Baptist hears words from heaven and speaks them on earth.[80]

Lütgert explains 3:31 on the basis that even on earth the Son can be understood to be in heaven, noting, as does Robinson,[81] that it can also be said of the disciples that they are not 'of the earth', but 'from above'; though of the Son it refers to eternal generation.[82] He points similarly to 3:13 as indicating Jesus' access to heaven while on earth: 'No one has ascended into heaven but the one who descended from heaven.'[83] Cadman points to Paul's being caught up into heaven as an analogy.[84] Barrett understands 3:13 to speak of Jesus' being on earth and in heaven at the same time;[85] and Odeberg explains the passage against the background of Jewish mysticism and proposes that 3:13 refer to a mystical ascent which will, in turn, set a pattern for mystical ascent of the disciples.[86]

Another line of argument runs from 1:18, where the participial phrase, *ho ōn eis ton kolpon tou patros* ('being in the bosom of the Father'), is read as referring to a permanent state of affairs, including therefore the relationship between Father and Son on earth, so that the participial phrase almost takes on a causal quality: 'No one has ever seen God; God, the only Son, being in the bosom of the Father, has made him known.' Accordingly, it is argued, the basis on which the Son knows the Father is this special relationship and the seeing of the Father in this sense may also have taken place on earth.[87] The view that *ho ōn* refers to Jesus' earthly life, not just to his present exalted state or present and pre-existent state, is widely held among scholars who do not espouse the approach to pre-existence we are examining.[88]

6:47 would, it is argued, also refer to an event on earth: 'Not that anyone has seen the Father except he who is from God; he has seen the Father' and similarly 5:37, 'You have never heard his voice nor seen his form.'[89] Brun also points to the context of 6:47 where Jesus argues that people taught of God come to him (6:45) and also to 8:47, 'He who is from God hears the words of God; because of this you do not hear, because you are not from God.'[90]

Brun also notes that, while people may hear God and be taught of him on earth, according to the gospel only the Son sees or has seen God. But, he argues, this cannot mean pre-existent seeing, for it is not unique to the Son to have seen God in heaven. The evangelist, he suggests, was probably fully aware of the wide range of traditions which speak of beings in heaven seeing the face of God. The distinctive seeing denied to all others, he argues, is the seeing of God on earth. Jesus as a man on earth is the sole exception and this is the case because he comes from above. His distinctive origins make it possible for him, as a human being on earth, to see the Father.[91]

This view also claims support from the consistent emphasis during the ministry of the Son's relationship with the Father. On earth he was not left alone, but worked with the Father. On earth he is one with the Father. Surely, it is argued, this must mean more than that he faithfully carried out the Father's commission which he remembered from the days of his pre-existence. Lütgert speaks of a fully conscious communication between Father and Son and Son and Father on earth.[92] Brun prefers to speak of visionary communication similar to what he finds in Philo or is present among inspired prophets who 'listen in' on the council of Yahweh.[93] How can the author assume a relationship of oneness exists between Father and Son, such as becomes the model for believers, in which no communication takes place? Had communication between Father and Son ceased at the point of the Son's coming into the world? Is the Son just an envoy a long way from home?

A further argument is found in the common interpretation of 1:51, 'You will see heaven opened and the angels of God ascending and descending upon the Son of Man.' According to this interpretation Jesus is predicting the revelatory nature of his ministry as a bridge between heaven and earth. It assumes Jesus engages both in receiving and in giving revelation.[94] Bultmann sees in it a symbol of uninterrupted oneness between Father and Son.[95]

Significance of arguments against pre-existence

The arguments for denying any role of pre-existence in the pattern of revelation deserve fuller attention than they have received in recent research, not least because, as Brun points out, it is in part in response to the issues they raise that Bultmann developed his influential analysis of Johannine christology.[96] Bultmann responded by declaring statements about pre-existent seeing and hearing and about pre-existence in general as mythological ways of saying that in the Son something beyond this world and beyond human resources is breaking in.[97] The *archē* ('beginning') in 1:1 and 1 John 1:1 are in effect the same.[98] Before considering such solutions, I first want to re-examine the arguments outlined above for their cogency.

Reviewing the arguments: seeing and hearing

Some of the arguments are particularly unconvincing. To these belong the argument from the analogies between the Jews and the devil, on the one hand, and the Son and the Father, on the other; and between the disciples and the Son, using 3:11 and parallels. These analogies cannot be pressed beyond the aspects of hearing, allegiance and obedience. There is no indication that the manner and timing of the hearing must be the same, nor that the nature of sonship or of the relationship is identical in each case.

Similarly the argument in relation to 1:18 that God's invisibility relates only to human beings on earth is unconvincing. It is true that the contrast is primarily between Jesus and human beings on earth, but the claim is that the Word made flesh has seen the Father because he was with him in the beginning. The other two passages which speak of the vision of God do so in close relationship to statements about Jesus' pre-existence. 'No one has seen there Father except he who is from the Father, he has seen the Father' (6:46). The Son has come from the Father and this must be seen as the ground for the claim that the Son, unlike any other human being, has seen the Father. 5:37f is also most naturally understood in this way, 'The Father who sent me has borne witness concerning me. His voice you have never heard and his form you have never seen and his word you do not have abiding in you, because in the one he has sent you do not believe.'

Seeing and Hearing in the context of coming and being sent

These claims must be seen and interpreted within the context of the pattern of statements which express the central structure of the author's christology, as the following sample texts show: 7:29, 'I know him, because I am from him and he sent me'; 18:37, 'I was born for this and for this I came into the world to bear witness to the truth'; 12:49, 'I have not spoken of my own accord, but the Father who sent me has given me the command what I am to say and speak'; 17:7f, 'Now they know that all which you have given me is from you. Because the words which you gave me I have given them, and they have received them and know truly that I came from you and they have believed that you sent me.'

The connection is also very clear in 3:31f, especially when we follow the shorter reading: 'He who comes from above is above all. He who is of the earth is of the earth and of the the earth he speaks; he who comes from heaven bears witness to what he has seen and heard.' But even the longer text makes the connection evident: 'He who comes from heaven is above all. What he has seen and heard to this he bears witness.' Similarly 8:42f assumes this connection: 'If God were your Father, you would love me, for I went out and have come from God; nor have I come of my own accord, but he sent me. Why do you not recognise my message? Because you cannot hear my word. You are of your father, the devil.'

The integrity of time and space in christology

Such texts as these, which we reviewed extensively in Part II, show that where Jesus speaks of having been taught or having seen or heard the Father in the past, he refers to pre-existence and not to a past event on the earth. This includes the texts like 8:26,28,38,40 cited as arguments above. Nor is there any reason why 3:13 should be an exception and refer to an ascent of the Son of Man while on earth,[99] let alone a constant state of ascending and descending as Lütgert proposes.[100] The reference to ascent is to Jesus' return to the Father as the context shows and the verse is one of a number in the gospel which contain anachronism (cf. already 3:11). The denial of spatial categories and therefore of categories of movement does not do justice to the gospel. If the Son remains both in heaven and on earth during his earthly ministry, this would make nonsense of statements of coming and going and rob others which imply a movement towards the presence of the Father in heaven as a return to glory of any meaning. Either the author has completely collapsed the spatial, demythologising it, as Bultmann suggests, or we must take time, place, and movement seriously and consistently.[101]

As far as the phrase, 'who is in the bosom of the Father' (1:18), is concerned, it is best taken as a reference to the present exalted status of Jesus, viewed (like 3:13 and the Baptist's witness in 1:15)[102] from the standpoint of the author,[103] not as a description also of Jesus' earthly relationship with the Father,[104] nor as such, taking *eis* in a dynamic sense to mean turned towards the Father, as de la Potterie and others suggest.[105] It describes the relationship of the Son with the Father in heaven as it now is since Easter and as it was before the Son's coming into the world. In that way it forms an inclusion with 1:1f ('In the beginning was the Word and the Word was with God and the Word was God. He was in the beginning with God.' cf. 1:18, 'The God, the only Son, who is in the bosom of the Father, he has made him known'). At the same time the phrase indicates why the Son can make the Father known: he was with God as the Word and became flesh to make him known. The author assumes a difference between the Son's heavenly being with the Father and his oneness with the Father on earth and this corresponds to our findings concerning glory and glorification. The Son manifested glory on earth, yet had also come from and returned to the glory he had with the Father from the foundation of the world (17:5).

This is not to deny the relationship the Son has with the Father on earth. The Son is not an envoy a long way from home, abandoned by his Father. The Father is present and at work in the works of the Son on earth. They are one. But this no more means that, in the case of Jesus, we should collapse the concept of heaven as the dwelling place of God than we should, in the case of other human beings. There has never been a major problem in speaking of a relationship between human beings and God and at the same time believing that this relationship will be richer and fuller in the world to come. The fourth evangelist assumes such a pattern.

Of the remaining arguments, 1:51, which refers to a vision of angels ascending and descending upon the Son of Man, need not refer to the Son as revealer in constantly receiving and giving revelation. It could equally refer to Jesus the revealer being the revelation because of what he has seen and heard already in pre-existence. We prefer, however, to read the verse as a reference to neither, but rather to Jesus' exaltation as Son of Man, as explained in IIIA4 above.

3:34 need not mean that Jesus gains inspiration for revelation from receiving the Spirit at his baptism, on the analogy with the disciples in 16:13-15. In its present context it cannot be separated from the notion of sending and pre-existence as the basis for revelation: 'Whom God sent speaks the words of God, for he does not give the Spirit to him by measure' (3:34 and cf. 3:31f). Similarly the following verse refers to the Son's pre-existent authorisation in the words, 'The Father loves the Son and has given all things into his hands.'

Relating pre-existence and continuing oneness with the Father

The dominant pattern throughout the gospel is that of the Son's having received revelation in his pre-existence which he brings to the world. Yet this happens only in such a way that the relationship with the Father remains a living one in which communication takes place, at least at the level at which it is possible for human beings to communicate with God, and doubtless more. How do these two aspects relate? The question must be considered in the light of our finding that the language of communication and revelation serves the end of setting forth Jesus as God's Son who presents people not with communication of revealed knowledge, but with himself and through himself with God and his offer of a relationship of allegiance and faith that brings life.

Function of pre-existent seeing and hearing for christology

Accordingly, statements about pre-existent receiving of revelation serve primarily to underline the fact that the Son has come from the Father, from the heavenly unity with the Father. The reference to the pre-existent life with the Father qualifies and validates the Son's claim to speak and act on God's behalf, in his person to offer God himself. Pre-existence remains central for the author's purpose,[106] but he uses the revealer envoy communication model only as a framework to present the Son's claim. This, then throws new light on the two exceptions to the normal pattern that statements about seeing and hearing refer to the Son's being with the Father in pre-existence, which have long been noted,[107] namely 5:19f,30. These speak in the present tense of Jesus' seeing and hearing, but refer to this not as acquisition of knowledge to be imparted, using the revealer envoy model, but rather to the Son's ability to judge as the Father judges or to act in accordance with his will. This sounds similar, but it is a different model. Accordingly they should not be made the basis for arguing a different time reference for all other passages and a denial of pre-existence. Nor do they represent a contradiction, as Bultmann supposed.[108]

5:19f,30   Resolution of a Conflict of Models

When we see that the author is employing the revelation envoy model in a non literal sense, the apparent contradiction between statements of this pattern and those like 5:19f,30, which focus on the Son's oneness with the Father on earth, is resolved and, with it, one of the major arguments against pre-existence. For in this instance the author is not employing the revealer envoy pattern, but apprenticeship imagery to describe not primarily revelation, but the giving of life. But ultimately both envoy and apprenticeship family relational imagery serves the same end: to establish the claim that in the Son the Father confronts the world with the opportunity for life.

Real pre-existence in space and time

However, unlike the statements in the revealer envoy model about information acquisition, those which speak of the Son's coming, being sent, returning show no sign of needing to be taken in a way that robs them of their implied sense of movement in space and time. It would not be consistent to explain the Logos motif, for instance, as expressing only the divine communication in the earthly ministry of Jesus and to deny to it the aspect of pre-existence, as does Dupont,[109] nor, to reduce the pre-existent Logos to an anhypostatic Logos which takes hypostatic form in Jesus[110] or enters him at his baptism.[111] Sending statements are not to be reduced to the equivalent of prophetic inspiration,[112] nor, as Appold, should we convert statements about Jesus' authorisation into statements about Jesus' continuing relationship with the Father.[113]

The author assumes the pre-existence of the Son[114] and uses it throughout as a basis for asserting the Son's authority to speak and act in a way that confronts the world and offers life in relationship with himself and with the Father. Statements like Jesus' existence before Abraham (8:58, hardly to be explained away as a reference to pre-existence of a Jungian 'self'),[115] his antedating John the Baptist (1:15, 30), his continuing as Son in the house forever (8:35),[116] his being seen by Isaiah (12:41), his pre-existent glory (17:5,24) and possibly 8:56[117] and 8:25, if it entails a reference to 1:1,[118] serve only to confirm what is announced in the prologue and presupposed in the central structure of the author's christology: the Son who was with the Father in the beginning came to make him known. This throws all the more weight on the nature of this relationship between Father and Son, especially since the revealer envoy communication model has been shown to be only a motif serving to express this claim. To this we turn in the following section.

3. The Nature of the Son in Relation to the Father

The central structure of the author's christology depends upon the pattern of the revealer envoy. This serves to underline the Son's claim of a unique relationship with the Father on the basis of which he has come into the world bringing life and light and truth. In this section we shall examine the nature of this unique relationship.

A Relationship Characterised by Love

We begin by noting that throughout the gospel love is a fundamental characteristic of this relationship. The Father loves the Son. In 3:35 it stands beside statements of equipping and authorisation: 'The one whom God sent speaks the words of God, for he does not give the Spirit by measure. The Father loves the Son and has given all things into his hand' (3:34f). In 5:20 it stands beside the statement that the Father is showing the Son what he is doing. In 10:17 it is said to be in response to the Son's obedient fulfilment of the task given him by the Father to lay down his life that he might take it up again for the sake of the sheep. In 15:9f it is the pattern for Jesus, in turn, to give love to his disciples, and for his exhortation that they should remain in that love by keeping his commands, as he remains in that love by keeping the commission given him. In 17:23 the goal of the community faith is that its oneness might bring the world to know that the Father sent the Son and that the Father has loved the disciples as he has loved the Son.

The relationship of mutual love between Father and Son is the source and the pattern for the relationships of love which are the goal and content of salvation. The similarity of pattern between the Father's love of the Son and the Son's love of the Father, on the one hand, and the relationships of love between the believers and the Father and the Son, and among believers themselves, on the other, is not a similarity in all respects. For the relationship between Father and Son is primary and pre-existent and the Son, unlike the believers, is pre-existent and unique.

The Prologue - Guide to the Relationship and to the Gospel

How is this unique sonship understood? The author doubtless intends the prologue to offer important information in the light of which the gospel is to be read, especially information about who the Son is. It was not a puzzle to be understood only at the end of a reading of the gospel, as it has become for us.[119] It is an overture,[120] a window,[121] a guide[122] and a key[123] for reading the gospel,[124] and for resolving its 'messianic secret'.[125] But without access to the extensive field of meanings shared by the author and his readers or hearers, we must be satisfied with constant cross references within the material of the gospel and with a consideration of a series of key passages before being able to place the statements of the prologue and others in the gospel of like kind within what we might claim is near to the Johannine perspective. Accordingly we shall look in particular at the prologue, itself; the disputes with the Jews in 5:17-47 and 10:22-39; Jesus' words to his disciples in 14:8-11; and his prayer in ch. 17. In the course of doing so we shall also take into account other references and more general considerations.

The Word was 'God'

The gospel begins with the words, 'In the beginning was the Word and the Word was with God and the Word was *theos* ('God').' 'The Word was *theos*' must not be isolated and made into a simple equation: the Word was God. Grammatically this is a possible translation, but not the only one. The statement's meaning, and so its translation, must be determined by its context. It could also be translated: 'the Word was a god' or 'the Word was divine'. Grammatical considerations alone fail to decide the question, since all three translations can be defended on grammatical grounds.[126]

The Word was God?

Against the first of these interpretations ('the Word was God') is the fact that the author has just said that the Word was 'with' God.[127] If 'Word' means little more than 'words', then it would be conceivable that the author could say: God's words were with him; they are, as his words, part of God himself, in that sense, they are God. Dupont comes near to this in claiming that the Logos concept refers not to a person but to God's communication of himself.[128] But the author goes on to speak of the Word as a person as distinct from God, so that this must be assumed also in the opening verses.

Nor is it likely that the author intends in his opening statement to make a gradual approach to what he wishes to say, so that 'the Word was with God' is merely a step along the way to the statement, 'the Word was God.' For it is precisely 'the Word was with God' which is repeated in 1:2.

The Word was a God?

The other two translations fit the context more smoothly at one level. Yet their evaluation cannot take place without our making assumptions about the author's wider frame of reference. In particular it is unlikely, given his context within the Christian community and its roots in Judaism, that he would mean that there is more than one God. Langbrandtner reckons with this as the position of the redactor, whereas the Grundschrift had thought of Jesus more as an extension of God into the world,[129] but such a view on the part of the redactor is unlikely and unsupported elsewhere. It is true, on the most natural reading of the text, that there are two beings here: God and a second who was *theos* but this second is related to God in a manner which shows that God is the absolute over against which the second is defined. They are not presented as two equal gods.[130]

The Word was divine?

This leads us to consider the third translation, 'divine', the equivalent of *theios*, suggested already by Origen,[131] and represented often by the phrase 'Gott von Art' or 'God of a kind'.[132] Should the author have been concerned to say the Word was divine, why did he write *theos* and not the more usual adjective, *theios*?[133] The order of 1:1c and the lack of the article may be idiomatic in relation to the use of predicate nouns, as Colwell suggests,[134] or it may, in addition, reflect an emphasis on quality shared without exact reciprocity.[135] This would suggest that the focus here lies not on the person, but on the quality or nature of the Word. Schnackenburg points to 1 Jn 5:20 ('We know that the Son of God has come and has given us understanding, so that we may know the truth and we are in the truth, in his Son, Jesus Christ. He is the true God and eternal life') and understands the use of *theos* for Jesus as expressing that in him God reveals himself and that he has the same nature as the Father.[136]

What was 'was'?

But what does 'nature' or 'quality' mean in this context? The New English Bible translates, 'what God was, the Word was.' It still leaves open the question: and what and how was that? Brown is right in pointing out that we are dealing with the language of doxology here.[137] Can we go beyond Bultmann's statement that here is paradox?[138] Is, as Haenchen argues, the anarthrous *theos* another indication of subordination of the Son to the Father in the gospel?[139] It would be easy to read 1:1-3 in isolation as a statement that the Logos had once been with, indeed been part of God and had ceased to be so, a kind of emanation, but passages such as 17:5,24 and those considered at the beginning of this discussion indicate much more of a personal relationship of union and love. The claim of shared originality ('in the beginning')[140] and the absence of any notion of the Son Logos as, for instance, 'firstborn' or 'first created' being, normally associated with Wisdom/Logos tradition, is astounding. It is no surprise that such statements provoke christological reflection in subsequent centuries. But our task must be to interpret as far as possible their meaning within the gospel without reading back into the text later attempts at a solution.

The nature of the relationship of Son and Father in the fourth gospel must rest on more than 1:1 and its grammatical interpretation. The term, *theos*, is applied similarly to Jesus in 1:18 and comes in the confession of Thomas in 20:28. But the issue is much wider than the use of *theos* even in the prologue and presents itself as a repeated focus of contention, as the Son makes his claims and the Jews make counterclaims accusing him of ditheism, an accusation constantly repudiated. But we return first to the prologue as presupposition and prelude to the gospel.

Analogous relationship in Logos Wisdom Torah tradition

It is widely recognised that the motif, Word, Logos, belongs within a tradition of thought reaching back to such passages as Prov 8:22-31 and reflecting speculation about wisdom or logos as the highest heavenly power in God's service. One strand of this tradition identifies heavenly wisdom with Torah, Law, and so personifies Torah.[141] In this stream Torah is God's and in that sense is God. It is not thought of literally as a person distinct from God, as we have it in the fourth gospel, but remains a personification. Closer to the notion of wisdom or the logos as a person is the stream which finds expression in Hellenistic Judaism (Wisdom, Philo).[142] This belongs within a wider tendency in Judaism to speak of the highest beings under God, sometimes to the extent that the kind of interchangeability already present in the Old Testament between the angel of the Lord and the Lord, which Justin later exploited so fully as a christological argument, extended to other high beings, including the Logos.[143] Incipient gnosticism doubtless heightened this tendency. It, too, used the Sophia/Logos speculation.[144] In Philo the logos is not only portrayed as a person, the highest heavenly being in the service of God, but can also be called *theos*, a second god (De Somn. I 229f; Leg. All. III 207f; Qu. Gen. II 62).[145] This is all the more interesting since Philo clearly does not understand this as compromising monotheism, which he stoutly defends.[146] Rather the bearing of God's name seems related to the bearing of God's power and functions.

Further analogies: angels, Christ, Messiah, rulers

A similar transfer of God's name to his highest servants is evident in circles of Jewish apocalyptic.[147] It sometimes meant that heavenly beings would be seen as being authorised to exercise divine functions such as the judging Melchisedek in 11QMelch, where 'proclaiming the acceptable day of the Lord' becomes 'proclaiming the acceptable year of Melchisedek'. It also became important within christological traditions of the church already in New Testament times, most notably in the Philippian hymn, where Jesus is given 'the name which is above every name, that at the name of Jesus every knee should bow and every tongue confess, that Jesus Christ is KYRIOS, to the glory of God the Father.' The practice of giving divine epithets to human rulers was also widespread and finds its particular expression in Israel when the king is addressed not only as 'Son of God' (Ps 2:7), but also as 'God' (Ps 45:6f). It became attached also to the hope for a future royal figure (Isa 9:6). Within the context of Christian messianic tradition it also came to be applied to Jesus (Heb 1:8f).[148]

Logos Wisdom Torah and the gospel

The parallels which share most in common with the prologue are those related to wisdom or logos. Torah imagery occurs in the final verses of the prologue and many of the images used of Jesus in the gospel are frequently used of Torah in these contexts,[149] so that this stream deserves to be taken seriously into account. This is all the more so if in its present context the prologue still refers to the coming of the Logos during Israel's history, which I doubt.[150] On the other hand, the Logos is no mere personification here and the opening verses of the prologue have strongest links with passages which use wisdom or logos motifs in relation to creation and the beginning of time. The two streams need not be seen as separate. The presence of elements of both make it likely that the logos wisdom tradition should be seen here. The wisdom logos stream becomes a major influence in Christian and gnostic reflection. Elsewhere in the New Testament it is present in hymnic traditions (Col 1:15f; Heb 1:2f).

The prologue stands within the wisdom logos stream and this stream also influences the imagery of the rest of the gospel elsewhere. Without clarifying further the context in which the stream influences the fourth gospel (conflict with the synagogue, influence from speculative Jewish Christianity or contact with early gnosticism), we can hold to the high probability that this stream lies beneath the prologue. Within this stream, at least in Philo, *theos* had been transferred as a title to the logos without compromise of monotheism. This procedure is also by no means without parallel in Judaism and Christianity. We may with some confidence assert that this also forms the background for the author's statement that 'the Word was *theos*'.

The logos-theos Son in the Prologue

We are therefore probably correct to assume that the use of the title *theos* for the Logos in 1:1 involves at least the understanding that the Logos is in the unique position of exercising functions and powers which belong to God. This would make good sense of the juxtaposition of statements in 1:1-2 and in no way jeopardise monotheism. Within the New Testament the closest parallel outside Johannine literature would be the use of kyrios for Jesus in Phil 2:11. This understanding of 1:1 also coheres well with the way the gospel presents the Son as primarily making the claim that a response to him is a response to God and as being the bearer of light and life and truth. But such an evaluation must wait until other passages have been considered.

Even if the sense in which the Logos is *theos* is to be explained by analogy with the Logos-Wisdom model, there remains the question: of what nature is then the Logos according to John? On what basis does the Logos bear these powers and functions? Was he thought of as the highest power under God, God's image and reflection, his firstborn, as Philo thought of the Logos, terms also used of Jesus in New Testament hymnic material elsewhere? Was he thought of as the highest angel, or as a being of unique kind, or as a being one with the Father in substance? Is his exercise of divine functions and powers rooted in his nature or in some way the result of authorisation, and, where the latter motif is present, how is it understood? Is it just a symbol? These questions of the gospel's christology must not be handled in abstract or answered from the annals of later christological discussion independent of close examination of the gospel itself.

The logos-theos Son in the Prologue: 1:1-13

1:2 repeats the statement that the Logos was with God and so confirms that the Logos is thought of primarily as a being distinct from God: 'he was in the beginning with God.' The repetition suggests that the emphasis is on primordial togetherness and the closing verse of the prologue, which forms an inclusio, matches this emphasis: 'No one has even seen God; *theos*, the only Son, who is in the bosom of the Father, he has made him known' (1:18). We shall return to this statement below.

1:3 tells of the function which the Logos bore as the one through whom all things were made. The second half of the verse could read, 'and without him was not anything made that was made', which would repeat with emphasis the point made in the first half. 1:4 would then continue as a statement of what was in the Logos: 'In him was life and the life was the light of people.' Alternatively, 1:3b may read, 'and without him nothing was made.' The prologue would then continue: 'What came about in him was life and the life was the light of people.' In the former, life is identified as something within the Logos. In the latter, life is identified with what came about in him. Both translations include a reference to the Logos's being present as life bringer. What may have once referred to his life in creation is now best taken primarily as a reference to the light which 'came about' or was present in the manifestation of the Logos on earth. Accordingly 1:5 makes this more explicit: 'The light shines in the darkness and the darkness has not accepted it.' This best refers to Jesus' rejection.[151] Whether read in this way, or as others prefer, with reference to the Logos's work in creation before the incarnation, the functions exercised and the qualities borne (life and light) are those belonging to God himself.

In 1:6-13 the same assumption is present, again, whether these verses refer already to the Logos in Jesus from his incarnation onwards, as I prefer, or only to pre-incarnational activity. The Logos stands in the place of God. Yet the distinction is preserved. Faith leads to people becoming not children of the logos, but children of God. I am not convinced that 1:13 originally had a singular verb and so referred to Jesus' birth.[152]

The logos-theos Son in the Prologue: 1:14-18

We shall examine 1:14-18 in greater detail in discussing the question of Jesus' humanity, but for the present context we note the Logos tents among his people much as God tents among his people in the wilderness, yet this motif already belongs to the wisdom stream and elsewhere tradition also speaks of God's Torah or shekinah or glory descending to dwell with his people. There is no confusion of being. The glory of the Son is 'glory as of the *monogenous* of the Father.' This is more than 'glory like that of a father's only son,' as Robinson suggests,[153] for this would be a bland anticlimax. Jesus' glory is related to his being the unique and only Son. It is a derived glory.

The use of *monogenēs*, 'the only one of his kind', for the Logos implies unique sonship (*monogenēs* of the Father).[154] 3:16 confirms this where *monogenēs* is used as an adjective directly qualifying 'Son'. 3:16 is related to a tradition evident elsewhere in the New Testament where the adjective *agapētos* ('beloved') expresses the uniqueness of Jesus' sonship (Mark 1:11; 9:7; 12:6; cf. Col 1:13; Eph 1:6; Rom 8:32).[155] It is because of this unique relationship of the Son to the Father that he is the bearer of light and life and here: glory, glory as of the unique Son of the Father. The closest parallel in the gospel is 17:22, 'The glory you have given to me I have given to them.' 1:16 belongs with 1:14, 'glory as of the unique Son of the Father, full of grace and truth....Because of his fullness we have all received, even grace upon grace.' This is also close to 5:26f, 'As the Father has life in himself, so he has also granted the Son to have life in himself and he has given him authority to make judgement.'

Light, life, glory, grace and truth all describe qualities which derive ultimately from God and are mediated through the Son.[156] Accordingly the author can contrast in 1:17 the two mediators, Moses and Jesus Christ. Sinai imagery is present in 1:14-18, in the tenting, the glory, the reference to Moses and Law and in the statement about seeing God.[157] The way in which it is used makes it difficult to see Torah wisdom as the primary basis for the prologue, because here Jesus is primarily being set in contrast to Torah. But as Edwards has convincingly pointed out,[158] *anti* in 1:16 means 'instead of', so that we see here grace acknowledged as once given in the Law through Moses now replaced and superseded by the grace that has come through Jesus Christ. It is still God's grace. Here is new revelation on a new basis. 1:18 makes this clear in bringing the prologue to its climax: 'No one has ever seen God; *monogenēs theos* ('God the only Son'),[159] who is the bosom of the Father, he has made him known.' *theos* is probably the reading to be preferred.[160] It forms an inclusion with 1:1 as does 'in the bosom of the Father'; cf. 'was with God' (1:1f). *monogenēs* and 'Father' catch up 1:14, 'the *monogenous* of the Father'. The 'bosom' imagery continues the family imagery ('Father', *monogenēs*, 'Son').

The picture is one of closest family intimacy. The juxtaposition of this image of family intimacy with the designation *theos* and the contrast with the 'no one' in the beginning of the verse suggest that the author is making the strongest possible distinction between the Son and all others and establishing the strongest possible base for the claim that the Son makes the Father known. But even here the distinctness of Father and Son is maintained. The *theos* not only echoes 1:1, but also functions within the same framework. There it was best understood along with its context as deriving, at least, from the wisdom stream of thought and as referring to the exercise of divine powers and functions by the Logos. Here it belongs in the language of family intimacy, more characteristic of the gospel as a whole, but similarly relates to the Son as bearer of light and life and revelation.

The logos-theos Son in the Prologue: Conclusion

The prologue offers us, therefore, an understanding of the Son as one who is life, light, glory, grace and truth to the world. He is what God is for the world. Thus he bears the designation *theos*. Yet in being what God is for the world, he is distinct from God. He was with God in the beginning, as now he shares the same intimacy with him in heaven. He is not another God, but the Son, the only one, deriving what he is for the world from God. By considering other passages in the gospel we can test what has emerged here and if possible supplement it. For anything more that is to be said of the nature of the Son as *theos* must be said in the light of the rest of the gospel. This will include not only the sole further occasion where *theos* is used again of Jesus, namely Thomas' confession (20:28), but also passages where Jesus explicates the basis of his claim.

The Son and the Father - 5:17-30

In ch. 5 Jesus' healing of a lame man on the sabbath provokes the anger of the Jews (5:16). Jesus responds: 'My Father is working up till now and I am working' (5:17). Jesus justifies his work on the sabbath by appealing to the belief that God also works on the sabbath. But in making this claim Jesus presupposes a relationship between himself and God which justifies his appeal. Why should a person claim to be able to do something on the basis that God does it? Can God be used as an example to follow in this way? Does this not obliterate the distinction between God and human beings? How can this be justified when it contradicts God's Law for human beings?

Jesus not only appeals to God as an example; he also claims that God is his Father and he, God's Son, in a way that goes beyond the usual understanding of these terms in Judaism. It is against this background that we must understand the reaction of the Jews: they seek to kill him, 'because he not only broke the sabbath, but was also saying that God was his own Father, making himself equal with God' (5:18). In other words there is implied in Jesus' response a distinctive quality of being like that expressed in the prologue. He is not arguing the correct application of the Law but setting himself apart from all others. How would the evangelist have understood the Jews' accusation that Jesus was 'making himself equal with God'?

This accusation forms the basis for the author's development of Jesus' explanation which follows. Jesus says, 'The Son can do nothing of his own accord except what he sees the Father doing. For what he does, this the Son likewise does' (5:19). This is not a statement about equality in the sense that it could be reversed to read: The Father can do nothing except what he sees the Son doing. The notion of equality is heavily qualified by the notion of dependence. The equality consists primarily in equal works, which had been the point of Jesus' claim in 5:17. 5:20 expands this

further: 'The Father loves the Son and shows him all that he is doing.' Jesus uses
apprenticeship imagery of himself and the Father,[161] rather than a parable, as
Robinson suggests.[162] The following verses continue in similar vein: both Father
and Son make alive (5:21); the Father has authorised the Son to judge (5:22), 'so
that all may honour the Son as they honour the Father. He who does not honour
the Son does not honour the Father who sent him' (5:23); the Son has been given
the right to have life in himself and so to judge (5:26f); and 5:30 concludes, 'I am
not able to do anything of myself. As I hear, I judge, and my judgement is just;
because I do not seek my own will, but the will of him who sent me.'

Equality grounded in complete obedience enabled by unique being

The Son's equality with the Father is grounded in and defined by his doing the
Father's will and fulfilling his commission. It is also grounded in the claim that he
is uniquely qualified to do so, since he is the Son of the Father, different from
other people. His being is distinctive and enables his doing. In his being he is
dependent and subordinate; in his doing he is equal. The inequality of dependence
of the unique Son is also emphasised as the basis for the equality of deed and word
in 5:36f.

This is substantially also the conclusion of Barrett,[163] and earlier Wetter, who cites this as a
major difference between Jesus and other divine figures claiming to be sons of God in the
world of the time.[164] Büchsel argues that this subordination applies only to the earthly Jesus
and speaks of the unity as the highest achievable by human beings on earth,[165] but this denies
both the use of dependency language for the pre-existence (sending, commissioning) and also
the difference in the nature of sonship presupposed in this passage. Similarly Sproston relates
subordination only to Jesus' humanity and not to the Son of the prologue.[166] Lindars comments
that the author is not always consistent, sometimes treating the relationship metaphysically,
sometimes functionally.[167] By contrast, Riedl suggests that the author operates with a binitarian
concept in which the Son as Son is seen as dependent on the Father without suggesting direct
subordination.[168] He speaks of a metaphysical unity of being ('Wesenseinheit') and of the
eternal generation of the Son.[169] But, as Barrett points out, this kind of interpretation reads later
christological formulations into the text.[170] Appold strongly emphasises equality and oneness,
but imposes here his own system upon the text when he denies any element of subordination,
claiming that 5:18 correctly interprets 5:17.[171] This is the case only if we take 5:19-21 as the
key to the understanding of 5:18. There is no reciprocal relationship here. The Father sends
and empowers the Son, not vice versa. On the other hand, Leistner and Miranda are surely
incorrect in arguing that the author denies the substance of the Jews' accusation of equality
altogether.[172] With Barrett, we see the author rejecting the Jews' meaning of equality with God,
but taking it up, like many statements with double meaning, as true in his own distinctive sense
of equality in subordination.[173] These are doubtless also real accusations hurled at the
Johannine community by Jewish critics.[174]

The Son and the Father - 10:22-39

In 10:30-39 the confrontation is similar to that of ch. 5. Jesus claims: 'I and the
Father are one' (10:30). This statement has often been seen as the hallmark of
Johannine christology and rightly so, but only if it is understood strictly within its
context in the gospel. Appold, for instance, makes it the basis of his claim that
oneness and equality are the centre of the gospel, but does so by denying its
context and even asserting that obedience of the Son to the Father is foreign to
Johannine christology.[175] Barrett also warns against reading too much into 10:30[176]
and Haenchen cautions similarly, noting that the motif of oneness occurs only here
and in ch. 17.[177]

Responding to the Jews' question about his messiahship, Jesus had answered that the works he did in his Father's name bore witness to him, but that the Jews had not believed in him because they were not his sheep (10:24-26). The sheep hear and follow Jesus and he knows them. They are safe in his hands (10:27f). This statement is then expanded in a way which equates the activity of the Son and the Father. In 10:28 Jesus said, 'No one shall snatch them from my hands'; in 10:29 he says: 'No one can snatch them from the Father's hands.' 10:30, 'I and the Father are one', is thus primarily related to the work of caring for the disciples.

Unfortunately the statement which lies between the two parallel claims of 10:28 and 10:29 has an uncertain textual tradition. The reading, 'My Father who has given (them) to me is greater than all' fits the context well and would make explicit the connection between the two claims. This would also be true of the reading, 'My Father, as regards what he has given me, is greater than all'. The more difficult reading is almost untranslatable because it makes 'greater' refer not to the Father, but to the relative pronoun, translated above, 'as regards what.' It could read, 'As for my Father, what he has given to me is greater than all.' It would then imply the Father's love as the motivation for his caring for the Son's disciples, though, nevertheless, also imply indirectly the Son's dependence on the Father. The conjunction of oneness and dependence is very evident in what follows.

10:22-39 - oneness in dependence

In response to Jesus' words the Jews seek his death (10:31). The Son's claim and the Jews' response echo 5:17f. There Jesus had said, 'My Father is working up till now and I am working'. The accusations of the Jews arose here, as we have seen, from the Son's claim also to keep his own, as the Father does (10:28f) and from his assertion that he and the Father are *hen*, one (10:30). The sense of the neuter en is functional unity, compared with the more strongly ontological claim which would be being made with the personal masculine *heis*, 'one'.[178] It assumes that to be in the hands of the Son is to be in the hands of the Father. But it also means more than this. For the disciples are safe only because being in the hands of the Son also means being in the hands of the Father. The identity of caring, or we might say, the equality of caring, is bound to the dependence of Son on Father. The Father guarantees the Son's caring is his caring. In that sense the Father and Son are one.

Jesus' defence of his claim also follows similar lines to his defence in 5:19f: 'I have shown you many works from the Father. For which of them do you want to stone me?' (10:32; cf. 5:20, 'The Father loves the Son and shows him all he is doing'). Jesus is also referring back to the works mentioned at the beginning of the encounter (10:25). The claim to oneness, like the statement of equality in 5:18, is, therefore, immediately interpreted as a oneness of works and in such a way that they derive from the Father.

The Jews fail to see the connection and retort: 'We do not want to stone you because of a good work, but for blasphemy, because you, though you are a human being, make yourself God' (10:33). The Jews have misunderstood Jesus' words, 'I and the Father are one', as though Jesus had said: 'I am God', in effect, 'I am the

Father'. But the author never has Jesus equate himself in this way with the Father.[179] Rather we have before us a typical example of the Johannine use of misunderstanding. Yet the following verses also indicate that their accusation, 'you, though you are a human being, make yourself God' (10:33), is true at one level, not in the sense that Jesus makes himself God, but that he is *theos*. A similar structure of thought is present here as in 5:18 where the accusation proves both false and true.

10:35-39 - the use of Psalm 82

In 10:35-38 Jesus argues the validity of his claim to be *theos*. He quotes Ps 82:6, 'Is it not written in your Law, "I said, you are gods." If he called them gods to whom the word of God came, and scripture cannot be contradicted, you say of the one whom God sanctified and sent into the world, that he blasphemes, because I said, "I am the son of God."' There are a number of extraordinary features in this reply. Jesus had not made the claim, 'I am the Son of God'. This must be a rephrasing of 'I and the Father are one' (10:30) understood in line with the Jews' accusation of his making himself *theos*, but taken in a Johannine way. This is just like 1:18 where being the only Son and being *theos* are juxtaposed. Accordingly we are faced with the same question: the nature of the Son as *theos*. The use of Ps 82 is intended to address this, or at least defend Jesus' claim. How does it do so?

Psalm 82 in 10:35-39 - the people of Israel, the judges?

Many exegetes point to the use of Ps 82 in rabbinic tradition, where it is taken as a reference to the people of God at Sinai, to whom indeed the word of God came, who for short time attained divine status.[180] Accordingly Jesus' argument would be: if it was valid to address the people of God as 'gods' at Sinai, then surely it is all the more valid to use this term of the one whom God sanctified and sent into the world. In the Psalm those addressed have also been understood as judges and this may be linked with Moses and the judges to whom the people came in the wilderness days, who acted as gods for them (Ex 4:16; 7:1; 21:6; 22:8f).[181] Boismard sees also a link between the coming of the word to the people as judges of Israel, and in that sense, prophets, and the idea of Jesus as the prophet par excellence.[182] The contrast with Sinai recalls 1:14-18 of the prologue and would maintain the contrast between the word coming then and the incarnation of the Word in the person of Jesus.

While, on these interpretations, a qualitative distinction between the people of Israel or the judges and Son is presupposed, nevertheless the comparison has the effect of watering down the use of *theos* and 'Son of God' considerably. It would be a long way below what the author usually means by the term, *theos*, when referring to Jesus.[183] The passage can hardly mean that Jesus was as much Son of God as any human being might become, except that Jesus was so from birth onwards, as Lütgert suggests.[184] Nor should the lack of article be taken as supporting such an interpretation, as if Jesus were saying, 'I am a Son of God', as Robinson proposes.[185] Such a use of 'Son of God' would be something of an anticlimax and stands in tension with the emphasis found in ch. 5 where the quality of Jesus' sonship is contrasted with that of normal human beings.

Psalm 82 in 10:35-39 - angelic 'elohim'?

Another interpretation avoids the blandness of this approach by referring to the way Ps 82 is used in Qumran. Emerton drew attention to 11QMelch, where the *elohim* ('gods') among whom God takes his place in council and holds judgement (82:1), whom he rebukes (82:2-5), and whom he addresses with the words, 'You are gods, sons of the most high all of you; nevertheless you shall die like men and fall like any human prince' (82:6f), are heavenly beings, angels.[186] This is also better Old Testament exegesis of the original. In 11QMelch Melchisedek assumes God's role as judge in the heavenly council. The original psalm, itself, uses the word *elohim*, which can mean either God, gods or angels, to refer to beings other than God. The LXX translates: *theoi*. Jesus' argument would then be as follows: if it was valid to address these heavenly beings as 'gods' or 'sons of God', is it not all the more valid for the one God sanctified and sent into the world, to be so addressed? The use of *theos* here would be similar to its use of the Logos in the prologue and would not have the effect of watering down the concept of sonship to the same degree as presupposed in the more common interpretation. It would, however, still conflict with the author's designation of Jesus as *monogenēs* in 1:18. It is a much more offensive claim than that assumed by the first interpretation, which the Jews should have had no difficulty in accepting. It makes better sense therefore in the context, since the Jews response was to seek Jesus' arrest (10:39).

Psalm 82 in 10:35-38 - Conclusions

On balance, the second interpretation coheres better with the context and the christology of the gospel as a whole. It would enable us to view angelology beside logos wisdom tradition as a possible background against which to interpret the nature of the Son as *theos*, but does not really lead us beyond that. All of the interpretations of Psalm 82 in 10:35-39 which we have considered imply some qualitative difference between the Son and others, whether they be the people of Israel, judges or other heavenly beings. They imply a claim about the Son's being. This is more than, though it includes, moral unity.[187] There are metaphysical claims implied here,[188] though they stop short of Sproston's assertion that here we have the paradox of full humanity and full divinity.[189] As in 5:19f, however, the author's argument is primarily about ethical and functional unity.[190]

10:36-39 - the unique intimacy of Father and Son

In the argument from Ps 82 the author also uses the shaliach envoy motif in 10:36, where the Son describes himself as the one sanctified and sent into the world.[191] This is the pattern of the familiar revealer envoy motif. When, therefore, Jesus refers to the claim to be 'Son of God' in the same verse, this is also primarily functional, but it also cannot be any less than what was implied in his claim to oneness with the Father and in a Johannine sense to be *theos*. The following verses then expound Jesus' claim in characteristically Johannine manner. Jesus says, 'If I do not do the works of my Father, do not believe me. If I do, and you do not believe me, believe the works, that you may come to know that the Father is in me and I am in the Father' (10:37f) Here we see oneness or equality at the level of works and at the same time the explicit claim that there is more here than functional unity; there is something more to believe, namely, the mutual indwelling of Father and Son. While the language of indwelling is also used of the relationship between believers and the Son, the context here indicates that what is being expressed is above all the unique intimacy of relationship between Father and Son such as we have it in 1:18.[192]

John 5 and 10 and christology

The controversies of ch. 5 and ch. 10 have their sequel in the trial before Pilate, where the Jews claim Jesus must die because, 'he has made himself the Son of God' (19:7) This is more than a false accusation about messianic claims, as Leistner suggests.[193] Pilate is filled with numinous fear and the evangelist, employing his characteristic narrative skills, has Pilate ask: 'Where do you come from?' (19:9). For in truth the readers know that the central focus of his sonship is: he is the Son come from the Father to make him known. It is this developed understanding of sonship which led, according to Martyn, to hefty conflict with the synagogue.[194] For this christology the community stood trial. The passages considered may also reflect an expansion of material originally at home in the tradition of Jesus' own trial or hearing before the Jews.[195]

As a whole, the christological controversies in ch. 5 and ch. 10 present a remarkably consistent picture. Jewish accusation that Jesus claims equality or identity with God is rejected at one level, but affirmed at another. In the process the author preserves the claim already expressed in the prologue of Jesus' unique sonship and his being *theos*, setting him apart from all others. At the same time he possesses this uniqueness of being in dependence upon and in subordination to the Father, as on the basis of his distinctive being he does the Father's works and fulfils his commission.

The Son and the Father: 14:8-11

In 14:8-11 Jesus responds to Philip's question, 'Show us the Father', by saying, 'Have I been with you so long, Philip, and you do not recognise me?' This is not a claim on the part of Jesus to be the Father. Rather, as the following comments show, he stands for the Father in the world: 'He who has seen me has seen the Father. How can you say, "Show us the Father"? Do you not believe that I am in the Father and the Father in me? The words which I say to you I do not speak of my own accord, but the Father remaining in me does his works. Believe me that I am in the Father and the Father in me; otherwise believe because of the works themselves' (14:9-11). Mutual indwelling and doing the works of the Father are motifs we have already encountered in 10:38. Seeing the Father by seeing the Son recalls 1:18, according to which the Son makes the Father known, whom no one except the Son has seen. The new element here, of the Father dwelling in the Son and therefore doing his works in him, is also only a combination of themes already present elsewhere. The Son is not an unconscious mouthpiece of the Father. It is the unique relationship between the two and the Son's willingness that the Father work through him and speak through him that makes possible the claim: anyone seeing me sees the Father.

The Son and the Father: ch. 17

In ch. 17 the Son prays to the Father. In itself this reflects subordination and dependency. Ricca exaggerates in describing Jesus the Son as characteristically the praying Son,[196] but, at least, with Lütgert and Wetter, we can say that it is consistent with the Johannine picture of Jesus the Son as humble and submissive to the Father.[197] The prayer illustrates the distinctiveness of Father and Son and of their relationship and comes closest to 1:1 and 1:18 in describing how the Son had shared the Father's glory before the foundation of the world and would share it again at his glorification. This implies a special claim about the being of the Son, setting him apart from all others. At the same time this distinctive being stands side by side with statements implying subordination. The Son is commissioned, passes on the glory, name, and words of the Father. His bearing the Father's name amounts to saying he bears the function and power of God himself. It comes close to what is expressed by *theos* in the prologue.

The confession of Thomas

In his encounter with the risen Jesus Thomas hails him with the words, 'My Lord and my God' (20:28). Probably an inclusio is intended with the use of *theos* in 1:1, but not in a way that isolates *theos*, as, for instance Wengst does, when he sees caught up in it the notion of the suffering God.[198] We have already noted that 20:28 must not be seen as different from the confession of Jesus as the Christ, the Son of God in 20:31, in a way that would make the latter an anticlimax. For Jesus is *theos* because he is the Son of God sent from the Father. Note the similar transition from 10:30,33 ('one', *theos*) to 10:36 ('Son of God'). Jesus is not *theos* in a way that obliterates the distinction between Father and Son or denies the subordination of the Son to the Father.

The 'I am' sayings and christology

Finally we should make mention of the passages where Jesus uses the words, 'I am', either absolutely, or with a predicate such as light, life, bread. It has been argued that these, and, in particular, the absolute occurrences, represent an allusion to the divine name.[199] This depends upon identifying in John some influence from an alleged use of the divine name in Isaiah and reflected in the LXX *egō eimi*, and possibly directly from its use in Exodus. Were this to be present, we should have here the extraordinary situation that Jesus would be pronouncing the divine name and so making the claim, either that he is Yahweh, the 'I am', or in this particular way uniquely represents him. Our review of the texts indicated that nowhere is such a sense demanded and that in each case a less extraordinary explanation is more natural. This is not to deny that the author (or his tradition) may not have modelled Jesus' self declarations on those of Yahweh in Isaiah, but, as there, the primary meaning in John is that Jesus is all he claims to be, as 8:28f aptly illustrates.[200] Alleged use of the divine name as a self appellation by Jesus fails to convince. This is also not to deny that, when Jesus presents himself as bread and light and life, a claim to offer what God alone can offer is intended. These are not divine titles,[201] but the claim entailed in this kind of self presentation amounts to the assertion, consistently made in the gospel, that the Son uniquely acts and speaks for the Father and it is this claim which lies behind statements without a predicate where Jesus claims, he is the one. The 'I am' statements reflect therefore the heart of Johannine christology; but they do not represent a novum: Jesus' self appellation with the name of God.

The Son's unique being and oneness with the Father

The passages considered thus far present a remarkably consistent picture. The first major point to emerge is that the Son has a unique relationship with the Father and has had since the beginning of time. It is a relationship of love. The unique relationship has to do with the unique being of the Son. He is called (*monogenēs*) *theos*, 'God the only Son', while not identical with God; he is (*monogenēs*) *huios*, 'the only Son', of the Father. As such he is dependent upon and subordinate to the Father; as such he is also uniquely able to fulfil the Father's commission and do his works and thereby present the Father's presence in the world. There is an ontological aspect.[202] Yet the precise nature of his being is left undefined.

Monotheism, christology and wisdom and related traditions

The closest analogy is in the logos/sophia stream, where *theos* could also be used of someone other than God without compromising monotheism. This doubtless paved the way for the kind of christology developed in John and the second century apologists pursued the Logos concept further.[203] As Dunn points out, it also helped ensure the preservation of monotheism.[204] Apocalyptic notions of heavenly beings exercising divine functions and so bearing the divine name also offer analogies. Both may have influenced the way in which the gospel speaks of the Son, but the gospel falls short of offering more than this.

Judaism had been tolerating a range of ways in which God's action was represented by personifications and presences, including glory, name, Spirit, angel of the Lord, wisdom, Shekinah, Torah, and these were never used in a way which implied abandonment of monotheism. They were either direct personifications or beings subordinate to God (angels and, mostly, Wisdom and Logos, though this is still in dispute).[205] The fourth gospel and its legacy would not have encountered difficulty with monotheism had it remained within such streams of thought. But, as it appropriated and formulated its christology, it shows a departure from such streams in three respects.

Christology and Wisdom: the differences

First, the Son Logos is co-eternal with the Father (was there 'in the beginning', not created like wisdom logos, the first of his works of old). This raises the question of shared being with the Father posed already through the formulation of the opening verses of the gospel, but presumed throughout. This would not in itself be a problem for monotheism of the time, but would force one to the personification option, present in a number of places where wisdom tradition is used in Judaism. In that sense this is not strictly a departure. It becomes such in the light of the Christian use of Wisdom to refer to a separate being.

The second is this use of Logos/Wisdom to refer to a being whose relationship with the Father can therefore be described in functional terms of obedience, being sent, coming and going. This, too, need not pose a problem if we were to take such statements as personification. God also sends his Spirit; the Spirit comes and goes.

The third and crucial departure is the identification of the man Jesus of Nazareth with the personal Logos Son. This is not presented in a manner which reduces the human Jesus to an appearance, as we shall see in IIIB4 below. And as we have seen, the central structure of the author's christology gives a major place to identity of being between the pre-existent one and the man Jesus. At this point both monotheism and, at the other pole of the paradox, Jesus' human personhood are threatened. The gospel does not work out solutions to the paradox and the author was unlikely to have been aware of the complexity of the problem which, above all, his gospel posed for the Church to follow. But he marked out the ground on which later theological edifices would rise, including the doctrine of the Trinity. He never ultimately surrendered the real human personhood of Jesus and he asserts at the beginning and assumes throughout the kind of intimacy of shared being between Son and Father otherwise preserved only for Jewish personifications of the divine. But even these poles of the paradox are scarcely defined or precise. For, on the one hand, he sometimes speaks of the Son as if he were a separate pre-existent being. It is hard to understand the envoy model descent ascent model otherwise. And, on the other, he sometimes speaks of the human Jesus as if he were no longer human, as we shall see in the next chapter. We see christology in a state of flux or, to change the metaphor, we can identify the two poles and also see how at times they bend to the point of breaking, but ultimately they remain in place and this was a significant contribution of the fourth gospel to the theology and christology of the Church to follow.

Not ditheism

Accordingly the gospel vigorously defends itself against the charge of ditheism, and assumes, legitimately so.[206] It even turns such accusations around ironically and responds to them always from a point of view which sets Jesus in a functional unity of subordination with the Father, without denying the Son's distinctive being. He does as the Father does, and this also includes exercise of miraculous powers normally reserved for God, such as walking on water, keeping his own, raising the dead, raising himself from the dead and being the bearer of glory.[207] Evans notes that the use of glory is the nearest the Hebrew tradition came to ontology.[208] But there is no merging of Jesus into God.[209] Nor is Jesus a divine emanation.[210] Yet neither are there two divine beings.[211]

Not begotten

There is also no word of the Son's eternal generation by the Father,[212], nor, on the other hand, any mention of a beginning of the Son's existence. Birth from above (3:3) is not such an allusion, but, like 1:12f, applies only to believers. Neither *monogenēs* nor 1:13 contains reference to the Son's birth. The former means 'only one, the unique one' and in relation to fatherhood and sonship, 'the only Son'; the latter would speak of the Son's birth only when the variant singular reading should prove original, and then need mean no more than the human birth of Jesus by a virgin.[213] The allusion to birth from above refers primarily to Christians in ch. 3, and even though there is a close analogy between the Son's being from above and the disciples' being 'from above', at no point is the language of birth applied directly to Jesus.[214]

Not incarnate awakened sonship

There is no indication that sonship belongs to Jesus only since the incarnation, as Lütgert argues, on the grounds that the prologue preserves the word Logos for the pre-existent being.[215] He treats the birth of Jesus as the point at which he is sent[216] and speculates that the Logos makes the Son aware of his original divinity.[217] It is true that the prologue uses the motif Logos in this way, but never elsewhere in the gospel is there the slightest indication that 'Son', let alone, 'Father', is inapplicable to the pre-existence and regularly the sending is associated with commissioning as an act which must be in pre-existence, for it is on the basis of it that the Son came from above in the first place.

Not adopted at birth or baptism

Lütgert is concerned to ward off views which see the unity of Father and Son as primarily one of will and thought, such as Holtzmann had propounded.[218] But his theory of a unity of being mediated by the Spirit, a position followed by Büchsel and Strathmann, also falls short of the Johannine conception.[219] He ends up with a Spirit mediated unity on earth, but a substantial unity of the Logos and God in pre-existence.[220] A modern, yet also ancient variant of this view is that propounded by Watson,[221] who identifies, like Fuller earlier,[222] the baptism of Jesus as the point when the anhypostatic Logos enters the human being, Jesus, and takes 1 John 5:6, with its reference to coming by water, to mean coming through baptism, a position therefore akin to Cerinthus.[223] 'Son' is also more than a metaphor to describe a functional unity and more than doxological, as if the evangelist is merely describing the human ideal, as Robinson and, earlier, Beyschlag suggest.[224]

Not later trinitarian syntheses

Nor have we indication in the gospel that Jesus operates with two egos, an 'I am' of pre-existence and an obedient human self, as Fuller proposes.[225] The gospel must be allowed to speak in its own terms without our reading in the christologies of later centuries.[226] Braun and Riedl, for instance, read the fourth gospel in line with the developments in later christological thought and claim that we have in John a binitarian metaphysical unity, one in which unity of being is combined with awareness of distinct subjects acting in love and oneness.[227] Blank holds the two in tension, speaking of an irreducable separateness in unity to be understood neither in mythological nor pantheistic terms, nor as a statement of simple identity.[228] He speaks of the 'christological implication' of the fourth evangelist's portrayal of Jesus.[229] Ibuki similarly stresses unity of being.[230]

Not oneness without real subordination

Baur had argued that the Son was not created, but was born of the Father and emphasised that such was the unity that no independent thought was possible,[231] but this denies the assumption of willing obedience we find throughout the gospel. It is nevertheless interesting to see the strength of the emphasis on oneness in

Käsemann and to find in Appold a survival of the view that obedience and
subordination are foreign to Johannine christology.[232] Yet Appold is hesitant to
define the nature of the oneness he stoutly defends. He denies it is metaphysical or
trinitarian, claims that more than a moral unity is presupposed for pre-existence,
and prefers to speak of a unity in which Father and Son have equivalent status,
'equivalent relationality' and mutually conditioned reciprocity.[233] He is right in
observing that the fourth gospel does not offer a precise definition, though in his
analysis he fails to do justice to the element of subordination. Pollard, too, claims
the author gives no precise definition.[234] Langbrandtner goes beyond the evidence
when he claims that for the Grundschrift the Logos is understood as an extension
of God, not a separate person, whereas the emphasis on distinct persons comes
first through the Redactor's addition of 1:3 and 1:14-18.[235]

The unique Son subordinate in oneness with the Father

The second most important point to emerge from our review of the passages is that
the Son is consistently presented as subordinate to the Father. This is not to be
explained away using two nature theory or by defining roles within the trinity on
the basis of the implied dependence in the imagery of 'Father' and 'Son'.[236] Nor is
subordination something limited to the earthly Jesus, as Lütgert's position
assumes.[237] Nor is there a kind of kenosis as Busse suggests, when he proposes that
the Logos surrenders its nature so that only through a unity of action one may
recognise God.[238] Precisely in his uniqueness of being as the Son of the Father
Jesus is also subordinate to the Father.[239]

Subordination and sending

The Father sent the Son. Above all Miranda and Bühner have emphasised the
importance of this motif and by implication the centrality of subordination in the
relation of Father and Son.[240] Miranda sees two streams merging in the gospel, that
of messianic and prophetic sending and that of the sonship of Jesus, in such a way
that a functional christology combines with one of distinctive relationship,
producing the christology of obedient sonship of the pre-existent sent one.[241]
Bühner identifies in the fourth gospel a combination of influences from the judicial
shaliach, the common envoy procedures, and the sent prophet and angel, and
Becker, importantly, notes that in John this sending stream must be seen as
merging with the distinctive wisdom stream.[242] One could say that this merging
accounts for much of the tension between the more strongly ontological
orientation of the logos traditions and the primarily functional orientation of the
sending tradition. Both aspects are present in each, but in different proportion.
Subordination is still common to both.

While the author uses the revelation-communication pattern in a non literal way,
he upholds the notion of the Son's obedience to a heavenly commission and his
continuing dependence on the Father during his earthly ministry. The author
assumes that the Son comes from the Father, from heaven to earth, completes his
commission, and then returns. With endless variation the author has Jesus repeat
this claim. The sending of the Son is central to Johannine faith.

Sending and oneness

Sending should not be seen as rivalling oneness as the centre of Johannine christology. Both Käsemann, and more particularly, Appold argue that sending is unable to integrate the whole of Johannine christology as oneness does.[243] At 5:19f a different image is employed. But their stress on oneness is given at the expense of motifs of subordination, sending, commissioning and obedience in the text. The problem with oneness is that it leaves too much undefined. The oneness between the Son and the Father is beyond dispute in the gospel. But what kind of oneness is it and in what way is it perceived to function? As a motif it is relatively rare. As a concept applied to the text it does integrate much of what is there in a way that is far more effective, than, say, Haacker's notion of Founder. But it is methodologically more satisfactory to identify the underlying structure of the author's thought than to seek one focal motif or to impose one overriding concept. By seeking the underlying structure we have been able to show how both oneness and sending belong, and to show what they mean in the gospel much more concretely than has been done by Appold. Haenchen's attack on the oneness motif, on the other hand, sees only the occurrence of the motif and fails to perceive the way in which Appold uses the notion.[244] Hahn is right in seeing three key elements in the gospel: oneness, sending, witnessing,[245] but that, too, does not go far enough, for it fails to show the integrating structure within which they belong.

Christocentric or theocentric?

It is consistent with the thoroughgoing christocentric interpretation of Käsemann and Appold that they fail to do justice to the notion of subordination and so make christology not theology the centre of the gospel. Lieu also emphasises the central role of Christ, especially compared with the first epistle where he is cast more in the role of founder and vicarious redeemer, but ultimately this central role of Christ in the gospel makes sense only because of the gospel's particularly theocentric approach in regard to its christology.[246] Haenchen and Becker strongly emphasise the sending motif and therewith theocentricity.[247] Barrett notes that the evangelist has the ministry of Jesus end with an openness for more to be said through the ministry of the Spirit and uses Davey's observations to show that the Son is dependent upon the Father for power and knowledge. Thus Christ remains strongly in the role of the mediator and revealer.[248] Scroggs exaggerates in claiming that we have in John complete subordination and complete equality.[249] Rather in his unique being, the Son, so superior to all others, acts in a unity of will and obedience with the Father which only his unique being makes possible.

The Son and the Father: Conclusions

Accordingly, we find within the gospel a christology of Jesus' sonship which does not easily fit the familiar categories. There is a definite ontological claim about the Son's being, which sets him apart from all others. As such, he is separate from God, yet as such, also uniquely able to do his works and speak his words. His relationship with the Father is one of love and obedience and, in obedient submission to the Father who sent him, he comes into the world offering to human beings all that the Father offers: light and life and truth. To receive him is to receive him who sent him. To see him is to see the Father. To enter a relationship of love with him is to do so also with the Father. To reject him is to reject the Father. Rejected by the world, he returns, ascending, exalted and glorified to the Father. He is vindicated; the world is judged; the Spirit is given; the disciples sent. He remains the unique Son, at one with the Father, always and obediently concerned to glorify the Father.

The undefined yet impressive emphasis on the unique being of the Son and his relationship with God raises, in turn, the question to what degree the author has defined the nature of this sonship in relationship to Jesus' humanity and to this we turn.

4. The Nature of the Son as Jesus of Nazareth.

We have considered the statements of the central structure of the author's christology which deal with the return of the Son to the Father, the nature of his 'revelation' as salvation event, the meaning of pre-existence and the nature of the Son in relation to the Father. The latter emphasised the unique being of the Son which also enabled him to fulfil his Father's commission in coming as the sent one into the world. As the sent one, making the Father known through his earthly ministry, he is Jesus of Nazareth. As we examined his nature as unique Son of the Father, so we now examine his nature as Jesus of Nazareth. How is his humanity portrayed in the gospel? And how is it likely that the author intended it should be understood? I distinguish these two questions, because an examination of what the artist has drawn may well reveal features belonging to the finished product which give an impression different from what the author intended, inasmuch as intentions are at all evident.

Real pre-existence and real coming

I want to begin with findings drawn from our analysis thus far. One is, that, the gospel employs revelation-communication language only as a way of claiming that the Son represents the Father's offer of life, and not literally as a description of an information giving process, whereas it uses the language of coming from pre-existent heavenly intimacy with the Father as a description of what actually happened. The Son, pre-existent with the Father, comes into the world, commissioned by him, to bring life to the world. This means, at the same time, that the author works with spatial and temporal categories, which enable him to describe movement from heaven to earth and earth to heaven. Believers look forward to the sight of the Son's glory in heaven, a vision not possible as long as they are on earth (17:24-26). Similarly Jesus, while on earth, had looked forward to his return to the Father in glory. Therefore theories of the Son somehow straddling heaven and earth during his earthly ministry or moving constantly between the two, as Lütgert proposed,[250] have no place in the author's christology. His oneness with the Father on earth never means his presence in heaven on earth. Behind the author's christology is a cosmological perspective according to which God is active and present on earth, but there exists a heaven in which God's being is more intensively present. This is the view common to all New Testament writers.

Real continuity of being

The Son's presence means therefore a departure from this heavenly presence. In this there is loss for the Son. Therefore also he looks forward to his return. In this he shared with human beings life on earth as distinct from life in heaven. Thus Thüsing speaks of the Son's giving up the glory of heaven.[251] The extent to which this represents humiliation will be addressed below when we also take into account the nature of his suffering and death. The Son's coming is a real coming in the sense that he does not cease to be the Son during his earthly ministry, but speaks and acts in full awareness of being the Son sent from the Father. Nowhere does the gospel indicate that this was an awareness awakened at some specific point in Jesus' ministry, as Lütgert suggested,[252] nor that the Logos or Spirit adopted[253] or became incarnate[254] in him only through the waters of baptism. Nor is there the slightest indication of duality in the Son as Jesus of Nazareth.[255] The Son is Jesus of Nazareth and Jesus of Nazareth is the Son, the one subject, the one Son who was with the Father from the beginning. The evangelist reveals no awareness of problems here. He does not ask: would the child Jesus have possessed the same full self awareness, the same knowledge? His interest is to tell of the Son's confrontation with the world in the event of his ministry and death.

Similarly the interest of the author is not to present Jesus as omniscient, though he tells of occasions of miraculous knowledge, nor as omnipotent, though he tells of miraculous deeds. His interest is to present him as a person demanding faith and allegiance toward himself and so towards God. It is for this that the Son came. And it is for this that he tells of the Son's pre-existence and sending. This consistent perspective throughout the gospel has important methodological implications. Miracles of knowledge and power have a subordinate role and must be weighted accordingly in examining the author's christology.

The Spirit and Jesus of Nazareth - adoption?

We begin our analysis by considering the significance of the Spirit for understanding the nature of the Son as Jesus of Nazareth. The fact that the author's account of the earthly life of Jesus concentrates only on the period following his baptism has led to a good deal of speculation about its significance, particularly as a way of explaining continuity of consciousness between the pre-existent Son and the earthly Jesus. This began with early gnostic teachers, like Cerinth, who proposed that the Son first entered the man, Jesus of Nazareth at this point (Iren Adv Haer I 14:6; Clem Alex Theod 43:5; 61:6). The same suggestion has been put forward again in more recent times by Watson.[256] Is John the Baptist's cry, 'Behold the lamb of God, who takes away the sin of the world', really saying that here is the body to be sacrificed, which the Son will now take upon himself or into which he will now enter? The narrative of the baptism contains nothing to support this view. For the Baptist goes on to speaks of his pre-existence, without any indication of a distinction of persons or of anhypostatic pre-existence only.

The Spirit and Jesus of Nazareth - establishing continuity?

More serious attention has been given from time to time to the theory that the coming of the Spirit in baptism established the continuity of consciousness between the Son as the man Jesus of Nazareth and the pre-existent Son as Logos. Cadman argues that the Spirit enabled Jesus to perceive himself as taken up into the Logos of God.[257] Lütgert identifies Spirit and Logos.[258] Weiss distinguishes between Jesus' receiving the Spirit for self awareness and his having received revelation already before baptism because of the Logos, citing the Baptist's words in 1:30f.[259] Büchsel sees the receiving of the Spirit as part of the process of incarnation.[260] Such views once had the support of a number of scholars and it is instructive to read the critical discussion in earlier writers like Holtzmann and before him Baur.[261] The baptism narrative also fails to support these views. There is not even the report of a vision, as in Mark. It would be a strange conflict of imagery if Jesus, on the one hand, claims that he tells what he had seen and heard and, on the other, knows that he needed to be reminded by the Spirit.

Jesus' baptism: bestowal or statement of what is?

Nevertheless the role of the Spirit in relationship to the Son during his earthly ministry is an important issue. The key texts are the Baptist's report of the descent of the Spirit in 1:32-34; the references to birth of the Spirit in 3:1-11; the statement about Jesus' receiving the Spirit in 3:34f; and the link between Jesus' words and the Spirit in 6:63. According to the Baptist's witness in 1:32-34, the descent of the Spirit enables the Baptist to identify Jesus as the pre-existent one, the lamb of God, the elect one or Son of God, and the one who baptises with the Holy Spirit. Beside this, the other distinctive feature, in comparison with the Synoptic accounts, is that the narrative explicitly adds that after its descent the Spirit not only descends but also remains on Jesus.

Already Baur argued that for John the descent of the Spirit is nothing more than a sign for the Baptist[262] and Holtzmann notes that already Matthew has turned it into a declaratory act for the sake of others.[263] Does the remaining of the Spirit on Jesus also symbolise his prophetic equipping with the Spirit from that point onwards,[264] or his equipping with the Spirit at his pre-existent commissioning onwards, as Bühner suggests?[265] Or is it a symbolic declaration of the permanent availability to him of the the Spirit through his eternal intimacy with the Father or the unique nature of his being? Burge, for instance, while acknowledging the tension which exists between Spirit possession tradition and the incarnation of the Son, the Logos, suggests that the Spirit should be understood here not primarily as a power, but as an attribute of his person.[266] The meaning of the dove's descent must be considered in the light of the other important statements about the Son and the Spirit in the gospel and to these we turn.

The Father gives the Spirit to the Son without measure (3:34)

In IIA2 we discussed the translations of 3:34b and argued for the view that it be understood as a statement about God's giving the Spirit to Jesus, not of Jesus' giving the Spirit to others. 'He whom God sent speaks the words of God; he does not give (him) the Spirit by measure. The Father loves the Son and has given all things into his hands' (3:34f). This could refer to a giving of the Spirit at baptism,[267] or in pre-existence at his sending as he is given all things (3:35),[268] but the present tense, *didosi* ('he gives'), makes it morely likely that it refers to a constant state. It is therefore to be taken closely with the present tense in the statement, 'The Father loves the Son' and with the perfect tense of, 'and has given all things into his hands' (3:35). We may detect a tension here between the image of permanent abiding and constant giving, but this should not be pressed and reflects the merging of different traditions. The focus is primarily on the fullness, 'without measure' (cf. 'all things' 3:35). This would also receive confirmation through 6:63 which shares with 3:34 a reference to Jesus' words and identifies them with spirit and by implication with the work of the Spirit: 'The Spirit is what makes alive, the flesh is of no profit; the words which I have spoken to you, they are spirit and they are life' (cf. 'He whom God sent speaks the words of God; for he does not give (him) the Spirit by measure' 3:34; similarly also 14:17). 3:34

favours therefore an interpretation which sees the descent of the dove in John as symbolising a permanent state of affairs. Correspondingly it is the one so identified who can baptise with the Spirit. He was of unique being and John recognises this.

The Son, born of water and the Spirit? 3:1-11

The earlier sections of ch. 3 should also not be seen as implying that Jesus was equipped or born of the Spirit at his baptism. The issue arises because in contrasting in 3:1-11 Nicodemus, on the one hand, and the disciples, on the other, the author makes statements which identify Jesus so strongly with his disciples, that one might easily apply what is said of them also to Jesus himself. This is particularly evident in 3:11, where Jesus says, 'What we know we speak and what we have seen to that we bear testimony and you do not receive our testimony.' Similarly the use of the wind simile in 3:8 raises questions of origin and destination in a way usually applied to the Son's coming and going. But there is no evidence that we should extend this further and see in 3:3 or 3:5, which describe birth by water and the Spirit, also a christological reference either to the Son's birth or to his receiving the Spirit by baptism.[269]

Permanent bestowal of the Spirit: Conclusion

The passages considered suggest that we best understand the Spirit as a constant gift of the Father to the Son and Jesus' baptism as a sign of this giving, of its permanence, and as a sign for the Baptist that Jesus is the expected one and the one whose pre-existent glory he affirms. The gospel does not make explicit whether there was a point when Jesus was first given the Spirit or whether the Spirit, like love, has been the constant gift of the Father to the Son from the beginning. The former might be understood in association with the Son's commissioning and authorisation, offering a close analogy with the disciples' receiving the Spirit and their commissioning. The latter is more probable and would see the Spirit as another way of describing that quality of eternal relationship of Son and Father which enables him to represent the gift of divine life to the world. Nowhere did we find evidence that the gospel uses Spirit as the mediator of awareness between the human Jesus and the pre-existent Logos or as the means whereby the Logos supposedly enters or takes up the human being Jesus of Nazareth at his baptism or an earlier point in time. The nature of the Son as Jesus of Nazareth is not such that he is a human being possessed of the Spirit, for the Spirit is the Father's gift to the Son. His nature as Jesus of Nazareth comes much more into focus when we turn to the theme of incarnation.

The Word became flesh: 1:14a in 1:14-18

The coming of the Son into the world is most frequently defined in association with incarnation, a term based on a single text, 1:14, 'And the Word became flesh.' It is unique in the gospel, but its position as part of the climax of the prologue demands that it be considered carefully as a christological statement. The statement in 1:14 may be set out as follows:

'(a) And the Word *egeneto* flesh
(b) and tented among us,
(c) and we beheld his glory,
(d) glory as of the only (Son) of the Father,
(e) full of grace and truth.'

It is not, itself, the climax, but forms the beginning of the prologue's climax which reaches to 1:18. 1:15 reports the Baptist's witness that the one referred to is the superior pre-existent one. 'John bears witness concerning him and has cried out saying, "This was the one of whom I said, He who comes after me is my superior, because he was before me."' In that sense, 1:15 expands the second half of 1:14 which speaks of the glory and eminence of the Son. 1:16f, in developing the contrast with the Law, also expands 1:14, taking up 14e: 'Because from his fullness we have all received grace replacing grace; for the Law was given through Moses, grace and truth came through Jesus Christ.' 1:18 also focusses on the salvific work of the Son. 'No one has ever seen God; God the only Son, who is in the bosom of the Father, he has made him known.' At the same time it echoes the language of 1:14d ('unique' *monogenēs* and 'Father') and puts 14c in different words, for to see the glory (14c) is to see the Father made known in the Son (18). I have translated *eskenōsen* as 'tented'(14b), since it doubtless alludes to the divine presence in the wilderness tabernacle. 14a is the primary link with what precedes, for it is the Logos of 1:1-3 who is being described in 14-18 as the only Son of the Father who makes God known.

Both 14a and 14b already contain or imply a reference to what is seen on earth (the Word, the divine presence), but primarily they describe how this comes to be. They are, in that sense, preparatory. The central focus of 1:14-18 is on the presence and presentation of God in the Son. Already Baur stressed the preparatory or subordinate role of 14a in comparison with 14cde[270] and the same point has been particularly emphasised by Käsemann.[271] What significance is to be attached, then, to the particular formulation in 1:14a? The author might easily have employed one of the gospel's more common formulations and said, that the Logos came or was sent into the world. The widely held assumption that he uses a traditional source here may well account for the difference of formulation, but this still calls for an explanation how the author might have understand these words and what weight we should give them in explicating his christology.

The Word became flesh: 1:14a and what precedes

When we read 1:14a also in relation to what precedes, we find that the prologue has already spoken of the coming of the Logos into the world: 'The true light, which gives light to every person, was coming into the world' (1:9); 'He came to his own and his own did not receive him' (1:11). Some interpret these as references not to his coming in Jesus, but to his work in the world of creation and with Israel.[272] Accordingly 1:14a would be a climax and emphasise that the Word came in a new way, 'in the flesh', in Jesus. I think it very likely that the author's tradition might have meant this once, when it existed as a variant of the Wisdom story applied to Jesus.[273] But in its present form the prologue refers already in 6-8 to John the Baptist and uses the present tense of *phainei* ('shines') in 1:5, so that the verses 9-11 most naturally read as descriptions of the coming of the Son in

Jesus of Nazareth.[274] Accordingly 1:14a represents another way of referring to the same event and not a contrast with previous ways in which the Logos might have come. The debate about the meaning of the prologue's statements of coming will continue and in following those who support the latter position I do not want to exclude from our discussion the former position. I shall, therefore look at the implications of both for our investigation.

The Word became 'flesh' - meaning?

If 1:14a represents a climax, on the former view, or, on the latter, a contrast with the previous descriptions of the same event of the Logos's coming into the world, there is still the question what the author means or intends by using the word, 'flesh'. Bultmann identifies here a deliberate paradox, the central theme of the gospel, the presence in human flesh of the divine Logos.[275] He also identifies it as deliberately antidocetic.[276] Richter identifies 1:14a as belonging to an antidocetic redaction of the gospel, of which he finds evidence also in 19:34f,39f; 20:24-29; 20:2-10; 6:51-58 and Thyen and Langbrandtner argue similarly.[277] If an emphasis on paradox, with or without the antidocetic motive, is present, then it is strange that the author passes away from it so quickly to place all the attention on glory and that in referring back to 1:14 in 1:15-18 he never returns to this theme. This also counts against seeing 1:14a as a major focus either as a climax or a contrast with the previous description of the coming of the Logos (Son) into the world. 1:14a may rather simply be a way of identifying the coming of the Logos in the man Jesus,[278] as the place where it was experienced.[279] According to Ruckstuhl the incarnation is implied, but carries no emphasis since it is already assumed in what has been said.[280] Or flesh is merely the basic where-with-all for communication among people, the manner of appearance, as Käsemann argued.[281] The statement is not primarily the highlighting of a paradox,[282] as Bultmann suggests, nor primarily an antidocetic declaration.[283] On the other hand, I would find it hard to rule out the possibility that these may be subordinate concerns, depending upon what precisely *sarx egeneto* means.

The Word 'became' flesh - meaning?

There is a variety of possible interpretations of the word *egeneto* in 1:14. The most common meaning of *ginomai* is 'become', so that 1:14a is regularly is translated: 'The Word became flesh'. But what does it mean to 'become'? It cannot mean a transformation of being in which the Logos became only what flesh is and ceased to be what flesh is not, for the author assumes a continuity of consciousness. This is widely recognised.[284] Büchsel therefore says it must mean that the Logos took upon himself human flesh.[285] But what does that mean? B. Weiss argued that 'flesh' is always personal, equipped with a soul ('beseelt').[286] This was in part a reaction against Baur, who had pointed out that the author might have written *anthrōpos* (a human being) instead of 'flesh' and, accordingly, claims that 'flesh' here should be understood as a covering ('Hülle').[287] This would allow a close parallel with 14b where tent imagery is present, tent being a common image for the human body. To see here, on the other hand, a kenotic christology of the kind found in Phil 2:6-11 scarcely fits the following context according to which what happened in 1:14 made divine glory visible.[288] The author offers us not a Son emptied of divine powers, but on the contrary one who is full of all authority and in himself brings divine life and light. The only loss of is the loss of having to depart from the intimacy of the heavenly divine presence.[289] The Son remains the Son on earth and never distinguishes between his nature and obedience as Son on earth and his nature and obedience as Son in heaven.

Käsemann returned to the position substantially represented already by Baur (see above), in arguing that 1:14a is primarily speaking of manner of appearance, human guise.[290] He reinforced his claim by correctly highlighting the centrality of 1:14c and thus challenged the role Bultmann and others had given to 1:14a. He went on to argue that the picture of Jesus in John's gospel is naively docetic.[291] But his espousal of the Baur interpretation of 1:14a is hardly convincing. The word *egeneto* usually carries with it more than this. It can mean little more than appearance (cf. 1 Jn 1:2)[292] and this is how later gnostic Christians interpreted this verse (cf. NH XIII 50:12-15; I 113:37; I.44,13f);293 and, as Berger shows,[294] the verb can mean 'come' of the Lord's coming into people (Barn 6:14-16) or 'come to appear' as in Justin's description of Logos appearing as the fire of the burning bush (Dial 127f). Many argue that here it must mean something like 'came on the scene of history,'[295] or be similar to Gal 4:4.[296] *egeneto* with *sarx* suggests a change in mode of being[297] and some see this as emphatically stressing a full entry into the human condition.[298]

The Word became flesh - to be read in the context of the gospel

On the other hand, the problem posed by 1:14a can never be solved in isolation from the the rest of the gospel.[299] Its interpretation has suffered far too much by people treating it as a key to the gospel, but not reading it first within the wider context to which it belongs. Accordingly, I shall consider the wider issue of Jesus' humanity in the gospel as a whole, bearing in mind the questions raised by 1:14a. In doing so, I want to keep in mind both aspects of the question with which we began: how does the portrait look to us and what, if anything, can we know of how the author would have interpreted it, assuming that the answer may not necessarily be identical in each case?

Jesus, a god at play in Galilee?

The problems of the Johannine picture of the humanity of Jesus have long concerned exegetes and came to the fore once again through the explosive essay of Käsemann.[300] Already earlier, scholars like Baur, Wrede, Holtzmann, Wetter, and Bousset had described the Son as being like a God striding across the world, rather than a human being.[301] The following features have led many to deny that we can speak of a real humanity of Jesus in the fourth gospel.

Supernatural knowledge and power: tradition and heightening

Jesus appears to have extraordinary capacity to know what is usually beyond the humanly possible.[302] He sees Nathanael under the fig tree when it was impossible for him normally to have seen him. He knows of the husbands of the Samaritan woman. He also has extraordinary miraculous power beyond what is evident in the Synoptic gospels. He not only feeds the 5000 and walks on the water; he also changes water into wine, raises Lazarus from the dead after four days, and performs a healing miracle at very great distance from the scene.

Some of these miracles show signs of having already been heightened before the author came to retell them, as in the Johannine version of the centurion's servant/official's son's healing at Capernaum. But, while the author constantly warns against faith centred solely on Jesus as miracle worker, he never suggests that the miracles had not happened, nor diminishes their fantastic character. Sometimes it seems he has himself heightened them.[303] He has also heightened the degree of Jesus' supernatural knowledge (eg. 5:6; 6:6, 15a; 11:11; 16:19; 18:29).[304] The author is doubtless responsible for a number of passages of typical Johannine irony, which often entail a heightening of the miraculous for their effect.

Miracles and the Evangelist

Wilkens notes that the raising of Lazarus as a miracle is made to perform an important role in his description of what led to the passion.[305] Wengst notes the role of Jesus' miraculous foreknowledge in assuring the reader that Jesus' passion was not an accident.[306] Langbrandtner argues that the author (of the Grundschrift) both heightens and criticises miracles (eg. 9:6f; 11:53), while at the same time maintaining that the miracles in themselves are irrelevant for faith.[307] Becker sees the author using a miracle source, but correcting its *theios anēr* christology.[308] Fortna sees the author doing little to combat *theios anēr* christology and, unlike Becker, sees the Signs Gospel (which include Becker's signs source material and more) as already docetic, with the evangelist heightening both the divinity and the humanity of Jesus and portraying the ministry more as an epiphany than had his source.[309] Schottroff speaks of the author retaining miracles in full force, but seeing in them the innerworldly irrelevant aspect of reality which calls forth a false innerworldly miracle based faith.[310] But they are hardly irrelevant for the author, for he, himself, heightens them. Nor, therefore, are they to be seen with Bultmann as merely a concession to human weakness.[311]

At the other extreme, Käsemann argues that the author would even find the miracles inadequate since they reflect so little of the divine glory.[312] Schnelle argues that the miracles serve the gospel's antidocetic purpose, but does so mostly in the form of assertions in summaries, with very little grounding in the text.[313] I fail to see how in John the miracles serve to emphasise the reality of the incarnation in a sense which could be seen as antidocetic by heightening their massive character, as he suggests.[314] At most, in this regard, they identify Jesus as the Christ who did these things and manifested divine glory, but that begs the question about the nature of this Jesus in regard to docetism. More relevant to an antidocetic stance would be Gnilka's comment that Jesus as miracle worker shows traits of humanity such as weeping and that miracles such as those of the fourth gospel are not found in gnosticism.[315]

Miracles remain miracles: manifestations of glory and symbols

There is little doubt that the miracles remain miracles in John and so present us with a Jesus of extraordinary knowledge and power. We are to read them as evidence that he is indeed the Son who has come from the Father. This is so even though their primary function for the reader is to be signs of the one who brings the bread of life, light, life and resurrection which they symbolise. At times, Baur claimed, real humanity almost disappears from view, as in 7:10,15; 8:59; 10:39; 6:10f, and ceases to be human flesh.[316] Consistent with this power he has authority to lay down his life and take it up again in resurrection and return to the Father (10:18; 2:19-22).

Miracles and the issue of real humanity

In itself the performance of miracles, including miracles of foresight, did not carry with it the implication that a wonder worker was not a human being, according to the popular anthropology of the day. Sometimes miracles were claimed as evidence that someone possessed divine nature and so ceased to that extent to be a mortal human being.[317] But often such miracles were seen as possibilities for human beings who, as prophets or wonderworkers, were gifted with divine powers or with the Spirit of God. In that sense the presence of such phenomena within the life of human beings in no way compromised their humanity. The difference between such figures and the Jesus of the fourth gospel is that Jesus is not pictured as one gifted with divine powers received on earth, but as a divine being acting in this way amongst men and women in the world with his own divine power. As

Barrett puts it, he is both too human and too divine to be a *theios anēr*.[318] At the
same time, the observation that miracles need not necessarily have been seen as
compromising humanity leaves open the possibility that the author could in some
way still hold that the Son who so worked was also human flesh and blood and did
not compromise what he perceived as humanity.

The discourses and dialogues and the issue of real humanity

More than the miracles exhibit superhuman ability: the discourses and dialogues
pose real problems for a human picture of Jesus. For in these we see Jesus
constantly taunting his opponents with double meaning as he asserts an authority
based on a premise they do not share, and behaving toward his conversation
partners in a way that takes full advantage of his superior knowledge and their
ignorance of his meaning to a degree that Robinson, for instance, speaks of an
impression of arrogance and megalomania.[319] The woman of Samaria is hopelessly
at sea with Jesus' cryptic remarks which she cannot have been expected to
understand. The Jesus of the dialogues and discourses is distanced and many see
him lacking any warmth of character.[320] Above all, Culpepper has documented this
emotional distance in John's characterisation: Jesus lacks compassion and
humanising traits, never really hungers, is little influenced by those around him,
seems incapable of giving a straight answer, knows shrewdly when to withdraw,
and has no real need of prayer except for confirmation and always remains in
control.[321] The humanity of the Lazarus episode is an exception.[322]

The Son's divine self awareness in life and death

Leaving aside the value judgements which often fall against the Johannine Christ
because of such behaviour, we note that the stance of superior knowledge derives
from Jesus' awareness of who he is. He is God's only Son who was pre-existent
with the Father and has come bearing his gift of life to the world. This is
superhuman knowledge. The author never attempts to show Jesus as having only
the knowledge available to a mere mortal. That would make the mission of the Son
impossible. It is true, the Son is not imparting heavenly revelations, as the story
pattern at first suggests; but he nevertheless offers himself as standing for God
because he knows himself as God's only Son come as the sent one from above.

This supreme confidence and awareness explains how sometimes his prayers take
the form of demonstrations for the sake of others of who he is (so 11:41f; cf.
12:30).[323] It also explains his attitude toward his death. For Jesus approaches death
aware of his authority to lay down his life and take it again. He knows his hour is
coming. He knows he will return to the Father. Confidence of return to the Father
and so confidence in the face of death can also characterise human beings,
particularly those with a firm assurance of life beyond. At that level Jesus sets a
pattern of confident faith for his disciples to follow. In itself, therefore, such
confidence does not conflict with the claim to be human. Yet the confidence of the
Son is not the same as that of believers. His is based in his own nature and
awareness as Son. It is assurance divinely given and knowledge supernaturally
available. Accordingly Jesus approaches his passion, conducts himself before the
Jews and before Pilate, and spends the last moments on the cross in the supreme
confidence derived from his self knowledge. In that sense it is, indeed, a

triumphant exit from life, with no cry of forsakenness, only a declaration that the task had been completed.[324] The more important issue is whether his suffering was real or just apparent and to this we shall return.

Jesus of Nazareth a real human being

On the other side of the ledger there are indications in the gospel that the author understands Jesus' humanity to be real. Jesus' conversation partners and his opponents always treat him as a human being[325] and Jesus never takes exception to this assumption. Even though he may at times have Jesus scold them for seeing him only in terms of human parentage, the author never has Jesus deny his human origins.[326] It is possible, as Wead suggests,[327] that the author knew of controversies surrounding Jesus' birth and therefore knew the tradition of the virginal conception; but it is equally possible he did not. The gospel gives no clear indication. What is apparent is that the offence Jesus caused was because of two facts which the author will not see compromised: the Son came from above and he is also Jesus, the man from Nazareth.[328]

Traits of humanity

Similarly Jesus does exhibit characteristic human needs. He is hungry, tired, thirsty; he loves, cries, is angry, needs and receives information, and possibly even changes his plans (11:6,11?). It is not convincing to argue that when in 4:34 Jesus speaks of having food to eat of which the disciples do not know, the will of God, he is thereby denying his need to eat.[329] Nor is it likely that his request of the Samaritan woman for a drink was a mere ploy for setting up his claims to be the water of life.[330] Sometimes statements about the Son's subordination to the Father are cited as evidence of Jesus' humanity, but as we have seen this belongs rather already to his relation as Son with the Father in pre-existence and has no implication for humanity in this sense.[331]

A suffering humanity

He approaches the passion with confidence, but also, in words which reflect Ps 6:3f and probably draw on Gethsemane tradition, speaks of being deeply troubled (12:27). Was this 'being troubled' an uncertainty about what he should pray? That in itself would be a human trait. Was it of the nature of despairing anxiety, as Lütgert suggests ('ratlose Angst')?[332] But this would deny Jesus' foreknowledge of events to come. Nor should the passage be seen as an embarrassment for the evangelist's christology.[333] Maybe it was Jesus' anxiety concerning his disciples whose suffering he had predicted.[334] But it is more likely that we have to do here directly with the prospect of the suffering which awaits him in his nonetheless confident journey through the cross to the Father. Confidence and real suffering are not incompatible. That real suffering is in view receives support from the fact that the author has added Old Testament passages which reflect suffering into the passion narrative.[335] Thüsing goes further and writes that the troubledness of 12:27 remains with Jesus throughout the passion, but there is little trace of this.[336] Fortna suggests that whereas the Signs Gospel (which he postulates as the evangelist's source) had an unmediated relationship between the miracles and the passion narrative, the author uses passages such as 12:27 and the last discourses to mediate between them in a way that directly emphasises Jesus' humanity.[337]

The author never mentions details of how Jesus' suffering pained him. The crucifixion is only briefly described. The mockery is portrayed in all its cruelty, but nothing is said of what Jesus felt. We can only speculate: would the author have believed that Jesus felt nothing of the horror and pain of all of this?[338] Or would he have believed that Jesus did experience it all, but saw it through in triumphant confidence? We cannot be absolutely sure, but the latter is more likely,[339] especially when taken together with Jesus' troubledness in prayer (12:27) and his view of what lay before him as a cup to be drunk (18:11). Accordingly the wretchedness of the mocked one to whom Pilate points with the words, 'Behold the man', is real, even if at the same time the reader knows the irony of the situation and knows Jesus' confidence. I am not, however, convinced by Moloney who sees here an allusion to the Son of Man title and evidence that Son of Man emphasises Jesus' humanity.[340]

If there is some real humanity present on the part of Jesus in the mockery, the same then must also be said of the crucifixion. The reference to blood and water flowing from the side of Jesus, secured by an eyewitness, also belongs here. Its meaning is debated (see the brief review in IIB5), but it most likely refers primarily either to the fact that Jesus really did die or to the fact that he really was flesh and blood.

Antidocetic interests in the gospel?

The context of either claim concerning 19:35 demands some opposing notion, such as that Jesus had not really died or that he was not fully human or both. This is an unusual emphasis in the gospel, rarely found elsewhere, or found in material seemingly the most recent in the gospel and similar to the apparent concerns of 1 John. Because we are concerned to find the strength of the gospel's portrait of Jesus' humanity, we shall consider here those theories which find an antidocetic thrust in the gospel.

Many see it as the work of redaction. Lorenzen argues for an antidocetic interest in the beloved disciple material, securing the reality of Jesus' suffering, death and resurrection.[341] Neugebauer, followed by Thyen and, more recently, Schnelle, argues for an antidocetic reading of 20:31 so that in essence it would be claiming (I think, quite unexpectedly, compared with similar confessional statements in 1:35-49; 11:27) that the Christ is Jesus, the man.[342] Richter and Thyen argue also for an antidocetic purpose in the Thomas episode which precedes[343] and a similar concern is suggested behind 6:51-58.[344] But in none of these is this, to my mind, finally convincing. Schnelle's major attempt to prove that the gospel is written after the epistle and in the light of the docetic problems it encountered has assembled a comprehensive range of arguments to support the hypothesis. But his attempt by its comprehensiveness succeeds on my assessment in being counterproductive of the hypothesis he seeks to prove. The argument from the use of the miracles, already alluded to above, and forming the major part of the book,[345] convincingly shows that miracles matter as an expression of the author's christology, but not that they are antidocetic. We are left then with the sacramental passages and with 1:14 discussed earlier. Where we might most expect the emphasis to show, namely in the major discourses, it is absent.

As it stands in the gospel, the commentary on the water and blood seems to me, nevertheless, to be strong evidence for an emphasis on Jesus' humanity as real humanity and his death as a real death. Whoever wanted to emphasise this would

184   Issues

certainly have understood 1:14 as indicating this real humanity, whether or not it,
too, carries antidocetic character.

The passion narrative: triumphant exit as Käsemann?

The role of the passion narrative and its significance for the reality of incarnation
in Johannine christology has been discussed already in relation to 12:27 and its
implications. I want here to review briefly the debate which Käsemann's
evaluation of the Johannine passion narrative has occasioned, before offering a
summary evaluation and returning to the question raised by 1:14.

Käsemann sees the passion in John as an account of the Son's triumphant exit.[346]
As such the passion, he says, fits awkwardly into Johannine christology and would
have become an irrelevant appendix for the author, had he not sprinkled it liberally
with traits of victory. U.B. Müller suggests that the author employs the passion
narrative not to depict real suffering, but to show up Jesus' opponents and that in
doing so he has made use of a tradition Müller identifies in 1:14,16, which had
seen the miracles as manifestations of divine glory.[347]

The passion narrative: responses to Käsemann

By contrast, Bultmann had spoken of the theologia crucis as not only including the passion
narrative, but also as extending over the entire ministry and as stated in its sharpest form in
1:14.[348] Thüsing had borrowed Kähler's phrase and described the gospel as a passion narrative
with an extended introduction.[349] He also affirms that both theologia crucis and theologia
gloriae are to be found in the gospel. In this way he distinguishes Johannine theology, therefore,
from that of the Philippian hymn.[350] De la Potterie does similarly and attacks Käsemann's
posing of the options as either glorious exit or humiliation and exaltation on the model of Phil
2,[351] preferring to speak of a humiliation of obedience. The fourth gospel presents us with the
unique Son who has come and returns, but in obedient fulfilment of his commission also
endures suffering. Thus Schnackenburg points out that the focus of the passion narrative is
neither on proofs of divinity, on the one hand, nor on humiliation of the kind found in
Philippians, on the other, but on fulfilment of the revelatory task.[352] Wilkens and Barrett speak
of the movement from heavenly glory as indicating loss and real exposure to abuse.[353]

Ibuki also denies the presence of humiliation christology, emphasising the centrality of the
glory of a constantly shared relationship, thereby also countering the triumphant portrait
Käsemann gives, but as we have seen, this fails to take into account the nuances of 'glory'.[354]
Similarly Riedl imports concepts foreign into the gospel when he describes incarnation as the
taking up of humanity into the divine or as the movement of divine glory into human flesh,
even in its suffering, without compromising either.[355] From a different angle Wengst, too,
imposes a foreign construction on the gospel in his thesis that the passion depicts the story of a
suffering God.[356] Sproston is closer to the mark in emphasising Christ's suffering as a model
for the disciples' suffering.[357] Hegermann, in response to Käsemann, relates elements of
victory in the passion to the fact that Jesus goes on to take away sin by exposing its full extent,
though this motif is more implicit than explicit in the narrative.[358] Leistner comes nearer to the
reality of the fourth gospel when he admits the elements of victory and power noted above, but
claims that at the same time the author believed in a real suffering and a real death.[359]

Our analysis above would confirm those who see in the Johannine passion
narrative neither triumphant exit nor abject humiliation, but a path of real
suffering, endured, however, with all the self confidence of the returning Son. The
author neither depicts subjective suffering as such (apart from 12:27) nor indicates
that the occurrences of affliction were any different in their affect on Jesus as a
human being than they would have been on any other person. The lack of interest

of the evangelist at this point counts rather for a normal human experience than against it. There are no hints of the later triumphant 'playing' of the Christ with his tormentors, such as we find when Christ and Jesus are no longer seen as one, as they are still in John. It is probably right to assume that the author was naively unaware of anything in his christology which would count against these being real experiences. But characteristically his interest centres on portraying Jesus as knowing himself to be God's only Son in every situation which confronts him and remaining faithful to his mission to the end.

Returning to 1:14a in the light of the gospel as a whole

What then does 1:14a mean in the light of the gospel? It cannot mean that human flesh is like a garment, a mere disguise to make communication possible. On the other hand, we can speak of a real humanity only in a qualified sense. For the Son who is Jesus of Nazareth remains the Son in full awareness of his being and of his commission to leave the intimacy of his heavenly glory with the Father and enter the world, and in full awareness that his deeds are wrought with the power that derives from his being as Son of the Father from the beginning of time.

Naive docetism?

Barrett speaks rightly of a struggle between the logos idea and the author's belief in the real humanness of Jesus which threatens to undermine the latter.[360] He suggests the author is, therefore, at the same time, both naively docetic and even more naively antidocetic.[361] Davey, too, had spoken of a tension without synthesis.[362] Others have responded to Käsemann's charge of naive docetism by noting its applicability to only certain parts or to sources. Baum Bodenbender denies it is applicable to the passion narrative. She argues that what Käsemann proposes is appropriate as a description of the source of the body of the gospel, whereas Bultmann's notion of paradox in incarnation fits the gospel itself.[363] Similarly Thyen and Langbrandtner describe the Grundschrift of the gospel in docetic terms.[364] Fortna, on the other hand, argues that the description, naive docetism, fits both the 'signs gospel' and the fourth gospel as we have it.[365] Scroggs see the gospel standing in a tradition in which the memory of the human Jesus acts as a restraint on what otherwise would quickly become a docetic christology.[366]

While the presence of miraculous powers need not be (or be seen by the author to be) in conflict with the claim that Jesus was a human being in the full sense, greater difficulties are created by the presence of the kind of self knowledge which the Son possesses. This might be somewhat alleviated with an anthropology which includes pre-existence for all humans, but that does not seem to be the case here.

The author portrays Jesus as a man with human passions and emotions. He affirms both: the real man who dies a real death with a real human body; and the Son with divine powers and knowledge, the unique pre-existent being who comes in obedient fulfilment of his Father's commission and through death returns to his former glory. The author never suggests that the Son's divine powers and awareness are compromised or lessened by his humanity, nor that we should think of Jesus of Nazareth as not a human being. We, from our standpoint, are aware of implications of one for the other. He, in his context, appears never to address this as an issue and may have been quite unaware of it. Against the Jews he constantly has Jesus assert his unique sonship, but never by denying his humanity. Assertion of Jesus' humanity against those who would deny it appears only rarely as an issue in the gospel, probably only in the reference to blood and water flowing from the side of Jesus and possibly indirectly in 1:14a. The author gives no indication of how precisely he would see Jesus' humanity and his unique sonship in relation to one another. I think, had we asked him, he would have answered uncompromisingly that Jesus was truly human. But he would not have surrendered his faith that here is also the Son come from the Father.

We can only wonder, then, how he might have solved the conflict which his portrait raises. He has similarly left open the relation of the Son to the Father. His portrait raised problems for generations to come. It is not that it is consistently docetic, even naively so. Nor is it consistently setting forth Jesus as fully human. It has elements of both. Viewed within the perspective of the anthropology of the day, the docetic tendencies lie really in the claims of Jesus to self awareness as the pre-existent Son come from the Father and not primarily in the miracles. Viewed within our contemporary understanding of humanity, it is above all the massively miraculous elements combined with the way they are related to Jesus' self awareness which seem to compromise the claim to normal humanity. We may dub their anthropology naive; but we must acknowledge, it seems to me, that the portrait still contains many clear indications that he was a human being and that the author saw him thus.

Portrait and Intention

It is instructive to distinguish between the portrait itself and the more elusive intention of the author. In response to Käsemann, Bornkamm had emphasised, amongst other things, that the Johannine christology is a projection of post Easter faith upon the ministry of the earthly Jesus.[367] Accordingly, he argued that the gospel must be seen from the perspective of Easter and the Paraclete, a perspective which understands the cross as paradox. It is this post Easter perspective, he argues, which leads to tension in the gospel's christological statements.[368] The bearing of this observation will vary, depending upon whether we are evaluating the portrait for its possible docetism or for the author's own intention or christology. All it does for the former is explain how the portrait came to be. It in no way invalidates an examination of the portrait with a view to evaluating its docetic character as Käsemann has done. As Schweizer pointed out, a post Easter perspective may produce a gospel where Jesus still cries the cry of deriliction on the cross, as in Mark, or produce one in which the post Easter glory casts its splendour on the earthly life in a way which endangers the historical Jesus, as in John.[369]

The Son as Jesus of Nazareth in the author's christology

Acknowledgement of the post Easter perspective is, however, relevant for the way we evaluate the author's intention, in that sense, his christology. This is particularly the case in John, because there are indications that he was aware in part of this process of projection, both in direct footnotes, such as 2:22 and 12:16, and in the creative shaping of his source material of which we shall say more in the following section.

In that sense we can agree with Nicol that the author has some awareness of the tension which results.[370] This is also the weakness of Käsemann's work, where he claims naive docetism without acknowledging the tension within the gospel.[371] The same must be said of Schottroff who denies the presence of docetism in the gospel because full real humanity is never denied by the author; it is only irrelevant;[372] though later she describes the Johannine Jesus as an inhuman figure, 'unmenschliche Gestalt'.[373] Von den Osten Sacken is nearer the mark in claiming that the author's intention was not docetic, but that the product of his work shows docetic features.[374] Nicol also rightly notes how the author's christological concern threatens to absorb history and so produce docetism, while, at the same time, the same concern gives the earthly Jesus of history a great importance, for it was in history that the glory was manifest.[375]

My assessment of the elusive intention of the author suggested that it would not have compromised either the unique sonship or the real humanity and was probably unaware of the problem in making both statements at once. Within the parameters which both offer he portrays the pre Easter Jesus from a post Easter perspective, without, it seems, intending to compromise either. For him, it seems, neither is dispensable, neither, irrelevant. Yet the resultant portrait raises problems of its own. Here traits of real humanity and unique sonship appear before us largely unmediated. If we fix our gaze at one point, we see Jesus the human figure; if we look at another, we see a divine being. This is the strength of Käsemann's use of the word, 'naive', to describe the docetism that appears, though my analysis suggests that even this is too simple and one sided in the way Käsemann presents it and fails to acknowledge the full extent of the tension in the portrait. In John's gospel we see christology in the making, with many of the tensions unresolved. In the following section I want to suggest that the resultant portrait is all the more complicated because of the author's creative and celebratory literary style, which has produced in many ways a timeless icon of faith. This will, in turn, have bearing on our evaluation of the author's sense of history and understanding of the historical Jesus.

The fourth gospel leaves unresolved the relationship of the unique Son and the humanity of Jesus. It simply asserts both. Subsequent history demanded closer definition and the Johannine Jesus became, not surprisingly, both the central figure of docetist Christianity and eventually also the central figure of those who opposed it. More recently many have constructed a history of the Johannine community which sees the division in the Johannine community, resulting in part from these two potential readings of the gospel and addressed by the members of one side in 1 John and perhaps already through redactional additions to the gospel itself.[376] In the

following section I want to suggest that it is crucial to define carefully the nature
of this document and that failure to do so leads and has led to major distortion of
its message.

IIIC. THE FOURTH GOSPEL IN THE LIGHT OF ITS

CHRISTOLOGY

1. The Gospel and the Jesus of History

How did the author mean his portrait of Jesus to be understood? We do not, of course, have access to the thoughts and intentions of ancient authors except in in so far as they have left direct or indirect indications of them in their writings. In this chapter I shall be examining these indications with the questions: Did the author write his gospel believing he was writing an accurate report of the events of the ministry of Jesus, including Jesus' words? Was he deliberately and consciously using the setting of the earthly historical Jesus in order to portray the Christ of the community's faith as experienced and understood in the period after Easter? Was he at all concerned about the Jesus of history or only about the Christ of faith? Would he have been aware of such a distinction?

It seems to me that the possible answers may be set out as follows:

(a) Objectively reliable historical reporting

The author believed he was writing an accurate report of the events of the ministry of Jesus, including Jesus' words, and occasionally makes his own commentary, which is clearly identified as such. The author was right in what he believed he was doing. This is substantially the position of Morris, Cadman and Riesenfeld.[1]

(b) Intentionally reliable historical reporting

This option is like (a) except for the concluding sentence. Scholars holding this position admit that the author would have been unaware that, in the process of writing, he was portraying Jesus in the light of his own and his tradition's post Easter faith. Thus Grundmann writes of the author taking over inspired words of the exalted Jesus from early Christian prophets as words of the earthly Jesus.[2]

(c) Intentionally creative portrait using historical tradition

The third position holds that the author was aware of using traditions which he believed faithfully depicted the words and deeds of Jesus or had their basis in authentic memory, but not only added commentary; that he also expanded, recreated or created from afresh dialogues and discourses in order to give new expression to who he believed Jesus to have been and to be; that he worked over narrative material similarly, and that he believed his work to be inspired by the activity of the Spirit in the community.

Thus Sidebottom quotes with approval Burkitt's claim that the author seems to have been aware where the historical Jesus tradition stopped and his own thoughts of what he 'must have said' began. A number of scholars see the author operating thus at two levels, one, that of the story in history, the other, that of deeper christological insight. Thus, Smalley, for instance, speaks of the author adding to his historical tradition of Jesus' words and deeds a layer of theological interpretation. In this he refers to Martyn's work, who emphasised, above all, that the interpretative level reflected the situation facing the Johannine church and not only its christology. Smalley also draws attention, like Dodd before him, to the author's concern to present the eternal in the temporal, so that the historical details are reworked in the light of the deeper meaning of the whole. Already Baur had noted that the author lives more with the idea than with history.

(d) Furthering a tradition of intentionally creative portrayal of the earthly Jesus of history

The fourth position is very close to the third, except that it is more willing to concede that already the author's traditions included elements which had been transferred back onto the earthly Jesus.

For instance, Mussner emphasises the historical witness which was borne by the apostolic office and which already combined memory plus interpretative anamnesis. 'Apostolic office' narrows the role of the disciples inappropriately, but others, too, identify a tradition of interpretation borne by disciples. Bornkamm emphasised the importance of the Paraclete sayings as illustrating the way the author would have seen his relationship, but also the relationship of those before him, to historical tradition. Indeed the Paraclete sayings serve as a justification or rationale of the creative shaping which has produced the gospel. Similarly Hahn speaks of a merging of horizons ('Horizontverschmelzung') and of the importance of the figure of the beloved disciple as a link with historical tradition, the 'implied author', as Culpepper brings out. Becker vividly illustrates the former by speaking of two slides projected onto a single screen. Blank, too, notes, that the author would not naively believe that the words of Jesus in ch. 5 were spoken by the earthly Jesus. In discussing the narrative of the wedding feast at Cana, Olsson speaks of a screening of the text, through which both salvation historical Sinai perspectives and post Easter perspectives leave their mark on the narrative, and describes this as a deliberate process on the part of the author, inspired by the Paraclete. The Paraclete and the beloved disciple are not merged into one; rather the beloved disciple stands out in the Johannine tradition in which the Paraclete is given to all.

In both the third and fourth position scholars acknowledge a sensitivity to history on the part of the author despite the subsequent layers of tradition and interpretation.

Mussner, in appealing to 'apostolic office', and Hahn, for instance, in pointing to the function of the beloved disciple, are emphasising this. Similarly Haacker argues against Käsemann's diminishing of the link with history and Hegermann points out that the author has not chosen to speak of the exalted one as presented, for instance, in the early chapters of Revelation, but has written a gospel centred on the earthly historical Jesus. Schnelle argues that the gospel form, which roots faith in history and links it with the earthly Jesus, also reflects an antidocetic concern of the evangelist. Onuki points out that the merging of horizons is the author's way of maintaining historical continuity and holding together the pre- and post Easter image of Jesus. Cullmann sees here an alternative method to that of Luke, who writes two successive volumes, noting how in John 3 the author moves almost imperceptibly from the pre- to the post Easter words of Jesus. While Schnackenburg rightly observes that this particular kind of merging is confined to this chapter, Cullmann's overall assessment of continuity combined in one volume without abandonment of the earthly historical Jesus has strong support. Brown notes how the signs have a similar duality of reference and points out that this includes also an awareness of time before and after Easter. Similarly Onuki argues for the author's consciousness of historical distance, and, like many others, points to passages like 2:21f and 12:16 where we have a more explicit expression of the issue of distance and difference in time between pre- and post Easter than in any of the other gospels. Others point also to the description of the Paraclete which implies historical awareness, especially in its function of bringing to remembrance what Jesus said,[26] although the overlap is present in the Paraclete's mediating also the words of the exalted Lord. Wead also points out that beside the beloved disciple there is also the community itself represented by the author's 'we' in 1:14, which illustrates historical awareness.[27] Culpepper, in particular, has analysed the importance of the author's statements on time in an excellent discussion which includes comments on the 'historical prolepses', such as 2:22 and 12:16, mentioned above.[28]

The presence of historical tradition in John has been especially emphasised by Robinson, following the lead of Dodd, though this also derives, in part, from Robinson's hypothesis of a very date for the gospel.[29] The issue of the presence of historically accurate material in the gospel need not logically hang together with the issue of date and the historical material is much better explained, to my mind, as coming to the author through the nature of his traditions than through direct authorship memory. Robinson, too, however, notes deliberate anachronism in the gospel with the resultant impression of docetism.[30] The author's awareness of temporal distance between his own day and the earthly Jesus is upheld by many. It is a different question to what degree this difference is discernable in specific passages, and a different question again to what degree what the author might have considered historical is in fact so.

(e) Furthering a tradition of creative portrayal of the living Christ without particular interest in the earthly Jesus of history

The fifth option is to deny that the author had any concern with the question of history at all and to maintain that the author used the traditions at his disposal and his own creative genius to portray the living Christ as experienced in the community of faith, and that he did so believing his work the fruit of the Spirit which had been working in this way in the community.

Bultmann's assertion that only the 'Dass', the sheer fact of Jesus' coming, not the 'Was', the details, matter for the author,[31] comes close to this position. Similarly Schlier notes there is no historical development in the Johannine picture of Jesus and suggests that the author has no interest in history, but seeks only to focus on the person of the Son.[32] Käsemann's position is similar, who speaks of the author clothing the dogmatic Christ in the earthly with no interest in the historical Jesus,[33] though he can argue against Bultmann that the miracles were not merely symbols.[34]

Against this option Barrett points out that the author was not satisfied with a timeless mediator in the manner of Philo, but remains committed to the human person Jesus as mediator.[35] Here, too, belong those who believe that the merging has gone to such a degree that the author virtually knew of no other Jesus than the exalted one and so can sometimes have Jesus use tenses, as in 3:13 about ascension, inappropriate for the earthly Jesus.[36] Others, like Nicholson, who acknowledge the fictional quality of much of the author's presentation of the earthly Jesus, nevertheless argue that the author has not created the fiction without also being concerned about the historical link.[37] The expansion of the Jesus tradition, not only through the revelations of the post Easter exalted Lord mediated by the Paraclete, but in particular through devices literary and otherwise to enhance communication and celebration should also be noted here. We return to these below.

What degree of historical interest?

I have identified five positions for the sake of overview. There is considerable variety within each and points where they merge, one into the other. There is a continuum of positions. Along that continuum the degree of interest in the earthly Jesus of history attributed to the author varies from the minimal position of Bultmann to those in the first position in whose mind it is one of the author's vital concerns. Was the author's interest only in the 'Dass', as Bultmann would have us believe? Does it include every detail recorded in the gospel? The answer lies, it seems to me, at neither extreme. We must also allow that the author may have weighted various historical elements differently.

Historical intention and historical achievement

Again, as in our discussion of the issues of the humanity of Jesus, we need to distinguish between the presence of what we, for our part, adjudge historically valuable material in the gospel and what the author, for his part, might have sensed as being historical, as distinct, for instance, from what he knew to be his own or the community's interpretative additions and embellishments. The focus of the present discussion is not on the historicity of John or Johannine tradition from our standpoint, but from the author's. What value did he place on the earthly Jesus as an historical figure? To what degree is his gospel history and to what degree conscious elaboration and embellishment of the tradition which lay before him?

Asking the questions

In what follows I shall defend a version of the fourth option and, in the course of doing so, present arguments which tell against the other four. I shall be pursuing the questions: what evidence is there that the author was aware of development in the Jesus tradition and, if so, how did he understand such development? What indications are there of the way he might have evaluated the products of this development, including his own gospel, in relation to historicity? And are there indications of criteria or of methods which the author employed when engaging in the interpretative process?

The Paraclete: evidence for awareness of historical and interpretative issues

In the last discourses Jesus promises the gift of the Paraclete to his disciples, 'He will teach you all things and bring all things to your memory which I have said to you' (14:26). 'He will bear witness concerning me' (15:26). 'He will convince the world with regard to sin, righteousness, and judgement' (16:8). 'He will lead you into all truth. For he will not speak of his own accord, but what he hears he will speak and he will declare to you the things which are coming. He will glorify me because he will take what is mine and declare it to you. All the Father has is mine; therefore I said, he will take what is mine and declare it to you' (16:13-15).

These logia reveal an awareness on the part of the evangelist that memory of the historical earthly Jesus and his words is an issue of relevance for the disciples.[38] As Porsch points out, this includes awareness that the disciples had not fully understood Jesus during his earthly ministry.[39] 16:13-15 also leaves open the possibility that not only the words of the earthly Jesus but also those of the risen Jesus will be mediated by the Spirit.

Bearers of the Paraclete - not a select few

There is no indication here of a select group, the apostolate, being made bearers of such revelation, as Mussner proposes,[40] as though the Paraclete were to be given to a chosen few. The verses may indicate the presence of inspired prophets in the Johannine community and in its tradition.[41] Schulz, for instance, suggests this in explaining the background of the 'I am' and the Son of Man sayings;[42] and Kundsin pointed to the parallels between the 'I am' sayings and the words of the exalted Jesus in Revelation 1-3.[43] But there is no indication that we should see the Paraclete promise as relating only to Christian prophets,[44] nor, with Minear, see the last discourses as applying only to the wandering charismatic disciple group.[45] The promises are to all the disciples without specifying a particular ministry. All are to abide in the vine and bear fruit; all need the comfort and encouragement of the second Paraclete, because all have been left by the earthly Jesus. Recall of what Jesus said and did is, of course, relevant only for those who were with Jesus, but the promise of 16:13-15 goes beyond memory of what was said and done.

Paraclete and *Methurgeman*?

In a recent monograph Franck seeks further elucidation of the function of the Paraclete in the community and its tradition with a novel theory which combines the idea of prophet and teacher or interpreter of scripture. He suggests, somewhat speculatively, that the Paraclete was modelled in a special way in the Johannine community on the person of the methurgeman, who traditionally translated the scripture into targum in the synagogue and so indirectly also preached.[46] The analogy is interesting and is consistent with the suggestions of Reim[47] and others concerning Targumic traditions in the fourth gospel. It would also explain, by analogy, the relationship of the work of the Paraclete and its bearers to the Jesus tradition and its interpretation. I am not convinced, however, that there is more than an analogy or parallel present.

Paraclete - an open door for new claims of revelation?

Being led into all truth and being told of things to come (16:13) might, if isolated from the context, seem to open the door for all manner of new revelation and, accordingly, Käsemann sees here a claim of charismatic enthusiasts.[48] But, as Haacker and Nicol point out, the context ties this revelation very closely to Jesus and may mean no more than the promise of greater understanding of who Jesus was and is.[49] Nicol includes in this both what Jesus once said and what he might well have said in the light of the full truth of who he is.[50] Schnackenburg speaks of a continuing revelation in the person of the exalted Jesus, but bound to him.[51] This leaves open the extent to which such revelation not only interprets the earthly historical Jesus, but also adds new christological insight. Boring argues similarly that Johannine prophetic activity retained the link with the historical Jesus and was never free floating.[52] Kremer sees the passage not as opening, but rather closing doors, especially against all other truth claims.[53] This may be so. On the other hand, I find Woll's thesis, in this regard, that much of the last discourses is aimed at countering the growing authority of charismatic prophets by subordinating the disciples, by highlighting the prior ascent and higher exaltation of Jesus and by tying the Paraclete promise to him, to be a construction going far beyond what the text justifies.[54]

The Paraclete and 'the things that are coming' - meaning?

The promise, that the Paraclete would also declare 'the things that are coming' (*ta erchomena*), might also indicate teaching in addition to what was given by the earthly Jesus. The expression may reflect Isa 41:22f, as de la Potterie and Porsch suggest, where it is used of future prediction.[55] It might refer to prophecy of the last days, such as we find in Revelation, but the relatively minor place of themes of future eschatology in John make this unlikely,[56] unlikely, at least, for the evangelist. It may have conveyed this meaning once in an earlier form, if one existed. Thüsing takes the expression to refer to the time of the Spirit,[57] which might include the ordeals to face the disciples.[58] It is also possible to see in it a reference to the events immediately to come in Jesus' ministry, namely Jesus' death and return to the Father, which the Spirit would interpret for the disciples,[59] perhaps seen also as eschatologial judgement.[60]

Historical awareness evident in 'footnotes'

However we measure the extent of any additional revelation to be given according to 16:13-15, all of the Paraklete sayings demonstrate a degree of historical awareness. This same awareness is also apparent in what Olsson and others have called Johannine 'footnotes'.[61] De Jonge points, in particular, to the following as illustrating awareness of two periods of history: 2:21f; 12:16; 13:7; 14:7b; and 20:9.[62] This tells against the view that the author had no interest in the historical Jesus. The author also reveals in passages like 20:29; 17:20; 10:16; 11:51f an awareness of the 'generation gap', as Nicholson puts it, between his own and earlier times, including the time of the historical Jesus and the disciples.[63]

2:22

In 2:22 we read, 'When Jesus was raised from the dead, the disciples remembered that he was saying this, and believed the scripture and the word which Jesus spoke.' They remembered Jesus' temple saying and believed it, because it had come true, but the author also implies, by his explanation of its meaning in 2:21, that they did not understand it until after Jesus' resurrection. The scripture they believed was doubtless Ps 69:10, which the disciples remembered, possibly during the incident of the temple expulsion, but more probably after Easter, 'Zeal for your house will consume me' (2:17). They saw its application to Jesus after Easter.

12:16

Similarly 12:16 displays an historical sensitivity, 'The disciples did not know these things at first; but when Jesus was glorified, then they remembered that these things were written concerning him and that they did these things to him.' It refers to Jesus' entry into Jerusalem, acclaimed by the crowds as royal messiah, and to the Zechariah prophecy, 'Fear not, daughter of Zion; behold your king comes, sitting upon the foal of an ass' (12:14f). This is all the more extrordinary since the Synoptic accounts present the narrative as messianic as though the disciples were fully part of the acclamation. The fourth evangelist distinguishes here between history and reflection.

8:28; 13:7; 20:7; 14:20; 16:25

8:28 has Jesus say to the Jews, 'When you have lifted up the Son of Man, then you shall know that I am the one and I do nothing of my own accord, but as the Father taught me so I speak.' This, too, promises (as a possibility) that knowledge of who Jesus is as the Son sent from the Father will come to some as a fruit of the exaltation. Similarly Jesus tells Peter in 13:7, 'What I am doing now you do not know now, but afterwards you will.' He will perceive the meaning of the footwashing. According to 20:7 the disciples did not understand the empty tomb because they had not yet understood the scripture about Jesus. Similarly in 14:20 Jesus promises the disciples that one day they shall know that he is in the Father and 16:25 promises deeper understanding. The promise to Nathanael of the vision of the Son of Man (1:50f) probably also belongs here, as does 6:62 with its promise of greater seeing, the ascension of the Son of Man.

'The hour is coming and now is'

Some would include here the sayings introduced with the formula, 'The hour is coming and now is' (4:23; 5:25; cf. 16:32). Thus Forestell and Thüsing take 'now is' as the author's own comment about the period following Easter.[64] But Blank is more convincing when he explains the now as a claim being made by the earthly Jesus based on his personal presence and Porsch points out that the narrative of Jesus' meeting with the Samaritan woman assumes that then and there the hour of fulfilment and hope was present.[65] Accordingly these sayings do not reflect a distinction between pre- and post Easter in the author's christology.

The significance of texts reflecting awareness of two periods in history

Whether indirectly in the words of Jesus or directly in his own words, the author often makes a clear distinction between two periods of time, between which is a watershed in understanding marked by Jesus' death, return to the Father, and the giving of the Spirit. None of the texts need mean anything more than that the author sees himself preserving authentic Paraclete-aided memory of what the historical Jesus actually said, plus enlightened comment and reflection, including Old Testament reflection, on what is reported. But there are indications within the gospel that this picture is inadequate. For, on the one hand, some changes have taken place within the tradition of which the author may have been aware, and on the other hand, he, himself, has effected significant changes which have altered the tradition.

Identifying distinctively Johannine tradition and interpretation

The distinction between what is the author's and what is tradition is difficult. Comparison with the synoptics enables us at least to identify elements peculiar to, or receiving a distinctive shape in, the fourth gospel. There is no need here to rehearse the evidence in full. Of primary importance is the pattern of christological statements we identified as the central structure of the author's christology in Part II. While the designations, 'Father' and 'Son' are not absent in the Synoptic gospels, there is no comparison with the extensiveness of their use in the fourth gospel. This is even more the case with statements about pre-existence, sending, coming and returning, which are either totally absent or used quite differently in the other three gospels. It is not just the presence of statements reflecting the revealer envoy pattern of the author's christology in the gospel itself, which sets John and the synoptics apart, but also their presence as explicit claims on the lips of Jesus. Whatever links may exist with the traditions present in these gospels, the Johannine gospel reflects a distinctive development. The Johannine Christ speaks Johannine language[66] and makes the christological claims of the Johannine community.[67] Neither the language nor the claims, in the way they are set forth here, can claim to represent accurately the Jesus of history. The language and christology of the synoptics would be scarcely explicable, should we have to assume their tradition reached back to the Johannine Christ.

The gospel in community

Community is an important perspective from which to understand the gospel. Meeks has shown this in pointing to the way the Johannine pattern of the descending ascending revealer serves more than christological affirmation. It also helps to reinforce the identity of the community estranged from the synagogue and from the world.[68] It represents a substantial modification of the Jesus tradition. Onuki has observed that the two parts of the gospel, Jesus' coming in chapters 1-12 and Jesus' going 13-21, also reflect the two fold movement of the community of faith: its reaching out into the world, where it also faces strangeness and alienation, and its withdrawing from the world for consolation and strength.[69] These help explain the shape of the gospel and the relevance of its christology to the community. But beside these dynamics which operate at a less conscious level in the community's development, there is also abundant evidence that the Jesus tradition has been quite consciously shaped and transformed to address its needs.

The author's creative development and embellishment of the tradition

While we cannot be sure of the extent to which the author would have been aware of the distinctive language of the Johannine tradition about Jesus, we are on surer ground when speaking of his own contribution.

> Culpepper notes, for instance, how the language the author uses in the so called Johannine footnotes (eg. 7:39; 12:16; 21:19; 7:30; 8:20) also corresponds largely to that of the last discourses[70] and Fortna postulates that these are the particular contribution of the author to bring together the disjointed parts of the 'signs gospel', the ministry and the passion narrative, in a way which spoke to the immediate needs of the Johannine community.[71] Onuki, too, stresses that the last discourses are primarily about the Johannine community and its situation.[72]
>
> It is particularly through literary analysis that the creative skill of the evangelist is being given the attention it deserves. Olsson, for instance, has shown through an analysis of the account of the wedding feast at Cana that this is a carefully composed piece of work written in the language of insiders.[73] Similarly Leroy has expounded the author's use of the techniques of misunderstanding and double meaning, their dependence for effect on a common in-group language and their function in reinforcing a sense of community.[74] He also shows how the author applies his technique sometimes in a way that the partners of Jesus are deliberately portrayed in a way that cannot have corresponded to reality.[75] Wead also highlighted the use of misunderstanding, and emphasised the use of irony and metaphor in the gospel.[76] Similarly

Lindars listed many of the deliberate techniques used by the author.[77] The recognition of literary technique in the fourth gospel is not new.[78] But in recent years it has come very strongly to the fore, represented especially through the work of Culpepper, Duke and O'Day, and scholars like de la Potterie.[79] They also emphasise the degree to which the effectiveness of such techniques depends heavily on a knowing community. This is especially so with the author's use of dramatic irony which both assumes a conversant group of hearers and reinforces their identity as community.[80] This gospel speaks the language of insiders for insiders.[81]

This is not the place to discuss the range of contributions being made in recent studies towards understanding the literary techniques of the gospel. But for the immediate purpose they offer abundant evidence of conscious literary skill on the part of the author with which he has shaped, composed, and created the material of the gospel. Instances of this skill are endless. The following are some examples: the author's use of symbolic allusion, for instance, in the Cana wedding pericope; the use of double meaning in the dialogue with Nicodemus, where *anōthen* ('from above' or 'again') works only in Greek; the drama of the Samaritan woman's meeting with Jesus, which depends so much for its effectiveness on double meaning and irony; the symbolic use of the feeding of the 5000; the brilliant multilevel drama of the healing of the blind man, a story of the light of the world and the blindness of those who oppose it; and not least the powerful irony woven into the passion narrative.[82]

From beginning to end the author's hand is to be seen in the reshaping of narrative and discourse. This is not to deny that literary techniques such as irony may not have been already present in the sources he used, such as, to some degree, surely in the passion narrative, as the Synoptic parallels show, and we must reckon with the possibility that such techniques had become the stock in trade of teachers and preachers of the Johannine community. But, for all of this, there can scarcely be any doubt that the author plays a major part in their being in the gospel.

Implications of evidence of creative literary techniques for understanding the nature of the gospel and its relation to history

The recognition of conscious literary shaping of the kind spoken of above, with its necessary impact on narrative and discourse content, has implications for the questions we face. It means that the author would have been to that degree aware that what he was producing was not primarily a historical report of what Jesus once said and did. At the same time we have to place beside this the author's concern for the Jesus of history. The gospel's central theme is that the Son of God has come from the Father to bring life. The fact of the historical Jesus, the event of the Son's coming in history, is of fundamental importance. This also means that the author would have believed that this Jesus would have made such claims. He probably saw himself as expanding upon a central christological claim already going back to Jesus himself. But beyond this, he also felt inspired and free to expand upon and elaborate the traditions he had received and saw this as part of the continuing work of the Paraclete. Accordingly it is doubtful that he would have understood the Paraclete promises to relate only to memory of the earthly Jesus.

Implications for understanding the 'unreal' elements in the portrait of Jesus' humanity

The author's use of literary and dramatic technique, such as irony, misunderstanding, and double meaning, also have a major affect on the portrait of Jesus as a human being, as we have briefly noted in the previous section. On the one hand, much of the superiority, indeed arrogance, seen in Jesus' behaviour in encounter with his contemporaries, is the product of the author's style of presentation. Such passages should not, therefore, be read as literal descriptions of the historical Jesus, nor should they be taken as indicators for the author's view of Jesus' actual humanity. Wead points out that it would be irrelevant to ponder what Nicodemus might have understood, as though ch. 3 were an historical dialogue, or what the disciples might have understood of 6:51-58.[83]

On the other hand, it is likely that the author develops such scenes in the belief that what they convey has a basis in the historical reality of Jesus as he perceived it. Above all, the author would have believed that the underlying christology reflected in these scenes was a valid one and truly corresponded to what was claimed by the historical Jesus himself. He was the Son from the Father. At most we may suggest that the manner of word play and other dramatic techniques of presentation, developed in order to assert this basic truth of the earthly historical Jesus, in end effect creates a story of Jesus in which unwittingly, that is, naively, the author makes it seem like Jesus is far less human than his own christology presupposes. This means saying that the medium affects the message, which then comes through in a way that the author did not realise.

Alternatively one would have to argue that the medium was christologically consistent with the message and that the author actually believed Jesus would have responded to people in exactly the way he presents. None of the indications of his awareness of the change in development between the time of the earthly Jesus and the post Easter period need imply otherwise. On such an alternative view, we have before us much more than unwittingly docetic tendencies. On balance, I think the awareness we must presuppose in the author's conscious employment of literary techniques counts against this. The question remains to what extent, then, he would have understood his creations as consistent with the way he would have thought Jesus to have been in reality during his earthly ministry.

The centrality of the historical event of the ministry of Jesus

To return to the issue of the author and the Jesus of history, the chief concern of the author is the one reflected in what we have traced as the central structure of his christology. It is not only the truth about the post Easter Christ of faith, nor is it simply that truth projected back into the scenery of the historical Jesus. Otherwise, as Haacker notes, we should expect a gospel focussing primarily on words to the disciples.[84] It is the story of the coming into the world of the Son of the Father, sent to bear the Father's challenge to the world. The Son's death and return to the Father represents not only the climax of this work, but also underlines its authenticity and significance, a perception given by the Spirit to the post Easter community.

The author is thus aware of history and of a development in understanding marked by Easter. But the event of fundamental importance is the Son's coming. Therefore the facts of Jesus' coming as the Son of the Father, his ministry in encounter with men and women, especially the Jews, his suffering and death on the cross at the hands of Pilate through the Jews, and his resurrection and return to the Father, these facts and a good many others are important for the author as historical events and necessary to his understanding of the gospel.

A hierarchy of significant historical data

The fact that Jesus encountered men and women is absolutely essential, though the details of each episode are not. The fact of Jesus' encounter with the Jews, in particular, is important because of its significance for his own community's relation with Judaism, though the details are not. This is why he can handle details of narrative and discourse so freely. Similarly the passion is essential for the author's historical claims; but details often reflect not history, but devotional edification.

There is for the author a complex hierarchy of historical data. He can take the trouble to inform readers of the detail of Jewish customs. He can also freely reconstruct narrative sources so that a bare torso of the original remains. The encounters of the historical Jesus with men and women, with Jews, with the world are central, even if the details are not. The basic fact of the coming of the Son, the sent one, is so much the centre, that the gospel is an endless variation on this theme, a persistence which already Baur noted, many in his day described as monotonous.[85]

Radical simplification and centering of the tradition

However we evaluate it, the effect of the author's undertaking is to simplify. This is true of the constant recurrence of the same pattern, as we noted in Part II. The encounters always centre around Jesus' claim to be the sent one and his call to receive what he offers in relationship with himself. The simplicity is also present in the symbols reflecting central human need like life, light, water, and bread. None of these is without an extensive traditio-historical background. But at the level of the evangelist's composition, they are consistently used to focus the message of the gospel on the gift of life in the Son.

The simplicity is more than a technique of communication; it reflects a centering or focussing upon what the author holds to be essential in such a way that other elements of the tradition are put in perspective in relation to that centre, even to the extent of being omitted altogether. This represents a theological method which has wide implications, not least for understanding what the gospel is and is not.

Accordingly the gospel is a presentation of a simple truth: the coming of the Son and so the coming of life through faith in him. It is interested in history in that it places this event firmly in history in the ministry of Jesus of Nazareth and assumes encounters like those present in the Johannine community. But beyond this, history is not the author's concern and stories and discourses serve not primarily, or even at all, to report what actually happened on this or that occasion, but to convey what happens and happened through the coming of the Son into the world. Each episode portrays the total event or an aspect of it as such.

The Gospel as celebration of faith

The dramatic irony, the word plays, the misunderstandings, so characteristic of the author's method, demand an audience which both knows the story and understands the Johannine language. In the scenes of ch. 4 where Jesus encounters the Samaritan woman, one can almost hear the laughter of the audience as the woman consistently fails to see what they had known all along and had been summarised for them also in the prologue. Many of the gospel episodes seem to be written like dramas to be acted out before a live audience.[86] Yet the gospel is not primarily dramatic entertainment. Nor is it primarily evangelistic, for its depends so much for its effects on having readers or hearers who understand. It is primarily the telling of a story to those who already know it. In that sense it does, indeed, resemble the great Greek dramas.[87] But its purpose seems much more to be the vehicle for edification and celebration. Duke speaks of devotional pleasure created through the fellowship of irony, considering as only a secondary possibility the persuasion of crypto Christians.[88] Culpepper speaks of the readers' enjoyment.[89] O'Day notes that the effect of the author's literary technique is to facilitate vision and emphasises the narrative mode as the vehicle of revelation.[90]

Faith's icon

The gospel is thus primarily faith celebrating faith and so making faith stronger. It is like an icon. Its context is the community of faith. It is doing, and doubtless sets out to do, precisely what was promised of the Paraclete: it calls to remembrance, leads into all truth about Christ, and takes what is his and declares it. But like the pattern of the envoy revealer, the focus is not primarily knowledge or information; it is encounter and relationship. The gospel is itself a work of christology, a portrait presented to the believer as a vehicle for evoking deeper faith commitment.

A mirror of unfaith

On the negative side it is a mirror of unfaith in which believers can see the conflicts of their own day. This accounts for the negative simplication and stereotyping of unbelievers. Such portrayals are to serve as comfort and encouragement for believers in their conflict with the world. Accordingly the issue of the Jews in history must be seen in much the same light as the issue of the Jesus of history within the gospel. The same unhistorical, simplifying elaboration overlays the stories based on actual conflicts, which the author believed Jesus faced during his ministry and in his passion. Here, too, it is the total response of rejection which shapes each episode and in such a generalising way that the hearers can make the connections with their own day. To read these narratives as history would be a gross distortion.

The last discourses and the gospel

The fourth gospel is thus a stylised presentation of the central significance of Jesus as the author sees it to have been, both in the earthly ministry and in the author's own day. It is stylised for the celebration and comfort of the faithful. For this reason the last discourses perform a distinctive role within this function. Bornkamm wrote that they help the community come to terms with the distance of history.[91] They also aid reflection on Jesus' ministry in terms of the central structure of the author's christology, offer comfort and hope, and set the terms of reference for the community of faith as called to be a community of love and commissioned to continue the Son's work in the world in the power of the Spirit. The final two chapters expand particular aspects of these themes, particularly those concerned with mission, order and historical distance.

John and the synoptics - similarities

The distinctiveness of the fourth gospel as a christological statement is evident when we compare it with the first three gospels. They, too, are written from a post Easter perspective. They, too, seek to come to terms with the tension between faith's growth in perception before and after Easter, Mark doing so, in particular, through the use of the motif of the messianic secret. Barrett notes therefore a common artificiality.[92] Leroy points to the presence of epiphany and misunderstandings in Mark.[93] Many of the questions we asked of the fourth gospel can be asked equally of them. The synoptic evangelists without doubt believed that when they wrote they included information about what actually happened during the ministry of Jesus. They, too, would have taken some traditions as historically accurate which had already been shaped and substantially modified by processes in the post Easter period of which they were unaware. They were also aware that there had been growth in understanding of who Jesus was after Easter. They, too, engaged in shaping, reordering, and supplementing the Jesus material that had come to them. And they, too, must have at least accepted the possibility that they were not the first to have done so.

John and the synoptics - differences

What then is the difference between their work and that of the fourth evangelist? Schnackenburg argues that there is no essential difference, except that in John statements are taken to their extreme ('Spitze').[94] Strathmann describes the three evangelists as painters, the fourth, as one who has produced a drawing or sketch.[95] Haacker points to the greater number of confessional statements in John.[96] Käsemann stresses the greater emphasis on divine glory.[97]

We have already noted the distinctive Johannine language. To this may be added major differences in the content and form of the material, in chronology, the absence in John of parables of the usual synoptic kind, of the kingdom of God as a central theme, and, conversely, in the synoptics, the absence of the kind of christological statements and symbols typical of John. Some of these differences will be explained by the distinctive history of the Johannine tradition and the Johannine community. But some major differences are doubtless attributable to the evangelist. These include the author's method of radically simplifying and centering and the extensiveness and nature of his reshaping of narrative and discourse material to serve as vehicles of a single christological statement. None of the other evangelists do this on anything like the same scale. There is in the synoptics some use of irony, above all in the passion narratives (eg. the title, 'King of the Jews'), and some use of symbolism (eg. in the feeding miracles, the stilling of the storm, and healings), but nothing on the scale of the fourth gospel. In the others we can identify christological concerns and trace redaction through preferred expressions and particular themes, but compared with John these are mere traces in what is basically a very conservative handling of the tradition.

Different soteriology and christology

It accords with these observations that another major distinction lies in the kind of soteriology which becomes central in the Johannine christological programme. While the author knows the wider tradition, his centre is the offer of life in relationship with the Father through the Son. Johannine salvation is thus relationship centred. Not definitive interpretation of Torah by God's Messiah, nor the promise of God's reign, nor the achievement of atonement, nor the gift of knowledge, nor defeat of the powers stands at the centre, but the coming of a person and the gift in that person to all who believe of life in relationship. Thus Blank emphasises the resolution of the traditional tensions between the now and not yet through a change of focus from eschatological hope to the person of Jesus.[98] This centrality of the person, in turn, makes central what in the other gospels is absent, namely the origin of the Son in pre-existent splendour with the Father and his heavenly commissioning.

The fourth gospel is unique among the gospels in its christology and soteriology. It shares with them the concern to tell the story of Jesus of Nazareth. It is even more explicitly aware of the issues of growth in understanding than they are, through the Paraclete sayings and through frequent references to historical distance throughout the gospel. It reflects a distinctive methodology, both in its simplification and centering and in its extensive freedom in reshaping traditional material using literary techniques such as irony and double meaning, all to state over and over again the central christological statement of the Son's coming with the gift of life. The result is a portrait of Jesus which has the character of an icon, a celebration and focus of faith. There is strong evidence that this is also how the author viewed his work. The Jesus of history remains central, not simply the fact of his coming, but also key encounters in which he engaged. Yet there the concern with history stops and faith's drama begins, in which scene by scene the central issues are rehearsed. This unique gospel demands to be understood in this light. Whenever people have approached its pages as if it were primarily history or doctrine or have failed to appreciate it as a celebration of faith, it has become a seedbed of controversy and conflict.

2. The Gospel, its Christology and its Community

The fourth gospel belongs to a community of faith. It spoke the language of that community. It encouraged, consolidated and celebrated the faith of the community through its unique portrayal of Jesus. It reinforced the community's identity as in, but not of, the world. It also challenged and confronted faith and understanding. Within all of this its christology played an important part.

The major part of this book has been considering the broad structure of Johannine christology and the issues of interpretation which arise within it. In it we have focussed on the text of the gospel as transmitted, which was once also the text of a community in the late first century. I want in this chapter to ask about the relationship between the author's christology and the community to which it once belonged. In doing so, I want also to take into account the important issues of the history of that community, the history of its christology and the history of the composition of the gospel itself. One short chapter cannot adequately treat the complex issues of any one of these three aspects. There exist excellent reviews of current research in these areas.[99] Rather it is my intention to begin with the structure of the author's christology and note questions and implications which I perceive arising in relationship to them.

The author's christology represents a synthesis. It combines various streams of thought. Sometimes these are identifiable and we can observe the degree to which they have merged. Occasionally we have detected tensions within the text between different traditions. By identifying these tensions and streams of thought, we can go on to ask how they arose and what they indicate about the development and background of christology, about the history and issues of the community, and perhaps, also about the history of composition of the gospel itself. In effect this means beginning with questions which emerge ultimately from the text itself and from the christological structure we have identified within it.

(a) The revealer envoy model

(i) The dominance of the revealer envoy model

The most important and outstanding feature of the author's christology is the dominance of the pattern of the revealer envoy, the coming and going of the Son, from and to the Father, a structure enunciated within the framework of a cosmic dualism of heaven, above, and earth, below. On the basis of this model the author reinterprets eschatology, integrates diverse christological traditions, focusses soteriology, and develops his pneumatology.

Thus eternal life, resurrection, and judgement are now, in relationship with the Son. Arguments with Jews about different kinds of messiahship are ultimately irrelevant and serve only to highlight their blindness to the one messiahship, which consists in Jesus' being the Son sent from the Father. Hopes for a prophet cease to be meaningful except in so far as they point to the one sent from above to tell what he has seen and heard. Here is much more than a Mosaic prophet teacher. Similarly the descent of the Spirit at Jesus' baptism is now only a sign of what is already his and a means of identification for the Baptist.

The distinctive wisdom logos imagery of the prologue also serves now to portray him from the beginning as the one who came to make God known. The traditions of family intimacy of the *monogenēs* Son of God and his sending serve the same end. Imagery of the Torah as water, bread, light and life, with which Jesus presents himself, now serves to express the gift of salvation which is relationship with the person of the Son. He is ('I am') the one who comes thus. Even the passion narrative with its strongly messianic colouring has been overlaid with the simplicity of the claim of the Son sent from the Father to bear witness to the truth. Likewise the miracles in their splendour manifest his glory and in their symbolism illustrate the life he brings.

Similarly he uses its pattern of sending also to describe the sending of the Spirit and the disciples. The Spirit Paraclete will be sent to make known what is the Son's word, to bring all that he has said to their memory and to lead the disciples into all truth. The disciples have been sent, as the Son was sent. They are to bear faithful witness with the aid of the Spirit of truth. The Spirit is not a second revealer; even less so are the disciples. The Paraclete and the disciples are witnesses to the one original and one only Son who has come as revealer envoy and returned, the gospel, itself, being the product of Paraclete and disciple fulfilling this work. Thus the revealer envoy pattern lends itself in part to the description of their sending, but retains its own absolute priority and dominance.

By using this model the author has radically simplified and centralised eschatology, christology, and pneumatology. The dominance of the model calls for an explanation. In seeking that explanation we should note also its role in simplifying and centralising soteriology and the peculiar modification which that brings to the model itself.

(ii) The modified revealer envoy model

In appropriating the revealer envoy model, the evangelist (or maybe already the tradition before him) has modified it in a significant way. The model logically demands the language of communication and revelation; the revealer reveals; the envoy tells what he has seen and heard. Whereas the author consistently employs the model using such language, he uses it now, not primarily about revelation as information giving, but as a means of portraying epiphany and encounter. What the Son comes to offer is primarily the gift of life in relationship with himself and with the Father. Only occasionally does he break from his dominant model, such as when he uses the apprenticeship Father Son pattern in 5:19f, and when he does, it is possible because of the distinctive modification of the model's basic statement. The primary focus in the modified revealer envoy model is life giving encounter. The coming and going remains intact, as does the cosmic dualism;[100] but the slavific event is not information giving; it is the offer of a life giving faith relationship.

This modification also brings with it, therefore, a modification of soteriology. The author's soteriology still includes the promise of following the path the redeemer has gone, in other words, going on after death to where he is, and to belong to him is not to belong to this world; it is to be born from above; yet the primary focus in the soteriology is not belonging to, and finally going to, the heavenly world, but life now in relationship with the Son and through the Son with the Father. The centre of focus moves from ascent to the heavenly world, transmortal salvation, which one might expect to be the focus of the message of a heavenly revealer envoy, to relationship with the person of the Son through faith. This relativises the significance of the cosmic dualism.

There is a strangeness, here. Why is that the envoy revealer pattern is both dominant and yet also appears as something which has had to be especially adapted? What has happened or what is the background for this? The question becomes more acute and more complex when we consider the understanding of the death of Jesus in relationship to the author's modified revealer envoy christology.

(iii) The modified revealer envoy model and the death of Jesus

The revealer envoy model, both when it is taken literally as a communication revelation model and when it is understood in a modified way as in the gospel, assumes by its structure that coming and going correspond and reflect little more than change of place, entry to and exit from earthly life. Our analysis has shown that the language of coming and going is frequently used throughout the gospel of the Son and his mission from the Father. Only exceptionally does the author go beyond the language of departure or going away when speaking of the end of the mission of Jesus as the Son. We might think of the use of language of glorification in relation to Jesus as the Son in 11:4 and, by implication, in 17:1,5; but mostly this kind of language to describe the end of Jesus' earthly life belongs within a distinctive cluster of terms associated with the title Son of Man. To these we shall return below. However, the fact remains that the revealer envoy model, which the author uses primarily in association with the language of Son and Father, and which speaks of the Son's coming from and returning to the Father, has by its very structure, little to say about Jesus' death and return to the Father beyond that it represents this return. It has little place for a soteriological significance to be attributed to Jesus' death. Structurally, persistence through suffering, even to death, need mean no more than faithful fulfilment of the revelatory task, without renegging under pressure. At most, the cross might reveal the extent to which the Son was willing to go and so might function symbolically as representative of the whole ministry. Structurally, it need mean no more than this.

Even with the author's own adaptation of the pattern, so that it represents the Son in encounter offering life in relationship to himself and not primarily information, this remains the case. For if the gift is already given by his presence, what more can his death and return add, especially when his presence is replaced or re-presented by the Spirit? In itself, the envoy christology presents the Son as the all sufficient life and nourishment and nothing more is to be done, except to ensure continuity and greater accessibility of the offer.

The modified revealer envoy model and vicarious atonement

Yet there are other statements in the gospel which attribute a more significant role to Jesus' death than this assumes. These stand in a certain tension with the revealer envoy model, even in its modified form. For instance, the revealer envoy model has no need, structurally, of vicarious atonement through an act of sacrifice or representative self giving on the part of the Son. For life is in the person of the Son and in relationship with him; the Logos is received or not received. Accordingly, we might expect that when they are used, they are largely incidental to the argument and this we found to be so. Then why are they even present?

The modified revealer envoy model and the casting out of the world's ruler

Another tradition in the gospel which interprets the climax of Jesus' earthly life sees his death as the casting out of the ruler of the world. It is located more centrally than the vicarious atonement traditions, since it is one of a number of statements which stand at the climax of a series of predictions about the 'hour' or 'time' to come and are introduced by the words, 'The hour has come' or 'Now is'. It appears in one of these, 12:31; it reappears in the summary of the Paraclete's proclamation to the world (16:11) and, apart from that it is hinted at in 14:31 and, anachronistically, in 16:32.

But why is this tradition there at all? Does the author indicate by it a particular achievement which actually changed cosmic power structures?[101] Is it such that, without it, the earthly gift of the Son could not have benefitted the recipients? Does it represent in some way the overcoming of the barrier between earth and heaven, for instance, the disempowerment of the one who bars the way, and thus the breaking open of the way? This would, indeed, fit the basic revealer envoy model in its unmodified form whose focus is access to the heavenly and transmortal salvation. Such a soteriology might well entail the necessity that revelation of the heavenly home be supplemented by an act which pioneered its access. But, were we to posit it as significant for the evangelist's soteriology, it would be extraordinary that an event of such crucial salvific significance is thematised only here in the gospel. It is much more likely, as we have argued above, that the author has now fully appropriated it to his modified revealer envoy model in a way that understands the disempowerment as exposure of the evil power in the event of Jesus' death for the evil that it is, as 16:8-11 suggests. With regard to the path to the Father, in John it is Jesus himself who is the way in his person, as he is also the door and the truth and the life.

Nevertheless the tradition of 12:31 still sits unevenly in its wider context and alerts us to its different character and origin. If traditions of atonement and of casting out the world's ruler are very much subordinated to the dominant revealer envoy model, this cannot be said in the same way of the Son of Man cluster of ideas.

(iv) The modifies revealer envoy model and 'the Son of Man cluster'

We noted in IIC9 and IIIA4 the concentration of Son of Man sayings and associated motifs on and around the climax of Jesus' ministry, his death and return, in what I have described earlier as 'the Son of Man cluster'.[102] Included in this cluster are the title, 'Son of Man', itself; lifting up/exaltation (*hypsoō*), glorification, ascending and descending (*ana- katabainō*) as distinctive vocabulary (whereas Son/Father sayings use other verbs); the judgement motif; the 'hour' (sometimes 'the time' or 'now'); and the promise of 'greater things'. These motifs occur frequently in association with 'Son of Man', individually, and sometimes in combination. Already this raises the questions: why this particular association of ideas? Where does it come from? Why the concentration on Jesus' 'hour'?

Different foci

But it is more than the presence of such a cluster of ideas and their concentration on the climax of Jesus' ministry which are noteworthy here. These also reflect a different focus in the application of key salvific motifs. On the one hand, the envoy model points to the saving presence of Jesus in his ministry, proclaims the glory of the Son manifest on earth, announces the offer of life as present in his person, and declares judgement to have come at the point of response to the encounter he brings. On the other hand, the language of the Son of Man cluster points forward to the 'hour' to come, looks upward to the glory of heaven with which the Son of Man will be glorified, promises the gift of life as something the Son of Man will give after his exaltation and through his flesh and blood, and declares judgement to have taken place at the climax of Jesus' ministry.

Merging traditions

I analysed in IIIA4 the way in which the author integrates, for instance, the two notions of glory, and in IIIA6 have shown how the 'greater' component of the 'hour' is set forth by the author largely in terms of the greater understanding brought by the Spirit and the mission this makes possible. Nevertheless there is evidence here of the envoy model and the Son of Man cluster being two different associations of ideas, represented by a distinctiveness of language. In the gospel we see the two streams coming together. Why is this so and what does it mean? How does the revealer envoy model which assumes such a dominant role in the author's christology relate to the Son of Man cluster of ideas? The closest the two sets of ideas come to merging is in John 17 where cluster terminology (eg. glorification) and Father Son terminology is no longer distinguishable (as it still is, for instance, earlier in the last discourse material in 13:31 - 14:31). We need to ask also why this is so at this point in the gospel. But we return first to the relationship between the revealer envoy model and the cluster in the gospel as a whole.

Not merely vestiges of tradition

The Son of Man cluster is particularly interesting because its language is present in clearly identifiable authorial footnotes, such as 7:39 and 12:16, referring to the coming of the Spirit who would mediate life and bring understanding. It cannot therefore be dismissed as a mere vestige of tradition. What is its present relationship to the envoy revealer model which the author adapts?

While I detect tension between these models, I do not find evidence of the author using one against the other. I see no evidence that he is using the title 'Son of Man' to highlight the humanity of Jesus, perhaps even correctively over against the envoy model.[103] This ignores that we are dealing with a cluster of ideas, not a title alone, and these do not point in such a direction; nor has the title this connotation in the gospel. It suggests the opposite. The evidence would be consistent, rather, with his approaching an already established revealer envoy model for portraying Jesus' ministry and supplementing it with the Son of Man material. Why has he done so? What did this cluster of ideas offer? Why was there need to offer any more than the revealer envoy christology anyway, given its presentation of an all sufficient salvation in the person of Jesus himself?

Meeting points

We come a step further when we look at passages where revealer envoy christology and Son of Man christology stand side by side. There is something slightly odd, where this happens, as can be seen, for instance, in the contrasts between 1:49 and 1:50f; 3:1-11 and 3:12; 6:60f and 6:62; 7:37 and 7:38f. The relationship is not polemical, nor corrective. But is the author really interested only in informing the reader of the historical differentiation between what the disciples understood before and after Easter? Or does the author point the reader to an even deeper understanding than that represented by Nathanael's traditional confession, Jesus' offer of new birth, and his gift of the bread and the water of life? What is the 'greater' represented by the vision of the Son of Man in heaven (1:51), the 'heavenly things' (which must include the Son of Man's ascension and exaltation of 3:13-15), the ascent of the Son of Man to where he was before (6:62), or the giving of the Spirit (7:38f)?

As we saw in IIIA6, the author expounds the promise of the 'greater event' primarily in terms of what the Spirit makes possible and brings to the community of faith. The greater event of the Son of Man's heavenly exaltation, glorification and ascent, will result in the drawing of all to himself, the possibility of deeper understanding of himself, of his coming and return, of the events of his ministry and of scripture witness to him. It will do so above all through making possible the Spirit. This is what Jesus means by his promise that the disciples will do 'greater' works than he (14:12). What then is the author doing, when he juxtaposes the revealer envoy model and the Son of Man cluster in such a way that the former is central and foundational and the latter is somehow 'greater'?

The gift then and its promised availability and abundance in the community of faith

The most probable explanation is that the author wants to stress the importance of the presence of the gift of life now being available and abundant in the post Easter community. He is not setting the event the Son of Man cluster describes over against Jesus, but, on the contrary, is using it as the means whereby to underline that what the Son brought then is now accessible for all in the community of faith. Occasionally this post Easter availability is mentioned directly such as in the promise in ch. 6 that the Son of Man will give life in his eucharistic flesh and blood (6:53; cf. 6:27; 3:14f); mostly it is simply presupposed. The gift of life then is the gift of life now. The Paraclete will mediate the gift of the presence of Christ, himself, the gift, to the disciples and bring them deeper understanding (14:16f). Nowhere does the author suggest that the salvation set forth in the revealer envoy christological model is inadequate or inferior. Confessing Jesus as the king of Israel and Son of God (1:49), being born from above (3:1-11), and receiving the bread and the water of life (6:60f; 7:37), are not now supplanted. But they now abound to all and they abound in and through the community of faith. And they are only possible now through the work of the Paraclete in this community. Or to use language which the author uses to link both together, the glorification of the Son of Man will make possible God's glorification in and through the disciples in mission, even as Jesus glorified God by his faithful fulfilment of his mission.

The author would, then, on my understanding, have employed the Son of Man cluster of ideas to point readers to the appropriation of all that Jesus already was in his earthly ministry now through the Spirit in the Church's mission and in its community. He sees the community of faith as the present place of the life and light Christ brought and therefore highlights this as the focus of the 'greater works', the fruit of 'the greater event' to which the Son himself looked forward and which he promised. The concern was not primarily with a competing view or a competing christology. Rather, it was with the life and light which the Son brought by his incarnation and through the greater event has enabled to be present and available in the faith community.

The ecclesial dimension of Johannine christology

This coheres well with the ecclesiological implications of the author's christology as a whole. For where the author employs the envoy revealer model, adapting it to focus primarily on relationship, this focus on relationship necessarily brings with it an increased focus on relationship, and thus on community as the vehicle of mission and the place of the life and presence of Christ. Meeks has shown also how the pattern of the descending ascending revealer might also reinforce community among those who, facing adversity and rejection of their mission, also identified themselves as strangers in the world.[104] The role of the Son of Man cluster would partly confirm this, but we should also note mission and fruit bearing as an important component in the Son of Man cluster or association of ideas (eg. 12:23f, 32). This points to an understanding of the community of faith as being much more actively the bearer of light and life to the world than Meeks's hypothesis of a withdrawn sectarian community envisages.[105]

This emphasis on the post Easter community's mission is also found above all in the first of the final discourses, where Jesus promises 'greater works' and speaks of the Spirit (14:12-17). In the remaining final discourse material in chs. 15-17 it continues, though with a much stronger emphasis on the maintenance of the community itself. The gospel is surprisingly ecclesiological in both the final discourses and in the final two chapters. This emphasis is also reflected in the author's concern to validate the community's integrity and witness through the Paraclete, the beloved disciple, the 'treasured legacy' of the mother of Jesus, the dependence on eyewitnesses and the reliability and adequacy of resourcing of the gospel itself.

The Son of Man cluster - its background

If this adequately accounts for the author's juxtaposition of the revealer envoy model and the Son of Man cluster, it raises at the same time important historical questions about the nature of these traditions. The relatively distinct association of motifs clustered around the Son of Man title indicates in all probability a pre-existing tradition. There is a strong concentration of exaltation christology within it and such christology elsewhere uses *hypsoō* and glorification terminology, usually however in association with a form of messianic christology (Acts 2:33; 5:31; Heb 5:5; Phil 2:11). There appears here to have been an association rather with Son of Man, perhaps also because of authorisation motifs (eg. 3:35) which originally belonged to an understanding of Jesus' exaltation[106] and are reflected in Matt 28:18 (cf. Dan 7:13f; perhaps originally the sense also of Matt 11:27a; Luke 10:22a). Traditional forensic associations of Son of Man are also evident in the gospel (5:27; 9:35, 39) and perhaps the parousia associations of the term have bequeathed the motifs of angelic service and heavenly glory (cf. 1:51; Mark 8:38; 13:26; 14:62). Beside this, there is the major expansion of Son of Man christology into pre-existence, evident in 3:13 and 6:62, which in the light of its distinctive vocabulary (present also in the manna discourse), must have already been established in the author's tradition. This expansion also results in some overlap with the revealer envoy model inasmuch as the 'descent' (*katabainō*) of the Son of Man is also related to revelation and the offer of life in both 3:13 and ch. 6. The Johannine Son of Man tradition demands closer research along these lines than space here permits.

The author has, therefore, employed the Son of Man cluster of ideas in order to point readers to the reality that the life then is even more fully present now in the post Easter mission and community of faith which lives from the benefits which flow from the Son's return to the Father, as the exalted, glorified, ascended Son of Man.

(v) The modified revealer envoy model, the Spirit and the miracles

We have noted above how the revealer envoy model integrates both the miracle tradition and the tradition of the giving of the Spirit. The miracles reveal the glory of the Son and symbolise who he is; the Spirit Paraclete bears witness to him. But in the process of integration, the understanding of Spirit and miracle tradition is seriously modified in a way which raises important questions about the nature of the Johannine christology and its community. It is striking that the work of the Spirit in John remains almost entirely at the level of information giving, acquaintance and confrontation with the truth, and mediation of presence in a personal way.[107] Where are the signs and wonders? Where are the charismatic gifts? There seems to be a concentration on teaching. Where are the public charismatic manifestations traditionally the markers for mission?

This is all the more striking because, by contrast, the gospel tells us that Jesus' ministry was one of signs enough to fill a universe of books, and the selection we have contains the most massively miraculous of all the canonical gospels. What has happened? Does this way of understanding the Spirit imply a similar balance should apply to our understanding of the christological material, the miracles of the gospel? What does this tell us, in turn, about the Johannine community? What has happened, that the community with the 'best' miracles of Jesus least sees the Spirit, and we may assume its community in the Spirit, in charismatic miraculous terms? Why have they lost their relevance?

Miracles and the 'agenda' of Salvation

The question of miracles includes more than the contrast between pneumatology and the account of Jesus' ministry in the body of the gospel. For the presentation of Jesus at many points exhibits a tension between what is happening in the miracles and what the revealer envoy model understands to be the mission of Jesus. Some of the miracles alleviate human sickness; one brings resuscitation of a dead person; others make provision for human need by way of food and drink; some more directly relate to Jesus' actions in regard to himself. At no point is there a suggestion that they should be doubted. On the contrary, they must be believed. Yet, aside from the miracles, there is nothing which indicates that the kind of agenda Jesus announces in the Lukan story to his home synagogue (Luke 4:16-20) and which is consistent with the portrait of Jesus in the other two synoptic gospels, is an agenda here in John. The miracles, as signs or works, manifest the Son's power and symbolise who and what he is, but, beyond that, they have ceased to be of paradigmatic value for the disciples, either in relation to a mission of healing and liberation or in relation to the manner in which such a mission should be exercised. The 'greater works' promised in 14:12 seem to bear no relation to signs and wonders of the apostolic church of Paul or of Luke; they indicate rather the fullness of life available through the Paraclete in the church and its fruit bearing mission.

The place of the miracles in Johannine christology and community

The miracles are not out of place in John, but they take their place in a manner which calls into question both their caritative role and their apologetic significance. The latter is present, but amid controversy, and frequently the wrong christological conclusions are drawn. The author implies that people should have read the miracles as proving that Jesus is what he claimed to be, as set out in the sayings material. Anything less than that is inadequate. But, beyondthat, he overlays them or through sayings material supplements them with symbolic interpretation, bringing them into line with, and making them serve, the central christological claim, that Jesus is the Son sent from the Father, even to the extent that the original story is left behind in the process (eg. 11:27). What lies behind this? Is this more than the will to integrate such stories within the dominant christological pattern? Does it reflect community conflict? How does the Johannine community relate to the kind of Christianity, so much evident elsewhere in the New Testament writings and their situations, for which signs and wonders and works of healing are manifestations of the Spirit and of the work of the apostles and have their natural precedent in the story of Jesus?

(vi) The modified revealer envoy model and other traditions

One of the remarkable features of Johannine christology is the dominance of the modified revealer model, on the one hand, as the centrepiece of its salvific

message, and the presence, on the other hand, of traditions which might easily
have been deemed on the basis of it to be superfluous. We have noted this already
in relation to traditions about Jesus' death as atoning or victorious and in relation
to Spirit and miracle tradition. It is also the case in relation to other traditions.
Probably some, at least, of the references to traditionally future eschatology belong
here.[108] They are now almost superfluous; for, since soteriology and eschatology
necessarily follow christology, future hope for believers will be fulfilled when they
join their Lord where he is (17:24); yet traditional motifs of eschatology persist.

The persistence of the tradition of Jesus as a real human being

More importantly, the revealer envoy model does not require more than an
appearance of the envoy among people in a form which makes communication or
encounter possible. There is strictly no need for a fully human Jesus. Yet the
gospel holds to both. The author adapts this model into the Jesus tradition which
speaks of a real human being. The 'play' of the Son with his contemporaries
always threatens to evaporate the humanity and the concentration of the full
meaning of the his coming into each single encounter makes human
characterisation of Jesus almost impossible. But the author seems in no doubt that
the full meaning of the incarnation includes the real human being, Jesus of
Nazareth.

**The persistence of the tradition of passion, resurrection and bestowal of the
Spirit by the risen one**

Similarly, the conclusion of the mission of the envoy need be no more than an exit,
but the author tells of suffering and real death. The model also had no particular
need for a human birth, nor for a descent of the Spirit. Yet these are present, the
latter sitting now somewhat awkwardly in the author's scheme. It is no surprise
that one solution of this tension, which the author does not adopt, was to see this as
the moment of the descent of the revealer envoy, leaving open the possibility that
ascent also occurred before the crucifixion. Such positions were consistent (though
not necessary) extrapolations of the revealer envoy model. This model would most
naturally see death as the point of return to the Father and find no place for a
passion narrative nor for an account of resurrection on the third day. It would be
consistent with the tradition of appearances of Jesus from heaven to his disciples,
but would need no separate act of bestowing the Spirit on earth by breath. Yet the
author persists in reaffirming these traditions, even though the 'rough edges' of
merged traditions sometimes show, as in the account of Jesus' words to Mary
Magdalene in 20:17. The model might also leave room for subsequent revealers,
but the second Paraclete never becomes this in John. It has no need for salvation
historical perspectives,[109] nor, necessarily for a doctrine of creation, but these, too,
seem part of the author's theology.[110]

(vii) Conclusion

Our discussion in the larger part of this book has explored the way the author
combines these traditions or streams of thought. Occasionally we have seen how
the perception of what the revealer envoy model requires has determined what
scholars have argued must be so in John. I have sought to weigh the significance

of the diverse ideas within John's christology and examine the degree of integration. At the same time this has exposed tensions. The author holds together diverse traditions. He makes central the revealer envoy model in a modified form, but uses it within a distinctively Christian setting. This surely explains the persistence of elements like the real humanity, suffering and death of Jesus, his baptism and the descent of the Spirit, his resurrection on the third day and his breathing of the Spirit, and the presence, incidentally, of traditions like that of vicarious atonement. These stand together with the basic christology: the revealer envoy model which proclaims the salvation event and the Son of Man cluster which secures and assures its ongoing availability and abundance in the community of faith. The 'rough edges' are apparent from time to time in the text and the integration is incomplete. The christology of the gospel is christology in development. The potential for greater dominance of the revealer envoy model at the expense of other traditions is already apparent and will be realised in gnosticism. The existence of this state of affairs calls for reflection on the story of this complex christology and its community.

(b) Johannine christology and the Johannine community

(i) Johannine christology and the synagogue

The christology of the fourth gospel has developed in a community of faith and reflects its story. In it there are traces of early conflicts with the synagogue over the claims for Jesus' messiahship and this has doubtless left its mark on the retelling of stories from the Jesus tradition. Of more recent date are: the apparent counter claims against mystical ascent related to Moses; the reflections of the charge of ditheism against the community's christological confession;[111] and the outright confrontation and bitterness expressed against the hardening Jewish stance against the community's proclamation, a stance moving progressively from persecution, to synagogue expulsion and finally to formal denunciation.[112]

Conflict with Judaism is still current,[113] though the break is past. In that respect John's gospel exhibits a similarly bitter, yet already distanced confrontation with Judaism as Matthew's gospel, yet gives less attention to justification of the Christian claim from the Old Testament. This is because the issue has ceased to be fought and rationalised on grounds of messianism and now focusses on transcendental claims about Jesus. The fourth gospel has not abandoned the Old Testament, but it is seen through the eyes of an author who stands within a stream which has linked Torah, wisdom and logos, and has begun to do what Justin did much more fully. It has begun to find the Old Testament heroes witnessing to and acquainted with the divine logos. They bore witness to the new which would replace the old. Failure to perceive this was to reject that same Logos.

Jewish influence

The evidence for Jewish heritage in the Johannine community is strong. The bitterness is hardly just paradigmatic and must spring from memory of hurt, rejection and also persecution. The Jewish heritage is also present in the earlier messianic concerns, the use of traditions later present in Targums, the apparent reaction to Jewish mystical claims about Moses, and the use of the Logos hymn and of images traditionally associated with personified wisdom as Torah in the discourses.

Samaritan influence?

How far Samaritan traditions, let alone Samaritan christianity, played a role in the formation of the community is uncertain, though the author assumes a link with Samaritan Christians in ch. 4.[114] I am not convinced that the early chapters of the gospel reflect its history[115] nor that there is sufficient evidence to show that the higher christology is due to Samaritan influence.[116] Links with early forms of Hellenistic Jewish Christianity of the type represented by Stephen are possible, but must remain hypothetical. Nor has it been convincingly shown that John the Baptist sectarians, against whom the gospel occasionally directs its attention, gave the gospel a significant legacy.

(ii) Johannine christology and the emerging Church

The representation of a range of christological traditions within the gospel, including those used incidentally, and the inheritance of material like that of the synoptic tradition, not least, the passion narrative, indicate that the Johannine church has had relationships with the wider Christian community, despite being sufficiently isolated for its distinctive forms to develop. The role given to Peter in relation to the beloved disciple suggests a continuing relationship, even if it assumes the Johannine group outruns the rest in wisdom and understanding,[117] and John 21 may reflect a stage of cautious realignment and affirmation of belonging with the wider Church.[118]

Distinctive developments of earlier tradition are apparent in: the Son of Man christology, both its focus on exaltation and its inclusion of pre-existence; the expansion of Spirit witness tradition through the Paraclete cycle; the use of wisdom Torah motifs to portray the significance of Jesus' ministry; and, above all, the expansion of Father Son revelation imagery into a full blown revealer envoy model with pre-existence playing a major role and ontology assuming a heightened significance. But the Johannine community seems still in loose association with the wider church as well as having received its early traditions and this traditional commitment continues to operate within the gospel with an established authority.

(iii) Johannine christology and miracle oriented Christianity

There are also indications within the gospel of criticism over against responses to Jesus which express themselves using largely messianic affirmations,[119] but which fail to go on to the insight that Jesus is the sent one from above. These are typically represented in Nicodemus (3:2; cf. also 2:23-25; 4:48).[120] The criticism is not an attack on miracles or on miracle based faith in itself, but it does attack a form of such faith which fails to draw the right conclusions and, given the observations already made about Johannine attitudes to the charismatic in Christianity, we may justifiably, I think, assume that these Christians belonged to such a miracle oriented group, whose christology kept it miracle focussed.[121] I do not consider the author to be concerned, here, with political zealot hopes linked with popular prophetic expectation, as Bittner suggests,[122] nor to be pitting a Moses against a Davidic messiahship, as Schillebeeckx argues.[123] His revealer envoy christology transcends such concerns. This miracle oriented messianic Christianity is inadequate because it fails to confess the one come from above. The evangelist had no qualms in using traditions they doubtless treasured, whether they existed as a collection or as individual units, and even heightened the impressiveness of their miracles, but for him the miracles were now past evidences of the heavenly envoy, manifestations then of the person who now meets them in community, not models of a continuing phenomenon for the faithful. The tensions with Christians of this kind are, I believe, reflected in the split portrayed in 6:60-71.

(iv) Johannine christology and revealer envoy christology

It is another question whether there had also existed a form of Johannine Christianity which had used the revealer envoy model in a more thoroughgoing and literal sense than the evangelist, as, for instance, Langbrandtner suggests in arguing for a gnostic Grundschrift.[124] This is not the place to pursue in detail possible gnostic influence in John or its extent. I have made some brief comments above in IIIB1. But two further observations are relevant. The envoy revealer model with its cosmic dualism, which the author has adapted, has a major place in the gospel and the author's merging of it with a developed Son of Man tradition in no way indicates that he has abandoned it. If gnostic influence lies behind the envoy revealer pattern which the author has adapted, he seems unaware or unconcerned about it, even though its application to Jesus is bound to lead to some degree of docetism. Religio-historical research continues to explore the sources the author or his tradition have employed in adopting this as the primary model and early gnosticism must be counted as a serious option.

The envoy messenger motif

At the same time I do not want to deny the possibility that the envoy revealer pattern, which in its existing form is based on cosmic dualism, has a complex history. The role of the 'shaliach' and messenger in the contemporary world, their stereotype protocol, and the application of these models to heavenly figures have been explored fully by Bühner;[125] they have probably contributed to the Johannine pattern of the sent one. Directly within the Christian community were also sent ones, namely, apostles and missionaries. The language of sending and authorisation was applied early both to Jesus and his disciples (eg. Matt 10:40; Luke 10:16; Jn 13:20). One might also compare the revealer function associated with Father Son language in Matt 11:27; Luke 10:22. Perhaps the charismatic prophet teacher model has, in its turn, at some stage influenced the portrait of Jesus in the tradition of the gospel. According to Boismard, the model of the Mosaic prophet shaped the christology of the earliest form of the gospel and continued its influence in the successive stages of its development.[126] Perhaps also the sending of prophets associated with the Wisdom tradition lies in the background (Luke 11:49-51). The tradition of the sending of the chosen or beloved Son appears in Johannine form in 3:16f and this is close to Gal 4:4 and Rom 8:3. But the form of sending christology which we have in John goes considerably beyond these and is different in the dualism it presupposes, in its soteriology, and above all, in its understanding of the role of pre-existence.[127]

While Paul presupposes pre-existence and later Pauline literature uses wisdom models of christology which presuppose it, in John pre-existence is made to be personally significant for the Son and soteriologically significant. In the revealer envoy model it is the basis on which the revealer has something to tell and in the modified form of the author it remains of major significance in expounding his origin and authority. This is something much closer to forms of early gnosticism as we know them. We noted above that the gospel leaves us with the distinct impression that the author modifies an existing model. While descent ascent patterns were common[128] and had already influenced his tradition, as illustrated by the Son of Man cluster, the foreignness of the model, which the modification presupposes, raises of necessity the question of influence, at least, from a community of ideas not fully compatible with the author's own and where cosmic dualism played a more significant role. This would be compatible with early gnostic influence.[129]

(v) Johannine christology and docetism

At one or possibly two points there seems to be a concern on the part of the author to emphasise Jesus' humanness as though it were being called into question. These are 19:34f and, just possibly, 1:14.[130] The former, particularly, 19:35, is strikingly odd and this gives it all the more weight. It has all the marks of a footnote added to the gospel to counter doubts or doctrines which called into question Jesus' real humanity and death. If this had been a major issue for the evangelist we should have more indication of it in the dialogues and discourses, but in these we find none, unless 6:51c-58 be read in this way. Even then its absence elsewhere in thematic material counts strongly against the hypothesis of Schnelle, for instance, who argues that the gospel has this as a major focus and follows the time of the epistle.[131] It seems to me more likely that the gospel writer is still innocently unaware of how a radical use of his envoy model could imperil the tradition and that this awareness arose at a later date, causing some supplementation, though I am not convinced that the supplements are as extensive as Langbrandtner has proposed.[132]

The gospel without antidocetic supplements could lead some directly to a one sided emphasis of the model and so to gnostic christology. Traditionally, 1 John has been adduced as evidence of this development having occurred and of a split in the community having taken place over this issue. Balz and Lieu may be right in arguing that we misread the epistle when we find in its confessions allusions to docetic doctrine.[133] Denying that Jesus came in the flesh may mean little more than denying Christ. On the other hand, the behavioural characteristics which the author addresses are consonant with a group whose christology had radicalised the dualistic envoy model, developed a triumphalist christology and consequently, like the Corinthians, have come to place a low value on human belonging and community.[134]

Given the importance of the post Easter community noted above and the movement in focus in the last discourses from mission in the first to community maintenance in chs. 15-17, we might well see the development of these chapters as a response to this emerging situation reflected in 1 John.[135] Lieu points out, for instance, that both in 1 John and in John 17 there is a tendency to focus on the message as once given and the community as its preserver, though differences between the two, such as the use of 'truth' and the understanding of revelation, make common authorship unlikely.[136] The increased focus on ecclesiology, especially in ch. 21, and in the person of the beloved disciple, may similarly reflect a later phase when the implications of an exalted and dualistic christology and soteriology threatened unity. Significantly, the epistle seems to have left behind the revealer envoy christology.[137] Correspondingly, its salvific focus moves to Jesus' death as vicarious and to traditional futuristic eschatology. It also shows no indication of tensions with Judaism. Its primary interest is with community identity and its maintenance by mutual love.

(c) Johannine christology and the composition of the gospel

Johannine christology also raises questions about the history of the gospel itself.[138] Here I can do little more than indicate what my analysis of the gospel christology might indicate. I have noted already the likelihood that 19:35 is a later addition and that christological considerations suggest the same for the final discourses beyond 13:31-14:31. There are other well known literary grounds to corroborate this, such as the ending of the latter and its easy connection with 18:1. 15:1-18 is also clearly composed differently from the rest of the gospel and speaks in the present tense about post Easter phenomena. Such straight anachronisms are surprisingly uncommon in John, even if, as a whole, the gospel portrait is materially anachronistic in the sense of having the earthly Jesus presented as we believe only the post Easter community came to know him. Similar straight anachronisms occur mainly in ch. 3, 4 and ch. 6 and these may reflect supplementation. Odd loosely attached pieces, such as those with which I began my study in II (3:31-36 and 12:44-50), reflect a process of composition. They reflect the revealer envoy model in summary form, perhaps from the hand of the evangelist, perhaps from earlier material, but now assume positions of major importance in the transmitted text.

The process of composition also reaches backward to earlier forms and I can only refer to discussion of the various theories. It is beyond the scope of this chapter to examine the various accounts of the origin of the miracle stories. From the perspective of christology they all seem to have been through a process of heightening, which would be consistent with their having been treasured and transmitted in the hands of those whose christology the author wants to supplement as inadequate,[139] but the author owns their massiveness and continues to heighten them through overlaying them with his own christology. This makes discussion of their possibly existing together as a separate body of material difficult; they could equally have been taken up singly[140] or in smaller groupings, such as the Cana miracles,[141] and at different times.[142] If so, we should then have to explain their common christological orientation as one existing within or in relationship to the author's community, and not as something separate. The former seems also likely because of the degree to which there is indication that their use in relationship to discourses has itself a history and is not first the creation of the evangelist.

Source theories should also take into account the evident modification on the author's part of an existing scheme and the degree to which this was reflected already in his sources, the degree to which Son of Man tradition reflects his redaction of earlier material, and the form in which the older Jesus tradition had reached him, which still keeps the new revealer envoy model from cutting adrift.

(d) Conclusion

The issues of the history and tradition of the Johannine community, its background and setting, and the history of the formation of the gospel, continue to be a field of intensive research and have been alluded to here only in summary form. The study of the christology of the gospel in the transmitted text underlines the importance of such research and raises central questions relevant for such study. At the same time it shows that the fourth gospel represents a stage in a history of developing Johannine christology in which dominant patterns are emerging and tensions are apparent. The Jesus tradition of John, heavily influenced by its Jewish heritage, is merging with a stream of cosmic dualistic thought which sees salvation made possible by the coming of a revealer envoy who tells of a heavenly place of rest. The distinctive adaptation of this revealer envoy model and the cosmic dualism it presupposes into the pattern of the envoy Son who offers life in relationship with himself and with the Father dominates the gospel's christology.

It is hardly a throughgoing synthesis, but it illustrates a compromise between this dualism and the Jesus tradition to the extent that the focus is moved from revelation to personal encounter, from place and heavenly station to person and personal relationship with him in the community of faith. This modified revealer envoy model linked with the Son of Man cluster forms the framework within which the author can reshape narrative and sayings tradition using creative literary skill and so making of the gospel both a proclamation and a celebration of faith. The focus, itself, on relationship and the use of Son of Man tradition, in particular, emphasises the gospel community of faith and its mission as the place of the mediated presence of the Son. Community and its maintenance emerge even more strongly in the later farewell discourses, where the distinctive traditions of Son of Man and Son have now merged. Perhaps these already reflect concern with the outworkings of an interpretation of the gospel which diminished the earthly and human community. Beyond the gospel we see a broken community regrouping in 1 John with a christology, by contrast, largely modified, focussed now not on the envoy revealer model, but more directly on God and the community itself and on Christ as its founder and saviour.

The gospel and its christology has continued its formative influence to our own day. In the chapter which follows I offer reflections on its use and abuse and the opportunities it affords for faith's celebration and communication today.

3. Johannine Christology and the Gospel Today

In this final chapter I wish to offer some reflections on the significance of the christology of the gospel for the life of faith in today's world. These include positive as well as negative comments about its influence and use, and hopefully some helpful suggestions about appropriate use of the gospel in the community of faith in the modern world.

Faith and history

The fourth evangelist demonstrates a way of handling issues of faith and history, which, I believe, deserves more serious attention. He remains committed to the fact of the earthly Jesus in history and the event of his ministry as the centre of faith. Yet he does not make faith dependent upon more than some basic details of history. The basic fact is that Jesus confronted his contemporaries with a claim that in him God offers to all people the gift of life in relationship to himself.

The gospel has Jesus express this claim in a distinctively Johannine way and has him make extensive personal claims to justify his authority. These include claims about his own being and origin in particular, such as we do not find in the other gospels and which have little claim to historical authenticity. Yet it seems to me that in having Jesus ultimately make the claim of God upon people in the form of offering them a life giving relationship, the evangelist accurately reproduces the central significance of Jesus for faith. He presented and embodied God's total claim. In him the claim and promise of God's reign presented itself.

By reducing or centering the message of Jesus upon this single claim, the author chooses a point of orientation for Christian proclamation which faithfully represents the essence of the message of Jesus.[143] The centre of Christian faith is thus, for John, a relationship with God the Father through Jesus Christ. The formal character of the Johannine claim about Jesus as the one sent from God, which comes to expression in so many variants in the gospel, has the effect of throwing all the weight upon theology in the strict sense. And the Johannine theology is of a God who loves and involves himself on behalf of the world which he has created. This, too, is simple.[144] It has a present and a future; but in both present and future the focus is on the relationship and the reward is the person of God himself and his glory.

By centering the gospel in this way the author makes faith less dependent upon history. The claim and the relationship are timeless in their relevance and so transcend the limits of history. Yet they are not timeless in the sense of not being involved in time and space. For it is in real history and a real person that this claim was brought to expression and the claim meets people today in real time and space. Hegermann is right in arguing that the fourth gospel does not present us with a timeless Jesus.[145] Bultmann, too, affirms that the revelation remains historical event, encounter with the preached word, not a matter of content, and argues that to make this possible the historical Jesus had to depart.[146] This must not, however, be played off against a significant informational content, which is basic for the author. Nevertheless, as Blank points out, it is the author's tendency to formulate words of Jesus in the light of the whole event which has the effect of liberating the word of Jesus from the confines of history.[147] And similarly, as Riedl notes, the death and resurrection free the event of revelation from its historical immanence in the event of the earthly Jesus.[148]

Theology and community

The understanding of salvation as primarily life in relationship, rather than a status or achieved security, makes the character of God central. God is loving. God is creator. Accordingly, when the gospel spells out the meaning of salvation it uses relationship language, such as love and mutual indwelling. Thus Forestell draws attention to salvation in John as a state of dynamic intercommunion, something much richer than forgiveness of sins.[149] And Bultmann and others have drawn attention to the explication of salvation in terms which embody basic human need: life, light, water, bread, truth, way.[150] While these function metaphorically, they convey the insight that what is offered by God in Christ is what the human being and the human community needs for the sake of its humanity before God, not a promise of distraction or escape from being human.

The centering upon relationship with God extends, consistently, to include relationships among believers and so lays the foundation for a profoundly community oriented understanding of the life of faith. This aspect comes too short in Bultmann's individualising existentialist interpretation. The evangelist also treats the community dimension of faith very simply, offering virtually no indication of how it should be worked out in reality. Concrete instructions are missing. In their place is the commandment of love. There are hints of sacramental life and real indications of a concern with order which authenticates the gospel, especially in the figures of Peter and the beloved disciple and in the writing of the gospel itself with its appeal to be trusted; but as a whole, the community receives only one simple rule of ethics, to love as they have been loved.

Faith and relationship

The Johannine understanding of faith is not one of obedience to laws; nor of adherence to a range of beliefs, except to the central one about who Jesus is and whom he represents. The focus of Johannine salvation is not a place of escape. In this it differs in emphasis from gnosticism with whose formulations it has otherwise much in common. Its salvation is not an experience, visionary or ecstatic. Nor does it centre upon forgiveness of sins, though it includes this; for this would be to remain at the level of dealing with the effects of unfaith, not its root and, on the fourth gospel's understanding, sin is primarily rejection of the gift of the person of Jesus. Nor is Jesus' death as atonement central, though this tradition is present in the gospel. The same must be said of the motif of casting out the ruler of this world. And even though the gospel employs stories of astounding miracles, in contrast to most other New Testament accounts, there is remarkably no hint whatever that the promised Spirit, the Paraclete, would guarantee such miraculous phenomena in the time of the Church.[151] The primary focus throughout is upon salvation as relationship in life with a person who loves and goes on loving even in the face of rejection and death and the living out of that relationship in

Christian community.

Faith and symbol

The Johannine gospel, more than any other, transposes faith into the language of existential symbolism, the language of metaphor, and so recognises that symbol and metaphor are the most effective language of faith's expression and communication. The use of this kind of language belongs together with the other tendencies we have been noting and would not really be possible without them. This is particularly so of the gospel's treatment of history, its method of simplification and centering, and its focus on relationship. The rich use of symbol and metaphor has won the gospel a major place in Christian history. It is precisely because it is less historical that it is historically more effective and, arguably, more faithful in portraying the meaning of the event of Jesus. It is a naive misuse of the gospel to preach it as history,[152] liable to lead to naively docetic Christianity. In its real character the gospel offers its own distinctive model for communication of faith today and challenges us to move away from strongly cognitive and intellectual formulations of faith to creative forms of self expression and communication that live in the language of art and symbol, the language of dream and metaphor where the deeper levels of our being find expression. The gospel invites emulation in the way it celebrates faith in the dramatic retelling of the stories of Jesus and the subtle irony with which it engages its audience in the tensions and the wonder of the Word in the world, including their contemporary one. Yet the balance of the gospel is to be preserved. It employs metaphor and myth in full awareness that here is also something to be believed; for something took place within real history and takes place within real history.

'In my Father's house'

The fourth gospel also has its dangers. While at its base is a theology of God as involved and loving, the future dimension of faith's hope, God's presence in its most intimate sense, is in heaven above and not in this world. Traditional eschatology is no longer the centre of faith, because faith's ultimate goal is the divine presence in heaven. This easily becomes: faith's ultimate goal is heaven, a place of escape from this world. The words, 'In my Father's house are many dwelling places' (14:2) are among the best known of the gospel and have frequently projected themselves to the centre of popular Christianity. The gospel does not put the focus here. Its dualism of 'above' and 'below' is subordinate to faith in the person, rather than the place, of God. One can cease to be 'from below' through responding to the challenge of God's offer in the Son. To be 'from above' is then primarily a way of describing a relationship with God, not a relationship with a place, even though the author still retains the spatial and temporal distinction between life now on earth and then in heaven. But when the emphasis is reversed, so that instead of God, the issues of space and time become central, something happens to people's attitude to the world. The world becomes merely a staging post and at worst a creation of evil powers.

Unearthed eschatology

This danger is also an indirect result of the replacement of traditional apocalyptic eschatology. Where salvation includes submission in faith to the God who promises to establish his reign of justice and peace, raise people from the dead, and transform heaven and earth, and where this is seen as an event already breaking into the present, there remains a lively concern with what is to be, and is being, transformed: heaven and earth, body and spirit, justice and peace now. The danger of reducing all of this to the simplicity of a relationship with its ultimate goal as God's heavenly presence is loss of these traditional perspectives. This lays open the possibility that the world will be devalued in itself. There is also the danger that Jesus himself is seen as not really a human being and the further consequence that concern with what belongs to human flesh, from human sexuality to human welfare and social justice in the widest sense, comes to be seen as irrelevant. The author's dramatic technique contributes further to this danger, since it often lifts Jesus above normal humanity and human interaction. The image of an unreal humanity in the dramatic portrayal of Jesus easily spawns unreal expectations of humanity, such that Christians who follow their master should always be at peace, never troubled, never depressed.

Political awareness?

Rensberger's observations about underlying political attitudes in the passion narrative which show Christ's kingship pitted against Jewish authority and against Roman authority are pertinent,[153] but nowhere are these political attitudes in direct focus and they remain incidental and at the level of general stance. Meeks's observations about the self consciously withdrawn character of the community and its christology more accurately portray the tone of the gospel,[154] though, it seems to me, mission to the world is still part of the community's self understanding more than Meeks allows.

My concern is not to say that the fourth gospel must lead to such conclusions, but that it can. For it is a gospel with loose ends. It does not present us with a rounded, systematically consistent, picture of Jesus. It reflects christology in a state of flux. The particular methods employed in its production, especially centering, simplifying, and literary techniques such as dramatic irony, mean that it can easily be misread and has been.

Dualism or theology

The dualism which seeks escape from this world can interpret the relationship centred salvation entirely in its own terms as 'making right connections' for eternal security. But relationship oriented faith includes relationship with God, with Christ, and with fellow believers. The key to the quality of that life in relationship is the understanding of God. Where God is thought of as promising an alternative to life in the world, then the community of faith will understand itself as community constituted by its not belonging to the world. Brotherly love becomes mutual support for survival and defence. The formal character of relationship oriented faith is thus vulnerable at the point of its theological premise, in the strict sense. This is why Lattke, following Käsemann, must explain away the usual sense of John 3:16, for their theories of the Johannine community see it as just such a community as we have described,[155] hardly one whose God loves the world as 3:16 might suggest. Where a community of faith is a self reproducing, self supporting, community, bent on escape from the world, its contacts with non believers will be limited to the invitation to them to join them in the flight. The fourth gospel has been, and is frequently, made to serve such a pattern of religion. Meeks notes that the combination of antiworldly sectarian self understanding with the Logos Sophia myth sets the stage for a Valentinian kind of gnosticism.[156] This is all the more possible because the gospel has no teaching about ethics outside of the community of faith. Traditional values preserved in apocalyptic eschatology, such as peace among the nations, justice for the poor and oppressed, redemption and transformation of the creation, are absent.

3:16 - rescuing the world's inhabitants?

Does, therefore, John 3:16 mean anything more than an indication of God's initiative to help people escape the world? Is mission, as Appold suggests, not unlike the gnostic preoccupation with gathering people out of the world?[157] Or does mission and fruitbearing mean being sent to share the gift of life now in the world, as Thüsing argues?[158] Much depends on the weight given to elements which do not share centre stage whether we see in the gospel an early form of gnostic faith or one more rooted in traditional Christianity. These elements include the statement about the creation of all things in the prologue, the extent of Jesus' real humanity, and the degree to which the gift of salvific life is related not only to the heavenly world, but, through the Logos and through God as creator, to creation itself. In my view these are sufficiently present as to indicate that the dualism has not gone so far as to deny inherent value to human life on earth and to Jesus' humanity.

As far as creation is concerned, I would agree with Schottroff that it is not denied by the author, though it does not come into his concerns.[159] But for the reasons set out above, I dispute her conclusion that the gospel is already gnostic in its dualism.[160] The matter is, however, by no means straightforward and the story which is at the centre of the author's christology, without its props, would grace a gnostic stage without too much modification, as history has shown. Already the first epistle of John is understood by many as attacking a form of Johannine christianity which displays in reality many of the dangers we have noted. The author attacks a lack of concern for temporal needs, an apparent denial of the human Jesus, and a spiritual perfectionism which results from an unrealistic view of ethics and spirituality.

The Centrality of Love

The focus in the last discourses, in particular, is not on recruiting disciples who shall go on a numbers drive to fill heavenly places, but on a quality of life lived already on earth in community. This is where the author's focus on person and personal relationship rather than place transcends dualistic concerns. While the notion of enabling grace, such as we find in Paul, is not so elaborated in John, there can be little doubt that the central story of Johannine christology is about an initiative of love in which through the Son God also offers life and love, calls people into relationship with himself, and sends them to be bearers of this life and love in the world. Despite its formal structure it is not a story about revelation of special gnosis, nor primarily a story about a promised future time or place. The dynamic quality of this life and love is so central that it strongly relativises any underlying dualism of time and place.

Antisemitism?

A further matter of concern has been the gospel's portrait of the Jews, which has left it open to be used as a vehicle of antisemitism.[161] It is one thing to grapple with the wonder of divine grace and seek an explanation in the direction of predestination of the astonishing blindness of people to its light. It is another when this is turned as a weapon to defame opponents and bolster one's self identity. Many find this happening in the author's presentation of Jesus' confrontation of the Jews in John 8, and the same kind of confrontation is undertaken in 1 John against those who 'have gone out from among us'. It is, of course, an error to take 'Jews' as a reference to all Jews by race or religion and find John to be antisemitic in that sense. The Johannine community itself probably included a large number of Jews and the Johannine Christ declares that salvation is of the Jews (4:22). Much of the time the author attacks the leaders of the Jewish people. But the author's overall methodology of simplification and dramatic enrichment has also produced a radically simplified and stereotyped image of the Jews whom Jesus confronted and failure to perceive the author's method and therefore the nature of the gospel leads, here, too, to dangerous distortion.

Faith's witness in faith's community

The New Testament witness reaches the heights in the Johannine portrait of Jesus the Son, who has come as the sent one from the Father to bear his word of life to all. The simplicity and power of of the Johannine portrait, its daring strokes and colours, make it a centrepiece and icon of faith. But the artist's achievement is at the expense of imprecision and ambiguity. The fourth gospel needs the epistles. It also needs the rest of the New Testament. It is primarily a document of faith's celebration, a drama enriching the community's self understanding and must be handled as such. Because it is so powerfully faith's self-expression, it is also powerfully faith's witness. It is a dangerous gospel when read without this understanding. But properly understood, it succeeds more than any other New Testament writing in identifying the heart of Christian faith, as life in relationship with the Son and the Father in the communion of love, love sent out into the world.

CONCLUSION

The concern of this study has been to approach the issues of Johannine christology by first analysing its central structure. This first step included noting christological structures in select passages, tracing the elements of these structures and collating their occurrence in the gospel, identifying christological summaries in the gospel, and reviewing the gospel as a whole in the search for significant structures. The central structure of Johannine christology, which emerged from these findings, may be expressed as follows:

The Father

sends and authorises the Son,

who knows the Father,

comes from the Father, makes the Father known,

brings light and life and truth,

completes his Father's work,

returns to the Father,

exalted, glorified, ascended,

sends the disciples

and sends the Spirit

to enable greater understanding,

to equip for mission,

and to build up the community of faith.

On the basis of this analysis we turned to an examination of the major issues which have emerged in Johannine research and which were identified in Part I. We also took into account questions which had been raised during the investigation of the structure of the christology, in Part II.

We began with a consideration of statements related to the death of Jesus and his return to the Father. We noted that the pattern of the Son's coming and return need, in itself, give no more significance to the death of Jesus than to see it as the point of exit. We saw, however, that it assumes a greater significance for the author. It represents the fulfilment of the Son's mission. We then considered whether this means that the author saw that fulfilment in terms of an act of vicarious or sacrificial atonement. We found this not to be so. The author uses traditions of vicarious atonement in the gospel, but mostly in an incidental manner and never as a major theme. Finishing the Father's work means faithfully fulfilling to the end the task of making the Father known and of presenting the world with his offer of light and life. Accordingly the cross is the point at which the issues of this claim come to a head: the world passes judgement on the Son. It is also the moment of supreme revelation. For in it the world and its ruler is judged, sin is revealed and the Son vindicated.

In the context of discussing Jesus' death we considered also the motifs of exaltation and glorification. We saw that they are best understood in the traditional sense of exaltation of the Son to the presence of God and to divine glory. The Pauline paradox of the cross as both suffering and glory is not found in John. Nor is the dual meaning of *hypsoō*, to mean lift up and exalt, an indication that the cross itself is being interpreted in this way, namely, as the Son's exaltation. The Johannine paradox does employ the dual meaning of *hypsoō*, but it does so by portraying the path to exaltation as the way of the cross. The world sees only the lifting up on the cross; faith sees exaltation through the event of the cross to the divine presence.

We found this understanding of Jesus' return to the Father as exaltation to glory to be also the most probable meaning of the heavenly vision promised believers in Jesus' words to Nathanael in 1:51. We noted also the association of exaltation with the motif of Jesus' ascent (and descent) and the regular association of these motifs with the title, Son of Man. We identified, thus, a 'Son of Man cluster' of motifs which include: the title, Son of Man; exaltation; glorification; ascension (and descent); 'the hour', 'the time', 'now'; judgement; and the promise of a 'greater event' to come. Son of Man, while used sometimes of Jesus' earthly ministry, seems primarily associated in John with motifs which describe the climax of Jesus' ministry, in particular his exaltation and its implications.

We then considered the resurrection tradition in the gospel and saw how the motif of the Son's coming and return had not produced, as it might have, a christology according to which Jesus ascended directly from the cross; rather traditions of return and resurrection merge, if sometimes awkwardly, as evidenced in Jesus' words to Mary, so that a pattern is preserved of death, resurrection on the third day, ascent to the glory of Father, appearances of the exalted glorified risen one, and the giving of the Spirit, the Johannine Pentecost.

The event, so described, is the 'greater event' to which the Son points forward during his ministry, often using the motifs of the Son of Man cluster. It is the 'greater' heavenly vision of the Son of Man served by angels in 1:51, which is greater than the confession of Jesus as Son of God. It is the 'heavenly things' of 3:12, explicated in 3:13-15 as the Son of Man's ascent and exaltation, greater than the 'earthly things' Jesus has been speaking of in 3:1-11, the announcement of new birth. It is the Son of Man ascending where he was before (6:62), greater than his descending as bread from heaven. It is the basis for 'greater works' by the disciples (14:12), greater than the works of the Son, because he goes to the Father.

We saw that the promise of the 'greater event' focusses not on the addition of a greater gift of life than was present in Jesus' ministry, nor on the realisation of what some see as only a proleptic offer of life during Jesus' ministry, nor on the fruits of an atonement not yet complete. Rather it interprets Jesus' return to the Father and the sending of the Spirit as the basis for greater availability, abundance and understanding of that gift of life, present in the person of the Son. Greater availability and abundance includes reference to mission and to the presence of the Son and the Father in the believers through the Spirit. Greater understanding includes the work of the Paraclete which calls to remembrance the words and work of Jesus, interprets them in the light of scripture, mediates the words of the exalted Lord to the community, and leads the disciples into all truth concerning who Jesus is and the meaning of his death and return to the Father. Ultimately the 'greater event' is what constitutes the community of faith as the place of the presence of the light and life made manifest in the incarnation of the Son. We also saw that the path of Jesus through suffering set a pattern for the community's own self understanding. Theirs, too, is the promise to follow that path and find themselves also where he is and share in his heavenly glory.

We turned then to the salvation event itself, the Son's making the Father known, and saw that the author uses, but significantly modifies, the revealer envoy model. The Son offers not information or revelation, but relationship. He presents himself as the light and life and invites the response of faith. This is the primary meaning of the 'I am' sayings, with and without predicate. The 'I am' of Isaiah 43 may stand as analogy, but 'I am' is not, itself, a pronunciation of the divine name, as often supposed. In the dialogues the Son repeatedly asserts that 'he is the one' who has come from the Father to make him known. His miracles, the signs, are to be understood as achievements indicative of his divine glory as Son of God sent from above and true faith sees them as such. They also function as symbols of the life he brings.

The modification of the revealer envoy model to one of encounter and of the offer of life in relationship also focusses attention away from salvation as place and so also modifies the significance of the dualistic framework in which it is expressed. Faith still looks to a future presence with the Son in heaven, but the relationship and the person is the centre, not time and place. Similarly salvation is not primarily contractual achievement through atonement, victory over powers, or imparting ecstatic experience, but the offer of life in a person. Christology is the centre of soteriology and also of eschatology.

The salvation event, considered as the presence of the Son, raises questions about who the Son is. In particular, we explored whether the author also modified the revealer envoy model in relationship to statements about the Son's pre-existence. We found the evidence for this was not strong. The noted discrepancy between the common statements about the Son's hearing and seeing in pre-existence what he says and does on earth and 5:19f, which speaks of a present seeing and hearing on earth, dissolves when it is realised that the language of seeing and hearing belongs to the envoy messenger motif which the author has modified. 5:19f uses apprenticeship imagery; the other statements use messenger imagery. Both are employed for the single purpose of saying that the Son represents the Father and does his work.

We found pre-existence to be important in the author's christology, not to explain how the Son received information and revelation, as a literal understanding of the revealer envoy would suggest, but for the Son's authorisation, origin, and ultimately, his being. We considered the question of the Son's being, both in relationship to the extraordinary statements of the prologue that he is *theos* and in relation to the way in which his being is asserted and defended in the dialogues. We saw a consistent defense against the charge of ditheism by appeal to the way the Son acted in complete obedience and subordination to the Father's will. Claims to be one or equal with the Father were always explained in these terms. On the other hand, we also saw that this went far beyond a functional christology which might see in Jesus a human being like any other, but perfectly in harmony with God. For the author presupposes an ontology which sets the Son apart from all mortals. It is his distinctive being, his distinctive origin, which enables him to come as the sent one and to be the light and life of God on earth.

The author never surrenders monotheism and accusations in this direction are treated almost playfully as a bad joke and exploited dramatically by the author. Yet the precise character of the Son's being *theos* is not defined. Its context in wisdom logos tradition suggests the analogy with these and other Jewish figures who may bear the title without surrender of monotheism, but such figures range from personifications to representative angels and kings. None brings together the two poles of reality present in Johannine christology: a real human being and an eternally existent heavenly Son. We rejected attempts to force a compromise in the Johannine material by, for instance, interpreting the pre-existent logos as anhypostatic. Johannine christology marks out the ground for later controversy and construction, but also in some sense sets the rules by affirming together: monotheism, the Son as distinct, yet *theos*, and the Son as Jesus of Nazareth.

Our discussion of the Son as Jesus of Nazareth took into consideration the battles fought over 'The Word became flesh' and its meaning and over the alleged naive docetism of the gospel. We found strong indications that the author would have affirmed Jesus' real humanity, including his real suffering and death. On the other hand, we also had to acknowledge that the Jesus of John's gospel is portrayed in ways which would normally call any claim to real humanity into question. This need not have been the case with the massive miracles, given the analogies of possessed human beings working wonders, but, because this is not the Johannine model and because the author constantly presents Jesus with both superhuman power and superhuman knowledge of his past and future, even in first century terms, John's Jesus would have been easily read as a mere appearance of a man. Both streams of thought are present: Jesus, remembered as a real human being, and Jesus, the eternally existent Son.

The Johannine gospel also, therefore, sets the rules, as it were, here for subsequent discussion: it affirms Jesus as Son and affirms his real humanity. We found it also useful to make a clear distinction between what the author probably intended in his portrayal and what was the result. Explanations that the post Easter perspective of faith influenced the portrayal help us with the former, not with the latter. We cannot help but see a much modified humanity in the portrait. But our discussion argued that in intention the author would not have denied Jesus' real humanity. The situation is further complicated by clear evidence of deliberate literary technique on the part of the author, with which he must have been aware he was modifying the portrait in ways that were unhistorical, even if not 'un-human'.

This latter observation also became important for understanding the author's approach to history in the gospel and for understanding the nature of the gospel itself. We noted the author's regular indications that Easter made a difference to the disciples' understanding of Jesus. The 'greater event' motif highlights this. The author seems aware of standing within a living tradition inspired by the work of the Paraclete who is leading him and his community into all truth concerning Jesus, past and present. But especially the self conscious literary techniques demanded that we saw the gospel not as history, but as a communication within a knowing community which has enough inside information to appreciate the irony and other devices being used.

The centrality of the Son's coming, his making the Father known, offering light and life and truth, makes the earthly Jesus of history of paramount importance: hence the writing of a gospel. The freedom to reshape the tradition for the community's celebration and to edify its faith by creating a dramatic, almost stereotypical presentation of Jesus and his conversation partners, scene after scene, means that the author's commitment to history was limited. We noted that the same simplifying and centering tendency evident in the author's understanding of the salvation event correspondingly affects his interest in history. Not the sheer fact of Jesus in history is enough. It is important that the story of his encounters be told and that of his death and resurrection; but the contours suffice. Details can vary with the artist's brush. The Johannine gospel is an icon of faith's celebration. Everywhere one looks, one sees a reflection of the whole. And what one sees is nothing less, the author would contend, than the light and life of the Son which shone among the disciples.

The analysis of the structure of the christology and its major issues also raises questions about the background of that christology and its community. This study focussed deliberately on the transmitted text of the gospel as it has been received. This was in part my not wanting to have the reader wade through a jungle of 'ifs' and 'buts'. It was also on methodological grounds: start first with the received text; then go beyond it. I am aware that this is not the only option. We undertake research in constant interplay between text and tradition. Nevertheless my aim in beginning this way was also to allow questions to arise from the analysis of the christology which might be pertinent to the issues of Johannine history, tradition and community. I addressed these in a summary manner in IIIC2.

We observed there that significant streams of christological thought merge in the gospel, but that at many points we can still see indications of where they have come from and sometimes see signs of turbulence where they mix. We noted first the dominance of the revealer envoy model and the way the author uses it to integrate a wide range of traditions. It is the overlay which covers the author's tradition, from the announcements of John the Baptist to the passion narrative. Prophetic, messianic, miracle focussed christology all served its primary message to declare Jesus the Son sent from the Father. Miracles in particular are not denied, but seem so totally transcended, both in the portrait of Jesus and in the description of the work of the Paraclete, that all the indications point to a complete absence of the charismatic miraculous in the Johannine church. It is also the context into which the author adapts wisdom christology. Even the sending of the Spirit and of the disciples is portrayed after the envoy pattern. We also saw the effect of this dominance on the author's understanding of salvation, eschatology and pneumatology, particularly in the modified form of the model which the author makes the centrepiece of his christology.

We noticed, too, the role of the Son of Man cluster in bridging the hermeneutical distance between the ministry of Jesus and the time of the evangelist, and above all, in underlining the importance of the community as the place of the presence of Jesus after Easter. We saw that the Son of Man traditions had already been expanded to include first exaltation and then also pre-existence. It was noteworthy that the Son of Man version of pre-existence and post-existence employed the distinctive descent ascent language. This probably indicated a development having taken place before the gospel, since in the gospel coming and returning is usually associated with the title, Son, and with a different set of verbs of movement.

The merging of the Son of Man cluster and the central story of the coming of Jesus as the revealer envoy still shows that both have an independent origin. This is particularly indicated by the fact that the author, while using the revealer envoy model with its dualistic cosmology, must significantly adapt it. Its independent existence seems also to be indicated by the way in which the author uses the distinctive Son of Man cluster to expand it and by the tensions which that produces in the understanding of such motifs as glory, judgement, and life. Altogether it is an extraordinary feature of John's gospel that it has at its centre a model which requires the death of Jesus to mean nothing more than his exit and his life on earth to be nothing other than an appearance; yet we find in the same gospel the persistence of a wide range of traditions including many vital to the author, like those attesting Jesus' humanity, death, resurrection, beside others, somewhat incidental, like vicarious atonement. The author obviously stands well rooted in the Jesus tradition and daringly adapts new material in the light of it.

We considered briefly indications of Jewish influence, reflections of a history of bitter conflict with the synagogue, and suggestions of Samaritan or Baptist traditions. We noted the significance of miracle based messianic Christianity, the relations with the wider church, the possibility of gnostic dualism as a background for the revealer envoy model and the suggestions of antidocetic emphasis in the gospel.

In the course of time the diverse and structurally divergent tendencies latent in the gospel would inevitably lead to new resolutions and some would be effected where the Jesus tradition was not so strong as it appears to be for the author. The christology of the gospel could be resolved in the direction of a strongly exalted christology like that at Corinth, if not like that of later docetism, and we recognised the probability, both that something like this will have occurred by the time of 1 John, and that response to it may already have led to expansion of the gospel through the later discourses and the antidocetic footnote of 19:35. In 1 John itself we see a reassertion of themes like vicarious atonement and future eschatology back into the mainstream and a probable marginalising of the revealer envoy model.

Finally we turned to the understanding and use of the gospel today, noting the strength of its simplifying, centering approach to christology for understanding history and faith. We also noted the dangers of reading (let alone preaching) it without some awareness of its special character and discussed the negative implications of its cosmic dualism and person centred salvation which left out of account the vision of a transformed world of justice and peace, present in Jesus' message of the kingdom. Nevertheless we saw in the gospel a challenge and a pattern for faith's celebration, a vehicle to enrich and stimulate faith, a unique witness which is to be treasured and read within the context of the canonical tradition and in the continuing community of faith. For this is the place of the presence of Jesus, according to its thought, and here its perspectives can be appreciated, its dangers counterbalanced, and its rootedness in Jesus tradition upheld.

NOTES

(In the notes monographs and articles are cited by author, shortened title and page number. Full bibliographical information for each work cited will be found in the Bibliography)

Notes to pp. 1 - 4

PART I Introduction

1. Kysar, 'The Fourth Gospel', 43.
2. 'Was ist seine zentrale Anschauung, seine Grundkonzeption?' in 'Bedeutung', 404. The article, 'Die Bedeutung der neuerschlossenen mandäischen und manichäischen Quellen für das Verständnis des Johannesevangeliums', appeared first in 1925 and represents the foundational statement of Bultmann's interpretation of Johannine christology developed later in his commentary, Das Evangelium des Johannes, first published in 1941, and in his Theologie des Neuen Testaments, first published in 1953. See also: 'Der religionsgeschichtliche Hintergrund des Prologs zum Johannesevangelium' (1923); 'Die Eschatologie des Johannes-Evangeliums' (1928); 'Untersuchungen zum Johannesevangelium' (1928/1930); the article, 'Johannesevangelium' in RGG III (1959) and the review article, 'Zur Interpretation des Johannesevangeliums' (1962).
3. 'Bedeutung', 407-455.
4. 'Bedeutung', 406f; Theologie, 365f, 389.
5. 'Bedeutung', 412-425, 459-465.
6. Johannes, 107; Theologie, 365, 369, 392f.
7. Johannes, 41f
8. Johannes, 42, 103f, 190.
9. Johannes, 190; Theologie, 191 n. 5.
10. Theologie, 387.
11. Johannes, 1, 103f, Theologie, 364.
12. Theologie, 415-418.
13. Johannes, 191f n. 5; Theologie, 385f, 414f.
14. Johannes, 26f, 39; Theologie, 420, cf. 379.
15. Johannes, 27f; Theologie, 370, 373.
16. Johannes, 189.
17. Johannes, 41f.
18. Johannes, 40f, 42, 75.
19. Johannes, 83.
20. Johannes, 79, 92; Theologie, 492.
21. Johannes, 232f, 261, 377, 432.
22. Johannes, 40; Theologie, 403.
23. Johannes, 325, 328, 330, 375f, 379.
24. Johannes, 341.
25. Johannes, 328, 375f; Theologie, 400.
26. Johannes, 325, 45.
27. Johannes, 189, 191 n. 5, 232.
28. Theologie, 387.
29. Theologie, 402; Johannes, 356.

Notes to pp. 5 - 8

30. Theologie, 408f.
31. Johannes, 430f, Theologie, 437, 395
32. Theologie, 400.
33. Johannes, 188, Theologie, 418.
34. Johannes, 410f.
35. Johannes, 66; Theologie, 406 n. 1.
36. Theologie, 408.
37. Johannes, 293, 372; Theologie, 405-407.
38. Theologie, 391f.
39. Johannes, 399; Theologie, 437.
40. Johannes, 330.
41. Johannes, 402.
42. Theologie, 412.
43. Johannes, 306f.
44. Johannes, 376f.
45. Johannes, 356 n. 24, 533; Theologie, 405.
46. Johannes, 298, 540.
47. Theologie, 418.
48. Theologie, 416f.
49. Theologie, 419.
50. Haenchen, 'Vater', 69; 'Das Johannesevangelium', 219; Johannes, 106; Käsemann, 'Prologue', 161; Letzter Wille, 54; Bornkamm, 'Interpretation', 116; Hegermann, 'Eigentum', 113.
51. Wilkens, Zeichen, 27, 30, 32, 44, 49, 66.
52. So Haenchen, Johannes, 106; similarly Schnackenburg, 'Frage', 205f; Appold, Oneness, 95, 100f; von den Osten-Sacken, 'Leistung', 161; Nicol, Semeia, 106.
53. Schnackenburg, John I, 517; similarly Nicol, Semeia, 99-103; Forestell, Word, 70; Appold, Oneness, 100.
54. Becker, 'Wunder', 144-148; Johannes, 119f; similarly Lattke, Einheit, 143.
55. Schottroff, Glaubende, 258f; similarly Langbrandtner, Weltferner Gott, 93-96, for the Grundschrift, cf. 111.
56. Käsemann, Letzter Wille, 17, 53, 53 n. 59.
57. Schottroff, Glaubende, 252-259; similarly Lattke, Einheit, 143; Schlier, 'Christologie', 85-88.
58. Käsemann, Letzter Wille, 22, 53f; cf. already Baur, Kritische Untersuchungen, 87, 313; and Holtzmann, Lehrbuch, 458; Bousset, Kyrios Christos, 217f.
59. Schweizer, 'Zeuge', 162f.
60. Bultmann, Theologie, 403.
61. Bornkamm, 'Interpretation', 112, 114; similarly von den Osten-Sacken, 'Leistung', 160; Wilkens, Zeichen, 51f, 66; Appold, Oneness, 111; cf. also Schweizer, 'Zeuge', 167.
62. Thüsing, Erhöhung, 335; similarly Haacker, Stiftung, 167f.
63. Bornkamm, 'Interpretation', 114.
64. As, for instance, Schottroff suggests, Glaubende, 279; similarly U.B. Müller, 'Bedeutung', 52 n. 15.
65. Käsemann, Letzter Wille, 61f. See also Schulz, Johannes, 211f; von den Osten-Sacken, 'Leistung', 157; Richter, Studien, 112, 114, (docetism in the gospel; antidocetism in redaction); similarly Thyen, 'Brüder', 536; Langbrandtner, Weltferner Gott, 38, 95f. Against docetism in John see Wilkens, Zeichen, 67; Bornkamm, 'Paraklet', 89; 'Interpretation', 117f.
66. Schweizer, 'Kirchenbegriff', 363f.
67. Käsemann, Letzter Wille, 22-24.

Notes to pp. 8 - 13

68. Bornkamm, 'Interpretation', 113, 117
69. Käsemann, Letzter Wille, 49 n. 53; Bultmann, Theologie, 392.
70. Richter, Studien, 152, 157f, 170, 179-182; Thyen, 'Brüder', 532; 'Entwicklungen', 259-299.
71. Schottroff, Glaubende, 272, 275; similarly U.B.Müller, 'Bedeutung', 52 n. 15; Schulz, Johannes, 211f.
72. Müller, 'Bedeutung',66f; Christologie, 13-36; similarly Becker, Johannes, 78.
73. Ibuki, Wahrheit, 193-198; similarly Schlier, 'Prolog', 195f, 282.
74. Robinson, Priority, 368-389; Watson, 'Christology'.
75. Mussner, Sehweise, 42f, 57, 81, 84.
76. Leroy, Ratsel, 71; similarly Olsson, Structure, 282f.
77. Martyn, 'History and Theology', 30, 129.
78. Martyn, 'History and Theology', 28; similarly Smalley, John, 178, cf. also 194f.
79. Riesenfeld, 'Gospel Tradition', 151f; Morris, John, 45-47.
80. Temple, Core, 286f.
81. Cadman, Open Heaven, 203f; similarly Brun, 'Gottesschau'; cf. also Robinson, Priority, 368-389.
82. Schnackenburg, John I, 23.
83. Schulz, Menschensohn, 179.
84. Grundmann, Zeugnis, 14.
85. Haacker, Stiftung, 59f.
86. de Jonge, Stranger, 8, 11f; Bornkamm, 'Paraklet', 87-89; Onuki, Gemeinde, 194.
87. So Haenchen, 'Vater', 74.
88. Bultmann, Johannes, 59.
89. See the discussion in von Wahlde, 'Jews'; also Pancaro, Law.
90. Schottroff, Glaubende, 230, 285f.
91. Schottroff, Glaubende, 228, cf. 232f.
92. Schottroff, Glaubende, 228, 285.
93. Schottroff, Glaubende, 272-274, 279.
94. Dodd, Interpretation, 142f, 445 n. 1.
95. Schottroff, Glaubende, 289, 295.
96. Haenchen, 'Das Johannesvangelium', 223f.
97. Käsemann, Letzter Wille, 95f n. 36b.
98. Langbrandtner, Weltferner Gott, 91-93; but see the criticism of this assessment of gnosticism by Onuki, Gemeinde, 53 and the review of Schottroff by Schenke in TLZ 97 (1972) 755.
99. Bergmeier, Glaube, 213-236.
100. Käsemann, Letzter Wille, 30f, 59; Appold, Oneness, 20, 272, 282f, 280f; similarly Ibuki, Wahrheit, 149, 358.
101. Haenchen, Johannes, 197; similarly Bornkamm, 'Paraklet', 69, 77-79; Miranda, Sendung, 37f, 42; de Jonge, Stranger, 141-150.
102. Riedl, Heilswerk, 421-423, 153, 201-205; Blank, Krisis, 36, 69, 72, 222-224.
103. Barrett, 'Father'; 'Theocentric'.
104. Haenchen, 'Vater', 72; Johannes, 226.
105. See Bultmann, Theologie, 414, 418.
106. Rengstorf, Art. 'apostellw', TDNT 1, 398-406; Kühl, Sendung; Borgen, Bread from Heaven, 158-162; also 'Agent'; Miranda, Vater; Sendung; Bühner, Gesandte.
107. Bühner, Gesandte, 310, 373-378.
108. Haenchen, Johannes, 218.
109. Cf. Hengel, Sohn Gottes, 73-77.
110. Haacker, Stiftung, 34-60.

Notes to pp. 13 - 18

111. So, for instance, Haacker, Stiftung, 90-134.
112. T.E. Müller, Heilsgeschehen, 130-132; also Miranda, Vater, 125f, 140; Sendung, 24f; Thüsing, Erhöhung, 68 n. 1, 164; Haacker, Stiftung, 169-173; Riedl, Heilswerk, 313f; Wilkens, Zeichen, 77; cf. also Richter, Studien, 305, 312 (for the Grundschrift); Langbrandtner, Weltferner Gott, 109 (for the redactor); similarly Becker, Johannes, 407.
113. Bultmann, Johannes, 188; Theologie, 418.
114. So Thüsing, Erhöhung, 14, 164, 171; Painter, 'Eschatology', 50f; 'Christ and the Church', 361f; Schillebeeckx, Christ, 405f, 410f.
115. Contrast Dauer, Passiongeschichte, 39.
116. Forestell, Word, 191; similarly Käsemann, Letzter Wille, 23; Painter, Witness, 63; Smalley, John, 224-226.
117. Hegermann, 'Eigentum', 119f, 126f; U.B. Müller, 'Bedeutung', 63.
118. T. Preiss, Life in Christ, 9-31. See also Blank, Krisis, 92f, 284f; Dauer, Passionsgeschichte, 247-249, 261; Hahn, 'Prozess', 68-85; Dahl, 'Church', 135; Meeks, 'Man from Heaven', 155.
119. Forestell, Word, 113; similarly Moloney, Son of Man, 38, 41.
120. Bornkamm, 'Interpretation', 114; 'Paraklet', 60.
121. Bornkamm, 'Interpretation', 113; Moloney, Son of Man, 176-178; Lindars, Son of Man, 147; similarly Ibuki, Wahrheit, 140f, 196, 230; Forestell, Word, 15, 36f; Dauer, Passionsgeschichte, 40, 238-240.
122. Thüsing, Erhöhung, 15, 21, 24-28, 33, 233, 240f.
123. Blank, Krisis, 139, 268f; Nicholson, Death, 99-101, 132-136; 141-151; similarly Riedl, Heilswerk, 160-162; Schnackenburg, John I, 394-397; Johannes II, 499-502.
124. Thüsing, Erhöhung, 300, cf. 302f, 305-307.
125. Thüsing, Erhöhung, 302, 308.
126. So correctly Becker, Johannes, 144.
127. Bultmann, 'Interpretation', 3f; Johannes, 398.
128. So Porsch, Pneuma, 75, 77f; Schnackenburg, Johannes II, 503; Riedl, Heilswerk, 155, 169.
129. So Thüsing, Erhöhung, 206-208.
130. Käsemann, Letzter Wille, 22.
131. Schulz, Johannes, 209, 238.
132. U.B. Müller, 'Bedeutung', 54, 58.
133. Thüsing, Erhöhung, 141f, 191f.
134. Blank, Krisis, 282.
135. Haenchen, Johannes, 109.
136. Haenchen, 'Das Johannesevangelium', 226f.
137. So Forestell, Word, 19.
138. Cf. Müller, Heilsgeschehen, 25, 33.
139. Haenchen, Johannes, 356; similarly Dodd, Interpretation, 442.
140. Bultmann, Theologie, 389.
141. Bultmann, Theologie, 360.
142. Bultmann, Johannes, 26-28.
143. Bultmann, Johannes, 139.
144. Hahn, 'Heil', 67-84; 'Juden', 430-438.
145. Borgen, Bread from Heaven; Logos was the true Light.
146. Meeks, Prophet-King.
147. Bultmann, Johannes, 187f; Theologie, 415.
148. Fortna, Signs.

Notes to pp. 18 - 22

149. Boismard/Lamouille, Jean; Becker, 'Wunder'; Johannes; U.B. Müller, Christologie; Richter, Studien; Martyn, 'Source Criticism'; Langbrandtner, Weltferner Gott; Brown, Beloved Disciple; Haenchen, Johannes; cf. also Lieu, Epistles, 171-216.
150. Ruckstuhl, Einheit.
151. Strecker, 'Anfänge'; Schnelle, Christologie.
152. Wengst, Gemeinde; cf. Kügler, 'Das Johannesevangelium und seine Gemeinde. Kein Thema für Science Fiction.' See the critical evaluation in Becker, 'Streit der Methoden', 53f; and the more positive responses of Schnackenburg, Johannes IV, 229; Reim, 'Lokalisierung', 73f; cf. also Klauck, 'Gemeinde', 198.
153. Meeks, 'Man from Heaven'.
154. Onuki, Gemeinde, 110-114; cf. also de Jonge, Stranger, 99f.
155. Becker, 'Dualismus'; Johannes, 147-151; 'Streit der Methoden', 46f.
156. Culpepper, Anatomy; Duke, Irony; O'Day, Revelation.

PART IIA Structure: Identifying the Central Structure

1. H.J. Holtzmann, Lehrbuch, 446; Haacker, Stiftung, 17f; Bultmann, Johannes, 1; Pollard, Christology, 13f; Wengst, Gemeinde, 101-103; Theobald, Anfang, 129; Schnelle, Christologie, 246.
2. Hooker, 'Prologue', 45.
3. Thyen, 'Literatur', ThR 39 (1974) 223.
4. Dunn, 'John', 334.
5. Culpepper, Anatomy, 108.
6. Bultmann, Johannes, 1; also Pollard, Christology, 6f.
7. Similarly Preiss, Life in Christ, 10; Beyschlag, Neutestamentliche Theologie II, 430f; Lütgert, Christologie, vii.
8. So Painter, 'Prologue', 48.
9. Käsemann, Letzter Wille, 23-25. See also Becker, 'Auferstehung', 138-140. Contrast Weder, 'Menschwerdung', 352.
10. Haacker, Stiftung, 21, 25-36.
11. Richter, Studien, 152, 173, 196; cf. also 66, 101-103, 141.
12. Smalley, 'Johannes 1,51', 313; similarly Moloney, 'Son of God', 180.
13. Breuss, Kana-Wunder, 26; Lütgert, Christologie, 18; Hofbeck, Semeion, 105. Cf. also Olsson, Structure, 101.
14. Weder, 'Menschwerdung', 325.
15. Ruckstuhl, Einheit, 249.
16. Appold, Oneness, 11f, 272, 280.
17. Ricca, Eschatologie, 106; Corell, Consummatum Est, passim.
18. Wetter, Sohn Gottes, 49-52, 155.
19. Lütgert, Christologie, 23-30, 36-40.
20. Bultmann, Johannes, 103f, 188-190; Theologie, 386f, 403f, 414.
21. Forestell, Word, 19-57.
22. Forestell, Word, 45f.
23. Eg: Kühl, Sendung, 77f; 82ff; Miranda, Vater, 18-52; Sendung, 29-35; Riedl, Heilswerk, 51 n. 41; Haacker, Stiftung, 92-97.
24. Ibuki, Wahrheit, 43.
25. Ibuki, Wahrheit, 146-149.
26. Schnackenburg, Johannes II, 153-157; cf. also Nicholson, Death, 52-60.
27. de Jonge, Stranger, 41, 132-135, 142-148; Moloney, Son of Man, 208.

28. Bühner, Gesandte, 198f, 212f; cf. also 202, 233, 261; similarly Robinson, Priority, 368f.
29. Becker, Johannes, 403-406.
30. Bornkamm, 'Paraklet', 77-79.
31. So Dodd, Interpretation, 309, 386; Beutler, Martyria, 313-315; Richter, Studien, 314, 337; Bornkamm, 'Paraklet', 77f; Meeks, 'Man from Heaven', 150.
32. Schnackenburg, John I, 380; 'Die "situationsgelösten" Redestücke'; similarly Blank, Krisis, 53-56; Moloney, Son of Man, 42.
33. Schnackenburg, John I, 4, 278, 280.
34. Olsson, Structure, 262.
35. Schulz, Johannes, 66.
36. Sanders and Mastin, John, 135; similarly Beasley-Murray, John, 53.
37. Bornkamm, 'Paraklet', 77f.
38. Becker, 'Streit der Methoden', 11.
39. Against Brown, John, 161; Lindars, John, 169; Boismard/Lamouille, Jean, 125 (for the redactor, not the 'IIA' gospel: so 119); Haenchen, Johannes, 232; Whitacre, Polemic, 97; Burge, Anointed Community, 83.
40. So Schnackenburg, John I, 382; Blank, Krisis, 66; Beutler, Martyria, 316; Beasley-Murray, John, 53.
41. So Bultmann, Johannes, 119; Barrett, John, 226; Schnackenburg, John I, 386f; Lindars, John, 170f; Bruce, John, 97; Johnston, Paraclete, 14; Ibuki, Wahrheit, 149f, 153; Beasley-Murray, John, 53f; Burge, Anointed Community, 83f.
42. Thüsing, Erhöhung, 153-156, 321; Porsch, Pneuma, 104f. See also Brown, John, 158, 161f.
43. Schnackenburg, John I, 388.
44. Schnackenburg, John I, 381; Brown, John, 157.
45. Olsson, Structure, 262
46. Brown, John, 160.
47. Schillebeeckx, Christ, 399f.
48. Schnackenburg, Johannes II, 523f.
49. Borgen, Logos, 44f.
50. So Boismard, 'Le caractère adventice'; see the discussion in Schnackenburg, Johannes II, 523-525.
51. So Becker, Johannes, 413-415.
52. So Dodd, Interpretation, 381-383; Barrett, John, 433.
53. On 'whence' and 'whither' sayings see further: Nicholson, Death, 53-55; de Jonge, Stranger, 142; Kieffer, 'L'Espace', 400f, 404; Culpepper, Anatomy, 170f; Dewailly, 'D'où es-tu?', 489-492.
54. So Kühl, Sendung, 54; Haenchen, Johannes, 107; Miranda, Sendung, 29; de Jonge, Stranger, 165.
55. Rengstorf, Art. 'apostello' TDNT 1; similarly Blank, Krisis, 70 n. 61; Bühner, Gesandte, 412f.
56. Radermakers, 'Mission', 100-121; similarly Riedl, Heilswerk, 55-57; Seynaeve, 'apostello', 389.
57. Thüsing, Erhöhung, 231f; Schnackenburg, Johannes III, 193f.
58. So Becker, Johannes, 518; Barrett, John, 502; Brown, John, 740.

Notes to pp. 35 - 45

59. Compare also the list of summary statements in Culpepper, Anatomy, 87f.
60. Ritt, Gebet, 5, 13; similarly Cadman, Open Heaven, 203.
61. See n. 57 above.
62. See n. 58 above.
63. See the discussion IIIA2 below.

PART IIB AND C Structure: Survey and Outline

1. So Olsson, Structure 72; Nicol, Semeia, 129; Wilkens, Entstehung, 39f; Porsch, Pneuma, 35; Dodd, Interpretation, 297; Smalley, John, 178; Hengel, 'Cana', 95-99.
2. So Breuss, Kana-Wunder, 30; Dodd, Interpretation, 299f; Boismard/Lamouille, Jean, 105f; Nicholson, Death, 46; Schnelle, Christologie, 88, 190; as the work of the redactor: Heekerens, Zeichen-Quelle, 72.
3. Barrett, John, 191; Cullmann, Worship, 66; Brown, John, 99f; Olsson, Structure, 101, 259; de Jonge, Stranger, 124; Heekerens, Zeichen-Quelle, 69; Schnelle, Christologie, 89. Cf. Hofbeck, Semeion, 95-97; Becker, Johannes, 111, Beasley-Murray, John, 35 for a contrary view.
4. Cullmann, Worship, 69; Mussner, 'Kultische Aspekte', 137; Brown, John, 110; Kee, Miracle, 234; Hengel, 'Cana', 102; as the work of the redactor: Langbrandtner, Weltferner Gott, 72; Heekerens, Zeichen-Quelle, 71-76; cf. Painter, 'John 9', 45; Schnelle, Christologie, 92 for a contrary view.
5. Cullmann, Worship, 70; Salvation, 279; Brown, John, 104; Lindars, John, 128, 134; Ellis, Genius, 42f.
6. So Schnackenburg, John I, 333; Nicholson, Death, 53; Kieffer, 'L'Espace', 401; Ellis, Genius, 43f; Schnelle, Christologie, 90, 95; cf. Barrett, John, 193.
7. So Bultmann, Johannes, 91; Brown, John, 121.
8. So de Jonge, Stranger, 40f; Nicholson, Death, 65.
9. So Meeks, 'Man from Heaven', 147; Nicholson, Death, 81f.
10. Duke, Irony, 101-103.
11. So Thüsing, Erhöhung, 59-61, 115; Brown, John, 88; Lindars, John 220, 222.
12. Schnackenburg, Johannes II, 125; Brown, John, 214, cf.88; Beasley-Murray, John 76; Becker, Johannes, 236-241 who sees a tradition originally referring to the exalted Jesus (5:19bc,21-23b) transferred by the evangelist to the earthly Jesus.
13. So Barrett, John, 281; 'Theocentric', 12f; Lindars, John, 247; Haenchen, Johannes, 311f; Bruce, John, 128.
14. Against Schnackenburg, Johannes II, 36, 68; Brown, John, 254f; Pokorny, 'Jesus', 217; Gnilka, 'Christologie', 101; Ellis, Genius, 110f whose structural analysis makes 6:16-21 the centre of the gospel (108).
15. So Heil, Jesus, 59, 67, 80.
16. Barrett, John, 286f; Schnackenburg, Johannes II, 49; Schenke, 'Vorgeschichte', 74, 86f; Wilckens, 'Lebensbrot', 226.
17. Wilckens, 'Lebensbrot', 224; Brown, John, 285, 291; Boismard/Lamouille, Jean, 204f; Haenchen, Johannes, 326; Beutler, 'Heilsbedeutung', 191f.

18. Lindars, John, 267; Schnackenburg, Johannes II, 83, 61f; Barrett, John, 298; Schnelle, Christologie, 223.
19. Schürmann, 'Schlüssel', 255, Weder, 'Menschwerdung', 348; Beasley-Murray, John, 94.
20. On the two foci of John 6 see Brown, John, 272-275; Wilckens, 'Lebensbrot', 226f. Weder, 'Menschwerdung', identifies three levels: messianic, Christ the true bread and the eucharist (329).
21. Dodd, Interpretation, 341f; Ellis, Genius, 128.
22. Lindars, John, 272; Schnackenburg, Johannes II, 104; Bruce, John, 163; Beasley-Murray, John, 96; Weder, 'Menschwerdung', 344; Lindars, Son of Man, 219f.
23. Brown, John, 300; Bornkamm, 'Tradition', 58 n. 16; Wilckens, 'Lebensbrot', 244; Weder, 'Menschwerdung', 345; Becker, Johannes, 216; Schnelle, Christologie, 214. Against Schnackenburg, Johannes II, 105f; Barrett, John 304f; Burge, Anointed Community, 105, 187.
24. So Bultmann, Johannes, 341; Bornkamm, 'Eucharistische Rede', 64; Schulz, Johannes, 110f; Meeks, 'Man from Heaven,' 153; Nicholson, Death, 58; Weder, 'Menschwerdung', 344.
25. So Thüsing, Erhöhung, 261f; Hofbeck, Semeion, 121 n. 144; Lindars, John, 273; Bruce, John, 163. Affirming both: Barrett, John, 303; Schürmann, 'Schlüssel', 258f; Schnackenburg, Johannes II, 105; Porsch, Pneuma, 206f; Beasley-Murray, John, 96.
26. So Thüsing, Erhöhung, 90f; Porsch, Pneuma, 75; cf. Haenchen, 'Vater', 75; Lindars, John, 284f.
27. So Bauer, Johannes, 123; Blank, Krisis, 230, 246, 227; Forestell, Word, 47; Riedl, Heilswerk, 234; Dauer, Passionsgeschichte, 244; Pancaro, Law, 60f; Harner, I am, 43-45; Lindars, John, 320f; Brown, John, 350f; Schnackenburg, Johannes II, 253f, 256; Boismard/Lamouille, Jean, 230; Moloney, Son of Man, 132; Bruce, John, 193; Beasley-Murray, John, 130.
28. So Bruce, John, 183; Boismard/Lamouille, Jean, 220; Nicholson, Death, 115, 117; cf. Schnackenburg, Johannes II, 256; Moloney, Son of Man, 133f; Miller, 'Christology', 263.
29. Barrett, John, 342; 'Theocentric', 12; 'Symbolism', 71f; Becker, Johannes, 208; Nicholson, Death, 113, 121.
30. Bultmann, Johannes, 265f; Riedl, Heilswerk, 365; Coppens, 'Fils de L'Homme', 54; Freed, 'Son of Man', 405; cf. Schnackenburg, Johannes II, 256.
31. So Brown, John, 367f; Schnackenburg, Johannes II, 300f; Pokorny, 'Jesus', 217; Becker, Johannes, 208; Forestell, Word, 47; Beasley-Murray, John, 139f.
32. So Barrett, John, 352; 'Theocentric', 12; 'Symbolism', 7f; Lindars, John, 336; Freed, 'Before Abraham', 52f, though his suggestion that we understand here a reference to the pre-existent Messiah Son of Man is not convincing.
33. So Brown, John, 375; Maddox, 'Function', 199; Duke, Irony, 124; Schnelle, Christologie, 138f.
34. Nicholson, Death, 152f.
35. So Schnackenburg, Johannes II, 485; Barrett, John, 425; Becker, Johannes, 387; Nicholson, Death, 128; cf. Bruce, John, 265f; Beasley-Murray, John, 212; Leon-Dufour, 'Père', who suggests Jesus prays to be brought through the hour (162-165).

Notes to pp. 51 - 62

36. On the meaning of 12:28 see also IIIA4.
37. So Thüsing, Erhöhung, 218f; de Jonge, Stranger, 137; Schnackenburg, Johannes IV, 151; Dupont, Christologie, 269-273; Moloney, Son of Man, 278; Reim, 'Targum', 8; Bittner, Zeichen, 96; cf. Dahl, 'Church', 129; Lindars, John, 439; Ellis, Genius, 206; Pamment, 'Doxa', 13; Whitacre, Polemic, 47; Bjerkelund, Tauta, 142, who also see here a reference to the glory of Jesus' ministry and death.
38. Cf. Barrett, John, 443.
39. Schnackenburg, Johannes III, 18; similarly Becker, Johannes, 420f.
40. Brown, John, 564; similarly Barrett, John, 439; Beasley-Murray, John, 233.
41. So Barrett, 'Theocentric', 12f; 'Symbolism', 71f; Becker, Johannes, 209; Nicholson, Death, 113.
42. Brown, John, 571; Boismard/Lamouille, Jean, 343; Schnackenburg, Johannes III, 31; Forestell, Word, 47; Bruce, John, 288; Pokorný, 'Jesus', 222.
43. So Lindars, John, 462; Schnackenburg, Johannes III, 54-57; Schulz, Johannes, 178f; Becker, Johannes, 449; Bruce, John, 292f; Beasley-Murray, John, 246.
44. Thüsing, Erhöhung, 233-239; similarly Brown, John, 610; Moloney, Son of Man, 195-197, 277.
45. Sanders and Mastin, John, 315; Kysar, Jesus, 67; cf. Barrett, John, 450.
46. Caird, 'Glory', 270f.
47. Schnackenburg, Johannes III, 57.
48. So Bultmann, Johannes, 471f; Hofbeck, Semeion, 154f; Thüsing, Erhöhung, 114f; Schnackenburg, Johannes III, 81; Brown, John, 633; Riedl, Heilswerk, 288; Ibuki, Wahrheit, 279f; Beutler, Angst, 49; Dietzfelbinger, 'Paraklet', 397.
49. Untergassmair, Im Namen Jesu, 86f, 123f; similarly Thüsing, Erhöhung, 115.
50. So Porsch, Pneuma, 247.
51. Beutler, Angst, 64f.
52. Boring, 'Prophecy', 114 n. 1.
53. So Porsch, Pneuma, 249f, 384.
54. van Hartingsveld, Eschatologie, 117.
55. So Porsch, Pneuma, 389; Onuki, Gemeinde, 73; Burge, Anointed Community, 138f.
56. Borig, Weinstock, 65f.
57. Thüsing, Erhöhung, 106-112, 119-121; similarly Bultmann, Johannes, 391; Onuki, Gemeinde, 126-130.
58. Mussner, 'Parakletssprüche', 154f; cf. Thüsing, Erhöhung, 329.
59. Minear, John, 84f, 92f, 14-23. Similarly by implication also Boring, 'Christian Prophecy', 113f.
60. So Schnackenburg, Johannes III, 113; Porsch, Pneuma, 194; Thüsing, Erhöhung, 119.
61. So Porsch, Pneuma, 269f; Ibuki, Wahrheit, 291; Scroggs, Christology, 88.
62. So Schnackenburg, Johannes III, 147; Painter, 'Farewell Discourses', 538f; Trites, Witness, 49f; Beasley-Murray, John, 280f; cf. also the review of alternatives in Carson, 'Paraclete', 547-566, who agrees that 'convict of' or 'convince of' gives the best sense, but, as Burge, Anointed Community, 209, notes, presses too hard

242 Notes

Notes to pp. 62 - 68

for a conformity of meaning among the genitives in having 'righteousness' refer ironically to the world's righteousness (558).

63. So Bultmann, Johannes, 434f; Blank, Krisis, 337; Schnackenburg, Johannes III, 149; Dietzfelbinger, 'Paraklet', 391f; Onuki, Gemeinde, 145; Beasley-Murray, John, 282.

64. So Preiss, Life in Christ, 21f.

65. So Bultmann, Johannes, 433; Theologie, 442; Blank, Krisis, 335; Barrett, John, 488f; T.E. Müller, Heilsgeschehen, 84; Thüsing, Erhöhung, 143; Painter, 'Farewell Discourses', 539f; Onuki, Gemeinde, 146; Carson, 'Paraclete', 553; Dietzfelbinger, 'Paraklet', 391f.

66. Against Porsch, Pneuma, 222-224, 274f, 280-286; de la Potterie, Vérité, 410; Berrouard, 'Paraclet', 361-389; Brown, John, 712; U.B. Müller, 'Parakletenvorstellung', 76; Becker, Johannes, 495.

67. So Barrett, John, 497; Schnackenburg, Johannes III, 185; Becker, Johannes, 505.

68. So Lindars, John, 573; Nicholson, Death, 68f; similarly Brown, John, 736.

69. Bultmann, Johannes, 494f; Barrett, John, 520; 'Theocentric', 12; Nicholson, Death, 112; cf. Schnackenburg, Johannes III, 254.

70. So Brown, John, 818; Boismard/Lamouille, Jean, 406; Schnackenburg, Johannes III, 253; Bruce, John, 341; Ellis, Genius, 251; Zimmermann, 'Egō eimi'; Forestell, Word, 47; Pancaro, Law, 60; Appold, Oneness, 82, 126; Reim, Studien, 172, 243f; Dauer, Passionsgeschichte, 41-43.

71. So Meeks, 'Man from Heaven', 159; Miller, 'Christology', 35; Minear, 'Diversity', 162.

72. Against Thüsing, Erhöhung, 30-33, 260, 290f; Dauer, Passionsgechichte, 249f, 274f; van Hartingsveld, Eschatologie, 64f; Kühl, Sendung, 118f; Wilkens, Zeichen, 72, 112; Ruckstuhl, Einheit, 257; 'Abstieg', 333f; Braun, Jean III, 137f, 216-218; Porsch, Pneuma, 76f, 206; Lindars, 'Passion', 77f; Schillebeeckx, Christ, 413; Meeks, 'Man from Heaven', 159; Miller, 'Christology', 34f.

73. Against Forestell, Word, 36, 71, 73; Moloney, Son of Man, 62f.

74. Against Bühner, Gesandte, 397; similarly Dodd, Interpretation, 442.

75. So Schnackenburg, Johannes III, 287, 296; de Jonge, Stranger, 66-69; Baum-Bodenbender, Hoheit, 66f; Beasley-Murray, John, 361.

76. Beutler, Martyria, 324; Ibuki, Wahrheit, 144f.

77. Dauer, Passionsgeschichte, 259f; Hahn, 'Prozess', 40f.

78. Schnackenburg, Johannes, III, 569f; also Baum Bodenbender, Hoheit, 66f; cf. Blank, 'Verhandlung', 62; Dauer, Passionsgeschichte, 249f, 259f; Hahn, 'Prozess', 40f; Duke, Irony, 106, 114, 132.

79. So Schnackenburg, Johannes, III, 85.

80. Baum Bodenbender, Hoheit, 62, 66, 79, 83.

81. So rightly Schnackenburg, Johannes, III 295f, 'Ecce Homo', 377-380; against Westcott, John, 269; Dodd, Interpretation, 437; Meeks, Prophet-King, 70f; Blank, 'Verhandlung', 75-77; Dauer, Passionsgeschichte, 264f; Evans, 'Passion', 60; Giblin, 'Hearing', 230; Suggit, 'Behold the Man', 333.

82. Moloney, Son of Man, 188.

83. Against Boismard/Lamouille, Jean, 434.

Notes to pp. 68 - 71

84. Against Suggit, 'Behold the Man', 334.
85. Against, Brown, John, 876; Meeks, Prophet-King, 69-72.
86. Against Gnilka, 'Christologie', 106f. See also the discussion of alternatives in Schnackenburg, 'Ecce Homo'.
87. Beutler, Martyria, 319; Boismard/Lamouille, Jean, 430f; Haenchen, Johannes, 541; Meeks, Prophet-King, 74f; and as one side of an instance of double meaning: Barrett, John, 544.
88. Dauer, Passionsgeschichte, 247, 249, 261; Hahn, 'Prozess', 68-85; similarly Porsch, Pneuma, 223-227; Beutler, Martyria, 365f; Appold, Oneness, 108f.
89. de la Potterie, 'Jésus roi et juge'; Giblin, 'Hearing', 234f; Nicholson, Death, 164.
90. Blank, 'Verhandlung,' 64f; Krisis, 269-274; Blinzler, Prozess, 346-356; Brown, John, 880f; Forestell, Word, 86 n. 115; Appold, Oneness, 134; Dauer, Passionsgeschichte, 155, 269-274; Hahn, 'Prozess', 48-50; Schnackenburg, Johannes III, 304f; Baum Bodenbender, Hoheit, 78f; Beasley-Murray, John, 341f.
91. Boismard/Lamouille, Jean, 442.
92. So Mussner, 'Kultische Aspekte', 143f; Brown, John, 921; Williams, 'Cultic Elements', 342f.
93. Critical appraisal of both in Schnackenburg, Johannes III, 317f.
94. So Boismard/Lamouille, Jean, 338, 443
95. Against Thüsing, Erhöhung, 68f.
96. Porsch, Pneuma, 327-330, 370; Braun, Jean III, 151f; Breuss, Kana Wunder, 24; Brown, John, 931; Beloved Disciple, 118; Dunn, 'Footwashing', 250; Moloney, Son of Man, 176; Culpepper, Anatomy, 134, 195.
97. Forestell, Word, 135; Riedl, Heilswerk, 112; Johnston, Paraclete, 11f; Schnackenburg, Johannes III, 332f; Beasley-Murray, John, 353; Burge, Anointed Community, 134.
98. Dodd, Interpretation, 230-238; Forestell, Word, 90; Dauer, Passionsgeschichte, 139-142; Johannes und Lukas, 230; Robinson, Priority, 152f.
99. Thüsing, Erhöhung, 171; Mussner, 'Kultische Aspekte', 142f; Klos, Sakramente, 75; Grigsby, 'Cross', 57-59; Baum Bodenbender, Hoheit, 54, 171; Bruce, John, 377; Ellis, Genius, 277f.
100. Against Boismard/Lamouille, Jean, 452; Brown, John, 953; Whitacre, Polemic, 62f.
101. So Bultmann, Johannes, 677; Lindars, John, 590; Apologetics, 96; Barrett, John, 558; Schnackenburg, Johannes III, 342.
102. Robinson, Priority, 152f; see also the convincing discussion in Dauer, Passionsgeschichte, 139-142.
103. Bultmann, Johannes, 525; Kremer, Osterevangelien, 162f; Moloney, 'Sacraments', 25; Ellis, Genius, 275f; Schnelle, Christologie, 229; cf. also Brown, John, 951f.
104. Wilkens, Zeichen, 74; Thüsing, Erhöhung, 167f; Klos, Sakramente, 78f; Minear, John, 75-78; Schnackenburg, Johannes III, 345; Burge, Anointed Community, 94.
105. Brown, John, 948-950; Beloved Disciple, 118f; Forestell, Word, 89f; Porsch, Pneuma, 338f.
106. So Brown, John, 948f; Boismard/Lamouille, Jean, 451.
107. So Richter, Studien, 134.

244   Notes

108. So Barrett, 'Theocentric', 13f; de Jonge, Stranger, 210f; Klos, Sakramente, 80;
     Schweizer, 'Zeugnis', 350f; Bruce, John, 376; Beasley-Murray, John, 356f;
     Gnilka, 'Christologie', 105; Schnelle, Christologie, 229.
109. For a full discussion of alternative interpretations of 1 John 5:6, see Brown, Epistles
     of John, 575-578.
110. So de la Potterie, Genèse, 30f; Minear, 'We don't know where'; Nicholson, Death,
     70f.
111. So Boismard/Lamouille, Jean, 459; Zeller, 'Ostermorgen', 158f.
112. So Brown, John, 987; Lindars, John, 602; Schnackenburg, Johannes III, 368;
     Kremer, Osterevangelien, 168.
113. Byrne, 'Beloved Disciple', 87-89, 92.
114. So Sanders/Mastin, John, 428.
115. So Thüsing, Erhöhung, 265; Brown, John, 992-994, 1011; Schnackenburg,
     Johannes III, 376; Onuki, Gemeinde, 86.
116. So de Jonge, Stranger, 4; Schnackenburg, Johannes III, 377; Kremer,
     Osterevangelien, 172; Perkins, Resurrection, 176; de la Potterie, 'Genèse', 34f;
     Byrne, 'Beloved Disciple', 84; cf. also Schneiders, Johannine Resurrection
     Narrative, 47-56, who sees in Mary's quest for the body an echo of the bride's
     quest in the Song of Solomon 3:1-4.
117. So de la Potterie, 'Genèse', 34f; Byrne, 'Beloved Disciple', 84; Dauer, Johannes und
     Lukas, 257, 259.
118. Similarly, Mlakuzhyil, Structure, 258.
119. Bühner, Gesandte, 166-180; Becker, Johannes, 208; 'Auferstehung' 150.
120. So Schweizer, Ego Eimi, 125-135.
121. So Wead, Devices, 76f.
122. So Barrett, 'Theocentric', 12; 'Symbolism', 71f.
123. So Barrett, 'Theocentric', 13; 'Symbolism', 69f; John, 342; Lindars, John, 320f.
124. So MacRae, 'Ego Eimi', 129, 132-134.
125. So also Bultmann, Theologie, 389; Dahl, 'Church', 127f; de Jonge, Stranger, 52, 57-
     60, 63-66, 84f, 96f; Appold, Oneness, 68f; Schnackenburg, John I, 155; Brown,
     'Beloved Disciple', 29; Painter, 'Christology', 45, 'John 9', 37; Dunn, 'John',
     321, 328f; Schnelle, Christologie, 117, 123; Mlakyzhyil, Structure, 256-258.
126. So Martyn, 'History and Theology', 131-134.
127. Against Moloney, Son of Man, 40, 183f, 210.
128. So Schnackenburg, Johannes II, 152; Scroggs, Christology, 68.
129. Schillebeeckx, Christ, 316-318, 412f.
130. Bittner, Zeichen, 154-167, 253, cf. 215.
131. See also Schnackenburg, Johannes IV, 62-64; de Jonge, Stranger, 152-159; Bühner,
     Gesandte, 251-256, 317; Isaacs, 'Prophetic Spirit', 404.
132. Against Mussner, 'Parakletssprüche', 154f.
133. Boring, 'Christian Prophecy', 120, 122.
134. Minear, John, 8-23 et passim.
135. Bornkamm, 'Paraklet', 77-79; Porsch, Pneuma, 237-239; Franck, Revelation, 80,
     83f; Burge, Anointed Community, 140-142; Isaacs, 'Prophetic Spirit', 393-401.
136. So also Bornkamm, 'Paraklet', 87.
137. Burge, Anointed Community, 41.

Notes to pp. 93 - 96

PART IIIA   Issues: The Death of Jesus

1. Käsemann, Letzter Wille, 124, 135; Schulz, Johannes, 209, 238; Lattke, Einheit, 142; U.B. Müller, 'Bedeutung', 48, 54; Appold, Oneness, 135; Becker, Johannes, 406f; Langbrandtner, Weltferner Gott, 97; cf. already Bultmann, Theologie, 406.
2. Thüsing, Erhöhung, 68f, 100; Wilkens, Zeichen, 73, 77; T.E. Müller, Heilsgeschehen, 34, 50, 74, 130f; Richter, Studien, 60, 291; Riedl, Heilswerk, 15; Miranda, Vater, 139-141; Sendung, 20, 28; Dauer, Passionsgeschichte, 282-292.
3. So Thüsing, Erhöhung, 58; Riedl, Heilswerk, 62f; Miranda, Vater, 126.
4. Käsemann, Letzter Wille, 23 n. 7; Appold, Oneness, 79; Haenchen, 'Das Johannesevangelium', 230; Johannes, 166f; U.B. Müller, 'Bedeutung', 63; Forestell, Word, 15f; cf. also Bultmann, Theologie, 406.
5. Becker, Johannes, 91f.
6. Painter, Witness, 63. Similarly Dodd, Interpretation, 233, 424; Bultmann, Theologie, 406f; Käsemann, Letzter Wille, 23 n. 7; Smalley, John, 225f; Appold, Oneness, 121f n. 3, 271-274; Schulz, Johannes, 237; Forestell, Word, 'the falling star' without parallel in the gospel (158); U.B. Müller, 'Bedeutung', 63f.
7. So, for instance, T.E. Müller, Heilsgeschehen, 112f, 130f, 134f; Schnackenburg, John I, 29; Johannes IV, 223; Thüsing, Erhöhung, 19-21, 51, 164; Blank, Krisis, 133f; Porsch, Pneuma, 42; Dauer, Passionsgeschichte, 292-294; Riedl, Heilswerk, 112f, 313f; Braun, Jean III, 137f, 216-218; Pancaro, Law, 441f; Haacker, Stiftung, 169-173; Richter, Studien, 42-45, 53, 58f, 291, 305, 312; Kühl, Sendung, 109f; Reim, Studien, 179; Miranda, Vater, 125f, 130, 132-141; Sendung, 20, 24f, 28; Schnider/Stenger, Johannes, 169; Williams, 'Cultic Elements', 340f; Wilkens, Zeichen, especially for the 'signs gospel', but not for the 'Reden', 112, 72-74, 77.
8. Riedl, Heilswerk, 112f, 313f.
9. Ibuki, Wahrheit, 158-160.
10. Onuki, Gemeinde, 90f.
11. Schnackenburg, John I, 157f; similarly Lindars, 'Passion', 72; Smalley, 'John 1:29-34', 326; Culpepper, Anatomy, 87f; Klaiber,'Interpretation', 312.
12. Forestell, Word, 160f.
13. Forestell, Word, 148f, 154; cf. similarly Porsch, Pneuma, 40f; Lindars, 'Passion', 72.
14. Hegermann, 'Eigentum', 119f, 126f.
15. Boismard/Lamouille, Jean, 47-60, 91f.
16. Dodd, Interpretation, 233, 236-238, pointing to the use of the ram lamb image in TestLevi 18:9; PsSol 17:29; 2 Bar 73:1-4. Cf also the discussion in Burrows, 'John the Baptist'.
17. Brown, John, 61-63; similarly Riedl, Heilswerk, 174f, 199; Beasley-Murray, John, 24f.
18. Forestell, Word, 158.
19. So Bultmann, Johannes, 66f; Theologie, 406; Barrett, John, 176; Schnackenburg, John I, 299; Brown, John, 61-63; Lindars, John, 109; Becker, Johannes, 97; Gnilka, 'Christologie', 106; Ellis, Genius, 33f; Grigsby, 'Cross', 54; Beutler, 'Heilsbedeutung,', 192; Beasley-Murray, John, 24f; Wilkens, Zeichen, 73f, 76f;

246 Notes

Notes to pp. 96 - 97

Forestell, Word, 165; also earlier: Lütgert, Christologie, 108-112. Against this: Hahn, 'Verständnis des Opfers', 75; Appold, Oneness, 79 n. 1.
20. So Barrett, John, 176; Schnackenburg, John I, 300; Brown, John, 61-63; Lindars, John, 109; Beasley-Murray, John, 24f; Riedl, Heilswerk, 179f; Haacker, Stiftung, 170f; Hahn, 'Verständnis des Opfers', 75; Jeremias, Art. *'amnos'*, TDNT I 338-341; Cullmann, Christologie, 66f; Schillebeeckx, Christ, 408f; Beutler, 'Heilsbedeutung', 192. Against this: Bultmann, Johannes, 66f; Becker, Johannes, 97; Haenchen, Johannes, 166.
21. Brown, John, 61; Lindars, John, 109; Jeremias, Art. *'amnos'*, TDNT I 338-341. Against this: Schnackenburg, John I, 298f; Haenchen, Johannes, 166.
22. Porsch, Pneuma, 40-42; Jeremias, Art. *'amnos'*, TDNT I 338-341; Art. *'pais theou'*, TDNT 5, 702; Boismard/Lamouille, Jean, 92; Burge, Anointed Community, 61.
23. Vermes, Scripture and Tradition, 223f; Le Déaut, La nuit pascale, 158; McNamara, Palestinian Targum, 164-168; Braun, Jean III, 137f, 162-165, 216-218; de Kruijf, 'Glory', 118, 122f; Lindars, Apologetic, 139, 146; Grigsby, 'Cross', 60; Schnackenburg, Johannes IV, 192.
24. Boismard/Lamouille, Jean, 92.
25. Beutler, 'Heilsbedeutung', 192.
26. Cf. Füglister, Pascha.
27. So Guilding, Jewish Worship, 61f; Grigsby, 'Cross', 53-57; Ellis, Genius, 272; Brown, John, 930.
28. So Dodd, Interpretation, 230-238, 424; Bultmann, Johannes, 524; Forestell, Word, 90-92, who interprets the passover typology only to mean Jesus passes to the Father (similarly Boismard/Lamouille, Jean, 337f for 13:1, but not for 19:34); Dauer, Passionsgeschichte, 137-143, who identifies passover typology as belonging only in the author's tradition; Johannes und Lukas, 230; Robinson, Priority, 152f;. See also the discussion in IIB5 above. Wilkens, Zeichen, sees 'the signs gospel' constructed around the Passover motif, with the signs corresponding to the plagues on Egypt and the cross as the Passover lamb sacrifice (73f,77). Others who support a passover interpretation include: Thüsing, Erhöhung, 19-21; Pancaro, Law, 350; Reim, Studien, 52, 179; Schnackenburg, Johannes III, 16; Fortna, 'Christology', 502; Wengst, Gemeinde, 109; Williams, 'Cultic Elements', 340f; Duke, Irony, 128; Beasley-Murray, John, 674.
29. Dodd, Interpretation, 235f; similarly Barrett, John, 176; Bruce, John, 52f; Lindars, John, 109; Forestell, Word, 162f; cf. Schnackenburg, John I, 299f; Porsch, Pneuma, 40; against Burney, Aramaic Origin, 107f; Jeremias, Art. *'pais theou'*, TDNT 5, 702; Cullmann, Worship, 63-65.
30. So Forestell, Word, 162f; Porsch, Pneuma, 40.
31. So U.B. Müller, 'Bedeutung', 63.
32. So Wilckens, 'Lebensbrot', 224, 227, 232; Beutler, 'Heilsbedeutung', 191f.
33. So T.E. Müller, Heilsgeschehen, 106; Hofbeck, Semeion, 120; Schnider/Stenger, Johannes, 163; Riedl, Heilswerk, 314; Ruckstuhl, Einheit, 357; Haacker, Stiftung, 173; Lindars, 'Passion', 73; John, 267; Son of Man, 152; Williams, 'Cultic Elements', 341; Bruce, John, 158; Weder, 'Menschwerdung', 348; Schnackenburg, 'Gedanke des Sühnetodes', 222; Beasley-Murray, John, 94; Schnelle, Christologie, 223.

Notes to pp. 97 - 99

34. Forestell, Word, 76; similarly in a non sacrificial sense: Schürmann, 'Schlüssel', 249-251.
35. So Wilkens, Zeichen, 98f; T.E. Müller, Heilsgeschehen, 56; Thüsing, Erhöhung, 279; Schnider/Stenger, Johannes, 164; Miranda, Sendung, 20; Haacker, Stiftung, 169; Barrett, John, 376; Schulz, Johannes, 151; Schnackenburg, 'Gedanke des Sühnetodes', 223; Beutler, 'Heilsbedeutung', 190f; Williams, 'Cultic Elements', 341.
36. So Bultmann, Johannes, 293; Schnackenburg, Johannes II, 372; Johannes IV, 110; Boismard/Lamouille, Jean, 271; Forestell, Word, 74f; Lattke, Einheit, 119-121; U.B. Müller, 'Bedeutung', 63f; Riedl, Heilswerk, 110; Becker, Johannes, 332; Busse, 'Johannes 10', 522f.
37. So also Appold, Oneness, 194, 271; Dauer, Passionsgeschichte, 39; Lindars, 'Passion', 73.
38. So T.E. Müller, Heilsgeschehen, 59f; Miranda, Sendung, 20,25; Schnackenburg, 'Gedanke des Sühnetodes', 223; Lindars, 'Passion', 73; Beutler, 'Heilsbedeutung', 190; Bruce, John, 251; Williams, 'Cultic Elements', 341; Ellis, Genius, 188.
39. So with hesitation, Dodd, Interpretation, 233, 246; Schnackenburg, Johannes II, 451; and confidently, Appold, Oneness, 121f, 194, 240, 272f; Forestell, Word, 82
40. Lindars, 'Passion', 73.
41. Against Lütgert, Christologie, 65, 169; T.E. Müller, Heilsgeschehen, 60-62; Haacker, Stiftung, 65, 169; Miranda, Sendung, 20; Beutler, 'Heilsbedeutung', 193; who see in 12:23 a reference to vicarious atonement. Cf. also Becker, Johannes, 400, who sees this as the work of the redactor.
42. Against Thüsing, Erhöhung, 24-28; Braun, Jean III, 175.
43. Rightly Maddox, 'Function', 188
44. So Schnackenburg, Johannes III, 124f; Thyen, Liebe, 467f, 481; Forestell, Word, 75.
45. Appold, Oneness, 194, recognises it as tradition but carrying no weight in the context; Forestell, Word, rejects the atonement motif here altogether (75).
46. T.E. Müller, Heilsgeschehen, 51f; Thüsing, Erhöhung, 9,14f; Riedl, Heilswerk, 145f; Miranda, Vater, 125f, 135-139; Sendung, 19; Lindars, John, 159; Haenchen, Johannes, 225; Schulz, Johannes, 60; Beasley-Murray, John, 51.
47. So Braun, Jean III, 157; Lindars, John, 159; Meeks, 'Man from Heaven', 156; Grigsby, 'Cross', 60; Ellis, Genius, 55f; Pamment, 'Doxa', 15; Schillebeeckx, Christ, 307.
48. So Lütgert, Christologie, 24; Bultmann, Theologie, 365; U.B. Müller, 'Bedeutung', 58f; Lattke, Einheit, 77, 84f, while acknowledging an originally vicarious tradition (70, 75); Segovia, Love Relationships, 167-169; Wengst, 'Formeln', 76; Nicholson, Death, 77; Scroggs, Christology, 75f; cf. also Schnackenburg, John I, 399.
49. So T.E. Müller, Heilsgeschehen, 50; Schnider/Stenger, Johannes, 163; indirectly, Dauer, Passionsgeschichte, 39.
50. Maddox, 'Function', 192; Wilckens, 'Lebensbrot', 224; Schnackenburg, John I, 395-397; Nicholson, Death, 99-101.
51. Against T.E. Müller, Heilsgeschehen, 61-65; Lindars, John, 528f; Miranda, Vater, 125f, Sendung, 25; Thüsing, Erhöhung, 187; Ibuki, Wahrheit, 137; Ritt, Gebet, 337; Porsch, Pneuma, 368; Riedl, Heilswerk, 109f; Ellis, Genius, 243; Beasley-Murray, John, 301.

248 Notes

Notes to pp. 100 - 103

52. See Loader, Sohn und Hoherpriester, 142-250.
53. Against Ellis, Genius, 131, 175, 268, 270; Thüsing, Erhöhung, 187; Brown, John, 767.
54. Bultmann, Johannes, 391, Theologie, 407, who sees in agiazw the language of sacrifice. Similarly Lindars, John, 375; 528f; 'Word', 62; Ellis, Genius, 243; Beasley-Murray, John, 301; but de la Potterie, Vérité, shows that this is not the case in the LXX (761f).
55. So Forestell, Word, 81; de la Potterie, Vérité, 767f, 770f; Appold, Oneness, 195.
56. Lindars, 'Passion', 72f.
57. Against Brown, John, 551; Richter, Fusswaschung, 289; Culpepper, Anatomy, 118; Bruce, John, 283; Beutler, 'Heilsbedeutung', 198.
58. Dunn, 'Washing', 249f, 252.
59. Segovia, 'John 13', 43-45.
60. Schnackenburg, Johannes III, 19, 21; 'Gedanke des Sühnetodes', 223.
61. Bultmann, Johannes, 358.
62. de la Potterie, 'Genèse', 38f.
63. Against Thüsing, Erhöhung, 324; Dauer, Passionsgeschichte, 39. So Schnackenburg, 'Frage', 208.
64. So Thüsing, Erhöhung, 231f; contrast Schnackenburg, 'Frage', 208.
65. Brown, John, 740; Becker, Johannes, 518.
66. Against T.E. Müller, Heilsgeschehen, 65-67; so Bultmann, Theologie, 408.
67. Wrede, 'Charakter', 29.
68. similarly Holtzmann, Lehrbuch, 523-526.
69. Bultmann, Theologie, 407.
70. Against Stevens, Theology, 224-233; Scott, Fourth Gospel, 207-212; Forestell, Word.
71. Beutler, 'Heilsbedeutung', 203f; Culpepper, Anatomy, 87f; Schnackenburg, John I, 157; Johannes II, 451; Johannes IV, 110, 114; 'Frage', 208; 'Gedanke des Sühnetodes', 219f, 224; Klaiber, 'Interpretation', 312.
72. Beasley-Murray, John, lxxxv.
73. Eg. Whitacre, Polemic, 157.
74. So Brown, Beloved Disciple, 119; Epistles, 79.
75. Segovia, Love Relationships, 196; Becker, Johannes, 407.
76. Schnelle, Christologie, 256.
77. Bornkamm, 'Interpretation', 114; similarly von den Osten-Sacken, 'Leistung', 160; Haacker, Stiftung, 167; and Thüsing, Erhöhung, 222, uses Kähler's phrase concerning Mark to describe John, too, as a passion narrative with an extended introduction.
78. So Schnackenburg, 'Gedanke des Sühnetodes', 224; Lindars, John, 322; 'Passion', 81f; Klaiber, 'Interpretation', 312.
79. Forestell, Word, 19f, 113, 191f; similarly Onuki, Gemeinde, 169f.
80. So Nicholson, Death, 4f; Morgan-Wynn, 'Cross', 221-223.
81. So de Jonge, Stranger, 66-69; Schnackenburg, Johannes III, 287, 296; Baum Bodenbender, Hoheit, 66f.

Notes 249

Notes to pp. 103 - 109

82. Against Thüsing, Erhöhung, 33, 260, 290f; Blank, 'Verhandlung', 62f; Dauer, Passionsgeschichte, 249f, 259f; Hahn, 'Prozess', 40f; Wilkens, Zeichen, 72, 112; Ruckstuhl, 'Abstieg', 334; Lindars, 'Passion', 77f; Schillebeeckx, Christ, 413; Kysar, Jesus, 60; Duke, Irony, 106, 114, 132.
83. Against Forestell, Word, 36, 61, 71, 73; Moloney, Son of Man, 62f; cf. also Bühner, Gesandte 397; and see the discussion in IIIB4 below.
84. Bultmann, Johannes, 293, 356; Theologie, 405, 408.
85. Baum Bodenbender, Hoheit, 79, 81, 83, 85.
86. Bultmann, Johannes, 356; Theologie, 400.
87. Against Käsemann, Letzter Wille, 19f.
88. Martyn, 'Source Criticism', 110.
89. Harvey, Trial, 53, 55, 57 et passim; see also Preiss, Life in Christ, 8-31; Dahl, 'Church', 135; Meeks, 'Man from Heaven', 155; Trites, Witness, 79-124; and Dauer, Passionsgeschichte, 247, 249. 261; Hahn, 'Prozess', 68-85, and de Jonge, Stranger, who emphasise the trial of the world in the trial of Jesus.
90. So Appold, Oneness, 110, 119; similarly, Hegermann, 'Eigentum', 127; Nicholson, Death, 49.
91. So Appold, Oneness 108, 111; Hegermann, 'Eigentum', 126; Dauer, Passionsgeschichte, 264, 267, 269.
92. Blank, Krisis, 282; cf. also Bultmann, Johannes 330.
93. So Becker, Johannes, 392, 406; Blank, Krisis, 282; Schnackenburg, Johannes II, 491; Dauer, Passiongeschichte, 241.
94. So Forestell, Word, 165; cf. also Nicholson, Death, 131.
95. So Becker, 'Auferstehung', 144, 149f.
96. So Lütgert, Christologie, 140; Preiss, Life in Christ, 19; Beasley-Murray, John, 214; cf. also the discussion in Blank, Krisis, 282-284.
97. van Hartingsveld, Eschatologie, 44.
98. Strathmann, Johannes, 183.
99. Bultmann, Theologie, 366; cf. also Schnackenburg, John I, 157f, Johannes II, 493f and Becker, 'Auferstehung', 149f.
100. Thüsing, Erhöhung, 194f; similarly Brown, John, 476f; Nicholson, Death, 129; Pamment, 'Doxa', 13.
101. So Bultmann, Johannes, 328; Schnackenburg, Johannes II, 486; Blank, Krisis, 278f; Riedl, Heilswerk, 173; Wilkens, Zeichen, 103; Untergassmair, Im Namen Jesu, 98f; Schillebeeckx, Christ, 412; Bruce, John, 266; Beasley-Murray, John, 212.
102. Thüsing, Erhöhung, 218f; de Jonge, Stranger, 137; Schnackenburg, Johannes II, 175f; Johannes IV, 451; Boismard/Lamouille, Jean, 329; Reim, 'Targum', 8; Bittner, Zeichen, 96.
103. Dahl, 'Church', 129; Hoskyns, John, 501; Lindars, John, 439; Whitacre, Polemic, 47; Ellis, Genius, 206.
104. Bultmann, Johannes, 346 n. 2; Pamment, 'Doxa', 13; Bjerkelund, Tauta, 142.
105. So also Lindars, John, 462; Hamerton-Kelly, Pre-existence, 235; Schnackenburg, Johannes III, 54-57; Schulz, Johannes, 178f; Bruce, John, 292f; Nicholson, Death, 149f; Beasley-Murray, John, 246.
106. Against Thüsing, Erhöhung, 236; Brown, John, 610.
107. Against Kysar, Jesus, 67.
108. Against Moloney, Son of Man, 195-197, 277.
109. Sanders/Mastin, John, 315; cf. also Barrett, John, 450.

110. Caird, 'Glory', 270f; against this: Schnackenburg, Johannes III, 57.
111. Moloney, Son of Man, 199f, 201, 277.
112. Thüsing, Erhöhung, 106; similarly Bultmann, Johannes, 325. Kossen sees an allusion
     to the servant imagery of Isa 49:3,5 here, so that Jesus represents Israel as a light
     to the Gentiles ('Greeks', 103-105, 108f).
113. Lindars, John, 427; Schnackenburg, Johannes II, 479f; Nicholson, Death, 151;
     Beasley-Murray, John, 211.
114. Against Moloney, Son of Man, 176-178; cf. also Scroggs, Christology, 73.
115. So Nicol, Semeia, 129; Brown, John, 431; Schnackenburg, Johannes II, 404f;
     Moloney, Son of Man, 210; Kremer, Lazarus, 30, 35f, 56f; Ellis, Genius, 184; cf.
     Lindars, John, who takes 11:4 to refer to the cross (387) and 11:40 to the glory of
     resurrection (400).
116. So also Brown, John, 610; Schnackenburg, Johannes II, 480; Johannes III, 54-57;
     Hamerton-Kelly, Pre-existence, 23f; Schulz, Johannes, 178f; Bruce, John, 292f;
     Nicholson, Death, 149-151; Beasley-Murray, John, 211, 246.
117. Cf. Hamerton-Kelly, Pre-existence, 199: 'whose finest hour was the hour of his
     death' and Dodd, Interpretation, who speaks of a progressive self renunciation
     reaching its climax at the cross (373f).
118. Bultmann, Johannes, 330; Theologie, 408. Similarly Bornkamm, 'Interpretation',
     113; von den Osten-Sacken, 'Leistung', 162; Lindars, John, 122, 157; Son of
     Man, 146f, 156; Moloney, Son of Man, 63f; Sproston, 'Christology', 79.
119. Dauer, Passionsgeschichte, 249f; Porsch, Pneuma, 79; Moloney, Son of Man, 63f,
     206f; Lindars, 'Passion', 77f; Son of Man, 147; Miller, 'Christology', 34f.
120. Bittner, Zeichen, 248; Pokorný, 'Jesus', 218, 222; Schnelle, Christologie, 208, 256.
121. Käsemann, Letzter Wille, 23, 49 n. 3, 124, 135; U.B. Müller, 'Bedeutung', 48, 54,
     65, 67f; Schulz, Johannes, 209, 237f; Appold, Oneness, 29, 54, 103, 123, 135;
     Becker, Johannes, 406; cf. already Bultmann, Theologie, 406.
122. So Ricca, Eschatologie, 131; Forestell, Word, 15; de la Potterie, Vérité, 198f, 771;
     Appold, Oneness, 32; Lindars, 'Passion', 79-81; Ibuki, Wahrheit, 141, 158;
     Moloney, Son of Man, 227f; Schillebeeckx, Christ, 419; Hegermann, Art. 'doxa',
     EWNT I, 840-843.
123. Blank, Krisis, 269; Dauer, Passionsgeschichte, 237; Dupont, Christologie, 263f.
124. So Riedl, Heilswerk, 155.
125. So Moloney, Son of Man, 228.
126. Against Schillebeeckx, Christ, 368f.
127. H.J. Holtzmann, Lehrbuch, 503, 505; similarly Westcott, John, 240f; Bernhard, John,
     563; Hoskyns, John, 506.
128. Schnackenburg, Johannes II, 505.
129. Käsemann, Letzter Wille, 22.
130. Schnelle, Christologie, 93, 182, 254.
131. Appold, Oneness, 30f; similarly Osborn, 'Theology', 76.
132. Bühner, Gesandte, 294.
133. B. Weiss, Lehrbuch, 609; similarly Dodd, Interpretation, 141.
134. Thüsing, Erhöhung, 214f, 222

Notes to pp. 113 - 115

135. Thüsing, Erhöhung, 185, 227f, 242f.
136. Thüsing, Erhöhung, 233, 240f.
137. Thüsing, Erhöhung, 181-186.
138. Bultmann, Johannes, 376f and Nicol, Semeia, 128.
139. Johnston, 'Ecce Homo', 131f, 135.
140. Theobald, Anfang, 37f; cf. also Becker, Johannes, 29f; Bornkamm, 'Paraklet', 117.
141. Bruce, John, 36; Onuki, Gemeinde, 106, 197-199, 210.
142. Schillebeeckx, Christ, 419; Käsemann, Letzter Wille, 48-54, 59; Appold, Oneness, 27f.
143. Hegermann, Art. 'doxa', EWNT I, 839f.
144. Caird, 'Glory', 269f, 272
145. So Schnackenburg, John I, 267; Johannes II, 505.
146. Bultmann, Johannes, 376, 398; similarly Appold, Oneness, 27f; Cadman, Open Heaven, 206; Bornkamm, 'Interpretation', 113; Smalley, John, 221; de la Potterie, Vérité, 459; and earlier: Baur, Kritische Untersuchungen, 203; Lütgert, Christologie, 21.
147. Bultmann, Johannes, 325; Cadman, Open Heaven, 38, 40.
148. Thüsing, Erhöhung, 246f; Lütgert, Christologie, 31; Nicol, Semeia, 122; de la Potterie, Vérité, 193; Blank, Krisis, 272; Ruckstuhl, 'Abstieg', 335.
149. So U.B. Müller, 'Bedeutung', 67f.
150. Thüsing, Erhöhung, 324; Nicol, Semeia, 122, 128.
151. So Hofbeck, Semeion, 104f, 143, 173-178; Wilkens, Zeichen, 110; Braun, Jean III, 206f; Schnackenburg, Johannes II, 503; similarly Käsemann, Letzter Wille, 22 and earlier Lütgert, Christologie, 21.
152. Schottroff, Glaubende, 272-277.
153. Käsemann, Letzter Wille, 19f.
154. Ibuki, Wahrheit, 191.
155. Forestell, Word, 70f.
156. Ibuki, Wahrheit, 192-196; Schlier, 'Prolog', 282; Riedl, Heilswerk, 138f. cf. also Thüsing, Erhöhung, 182, 242f, 246; de la Potterie, Vérité, 198f.
157. So Schnackenburg, Johannes II, 503; Whitacre, Polemic, 109; Hegermann, Art. 'doxa', EWNT I, 840f.
158. Moloney, Son of Man, 227; Pamment, 'Doxa', 14.
159. Wilkens, Zeichen, 113.
160. Richter, Studien, 193, 284f.
161. Becker, Johannes, 518.
162. U.B. Müller, Christologie, 32-35.
163. Riedl, Heilswerk, 123-127.
164. Riedl, Heilswerk, 169-171, 178f. Similarly, Braun, Jean III, 209f, 216f, 220f; Porsch, Pneuma, 76-78; Cadman, Open Heaven, 13.
165. Baur, Kritische Untersuchungen, 253; Bultmann, Johannes, 398.
166. Against Dupont, Christologie, 235f, 267f, 288-290. See also the criticism by Braun, Jean III, 201.
167. Bultmann, Johannes, 83. So Nicol, Semeia, 106; Haenchen, Johannes, 106; 'Das Johannesevangelium', 219-221; Schottroff, Glaubende, 245f, 255f, 259f; von den Osten Sacken, 'Leistung', 161; Bornkamm, 'Interpretation', 116; Wilkens, Zeichen, 28f, 44-49; Schulz, Johannes, 212; Appold, Oneness, 88-91; earlier: Lütgert, Christologie, 10.

Notes to pp. 115 - 118

168. Schottroff, Glaubende, 252-256, 258f; similarly, Langbrandtner, Weltferner Gott, 93-96.
169. See Bertram, Art. '*hypsoō*', TDNT 7, 610 n. 38; Black, 'Son of Man', 7; Thüsing, Erhöhung, 36f; Moloney, Son of Man, 61 n. 102; Lüdemann, Art. '*hypsoō*', EWNT III, 982; Beasley-Murray, 'John 12,31-32', 71f.
170. So Wead, Devices, 34f; Meeks, 'Man from Heaven', 155 and 171 n. 63.
171. So Riedl, Heilswerk, 100f; Richter, Studien, 61, 74-79, 116; Dauer, Passionsgeschichte, 231; U.B. Müller, 'Bedeutung', 57f, 67; Christologie, 49f; Wengst, Gemeinde, 63-65; Nicholson, Death, 143f.
172. Thüsing, Erhöhung, 15,21.
173. Thüsing, Erhöhung, 24.
174. So Dodd, Interpretation, 247; Schnackenburg, 'Son of Man', 130; John I, 397, 536; Johannes II, 505; Black, 'Son of Man', 6f; Thüsing, Erhöhung, 36; Brown, John, 146; Smalley, 'Son of Man', 291; Reim, Studien, 174-176; Forestell, Word, 64f; Beutler, 'Psalm 42/43', 57; Richard, 'Double Meaning', 105; Beasley-Murray, John, lxxxiv.
175. Caird, 'Glory', 274f; Klaiber, 'Interpretation', 316.
176. So among others Dodd, Interpretation, 306; Schulz, Menschensohn, 108; Johannes, 59f; Wilkens, Zeichen, 103f, 110; Barrett, John, 214, 427; 'Paradox', 109; Blank, Krisis, 84f, 261, 287; Schnackenburg, John I, 394-397; Johannes II, 156, 492f, 499-502; Johannes IV, 112; Käsemann, Letzter Wille, 46f; Coppens, 'Fils de L'Homme', 48; Becker, Johannes, 402-404; U.B. Müller, 'Bedeutung', 56-60; Brown, John, 40, 84, 168; Smalley, 'Son of Man', 291; Maddox, 'Function', 191; Appold, Oneness, 52f; Riedl, Heilswerk, 364; Bertram, Art. '*hypsoō*', TDNT 7, 610; Boismard/Lamouille, Jean, 51, 124, 319; Nicholson, Death, 75, 99-101, 119, 132-136; Lüdemann, Art. '*hypsoō*', EWNT III, 982; Gnilka, 'Christologie', 104; Bruce, John, 88, 182, 267, but cf. 195; O'Day, Revelation, 111f; Beasley-Murray, John, lxxxivf, 50f, 54, 76, 131f; 'John 12,31-32', 71-73; Burge, Anointed Community, 132.
177. Against Moloney, Son of Man, 63f; Lindars, Son of Man, 146, 156.
178. Cf. Pamment, 'Doxa', 16, who makes a link with the use of *doxa* in Isa 53:2; similarly Reim, 'Targum', 2.
179. Bultmann, Johannes, 189, 331.
180. Bittner, Zeichen, 254.
181. Bühner, Gesandte, 396f.
182. Against Meeks, Prophet-King, 287-292; 'Man from Heaven', 156; Thüsing, Erhöhung, 1-12; Forestell, Word, 63; Riedl, 'Menschensohn', 360; Ruckstuhl, 'Abstieg', 333; Moloney, Son of Man, 60-64, 140f, 228f; Lindars, Son of Man, 146, 156f; Baum Bodenbender, Hoheit, 265f cf. 256; Ellis, Genius, 153, 204.
183. Against Moloney, Son of Man, 63, 176-178, 207, 210; Lindars, 'Passion', 79; Son of Man, 147; Pokorný, 'Jesus', 218, 222; Pamment, 'Doxa', 13-16; Miller, 'Christology', 34f; Bittner, Zeichen, 248; Bjerkelund, Tauta, 124, 128; Schnelle, Christologie, 208, 250.
184. Pamment, 'Doxa', 13f.
185. Thüsing, Erhöhung, 24-28, 33, 302f; similarly Jervell, Jesus, 58, 60, 72; Schillebeeckx, Christ, 409f.

Notes to pp. 118 - 120

186. Thüsing, Erhöhung, 8f, 24, 26, 33, 293, 302f, 307.
187. Thüsing, Erhöhung, 300.
188. Thüsing, Erhöhung, 305-307.
189. Thüsing, Erhöhung, 303.
190. Moloney, Son of Man, 54f.
191. Odeberg, Fourth Gospel, 72-78.
192. Meeks, Prophet-King, 297, 301; 'Man from Heaven', 147; Haacker, Stiftung, 108-110; Miranda, Vater, 80; Borgen, 'Agent', 131f; 'Son of Man', 133-138; Whitacre, Polemic, 52; Segal, Two Powers, 213-214; Dunn, 'John', 326f.
193. Blank, Krisis, 77; Dahl, 'Church', 137; Forestell, Word, 43; Meeks, 'Man from Heaven', 147; Michel, 'Aufgestiegene', 349, 352f; Dunn, 'John', 322-325 (especially Merkabah mysticism); Reim, 'Targum', 7 (ascending angels).
194. Borgen, 'Agent', 129-131.
195. Bultmann, Johannes, 146-153; Blank, Krisis, 77f.
196. Moloney, Son of Man, 54f, 244. So also Sidebottom, Christ, 120; Ruckstuhl, 'Abstieg', 325; Lindars, Son of Man, 150.
197. Specifically in relation to Moloney: Barrett, John, 213; 'Paradox', 110; Nicholson, Death, 93-95; Painter, 'Christology', 59; cf. also Borgen, 'Son of Man', 139.
198. Bühner, Gesandte, 304-307, 380f, 392f; Borgen, 'Son of Man', 139-141. For criticism see Dunn, 'John', 329f; Moloney, Son of Man, 232f, 240f; Schnackenburg, Johannes IV, 105; Schnelle, Christologie, 207.
199. Cadman, Open Heaven, 30.
200. Borsch, Son of Man, 273, 275 n. 2.
201. Lütgert, Christologie, 42, 46f; Strachan, Fourth Gospel, 137f; Robinson, Priority, 371; cf. also Barrett, John 187; 'Paradox', 110f.
202. So Thüsing, Erhöhung, 256; Coppens, 'Le Fils de L'Homme', 35 arguing for its originality; cf. also Barrett, John, 213; Brown, John, 16; Schnackenburg, John I, 394; Nicholson, Death, 97f. See also Mees, 'Lectio brevior', 115 and 'Erhöhung', 34.
203. So Barrett, John, 213; Brown, John, 132; Sanders/Mastin, John, 126; Bruce, John, 87f; Haenchen, Johannes, 224; Schulz, Johannes, 59; Painter, 'Christology', 59.
204. See also Nicholson, Death, 92f.
205. Moloney, Son of Man, 123, 244-247.
206. So Bühner, Gesandte, 391f; Richter, Studien, 361f; Forestell, Word, 23f; Schulz, Menschensohn, 102f.
207. So Lütgert, Christologie, 47; Cadman, Open Heaven, 28; Schulz, Menschensohn, 102f; Bultmann, Johannes, 75; Dodd, Interpretation, 296; Brown, John, 83f, 97; Haenchen, Johannes, 182; Schnackenburg, John I, 321f, 413; 'Son of Man', 131; Forestell, Word, 67; Reim, Studien, 104; Appold, Oneness, 53f; Hahn, 'Jüngerberufung', 173; Lindars, 'Passion', 77; Boismard/Lamouille, Jean, 99; Bühner, Gesandte, 391f; Olsson, Structure, 102-104; Richter, Studien, 366; Dunn, 'John', 326; Bittner, Zeichen, 76; Pamment, 'Son of Man', 59; de Jonge, Stranger, 13, 59; Schnelle, Christologie, 87f; Burge, Anointed Community, 86; Scroggs, Christology, 70.
208. So Bauer, Johannes, 42; Maddox, 'Function', 190f; Higgins, Son of Man, 159f; Dahl, 'Church' 133; Bruce, John, 88; Painter, Witness, 55f; 'Church and Israel', 109f; 'Christ and the Church', 361; Coppens, 'Le Fils de L'Homme', 45. Cf. Smalley,

Notes to pp. 120 - 123

John, who sees both present (312). See now also my recent extended discussion: "Greater Things".
209. Derrett, Law, 416; Moloney, Son of Man, 38-40; Pamment, 'Son of Man', 59; Trudinger, 'Ladder', 119; Bruce, John, 88.
210. So Brown, John, 88; Moloney, Son of Man, 38-40; Lindars, John, 122; Son of Man, 148f; Ellis, Genius, 58; Beasley-Murray, John, 35.
211. So Moloney, Son of Man, 67; Lindars, Son of Man, 148f; Meeks, 'Man from Heaven', 146f.
212. Schnackenburg, 'Menschensohn', 126; also John I, 393; Johannes II, 156, 166f, 256.
213. Schnackenburg, 'Menschensohn', 126; similarly Preiss, Life in Christ, 16f.
214. Against Dodd, Interpretation, 245.
215. Schnackenburg, 'Menschensohn', 127f.
216. Schnackenburg, Johannes IV, 173.
217. Cullmann, Christologie, 192.
218. So Blank, Krisis, 257; Schenke, 'Vorgeschichte', 86f.
219. So Moloney, Son of Man, 114.
220. So Schnackenburg, Johannes II, 50f; Bruce, John, 162.
221. Schnackenburg, 'Menschensohn', 129f, 132; John I, 393; similarly Barrett, 'Symbolism', 73f; Boismard/Lamouille, Jean, 51; Nicholson, Death, 142.
222. Schnackenburg, Johannes IV, 112; similarly, Gnilka, 'Christologie', 103.
223. Schnackenburg, 'Menschensohn', 136.
224. Maddox, 'Function', 201f; similarly Culpepper, Anatomy, 39.
225. Maddox, 'Function', 193; similarly Dunn, Christology, 56.
226. Moloney, Son of Man, 211-213. See also Lindars, Son of Man, 150f, who largely follows Moloney (so 218 n. 2.)
227. Moloney, Son of Man, 179, 207.
228. Moloney, Son of Man, 226f.
229. Moloney, Son of Man, 195, 229 n. 27.
230. Moloney, Son of Man, 202-207; similarly Pamment, 'Son of Man', 58, 62, 64.
231. Schnelle, Christologie, 224. Against this: Wilckens, 'Lebensbrot', 237; Schnackenburg, Johannes II, 91.
232. So de la Potterie, 'Genèse', 36f; Woll, Johannine Christianity, 41; Burge, Anointed Community, 136f.
233. Against Barrett, John, 565f.
234. Against Onuki, Gemeinde, 86.
235. Against Sanders/Mastin, John, 428. So rightly Thüsing, Erhöhung, 265; Brown, John, 992-994, 1011; Schnackenburg, Johannes III, 376; Onuki, Gemeinde, 86.
236. Kremer, Osterevangelien, 173f, 183; Schillebeeckx, Christ, 918; cf. also Brown, John, 1011.
237. Schnackenburg, Johannes III, 376f; Minear, John, 128.
238. See the excellent discussion in Brown, John, 1011-1016; also Beloved Disciple, 54; Schnackenburg, Johannes III, 378; Johannes IV, 110; Nicholson, Death, 69-73, 199.
239. So Lindars, John, 607f; Meeks, 'Man from Heaven', 159; Zeller, 'Ostermorgen', 160.
240. Dodd, Interpretation, 241f
241. Wilkens, Zeichen, 113.
242. Lindars, 'Passion', 79.
243. So rightly Schillebeeckx, Christ, 417; Beasley-Murray, John, 73.

Notes to pp. 123 - 132

244. Bultmann, Theologie, 408-411.
245. Haenchen, 'Vater', 73, 75; Johannes, 109.
246. Thüsing, Erhöhung, 161, 164, 324.
247. Dauer, Passionsgeschichte, 39.
248. Schnackenburg, Johannes II, 217.
249. Haacker, Stiftung, 164-168, cf. 156, n. 806.
250. Forestell, Word, 19.
251. Becker, Johannes, 403-405.
252. Dodd, Interpretation, 372.
253. Painter, Witness, 89f; 'Eschatology', 50f; 'Christ and the Church', 361f.
254. Nicholson, Death, 119.
255. Schillebeeckx, Christ, 405f, 410f.
256. Johnston, 'Ecce Homo', 135f.
257. Hamerton-Kelly, Pre-existence, 233f.
258. Onuki, Gemeinde, 206
259. Bultmann, Johannes, 395; similarly Dahl, 'Church', 124f; Childs, Canon, 135.
260. Segovia, 'Structure', 490f; cf. also Nicholson, Death, 68f.
261. Bultmann, Johannes, 430f; Theologie, 395, 437.
262. Baur, Vorlesungen, 379.
263. Porsch, Pneuma, 66-68; similarly de Jonge, Stranger, 9.
264. Ibuki, Wahrheit, 300, 324.
265. Hofbeck, Semeion, 147, 177, 219.
266. T.E. Müller, Heilsgeschehen, 25, 33, 80-82, 132.
267. Thüsing, Erhöhung, 161, 164, and esp. 321-324.
268. Thüsing, Erhöhung, 283.
269. Thüsing, Erhöhung, 164.
270. Blank, Krisis, 141.
271. Porsch, Pneuma, 246f; Boismard/Lamouille, Jean, 357, pointing to the parallel in 2 Jn 2. For a contrary view cf. Boring, 'Christian Prophecy', 114 n. 1.
272. Beutler, Angst, 64f.
273. So Porsch, Pneuma, 71f, 208, 246f.
274. So Porsch, Pneuma, 105, 109f, 144.
275. So Hahn, 'Wasser', 53f; Reim, Studien, 85.
276. So Schnackenburg, Johannes II, 213f; Painter, Witness, 64f; Haacker, Stiftung, 51; Boismard/Lamouille, Jean, 52; Bruce, John, 181f; Beasley-Murray, John, 116.
277. So Thüsing, Erhöhung, 161; Brown, John, 329; Burge, Anointed Community, 91-93.
278. So Hahn, 'Wasser', 53, 60; Porsch, Pneuma, 70; cf. Ibuki, Wahrheit, 324.
279. So Porsch, Pneuma, 68-70.
280. Cf. Hahn, 'Wasser', 66f
281. Thüsing, Erhöhung, 263-268; Porsch, Pneuma, 249f, 343, 371-376, 386; see also Dauer, Johannes und Lukas, 238-241.
282. So Porsch, Pneuma, 374.
283. So Porsch, Pneuma, 359-362; Schnackenburg, Johannes III, 386; Onuki, Gemeinde, 89; Dauer, Johannes und Lukas, 242-245; Perkins, Resurrection, 178.
284. So Thüsing, Erhöhung, 274.
285. Forestell, Word, 98-101, 157.
286. So Haacker, Stiftung, 62, 150; against de la Potterie, 'Genèse', 38.
287. Wengst, Gemeinde, 114f, 120.

256   Notes

Notes to pp. 132 - 139

288. U.B. Müller, 'Bedeutung', 68f.
289. Hegermann, 'Eigentum', 130f.
290. Martyn, 'Source Criticism', 111-113; see also Minear, John, passim.
291. See Evans, 'Quotation Formulas', 82.

PART IIIB   Issues: The Salvation Event

1. Baur, Vorlesungen, 372, 377.
2. Wetter, Sohn Gottes, 5f, 151f; Büchsel, Johannes, 16.
3. Bultmann, Johannes, 103f, 111, 188; Theologie, 414, 418-420.
4. Bultmann, Johannes, 188; Theologie, 418.
5. Bultmann, Theologie, 420.
6. Lütgert, Christologie, 17; similarly, Hofbeck, Semeion, 190-193.
7. Haenchen, 'Vater', 72; Johannes, 232; similarly Scroggs, Christology, 66f.
8. Haenchen, 'Das Johannesevangelium', 222f, 226.
9. Käsemann, Letzter Wille, 47f, 87-89; Ibuki, Wahrheit, 44-46; de la Potterie, Vérité,
   1011, 240; von den Osten-Sacken, 'Leistung', 161; Riedl, Heilswerk, 26f.
10. So T.E. Müller, Heilsgeschehen, 112, 135; Blank, Krisis, 133f; Riedl, Heilswerk, 314;
    Wengst, Gemeinde, 119f.
11. Brown, John, 32.
12. Schnackenburg, John I, 155, 392.
13. Becker, 'Auferstehung', 142-144, 149f.
14. Weder, 'Menschwerdung', 353.
15. So Schnackenburg, Johannes IV, 114f; similarly Thüsing, Erhöhung, iii.
16. Meeks, 'Man from Heaven', 143-146, 154, 161f; cf. also Talbert, 'Descending and
    Ascending Redeemer', 425.
17. O'Day, Revelation, 35-42, 45f; similarly Scroggs, Christology, 60f.
18. Haenchen, 'Das Johannesevangelium', 219
19. Schweizer, 'Zeuge', 161; Jesus, 160; cf. also Preiss, Life in Christ, 11, 17;
    Schillebeeckx, Christ, 312, 314.
20. So Bultmann, Johannes, 116.
21. Bultmann, Theologie, 393f, 415.
22. Eg. Käsemann, 'Prologue', 102; Schulz, Johannes, 210; Lieu, 'Epistles', 201.
23. Forestell, Word, 57
24. Forestell, Word, 172.
25. Ibuki, Wahrheit, 115.
26. Haacker, Stiftung, 163-165.
27. T.E. Müller, Heilsgeschehen, 33, 138f.
28. Bultmann, Johannes, 190; Theologie, 415.
29. So Dodd, Interpretation, 194; Haenchen, 'Vater', 73; Barrett, John, 98; 'Father', 21-
    26; Hahn, 'Sehen', 128; Ritt, Gebet, 459; Schnackenburg, 'Fleisch', 8 and see
    IIIB3 below.
30. Porsch, Pneuma, 151.
31. Käsemann, 'Prologue', 124; Letzter Wille, 107-109; Schottroff, Glaubende, 288;
    Lattke, Einheit, 50f, 70.
32. So Bultmann, Theologie, 367; Klaiber, 'Interpretation', 319-321; Segovia, Love
    Relationships, 169; Schnelle, Christologie, 210f; Scroggs, Christology, 76f.
33. Ibuki, Wahrheit, 174.

34. So Bultmann, Johannes, 92; Forestell, Word, 70; Appold, Oneness, 100; Schnackenburg, John I, 506, 519f; Brown, John, 528; Nicol, Semeia, 99-103.
35. So Bultmann, Johannes, 83 n. 7; Theologie, 396; Schnider/Stenger, Johannes, 82, 84-86; Haenchen, Johannes, 107; Richter, Studien, 343; Untergassmair, Im Namen Jesu, 47; Fortna, 'Christology', 493; Barrett, 'Symbolism', 76f; Schnelle, Christologie, 202.
36. Bittner, Zeichen, 128-132.
37. Against Bultmann, Theologie, 397. So rightly Wead, Devices, 19; Nicol, Semeia, 106; Pokorný, 'Jesus', 218; Schnelle, Christologie, 150.
38. Schottroff, Glaubende, 48; Langbrandtner, Weltferner Gott, 93-96.
39. So rightly Wead, Devices, 24; Gnilka, 'Christologie', 99; Schnelle, Christologie, 94-98, 148-151, 183, 191.
40. Similarly Hofbeck, Semeion, 180, 182; Schnackenburg, 'Frage', 205f; Käsemann, Letzter Wille, 17, 53; Lohse, 'Miracles', 72; Segovia, Love Relationships, 194; Lona, 'Glauben' 179; Fortna, 'Christology', 491.
41. Kee, 'Myth and Miracle', 145-164; Miracles, 221; 'Christology', 181, 190.
42. On this see the essay by de la Potterie, 'Genèse'.
43. Bultmann, Johannes, 27f; Theologie 370, 373-375, 429; similarly Ibuki, Wahrheit, 38-54, 114f; Painter, 'John 9', 55; Scroggs, Christology, 101f.
44. Bergmeier, Glaube, 213-216; similarly Haenchen, 'Das Johannesevangelium', 224f.
45. Langbrandtner, Weltferner Gott, 91-93; Haenchen, 'Das Johannesevangelium' 223f; Schottroff, Glaubende, 289, 295; Hofrichter, 'Gnosis', 17f.
46. Bultmann, Johannes, 26f, 39; Theologie, 420, cf. 379; Wilkens, Zeichen, 120; Blank, Krisis, 96-99, 145-149; Hegermann, 'Eigentum', 120; Porsch, Pneuma, 128-130; Schottroff, Glaubende, 229; Langbrandtner, Weltferner Gott, 100 (of the 'Grundschrift').
47. So rightly Onuki, Gemeinde, 53. See also H.M. Schenke's review of Schottroff in ThZ 97 (1972) 751-755, esp. 755.
48. So rightly Onuki, Gemeinde, 54 against Käsemann, Letzter Wille, 114.
49. Becker, 'Dualismus'; Johannes, 147-151.
50. See, in particular, Nicol, Semeia, 146f; von den Osten-Sacken, 'Leistung', 157; Brown, Community.
51. So Bultmann, Theologie, 394; Preiss, Life in Christ, 29; Ibuki, Wahrheit, 355; Riedl, Heilswerk, 26f; de la Potterie, Vérité, 1011.
52. Becker, 'Johannes 17', 76-78; Johannes, 519; similarly Langbrandtner, Weltferner Gott, 68f; cf. Untergassmair, Im Namen Jesu, 67f.
53. Bultmann, Theologie, 418; similarly Käsemann, Letzter Wille, 109, 116; Haenchen, 'Das Johannesevangelium', 282; Schweizer, Ego Eimi, 132-135; Lieu, Epistles, 241f; Painter, 'John 9', 44-46; Gnilka, 'Christologie', 101.
54. Bultmann, Johannes, 26f; similarly Käsemann, Letzter Wille, 109; von den Osten-Sacken, 'Leistung', 159.
55. Painter, 'John 9', 49-55.

Notes to pp. 142 - 148

56. Bultmann, Johannes, 39.
57. Appold, Oneness, 276-278. And see the criticism by Onuki, Gemeinde, 57-62.
58. So rightly Schnackenburg, Johannes II, 54; 'Frage', 204; Onuki, Gemeinde, 65-70.
59. So Porsch, Pneuma, 382; Moule, 'Neglected Factor', 156f, 159; Forestell, Word, 132-134; van Hartingsveld, Eschatologie, 153; de Jonge, Stranger, 173f, 188; Schnelle, Christologie, 146; Beasley-Murray, John, 79; Burge, Anointed Community, 143-146. Against Fischer, Himmlische Wohnungen, 330-332, 346-348; Heise, Bleiben, 100, 173; Scroggs, Christology, 98f.
60. So rightly Scroggs, Christology, 58f; Gnilka, 'Christologie', 94f; Becker, Johannes, 147-151; 'Dualismus', 71-87; 'Auferstehung', 147f; 'Streit der Methoden', 46f.
61. So rightly Barrett, John, 108; cf. Schottroff, Glaubender, 272-274.
62. Gnilka, 'Christologie', 96f, 102; Onuki, Gemeinde, 41f; Painter, 'John 9', 54; Scroggs, Christology, 58f.
63. So Onuki, Gemeinde, 53f.
64. Against Käsemann, Letzter Wille, 114; Evans, 'Passion', 65.
65. Becker, 'Auferstehung', 149f.
66. Schnackenburg, John 1, 155.
67. So rightly Schillebeeckx, Christ, 339; Wilckens, 'Lebensbrot', 234.
68. Against T.E. Müller, Heilsgeschehen, 35, 67-70; Thüsing, Erhöhung, 132f; Richter, Studien, 43f, 53, 58f; and see IIIA2 above.
69. So Bultmann, Theologie, 408f; Lattke, Einheit, 149; Becker, Johannes, 423.
70. Bultmann, Johannes, 187f, 190, 191 n. 5; Theologie, 414f; similarly Cadman, Open Heaven, 4-6; cf. also Robinson, Priority, 389.
71. Lütgert, Christologie, 25-30; Brun, 'Gottesschau', 1 and passim; Robinson, 'Trinity', 174; Priority, 368-389; similarly Büchsel, Johannes, 15f; Cadman, Open Heaven, 3f; and earlier Beyschlag, Neutestamentliche Theologie II, 96ff.
72. So Lütgert, Christologie, 26f; Brun, 'Gottesschau', 1,3f; Büchsel, Johannes, 16; Cadman, Open Heaven, 4; Robinson, Priority, 372; earlier H.J. Holtzmann, Lehrbuch, 452.
73. Blank, Krisis, 117; Thüsing, Erhöhung, 213.
74. So Lütgert, Christologie, 25f; Brun, 'Gottesschau', 4; Cadman, Open Heaven, 4; H.J. Holtzmann, Lehrbuch, 452.
75. So Lütgert, Christologie, 27f; Brun, 'Gottesschau', 4; Cadman, Open Heaven, 5; Robinson, Priority, 370.
76. So Lütgert, Christologie, 30; Brun, 'Gottesschau', 1,17f; H.J. Holtzmann, Lehrbuch, 452.
77. So Brun, 'Gottesschau', 5.
78. So Lütgert, Christologie, 30; Brun, 'Gottesschau', 6; Cadman, Open Heaven, 6; of receiving the revelation on earth, though not denying pre-existence: Strathmann, Johannes, 79.
79. H.J. Holtzmann, Lehrbuch, 452f.
80. Brun, 'Gottesschau', 20f; similarly Robinson, Priority, 371.
81. Robinson, Priority, 370f.
82. Lütgert, Christologie, 31, 36-38.
83. Lütgert, Christologie, 42, 46f; similarly, Beyschlag, Neutestamentliche Theologie II, 100f; Büchsel,

Johannes, 16, 53; as possible: Brown, John, 17; cf. Barrett, 'Paradox', 110f, who
using 3:13 with 1:51 to say that the addition to 3:13, 'who is in heaven', would be
consistent with John's view of the earthly Jesus.
84. Cadman, Open Heaven, 30.
85. Barrett, John, 73, 187; 'Paradox', 110f; cf. also Dodd, Interpretation, 258f; Kieffer,
'L'Espace', 405f.
86. Odeberg, Fourth Gospel, 114.
87. So Lütgert, Christologie, 32; Brun, 'Gottesschau', 7f, 14-16; Beyschlag,
Neutestamentliche Theologie II, 426; Büchsel, Johannes, 16; Cadman, Open
Heaven, 10; Robinson, Priority, 371.
88. Westcott, John, 15; Lindars, John, 99; Käsemann, 'Prologue', 163; Letzter Wille, 27f;
Schillebeeckx, Christ, 361; Beasley-Murray, John, 4.
89. So Lütgert, Christologie, 34; Brun, 'Gottesschau', 7, 10-13, who also takes 8:37f in
this way (8f); H.J. Holtzmann, Lehrbuch, 452; Robinson, Priority, 372.
90. Brun, 'Gottesschau', 10f; similarly Robinson, Priority, 369f.
91. Brun, 'Gottesschau', 13f.
92. Lütgert, Christologie, 36, 47f; similarly Büchsel, Johannes, 14,16.
93. Brun, 'Gottesschau', 6-8.
94. So Lütgert, Christologie, 42; Brun, 'Gottesschau', 16 n. 1; Büchsel, Johannes, 16;
Strathmann, Johannes, 53.
95. Bultmann, Johannes, 75; similarly Appold, Oneness, 53.
96. Brun, 'Gottesschau', 1.
97. Bultmann, Johannes, 191.
98. Bultmann, Theologie, 387.
99. Against Odeberg, Fourth Gospel, 114.
100. Lütgert, Christologie, 42, 46f.
101. So rightly, Woll, Johannine Christianity, 27f; Fuller, 'Theology', 107 against
Schillebeeckx, Christ, 403; cf. also Robinson, 'Christology', 75; and n. 85 above.
102. So Beutler, Martyria, 248; Theobald, Anfang, 57; de la Potterie, 'Prologue', 367.
103. So Thüsing, Erhöhung, 209; Schnackenburg, John 1, 281; Bühner, Gesandte, 376;
Haenchen, Johannes, 132; Theobald, Anfang, 119; Painter, 'Prologue', 470;
earlier H.J. Holtzmann, Lehrbuch, 450.
104. Against Westcott, John, 15; Bultmann, Johannes, 56; Käsemann, 'Prologue', 163;
'Letzter Wille, 27f, 124; Lindars, John, 99; Beasley-Murray, John, 4.
105. de la Potterie, 'L'emploi dynamique de eis', 366-387; Vérité, 73-74; 'Prologue',
363f, 369; Moloney, 'John 1:18', 65, 67f. Against this Schnackenburg, Johannes
II, 234; 'Fleisch', 2 n. 5; Haenchen, Johannes, 116; Bruce, John, 45; Schnelle,
Christologie, 233.
106. So Schnackenburg, Johannes IV, 109; Scroggs, Christology, 106.
107. See n. 71 and 72 and also Brown, John, 214; Schulz, Johannes, 187f; Beasley-
Murray, John, 53, 76.
108. Bultmann, Theologie, 190f.
109. Dupont, Christologie, 48f.
110. Against Robinson, 'Trinity', 174; 'Christology', 75, 77; Priority, 379-381; cf. also
Schillebeeckx, Christ, 403, 431; Harvey, Constraints, 178.

Notes to pp. 153 - 157

111. Against Fuller, 'Christmas', 70; Schoonenberg, 'Prologue', 409, 411f; and most radically, Watson, 'Christology', 114-116; cf. Brown, Beloved Disciple, 152f; Epistles, 121f.
112. Against Robinson, 'Christology', 75.
113. Appold, Oneness, 62.
114. So Haenchen, 'Das Johannesevangelium', 218; Thüsing, Erhöhung, 209; Haacker, Stiftung, 14; Bühner, Gesandte, 378-380; earlier B. Weiss, Lehrbuch, 602, 605f; H.J. Holtzmann, Lehrbuch, 451-453.
115. Against Robinson, Priority, 389.
116. So Lindars, 'Slave', 274, 281.
117. So Schnackenburg, Johannes II, 299; cf. Brown, John, 367.
118. Miller, 'Christology', 263.
119. Bultmann, Johannes, 1.
120. So Bultmann, Johannes, 1; Pollard, Christology, 13f.
121. Dunn, 'John', 334.
122. So H.J.Holtzmann, Lehrbuch, 446; Haacker, Stiftung, 17f; Wengst, Gemeinde, 101-103; Thyen, 'Literatur', ThR 39, 223; Schnelle, Christologie, 246.
123. Theobald, Anfang, 129.
124. Contrast Beyschlag, Neutestamentliche Theologie II, 430f; Lütgert, Christologie, vii.
125. Hooker, 'Prologue', 45.
126. On the grammatical issues see Westcott, John, 3; Colwell, 'The Use of the Article', 33; Moule, Idiom Book, 115f; Harner, 'Qualitative Anarthrous Predicate Nouns', 75-87; Mastin, 'Neglected Factor', 35f; Haenchen, Johannes, 118; Bruce, John, 31; Fennema, 'God the only Son', 128-131; Hofius, 'Struktur', 16f.
127. So Bauer, Johannes, 6; Schnackenburg, 'Fleisch', 3; Barrett, 'Father', 23; Bruce, John, 31; Theobald, Anfang, 43f; Hofius, 'Struktur', 16; Mastin, 'Neglected Factor', 36; Fennema, 'God the only Son', 129, cf. also on 1:18, 130f. Contrast also the translation in Schillebeeckx, Christ, 317, 'God was the Word'!
128. Dupont, Christologie, 48f.
129. Langbrandtner, Weltferner Gott, 40-42.
130. So rightly Cullmann, Christologie, 317; Schnackenburg, John 1, 234f; Theobald, Anfang, 43-45; Fennema, 'God the only Son', 130.
131. Cited in Mastin, 'Neglected Factor', 35.
132. So Schulz, Johannes, 19; Haenchen, Johannes, 117f.
133. So Dodd, Interpretation, 280; similarly Schnackenburg, John 1, 234f; Theobald, Anfang, 43f, 47; Hofius, 'Struktur', 17
134. Colwell, 'The Use of the Article', 33.
135. So Westcott, John, 3; Moule, Idiom Book, 115f; Harner, 'Qualitative Anarthrous Predicate Nouns', 75-87; Mastin, 'Neglected Factor', 35f; Fennema, 'God the only Son', 129f; Beasley-Murray, John, 10f; Hofius, 'Struktur', 16f.
136. Schnackenburg, 'Fleisch', 3; Barrett, John, 156; Bruce, John, 31.
137. Brown, John, 1047.
138. Bultmann, Johannes, 16.
139. Haenchen, Johannes, 118.
140. So Theobald, Anfang, 49, 'Gleichursprünglichkeit'.
141. See Schnackenburg, John 1, 484f; Brown, John, 523f; Borgen, Bread from Heaven, 104; Weder, 'Menschwerdung', 340;

Notes to pp. 157 - 159

Dunn, 'John', 332f; Painter 'John 9', 49f; cf. also the possible influence of rabbinic traditions concerning the Memra: Hayward, 'Holy Name', 16-23; Theobald, Anfang, 46; Reim, 'Targum', 5f; cf. Barrett, John, 153: 'a blind alley'.

142. See Bultmann, 'Prologue', 20-30; Dodd, Interpretation, 54-73; Schnackenburg, John 1, 485-487; Brown, John, 521-523; Theobald, Anfang, 98-109; Ruckstuhl, 'Prolog', 454; Dunn, 'John', 330f, Christology, 242, 344f, 349 arguing, I think, unconvincingly that all uses before John are metaphorical; cf. Segal, 'Pre-Existence', 92-94; Fuller, 'Theology', 110f.

143. See further Fuller, 'Theology', 110f; Talbert, 'Descending and Ascending Redeemer, 439; Fossum, 'Christology'.

144. See esp. Wilson, 'Nag Hammadi', 298; Evans, 'Prologue', 399.

145. So Dodd, Interpretation, 280; Bauer, Johannes, 6; Haenchen, 'Das Johannesevangelium', 218; Johannes, 116; Schnelle, Christologie, 234; Fuller, 'Theology', 110f; cf. Theobald, Anfang, 43-45.

146. So Lindars, John, 77.

147. See Hengel, Sohn Gottes, 73-76.

148. See Loader, Sohn und Hoherpriester, 25f.

149. So Brown, John, cxxii-cxxv; Weder, 'Menschwerdung', 340; Painter 'John 9', 49f; Reim, 'Targum', 5f.

150. Against Eltester, 'Logos', 124-134; Haenchen, Johannes, 120-133; Hofius, 'Struktur', 21; Kysar, Jesus, 17. As the meaning belonging to the original tradition used by the author: Theobald, Anfang, 109-115; Schnackenburg, 'Logos Hymnus', 84-90; Onuki, Gemeinde, 105; Ruckstuhl, 'Prolog', 452f.

151. So Käsemann, 'Prologue', 165f; Schnackenburg, John I, 227; 'Prolog', 40, 42; Ruckstuhl, 'Prolog', 452f; Theobald, Anfang, 117-126; Onuki, Gemeinde, 42; Ellis, Genius, 22.

152. Against Vellanickel, Divine Sonship, 112-132; Boismard/Lamouille, Jean, 72; de la Potterie, Vérité, 206. So Mees, 'John 1,12.13', 107-115; Pryor, 'Virgin Birth', 296-318; cf. Hofrichter, who has modified his support for the singular reading expressed in Nicht aus Blut, passim, and argues now for the singular reading having belonged to the original pre Johannine prologue to which he attributes then unbelievable influence on Christianity and gnosticism (Anfang, 45-54).

153. Robinson, 'Christology', 70; Priority, 321; also citing Dodd in approval: 'Christology', 78 n. 99. See also the criticism of de la Potterie, Vérité, 178.

154. So Hahn, 'Beobachtungen', 241-244; de la Potterie, Vérité, 189f; Dahms, 'Monogenēs', 228, 230; Fennema, 'God the only Son'', 126f.

155. See also de Kruijf, 'Glory', 114.

156. So also Schnelle, Christologie, 342.

157. Schnackenburg, 'Fleisch', 7f; Hooker, 'Prologue', 53-58; Theobald, Anfang, 38f; Mowvley, 'John 1:14-18', 135-137; Thyen, 'Brüder', 533; Bühner, Gesandte, 375.

158. Edwards, 'charin anti charitos'; see also Theobald, Anfang, 60f.

159. For this translation, see Fennema, 'God the only Son.'

160. So Cullmann, Christologie, 317; Brown, John, 17; Lindars, John, 98f; Bruce, John, 45; Mastin, 'Neglected Factor', 37-41; Fennema, 'God the only Son', 126-128, 131; contrast Barrett, John, 169; Schnackenburg, John I, 280; Haenchen, Johannes, 132; Beasley-Murray, John, 2f.

Notes to pp. 159 - 166

161. So Schnackenburg, Johannes II, 129; Haenchen, Johannes, 276.
162. Cf. Dodd, Historical Tradition, 386 and Robinson, 'Christology', 71, who see a parable in 5:19f; Lindars, 'Slave', 272, in 5:19 only.
163. Barrett, 'Father', 23f; similarly Brown, John, 218f; Preiss, Life in Christ, 25; Moloney, Son of Man, 209; Haenchen, Johannes, 275f; Painter, 'Text and Context', 32; Beasley-Murray, John, 74f; Scroggs, Christology, 79.
164. Wetter, Sohn Gottes, 174.
165. Büchsel, Johannes, 75; cf. also Schillebeeckx, Christ, 403, 431.
166. Sproston, 'Christology', 81f.
167. Lindars, John, 56.
168. Riedl, Heilswerk, 422.
169. Riedl, Heilswerk, 201f, 213.
170. Barrett, 'Father', 19-22.
171. Appold, Oneness, 23.
172. Leistner, Antijudäismus, 126; Miranda, Sendung, 45.
173. Barrett, 'Father', 23f; John, 72; similarly Bultmann, Johannes, 184f; Schnackenburg, Johannes II, 128; Kysar, Jesus, 35.
174. So de Jonge, Stranger, 148f who notes that the charge was also laid against Caligula.
175. Appold, Oneness, 23, 24 n. 1, 272.
176. Barrett, 'Father', 150.
177. Haenchen, Johannes, 107f.
178. Beasley-Murray, John, 174; Brown, John, 232f.
179. So rightly, Miranda, Sendung, 78; Lindars, 'Behind the Fourth Gospel', 70; Jervell, Jesus, 21.
180. So Dahl, 'Church', 130; Riedl, Heilswerk, 260f; Schnackenburg, Johannes II, 390; Mann, 'Exégèse', 532; Beasley-Murray, John, 176f; Hanson, 'Citations' 160, who also identifies the 'Word' as the Logos (161). Against this Schnackenburg, Johannes II, 391.
181. Brown, John, 409f; Robinson, Priority, 373f.
182. Boismard, 'Prophete', 170; Boismard/Lamouille, Jean, 275.
183. So Barrett, 'Father', 25; similarly Davey, Jesus, 36f.
184. Lütgert, Christologie, 58-60; Büchsel, Johannes, 75; similarly Robinson, Priority, 311, 375.
185. Robinson, 'Christology', 72.
186. So Emerton, 'Psalm 82 and John 10', 329-332; 'Melchisedek and the Gods', 399-401; similarly Bühner, Gesandte, 393-395.
187. Against Robinson, Priority, 375.
188. So Barrett, John, 382; Brown, John, 408.
189. Sproston, 'Christology', 84f.
190. Barrett, John, 382; Brown, John, 408; Lindars, John, 370f; Busse, 'Johannes 10', 524.
191. So Brown, John, 411.
192. On 'en' language see Borig, Weinstock, 210-213, 217; Malatesta, Interiority and Covenant.
193. Leistner, Antijudäismus, 126-129; cf. also Miranda, Sending, 78.
194. Martyn, 'Glimpses', 104f. Cf. also Brown, Beloved Disciple, 44-47; de Jonge, Stranger, 148f.
195. So Lindars, Behind the Fourth Gospel, 70; John, 365; Schnackenburg, Johannes II, 128, 388; Boismard/Lamouille, Jean, 273f.
196. Ricca, Eschatologie, 108.
197. Lütgert, Christologie, 92-95, 105; Wetter, Sohn Gottes, 176.

198. Wengst, Gemeinde, 103f
199. So Zimmermann, '*Egō Eimi*', 60-69; Brown, John, 535-538; Harner, 'I am', 6-15; Schnackenburg, Johannes II, 64-70; Moloney, Son of Man, 131f; Gnilka, 'Christologie', 100; McArthur, 'Christological Perspectives', 80; Beasley-Murray, John, 89f. Cf. Delebecque, Jean, who finds allusions to the divine name also in the use of the participle of the verb to be in 1:18; 3:13; and also in 8:25. On the latter see Schnackenburg, Johannes II, 254.
200. So Barrett, John, 342; 'Theocentric', 12f; 'Symbolism', 69-72; Lindars, John, 320; Bühner, Gesandte, 166-174; Becker, 'Auferstehung', 150; Johannes, 208. Cf. also IIIC6 above.
201. Against Schweizer, Ego Eimi, 125-127, 135; so Zimmermann, '*Egō Eimi*', 57f; Wead, Devices, 76f.
202. So de Jonge, Stranger, 150; Mastin, 'Neglected Factor', 49; Fuller, 'Theology', 114.
203. So Dunn, 'John', 334f; Osborne, 'Christology', 58; Fuller, 'Theology', 109f.
204. Dunn, 'John', 336f.
205. See Dunn, Christology, 163-176, who argues for personification in the use of Sophia right up to but not including the fourth evangelist. Countering, rightly, that this sets the limit too late: Segal, 'Pre-existence', 93; Fuller, 'Theology', 108-111.
206. So de Jonge, Stranger, 148f; Ellis, Genius, 140; Lindars, John, 77.
207. So Boismard/Lamouille, Jean, 52.
208. Evans, 'Passion', 65.
209. Lieu, Epistles, 202.
210. So Haenchen, Johannes, 275f.
211. So Cullmann, Christologie, 272f; Barrett, 'Theocentric', 13.
212. Against Riedl, Heilswerk, 213; Vellanickel, Sonship, 112f, 130f.
213. See n. 152 above.
214. Cf. Nicholson, Death, 81.
215. Lütgert, Christologie, 60, 64f, 77.
216. Lütgert, Christologie, 24, 41, 60.
217. Lütgert, Christologie, 54, 56, 67. Similarly Beyschlag, Neutestamentliche Theologie II, 425; B.Weiss, Lehrbuch, 609, 613; Cadman, Open Heaven, 11-13, 16; Brun, 'Gottesschau', 15.
218. H.J. Holtzmann, Lehrbuch, 493f.
219. Lütgert, Christologie, 51f, 99; cf. Büchsel, Johannes, 59; Strathmann, Johannes, 79.
220. Lütgert, Christologie, 69; similarly Cadman, Open Heaven, 16; and earlier, Beyschlag, Neutestamentliche Theologie II, 425.
221. Watson, 'Christology', 113f.
222. Fuller, 'Christmas', 70; also Schoonenberg, 'Prologue', 409-411; Brown, Beloved Disciple, 152f; Epistles, 77f.
223. Watson, 'Christology', 118.
224. Robinson, 'Christology', 71f; 'Trinity', 177; Priority, 311; Beyschlag, Neutestamentliche Theologie II, 425; similarly Harvey, Constraints, 178; Schillebeeckx, Christ, 431.
225. Fuller, 'Theology', 116.
226. So Schnackenburg, Johannes II, 107; Mastin, 'Neglected Factor', 49; Barrett, 'Father', 19-21; Dunn, 'John', 30f.
227. Braun, Jean 70; Riedl, Heilswerk, 421-423, cf. also 201, 205, 277; cf. also Fuller, 'Theology', 116.
228. Blank, Krisis, 222-224.

264 Notes

Notes to pp. 169 - 175

229. Blank, Krisis, 347.
230. Ibuki, Wahrheit, 115, 123, 149, 174, 206.
231. Baur, Vorlesungen, 357f, 367. Cf. similarly Scroggs, Christology, 79, on Jesus' freedom as Son.
232. Käsemann, Letzter Wille, 59, 105; Appold, Oneness, 20-22; agreeing: Osborn, 'Theology', 76.
233. Appold, Oneness, 272, 283, 22.
234. Pollard, Christology, 17.
235. Langbrandtner, Weltferner Gott. 42, 89-92, 108f.
236. Cf. Mastin, 'Neglected Factor', 50.
237. Lütgert, Christologie, 69; similarly Cadman, Open Heaven, 16; Braun, Jean, 141f.
238. Busse, 'Johannes 10', 524.
239. So Barrett, 'Father', 23-25.
240. So Miranda, Vater; Sendung; Bühner, Gesandte; see also Borgen, Bread from Heaven, 158-162; Haenchen, Johannes, 107f; Bruce, John, 130; Barrett, 'Theocentric', 6f; Robinson, Priority, 350; Schnelle, Christologie, 209.
241. Miranda, Sendung, 34, 38, 41-45, 67; similarly the emphasis on the prophetic background of the sending motif in Borgen, Bread from Heaven, 158-162; Boismard/Lamouille, Jean, 49f; Bruce, John 167f; Isaacs, 'Prophetic Spirit', 402f.
242. Bühner, Gesandte, 213-215; 233f, 264-266, 335; Becker, Johannes, 55; 'Auferstehung', 142; cf. also critically Schnelle, Christologie, 209f, who stresses the wisdom background of sending.
243. Käsemann, Letzter Wille, 30, 59, 105; Appold, Oneness, 20-22, 283; cf. the criticism in Haacker, Stiftung, 93 n. 76; Barrett, 'Father', 25f.
244. Haenchen, Johannes, 107.
245. Hahn, 'Prozess', 95.
246. Lieu, Epistles, 201-206; similarly Robinson, Priority, 350f.
247. Haenchen, Johannes, 107f; Becker, Johannes, 147f.
248. Barrett, 'Theocentric', 6f; 'Father', 22f; similarly Lieu, Epistles, 202.
249. Scroggs, Christology, 242.
250. Lütgert, Christologie, 49.
251. Thüsing, Erhöhung, 222f, 225.
252. Lütgert, Christologie, 54, 56, 67.
253. Watson, 'Christology', 114.
254. Fuller, 'Christmas', 70; Schoonenberg, 'Prologue', 409.
255. Against Fuller, 'Theology', 116.
256. Watson, 'Christology', 114.
257. Cadman, Open Heaven, 6-8
258. Lütgert, Christologie, 25
259. B.Weiss, Lehrbuch, 613 n. 15, 614.
260. Büchsel, Johannes, 40; similarly Fuller, 'Christmas', 70; Schoonenberg, 'Prologue', 409.
261. H.J. Holtzmann, Lehrbuch, 451, 464, 508f; Baur, Vorlesungen, 366.
262. Baur, Vorlesungen, 107; similarly Porsch, Pneuma, 104; Braun, Jean III, 68f.
263. Holtzmann, Lehrbuch, 509.
264. Miranda, Sendung, 40, 54; similarly Schnackenburg, John, 386.
265. Bühner, Gesandte, 304.
266. So Burge, Anointed Community, 72f, 87.

Notes to pp. 175 - 179

267. So Büchsel, Johannes, 59; Strathmann, Johannes, 79; Dodd, Interpretation, 311; Schnackenburg, John I, 386; Miranda, Sendung, 40.
268. So Lindars, John, 171; Bruce, John, 97; Burge, Anointed Community, 83.
269. Cf. Nicholson, Death, 81.
270. Baur, Vorlesungen, 363f; Kritische Untersuchungen, 94-96.
271. Käsemann, Letzter Wille, 23f; similarly Schnackenburg, Johannes, II, 511f; Hamerton-Kelly, Pre-existence, 206; Bergmeier, Glaube, 210f; Haacker, Stiftung, 26f.
272. So Eltester, 'Logos', 124-134; Hofius, 'Struktur', 21; Kysar, Jesus, 17.
273. So also Schnackenburg, 'Logos-hymnus', 84-89; Theobald, Anfang, 109-115; Ruckstuhl, 'Prolog', 452f.
274. So Bultmann, Johannes, 26-38; Schnackenburg, John I, 227; Käsemann, 'Prologue', 165f; Theobald, Anfang, 117, 126; Ruckstuhl, 'Prolog', 452f.
275. So Bultmann, Johannes, 40f; Theologie, 403; similarly Bousset, Kyrios Christos, 220; Bauer, Johannes, 22; Braun, Jean III, 65; Hamerton-Kelly, Pre-existence, 199, 207; Demke, 'Prolog', 63; Schnackenburg, 'Fleisch', 5; John I, 266; Zimmermann, 'Prolog', 262f; Weder, 'Menschwerdung', 352, 256; Barrett, 'Paradox', 105; Painter, 'Prologue', 470; Hofius, 'Struktur', 24.
276. Bultmann, Johannes, 41f; Theologie, 392; similarly Bauer, Johannes, 23; Schnackenburg, John I, 170, 269; Lindars, John, 79, 94; Neugebauer, Entstehung, 29; Bruce, John, 39; Gnilka, 'Christologie', 103f; Hofrichter, Im Anfang, 52; Schnelle, Christologie, 242f, arguing that 'tented' is also antidocetic.
277. Richter, Studien, 157f, also 110f, 134, 179-182; Thyen, 'Brüder', 532, and 534; 'Entwicklungen', 260f; Langbrandtner, Weltferner Gott, 44, 108, and 9f, 17, 32, 36; cf. also similarly Painter, 'Opponents', 65, 68.
278. Theobald, Anfang, 55.
279. So de Jonge, Stranger, 207f.
280. Ruckstuhl, 'Prolog', 451.
281. Käsemann, 'Prologue', 159f; Letzter Wille, 24.
282. So also Hamerton-Kelly, Pre-existence, 207; Nicol, Semeia, 131-133; Dupont, Christologie, 51f.
283. So also Käsemann, Letzter Wille, 27; Schottroff, Glaubende, 276f; Müller, Christologie, 25: Bergmeier, Glaube, 210; Theobald, Anfang, 35; Becker, Johannes, 77; 'Auferstehung', 140f; Painter, 'Christology', 50; Berger, 'Wort', 166; Schnackenburg, Johannes IV, 113.
284. So Hamerton-Kelly, Pre-existence, 206; Büchsel, Johannes, 32; Schnackenburg, 'Fleisch', 4; Barrett, John, 169.
285. Büchsel, Johannes, 32.
286. B. Weiss, Lehrbuch, 612f; similarly Holtzmann, Lehrbuch, 464.
287. Baur, Kritische Untersuchungen, 233. Cf. Cullmann, Christologie, 192, who argues that *anthrōpos* was not used because of possible associations with Anthropos figures.
288. So Ibuki, Wahrheit, 190f; Wilkens, Zeuge, 110; Riedl, Heilswerk, 155; earlier Beyschlag, Neutestamentliche Theologie II, 432.
289. So Haenchen, Johannes, 144f; Wilkens, Zeichen, 110.
290. Käsemann, Letzter Wille, 24; similarly Schulz, Johannes, 31f, 212.

291. Käsemann, Letzter Wille, 61f.
292. So Schulz, Johannes, 32; similarly Schillebeeckx, Christ, 365.
293. So Pagels, John, 37; Brown, Beloved Disciple, 111f, 152f.
294. Berger, 'Word', 162.
295. Barrett, John. 169.
296. Painter, 'Prologue', 37; 'Christology', 49; U.B. Müller, Christologie, 25.
297. Schnackenburg, John 1, 267; Hofius, 'Struktur', 24.
298. Cranfield, 'John 1:14', 215; Dunn, 'John', 347; Beasley-Murray, John, 13f; Schnelle,
     Christologie, 241f
299. So Schillebeeckx, Christ, 365.
300. Käsemann, Letzter Wille.
301. Baur, Kritische Untersuchungen, 87, 313; Wrede, Charakter, 39; H.J. Holtzmann,
     Lehrbuch, 458; Wetter, Sohn Gottes, 149; Bousset, Kyrios Christos, 217f; cf. also
     Käsemann, Letzter Wille, 22; Schulz, Johannes, 211; Miranda, Vater, 54; Martyn,
     'Glimpses', 102; Langbrandtner, Weltferner Gott, 38, 95f (of the Grundschrift);
     and with extensive character illustration: Culpepper, Anatomy, 108-112.
302. So already Baur, Kritische Untersuchungen, 233; Vorlesungen, 358; H.J. Holtzmann,
     Lehrbuch, 453-458; similarly Nicol, Semeia, 132.
303. So Wrede, Charakter, 7f; Wetter, Sohn Gottes, 71; Käsemann, Letzter Wille, 17;
     Schulz, Johannes, 212; Klaiber, 'Interpretation', 317; Schnelle, Christologie, 105,
     116, 183; see also Hegermann, 'Eigentum', 113.
304. So Fortna, 'Christology', 394; Schnelle, Christologie, 184.
305. Wilkens, Zeichen 51f.
306. Wengst, Gemeinde, 104f.
307. Langbrandtner, Weltferner Gott, 94f.
308. Becker, Johannes, 119f.
309. Fortna, 'Christology', 493, 495f.
310. Schottroff, Glaubende, 251, 254, 269.
311. Bultmann, Johannes, 173.
312. Käsemann, Letzter Wille, 53 n 59; cf. also Appold, Oneness, 95.
313. Schnelle, Christologie, 94, 140, 148, 184f, 188, 194.
314. Against Schnelle, Christologie, 94f, 148.
315. Gnilka, 'Christologie', 99.
316. Baur, Vorlesungen, 304f, 365; similarly H.J. Holtzmann, Lehrbuch, 458-461.
317. See the extensive material gathered by Wetter, Sohn Gottes, 6-8 and passim; see also
     Bauer, Johannes, 23f; Käsemann, Letzter Wille, 17; and Kee, Miracle.
318. Barrett, 'Theocentric', 13; similarly Fortna, 'Christology', 495.
319. Robinson, 'Christology', 68.; similarly Strathmann, Johannes, 3; Käsemann, Letzter
     Wille, 22f, 20, 48.
320. Lindars, John, 53f, 62; cf. also Käsemann, Letzter Wille, 22f, 48.
321. Culpepper, Anatomy, 108-112; similarly Käsemann, Letzter Wille, 22f; Brown,
     Beloved Disciple, 114-116; du Rand, 'Characterisation', 29.
322. Culpepper, Anatomy, 111.
323. So Appold, Oneness, 123, 205f.
324. So Nicol, Semeia, 132; Appold, Oneness, 136, 120, 125f; U.B. Müller, 'Bedeutung',
     54, 56; Strathmann, Johannes, 3;

Notes to pp. 183 - 184

Lattke, Einheit, 142; Haenchen, 'Vater', 77; Langbrandtner, Weltferner Gott, 96 (of the Grundschrift); Wengst, Gemeinde, 104f.
325. So Bousset, Kyrios Christos, 219f; Barrett, 'Theocentric', 3; Wengst, Gemeinde, 100f; Scroggs, Christology, 80f.
326. So H.J. Holtzmann, Lehrbuch, 467f; Baur, Vorlesungen, 365; Nicol, Semeia, 132; de Jonge, Stranger, 92-94; Schweizer, Jesus, 156; O'Grady, 'Human Jesus', 63; Robinson, Priority, 367; Johnston, 'Ecce Homo', 130.
327. Wead, Devices, 62f.
328. So Dewailly, 'D'où es-tu?', 493f; Weder, 'Menschwerdung', 356.
329. Against Käsemann, Letzter Wille, 22f; Culpepper, Anatomy, 109f; Cf. Nicol, Semeia, 132.
330. Against, for instance, Dauer, Passionsgeschichte, 287.
331. So rightly Baur, Vorlesungen, 367f; Wetter, Sohn Gottes, 119; de la Potterie, Vérité, 990 n. 254 and see IIIB3 above.
332. Lütgert, Christologie, 101.
333. Against Schnackenburg, Johannes II, 485.
334. So Nicholson, Death, 128.
335. So Beutler, Angst, 25-36; Whitacre, Polemic, 63.
336. Thüsing, Erhöhung, 81; cf, Lütgert, Christologie, 101.
337. Fortna, 'Christology', 501f.
338. Cf. Evans, 'Passion', 62.
339. So Lütgert, Christologie, 110; Schnackenburg, Johannes II, 512; Bornkamm, 'Interpretation', 114; Wilkens, Zeichen, 62, 67; Barrett, 'Theocentric', 11; Schweizer, Jesus, 156; Onuki, Gemeinde, 203; Baum Bodenbender, Hoheit, 268-270; Johnston, 'Ecce Homo', 134.
340. Moloney, Son of Man, 254f and see the discussion of Son of Man in IIIA4 above.
341. Lorenzen, Lieblingsjünger, 106-108; similarly Onuki, Gemeinde, 203.
342. Neugebauer, Entstehung, 28f; Thyen, 'Entwicklungen', 260f; Schnelle, Christologie, 155. Against this reading: de Jonge, Stranger, 207.
343. Thyen, 'Brüder', 534; Richter, Studien, 180; similarly, Schnelle, Christologie, 160. Against this: de Jonge, Stranger, 207; Pokorny, 'Jesus', 219; Dauer, Johannes und Lukas, 293.
344. So Schenke, 'Vorgeschichte', 86f; Beutler, 'Heilsbedeautung, 192; Weder, 'Menschwerdung', 348f; Schnelle, Christologie, 223. Against this: Schnackenburg, Johannes II, 91f; Wilckens, 'Lebensbrot', 238f; Moloney, 'Sacraments', 23; cf. also de Jonge, Stranger, 208f.
345. Schnelle, Christologie, 87-194.
346. Käsemann, Letzter Wille, 23, 49 n. 53; similarly Schulz, Johannes, 237; U.B. Müller, 'Bedeutung', 65; Appold, Oneness, 52, 103, 123; and against this Schweizer, Jesus, 156.
347. U.B. Müller, 'Bedeutung', 65-67.
348. Bultmann, Theologie, 403, 405, 411.
349. Thüsing, Erhöhung, 222; similarly Schnelle, Christologie, 256.
350. Thüsing, Erhöhung, 3.
351. de la Potterie, Vérité, 990 n. 254.
352. Schnackenburg, Johannes II, 512; Forestell, Word, 225.
353. Wilken, Zeichen, 110; Barrett, 'Father', 32; similarly Haenchen, Johannes, 144f.
354. Ibuki, Wahrheit, 191-196; and see IIIB4 above.

355. Riedl, Heilswerk, 155.
356. Wengst, Gemeinde, 102f.
357. Sproston, 'Christology', 79f.
358. Hegermann, 'Eigentum', 116f, 119.
359. Leistner, Antijudäismus, 145-150.
360. Barrett, 'Theocentric', 11f.
361. Barrett, 'History' 129f; similarly Lieu, Epistles, 204f.
362. Davey, Jesus, 14.
363. Baum Bodenbender, Hoheit, 284-286.
364. Thyen, 'Brüder', 536; Langbrandtner, Weltferner Gott, 38, 95f; similarly Martyn,
     'Church', 110.
365. Fortna, 'Christology', 494.
366. Scroggs, Christology, 61.
367. Bornkamm, 'Paraklet', 89; 'Interpretation', 114; similarly Robinson, 'Christology',
     67.
368. Bornkamm, 'Interpretation', 117; similarly Haenchen, 'Vater', 75f; Hegermann,
     'Eigentum', 113; Onuki, Gemeinde, 200.
369. Schweizer, 'Zeuge', 167f.
370. Nicol, Semeia, 135f.
371. Käsemann, Letzter Wille, 61f.
372. Schottroff, Glaubende, 274.
373. Schottroff, Glaubende, 290f.
374. Von den Osten Sacken, 'Leistung', 157.
375. Nicol, Semeia, 136; similarly Schweizer, 'Zeuge', 145.
376. So Richter, Studien, 112, 141, 357; Mealand, 'Christology', 453; Nicol, Semeia, 149;
     Thyen, 'Brüder', 536; Langbrandtner, Weltferner Gott, 38, 95f; Brown, Beloved
     Disciple, passim; and see also IIIC2 below.

PART IIIC   Issues: The Gospel in light of its Christology

1. Morris, John, 41-46; Cadman, Open Heaven, 203f; Riesenfeld, 'Gospel Tradition',
    151; Temple, Core, 286f; Delebecque, Jean, 18f; cf. Schnackenburg, John I, 19-
    22.
2. Grundmann, Zeugnis, 14; cf. Schnackenburg, John I, 23f.
3. Burkitt, Christianity in the Light of Modern Knowledge, 209, cited in Sidebottom,
    Christ, 11; similarly Ricca, Eschatologie, 28; T.E. Müller, Heilsgeschehen, 79.
4. Smalley, John, 192-195; similarly, T.E. Müller, Heilsgeschehen, 79. Cf. also Martyn,
    History and Theology; 'Source Criticism', 103-114; Nicholson, Death, 157-159;
    Onuki, Gemeinde, 99, 165.
5. Dodd, Interpretation, 142f, 444f.
6. Baur, Kritische Untersuchungen, 314.
7. Mussner, Sehweise, 23,42f; 'Parakletsspruche', 154f.
8. So Käsemann, Letzter Wille, 70f; Haacker, Stiftung, 157-161 in criticism of Mussner
    and Käsemann.
9. Bornkamm, 'Paraklet', 87f; 'Interpretation', 114, 117; similarly Nicol, Semeia, 27; de
    Jonge, Stranger, 11f; Klauck, 'Gemeinde', 213f.
10. Kremer, 'Verheissung', 259f; Painter, 'Farewell Discourses', 531; Dietzfelbinger,
    'Paraklet', 405, 407.
11. Hahn, 'Sehen', 140; similarly Onuki, Gemeinde, 12-14, 203.
12. Culpepper, Anatomy, 47; cf. also his work, Johannine School.
13. Becker, Johannes, 57.

Notes to pp. 190 - 193

14. Blank, Krisis, 117.
15. Olsson, Structure, 271, 279, 281.
16. So Klauck, 'Gemeinde', 213f and see the discussion about Johannine bearers of the Paraclete to follow in the next pages.
17. Haacker, Stiftung, 159f.
18. Hegermann, 'Eigentum', 129; similarly Barrett, 'Theocentric', 7; Onuki, Gemeinde, 50f, 205; Klaiber, 'Interpretation', 306.
19. Schnelle, Christologie, 250.
20. Onuki, Gemeinde, 202, 205.
21. Cullmann, Salvation, 271; similarly Childs, Canon, 135.
22. Schnackenburg, 'Frage', 205.
23. Brown, John, 530; similarly Cullmann, Salvation, 272f; Schnackenburg, 'Frage', 205f.
24. Onuki, Gemeinde, 12-14, 165.
25. Onuki, Gemeinde, 58f; similarly Robinson, Priority, 35; Franck, Revelation, 48; Cullmann, Salvation, 274; Woll, Johannine Christianity, 28f; Nicholson, Death, 157f.
26. So Lieu, Epistles, 177f; Burge, Anointed Community, 216.
27. Wead, Devices, 10f.
28. Culpepper, Anatomy, 54-70, esp. 67.
29. Robinson, Redating, 254-311, and, most extensively, Priority, passim.
30. Robinson, 'Human Face', 67f; Priority, 35.
31. Bultmann, Theologie, 419.
32. Schlier, 'Christologie', 86f.
33. Käsemann, Letzter Wille, 96 n. 37; Lattke, Einheit, 143; contrast Wead, Devices, 24; Nicholson, Death, 157-159.
34. Käsemann, Letzter Wille, 54
35. Barrett, 'Theocentric', 9f.
36. So Thüsing, Erhöhung, 256; Riedl, Heilswerk, 154.
37. Nicholson, Death, 157-159.
38. So Bornkamm, 'Paraklet', 87-89 and see n. 25 above.
39. Porsch, Pneuma, 262, 264f.
40. Mussner, 'Parakletssprüche', 154f.
41. So Kundsin, 'Reden', 268-284; Käsemann, Letzter Wille, 70f; Leroy, Rätsel, 180; Aune, Cultic Setting, 101; Smith, 'Johannine Christianity', 244; Onuki, Gemeinde, 80f; Boring, 'Christian Prophecy', 113f; Franck, Revelation, 120-122; Minear, John, 20-23; contrast Schnackenburg, Johannes IV, 56-58.
42. Schulz, Johannes, 86, 91-94; see also his earlier work, Menschensohn.
43. Kundsin, 'Reden', 268-284; similarly Boring, 'Christian Prophecy', 115; contrast Burge, Anointed Community, 218.
44. So rightly Klauck, 'Gemeinde', 213f; Franck, Revelation, 127-129; Isaacs, 'Prophetic spirit', 406f; Schnackenburg, Johannes IV, 57f; against Boring, 'Christian Prophecy', 113.
45. Against Minear, John, 20-23 et passim.
46. Franck, Revelation, 132-140.
47. See Reim, 'Targum' and also the essays in Borgen, Logos was the true Light.
48. Käsemann, Letzter Wille, 70f.
49. Haacker, Stiftung, 154f, 158-160; Nicol, Semeia, 126, 130; similarly Mussner, 'Parakletssprüche', 150-152; de la Potterie, Vérité, 424, 438; Porsch, Pneuma, 295; Ibuki, Wahrheit, 300f; T.E. Müller, Heilsgeschehen, 83; Franck, Revelation, 74.

270   Notes

Notes to pp. 193 - 200

50. Nicol, Semeia, 126, 130; similarly Scroggs, Christology, 88, 91.
51. Schnackenburg, Johannes III, 154.
52. Boring, 'Christian Prophecy', 117f.
53. Kremer, 'Verheissung', 256.
54. Woll, 'Preparation', 237f; Johannine Christianity, 105, 124.
55. de la Potterie, Vérité, 450; Porsch, Pneuma, 298.
56. So rightly Schnackenburg, Johannes III, 154.
57. Thüsing, Erhöhung, 151f.
58. So de Jonge, Stranger, 25; similarly in part Kremer, 'Verheissung', 258.
59. So Kremer, 'Verheissung', 258; Onuki, Gemeinde, 150f; Burge, Anointed Community, 215.
60. So Isaacs, 'Prophetic Spirit', 398.
61. Olsson, Structure, 262; similarly Wead, Devices, 6-9; Nicholson, Death, 32f; Bjerkelund, Tauta, 97; Minear, John, 9f.
62. So de Jonge, Stranger, 8, 17.
63. Nicholson, Death, 36f.
64. Forestell, Word, 34; Thüsing, Erhöhung, 98, 163; Dahl, 'Church', 125f.
65. Blank, Krisis, 136; Porsch, Pneuma, 139, 143, 147f; similarly Riedl, Heilswerk, 20-22; Bornkamm, 'Paraklet', 88; Barrett, 'Theocentric', 15.
66. So Schnackenburg, John I, 21f; similarly Leroy, Rätsel, 46f, 71-73, 79; Olsson, Structure, 282; Culpepper, Anatomy, 86; Onuki, Gemeinde, 26.
67. Mussner, Sehweise, 84.
68. Meeks, 'Man from Heaven', 162f; cf. the critical appropriation of the thesis in de Jonge, Stranger, 99.
69. Onuki, Gemeinde, 110-114.
70. Culpepper, Anatomy, 36.
71. Fortna, 'Christology', 503.
72. Onuki, Gemeinde, 165.
73. Olsson, Structure, 282.
74. Leroy, Rätsel, 46f, 71-73, 79, 158-160; similarly Culpepper, 152-197, esp. 164; 179f; Duke, Irony, 142-147; Richard, 'Double Meaning'.
75. Leroy, Rätsel, 62.
76. Wead, Devices, 30-46, 47-70, 71-93.
77. Lindars, 'Traditions', 111f.
78. eg. Strathmann, Johannes, 59.
79. Culpepper, Anatomy; Duke, Irony; O'Day, Revelation; de la Potterie, 'Genèse'; 'Prologue'.
80. So Culpepper, Anatomy, 179f; Duke, Irony, 27; O'Day, Revelation, 30.
81. So Meeks, 'Man from Heaven', 162; Culpepper, Anatomy, 28; Minear, John, 19.
82. See also Leon Dufour, 'Symbolism', 443-445.
83. Wead, Devices, 8f.
84. Haacker, Stiftung, 59f.
85. Baur, Kritische Untersuchungen, 295; cf. also Wrede, 'Charakter', 13; Wetter, Sohn Gottes, 135; Strathmann, Johannes, 2; Sanday, Criticism, 206; Preiss, Life in Christ, 10; Hengel, Cana, 87.
86. Similarly Nicholson, Death, 38.

Notes to pp. 200 - 214

87. Cf. Strachan, Fourth Gospel, 32-34.
88. Duke, Irony, 152, 154.
89. Culpepper, Anatomy, 175f.
90. O'Day, Revelation, 31.
91. Bornkamm, 'Interpretation', 112.
92. Barrett, John, 32; on the use of the messianic secret motif in John see also Barrett, 'Paradox', 108; Schnackenburg, 'Menschensohn', 126; Hooker, 'Prologue', 46-51; Schillebeeckx, Christ, 368; Fortna, 'Christology', 503.
93. Leroy, Rätsel, 163 n. 14.
94. Schnackenburg, Johannes I, 14; John I, 24; similarly Smalley, John, 213.
95. Strathmann, Johannes, 4.
96. Haacker, Stiftung, 58 n. 258.
97. Käsemann, Letzter Wille, 22f, 28.
98. Blank, Krisis, 165-167; similarly Käsemann, Letzter Wille, 42.
99. See Kysar, 'The Fourth Gospel'; Becker, 'Streit der Methoden'.
100. On the importance of cosmic dualism for understanding Johannine christology see Becker, 'Dualismus'; Johannes, 147-151; 'Auferstehung', 142f; 'Streit der Methoden', 46f.
101. So Forestell, Word, 165 and see the discussion in IIIA3 above.
102. Loader, 'Central Structure', 196-199.
103. For this suggestion of Moloney, Son of Man, 247-256, and others see the discussion at the conclusion of IIIA4 above.
104. Meeks, 'Man from Heaven'.
105. So de Jonge, Stranger, 99f; see also Onuki, Gemeinde, 110-114.
106. So Becker, Johannes, 158.
107. See also Dietzfelbinger, 'Paraklet', 402.
108. On the redactional addition of some future eschatology statements see Schnackenburg, Johannes IV, 94.
109. As the Johannine position: Becker, Johannes, 58; Schmithals, 'Prolog', 39f; Haenchen, Johannes, 35; Schnelle, Christologie, 43. Contrast Edwards, 'Charin anti charitos'.
110. Cf. Becker, Johannes, 148, who cautions against interpreting Johannine dualism on the basis of creation statements of the prologue.
111. So Martyn, 'Source Criticism', 105f; Onuki, Gemeinde, 33; Witkamp, 'Tradition', 33.
112. On the historical issues of synagogue expulsion and the cursing of the minim and Nazoreans in the 18 Benedictions see Horbury, 'Benediction'.
113. Against Käsemann, Letzter Wille, 102 n. 41; Schnelle, Christologie, 42.
114. Cf. Meeks, Prophet King, 216-220; Schillebeeckx, Christ, 312-317.
115. Against Brown, Beloved Disciple, 26-50.
116. Cf. Cullmann, Johannine Circle, 43-56; Brown, Beloved Disciple, 36-40.
117. See Brown, Beloved Disciple, 81-88.
118. So Klauck, 'Gemeinde', 216.
119. So for his 'Signs Gospel' Fortna, 'Signs', 228; cf. also similarly Nicol, Semeia, 88-90; and contrast Becker, Johannes, 117-120, emphasising *theios anēr* christology.
120. So de Jonge, Stranger, 39f; cf. also Painter, 'John 9', 37.
121. See also Martyn, 'Source Criticism', 106f, who sees the author both correcting signs based faith of the 'signs gospel' and securing christological affirmation against its vulnerability to Jewish argument.

Notes to pp. 215 - 223

122. Bittner, Zeichen, 285-289.
123. Schillebeeckx, Christ, 312-321.
124. Langbrandtner, Weltferner Gott.
125. Bühner, Gesandte; see also Miranda, Sendung.
126. Boismard/Lamouille, Jean.
127. Against deriving the revealer envoy model from Wisdom: Becker, Johannes, 55.
128. So Talbert, 'Descending and Ascending Redeemer'.
129. So Martyn, 'Source Criticism', 114f; Becker, Johannes, 53f; cf. also Fischer, 'Christus'; Barrett, 'Gospel of Truth'; Beasley-Murray, John, lvf.
130. See the useful evaluation of possible antidocetic passages by de Jonge, Stranger, 207-210.
131. Schnelle, Christologie; similarly Strecker, 'Anfänge'.
132. Langbrandtner, Weltferner Gott, 108-113; cf. also Thyen, 'Entwicklungen'; Richter, Studien, 357f, 409f.
133. Lieu, Epistles, 81f, 211; Balz, 'Theologie', 53-55. See also the brief discussion in my Johannine Epistles.
134. Similarly Balz, 'Theologie', 55f.
135. For discussion of stages of composition in the last discourses relating to the situation of 1 John see Segovia, 'Love Relationships', 191-195; 'John 15', 125f; 'John 15:18 - 16:4a'; Painter, 'Farewell Discourses'; Kaefer, 'Discours'; cf. also Becker, 'Streit der Methoden', 29-31.
136. Lieu, Epistles, 179, 211-215.
137. Lieu, Epistles, 199f.
138. See the excellent discussion of method and theories in Becker, 'Streit der Methoden', 28-39; and Schnackenburg, Johannes IV, 90-102. See also the defense of the traditional position on John in Hengel, Johannine Question, and my review in Kings Theological Review
139. So Becker, Johannes, 119f.
140. So Barrett, 'Symbolism', 76.
141. Cf. Schnelle, Christologie, 107, 170-182; and Bjerkelund, Tauta, 65, who argue that the traditional markers of a signs source, 2:11 and 4:54, derive from the author.
142. Cf. Heekerens, Zeichen-Quelle, 43 et passim, who argues that the Cana signs have been introduced into the gospel at the stage of the final redaction.
143. So Blank, Krisis, 349.
144. So similarly Gnilka, 'Christologie', 101.
145. Hegermann, 'Eigentum', 129.
146. Bultmann, Johannes, 238f, 261, 430-432.
147. Blank, Krisis, 139f.
148. Riedl, Heilswerk, 21.
149. Forestell, Word, 122,155.
150. Bultmann, Theologie, 418; Käsemann, Letzter Wille, 106, 112.
151. So Dietzfelbinger, 'Paraklet', 402.
152. So rightly Dunn, 'John', 314.
153. Rensberg, 'Politics', 411 et passim.
154. Meeks, 'Man from Heaven'.
155. Lattke, Einheit, 2, 50f, 162-169, 188; Käsemann, Letzter Wille, 124f, 139. See also the criticism by Miranda, Sendung, 22f; Thyen, 'Brüder', 537; 'Liebe', 467f; Segovia, Love Relationships, 169; Klaiber, 'Interpretation', 319f; Schnelle, Christologie, 210f.

156. Meeks, 'Man from Heaven', 165.
157. Appold, Oneness, 266, 278, 288
158. Thüsing, Erhöhung, 138-140.
159. Schottroff, Glaubende, 233.
160. Against Schottroff, Glaubende, 236-241 and see the discussion IIIC1 above.
161. See the discussion in von den Osten-Sacken, 'Leistung', 166-168; Bergmeier, Glaube, 260 n. 421; Thyen, 'Brüder', 541; 'Heil', 182f; Grässer, 'Antijüdische Polemik', 50-69; Schramm, *IOUDAIOS*; Leistner, Antijudäismus; Hahn, 'Heil'; 'Juden'; Lowe, Ioudaioi; Ashton, 'Identity'; von Wahlde, 'Jews'; Culpepper, 'The Jews'.

BIBLIOGRAPHY

Aland K. 'Der Text des Johannesevangeliums im zweiten Jahrhundert' In: Studien zum Text und zur Ethik des Neuen Testaments. Festschrift für H. Greeven. Edited by W. Schrage (BZNW 167, Berlin: de Gruyter, 1986) pp. 1-10.

Appold, M.L. The Oneness Motif in the Fourth Gospel (WUNT II, 1, Tübingen: JCB Mohr, 1976)

Ashton, J. 'The Identity and Function of the IOUDAIOI in the Fourth Gospel' NovT 27 (1985) 40-75

Ashton, J. (ed.) The Interpretation of John (Issues in Religion and Theology 9, London/Philadelphia: SPCK/Fortress, 1986)

Ashton, J. 'The Transformation of Wisdom' NTS 32 (1986) 161-186

Aune, D.E. The Cultic Setting of Realized Eschatology in Early Christianity (SupplNovT XVIII, Leiden: Brill, 1972)

Bacon, B.W. The Fourth Gospel in Recent Research and Debate (New Haven, 1928)

Bailey, J.A. The Traditions Common to the Gospels of Luke and John (SupplNovT VII, Leiden: Brill, 1963)

Balz, H. 'Johanneische Theologie und Ethik im Lichte der "letzten Stunde"' In: Studien zum Text und zur Ethik des Neuen Testaments. Festschrift für H. Greeven. Edited by W. Schrage (BZNW 167, Berlin: de Gruyter, 1986) pp. 35-56.

Bammel, E. 'Jesus und der Paraklet in Johannes 16' In: Christ and the Spirit. Studies in Honour of C.F.D. Moule. Edited by B. Lindars and S.S. Smalley (London: SCM, 1973) pp. 199-217

Bampfylde, M. 'More Light on Jn XII 34' JSNT 17 (1983) 87-89

Barrett, C.K. 'Christocentric or Theocentric? Observations on the Theological Method of the Fourth Gospel' In: Essays on John (London/Philadelphia: SPCK/Westminster, 1982) pp. 1-18

Barrett, C.K. Essays on John (London/Philadelphia: SPCK/Westminster, 1982)

Barrett, C.K. '"The Father is greater than I" John 14.28: Subordinationist Christology in the New Testament' In: Essays on John (London/Philadelphia: SPCK/Westminster, 1982) pp. 19-36

Barrett, C.K. '"The flesh of the Son of Man" John 6.53' In: Essays on John (London/Philadelphia: SPCK/Westminster, 1982) pp. 37-49

Barrett, C.K. The Gospel according to St. John (2nd edn., London: SPCK, 1978)

Barrett, C.K. 'History' In: Essays on John (London/Philadelphia: SPCK/Westminster, 1982) pp. 116-132

Barrett, C.K. 'Paradox and Dualism' In: Essays on John (London/Philadelphia: SPCK/Westminster, 1982) pp. 98-115

Barrett, C.K. 'Symbolism' In: Essays on John (London/Philadelphia: SPCK/Westminster, 1982) pp. 65-79

Barrett, C.K. 'The Theological Vocabulary of the Fourth Gospel and the Gospel of Truth' In: Essays on John (London/Philadelphia: SPCK/Westminster, 1982) pp. 50-64

Bassler, J.M. 'The Galileans: A Neglected Factor in Johannine Community Research' CBQ 43 (1981) 243-275

Bauer, W. Das Johannesevangelium (Handbuch z. NT 6, Tübingen: JCB Mohr, 1933)

Bauer, W. 'Johannesevangelium und Johannessbriefe' ThR NF1 (1929) 135-160

Baum-Bodenbender, R. Hoheit in Niedrigkeit. Johanneische Christologie im Prozess Jesu vor Pilatus (Joh 18,28-19,16a) (FzB 49, Würzburg: Echter, 1984)

Baur, F.C. Kritische Untersuchungen über die kanonischen Evangelien (Tübingen: Fues, 1847)

Baur, F.C. Vorlesungen über neutestamentliche Theologie (Darmstadt: Wiss. Buchgesellschaft, 1973)

Beasley-Murray, G.R. John (WordBibCommentary 36, Waco: Word, 1987)

Beasley-Murray, G.R. 'John 3:3,5. Baptism, Spirit and Kingdom' ExpT 97 (1986) 167-170

Beasley-Murray, G.R. 'John 12,31-32. The Eschatological Significance of the Lifting Up of the Son of Man' In: Studien zum Text und zur Ethik des Neuen Testaments. Festschrift für H. Greeven. Edited by W. Schrage (BZNW 167, Berlin: de Gruyter, 1986) pp. 70-81

Becher, H. Die Reden des Johannesevangeliums und der Stil der gnostischen Offenbarungsrede (FRLANT 68, Göttingen: V & R, 1956)

Becker, 'Aufbau, Schichtung und theologiegeschichtliche Stellung des Gebetes in Joh 17' ZNW 60 (1969) 56-83

Becker, J. 'Ich bin die Auferstehung und das Leben. Eine Skizze der johanneischen Christologie' TZ 39 (83) 138-151

Becker, J. 'Beobachtungen zum Dualismus im Johannesevangelium' ZNW 65 (1974) 71-87

Becker, J. Das Evangelium des Johannes (OekTK 4/1+2, Gütersloh: Mohn, 1979/1981)

Becker, J. 'Das Johannesevangelium im Streit der Methoden (1980-1984)' ThR 51 (1986) 1-78

Becker, J. 'Aus der Literatur zum Johannesevangelium (1978-1980)' ThR 47 (1982) 279-301

Becker, J. 'Wunder und Christologie' NTS 16 (1969/1970) 130-148

Berger, K. 'Zu "Das Wort ward Fleisch" Joh I 14a' NovT 16 (1974) 161-166

Bergmeier, R. Glaube als Gabe nach Johannes (BWANT 12, Stuttgart: Kohlhammer, 1980)

Berrouard, M.F. 'Le Paraclete, Défenseur du Christ devant la conscience du croyant (Jo. XVI.8-11)' RSPT 33 (1949) 301-349

Bernhard, J.H. A Critical and Exegetical Commentary on the Gospel of St. John. 2 Vols. (ICC, Edinburgh: T & T Clark, 1929)

Bertram, G. Art. 'hypsoō' TDNT 7, 606-613

Beutler, J. Habt keine Angst. Die erste johanneische Abschiedsrede (Joh 14) (SBS 116, Stuttgart: KBW, 1984)

Beutler, J. 'Die Heilsbedeutung des Todes Jesu im Johannesevangelium nach Joh 13, 1-20' In: Der Tod Jesu. Deutungen im Neuen Testament. Edited by K. Kertelge (QD 74, Freiburg: Herder, 1976) pp. 188-204

Beutler, J. MARTYRIA. Traditionsgeschichtliche Untersuchungen zum Zeugnisthema bei Johannes (FrankThStud 10, Frankfurt: Knecht, 1972)

Beutler, J 'Psalm 42/43 im Johannesevangelium' NTS 25 (1979) 33-57

Beyschlag, W. Neutestamentliche Theologie II (Halle, 1896)

Bittner, W.J. Jesu Zeichen im Johannesevangelium. WUNT 2.26 (Tübingen: JCB Mohr, 1987)

Bjerkelund, C.J. TAUTA EGENETO. Die Präzisierungssätze im Johannesevangelium (WUNT 2.40, Tübingen: JCB Mohr, 1987)

Black, M. 'The "Son of Man" Passion Sayings in the Gospel Tradition' ZNW 60 (1969) 1-8

Blank, J. Krisis. Untersuchungen zur johanneischen Christologie und Eschatologie (Freiburg: Lambertus, 1962)

Blank. J. 'Die Verhandlung vor Pilatus. Joh 18,28-19,16 im Lichte johanneischen Theologie' BZ 3 (1959) 60-81

Blinzler, J. Der Prozess Jesu (4th edn., Stuttgart: KBW, 1969)

Bogart, J.L. Orthodoxy and Heretical Perfectionism in the Johannine Community as evident in the First Epistle of John (SBLDS 33, Missoula, 1977)

Boismard, M.-E. 'Le caractère adventice de Jo., XII, 45-50' In: Sacra Pagina II (Paris: Gembloux, 1959) pp. 189-192

Boismard, M.-E. 'Jésus, le Prophète par excellence d'après Jean 10,24-39'. In: Neues Testament und Kirche. Festschrift für R. Schnackenburg. Edited by J. Gnilka (Freiburg: Herder, 1974) pp. 160-172

Boismard, M.-E and Lamouille, A. L'Évangile de Jean. Synopse des Quatres Évangiles en Français, Tome III (Paris: Cerf, 1977)

Borgen, P. Bread from Heaven. An Exegetical Study of the Concept of Man in the Gospel of John and the Writings of Philo (SupplNovT X, Leiden: Brill, 1965)

Borgen, P. 'God's Agent in the Fourth Gospel' In: Logos was the True Light (Trondheim: Tapir, 1983) pp. 121-132.

Borgen, P. Logos was the True Light and Other Essays on the Gospel of John (Trondheim: Tapir, 1983)

Borgen, P. 'Logos was the True Light' In: Logos was the True Light (Trondheim: Tapir, 1983) pp. 95-110

Borgen, P. 'Observations on the Targumic Character of the Prologue' In: Logos was the True Light (Trondheim: Tapir, 1983) pp. 13-22

Borgen, P. 'Some Jewish Exegetical Traditions as Background for Son of Man Sayings in John's Gospel' In: L'Évangile de Jean. Sources, Rédaction, Théologie. Edited by M. de Jonge (BibEphThLov XLIV, Leuven: Gombleux, 1977) pp. 243-258.

Borgen, P. 'The Son of Man Saying in John 3:13-14' In: Logos was the True Light (Trondheim: Tapir, 1983) pp. 133-148

Borig, R. Der wahre Weinstock (StANT 16, München: Kösel, 1967)

Boring, M.E. 'The Influence of Christian Prophecy in the Johannine Portrayal of the Paraclete and Jesus' NTS 25 (1978) 113-123

Bornkamm, G. 'Die eucharistische Rede im Johannes-Evangelium' In: Geschichte und Glaube. Erster Teil. Gesammelte Aufsätze, Band III (München: Kaiser, 1968) pp. 60-67

Bornkamm, G. 'Zur Interpretation des Johannesevangeliums' In: Geschichte und Glaube. Erster Teil. Gesammelte Aufsätze, Band III (München: Kaiser, 1968) pp. 104-121

Bornkamm, G. 'Der Paraklet im Johannes-Evangelium' In: Geschichte und Glaube. Erster Teil. Gesammelte Aufsätze, Band III (München: Kaiser, 1968) pp. 68-89

Bornkamm, G. 'Vorjohanneische Tradition oder nachjohanneische Bearbeitung in der eucharistischen Rede Johannes 6' In: Geschichte und Glaube. Zweiter Teil. Gesammelte Aufsätze, Band IV (München: Kaiser, 1971) pp. 51-64

Borsch, F.H The Son of Man in Myth and History (London: SCM, 1967)

Bousset, W. Kyrios Christos (Nashville: Abingdon, 1970)

Braun, F.-M. Jean Le Théologien. Tome III (Paris: Gabalda, 1966)

Breuss, J. Das Kana Wunder (BiblBeiträge 12, Fribourg: SchweizKathBibelwerk, 1976)

Brown, R.E. The Community of the Beloved Disciple (New York: Paulist, 1979)

Brown, R.E. The Epistles of John (AncB 30, New York/London: Doubleday/Chapman, 1983)

Brown, R.E. The Gospel according to John (AncB 29/29A, 2 vols, New York/London: Doubleday/Chapman, 1966/1970)

Bruce, F.F. The Gospel of John (Grand Rapids: Eerdmans, 1983)

Brun, L. 'Die Gottesschau des johanneischen Christus' Symboloae Osloenses 5 (1927) 1-22

Büchsel, F. Das Evangelium nach Johannes (NTD 4, Göttingen: V & R, 1934)

Bühner, J. Der Gesandte und sein Weg im 4. Evangelium (WUNT II 2, Tübingen: JCB Mohr, 1977)

Bultmann, R. 'Die Bedeutung der neuerschlossenen mandäischen und manichäischen Quellen für das Verständnis des Johannesevangeliums'. In: Johannes und sein Evangelium. Edited by K. H. Rengstorf, (Wege der Forschung LXXXII, Darmstadt: Wiss. Buchgesellschaft, 1973) pp. 402-465; first published in ZNW 24 (1925) 100-146

Bultmann, R. 'Die Eschatologie des Johannes-Evangeliums' Zwischen den Zeiten 6 (1928) 4-22

Bultmann, R. Das Evangelium des Johannes (KEKNT, Göttingen: V & R, 1968; first published 1941; ET: The Gospel of John. Oxford: Blackwell, 1971)

Bultmann, R. 'Johannesevangelium'. In: RGG III, 1959, 840-850

Bultmann, R. 'Zur Interpretation des Johannesevangeliums' TLZ 87 (1962) 1-8

Bultmann, R. 'Der religionsgeschichtliche Hintergrund des Prologs zum Johannesevangelium' In: EUCHARISTERION. Festschrift für H. Gunkel. 2. Teil (Göttingen: V & R, 1923) pp. 3-26 (ET: slightly abbreviated: 'History of Religions Background of the Prologue to the Gospel of John' In: The Interpretation of John. Edited by J. Ashton. Issues in Religion and Theology 9, London/Philadelphia: SPCK/Fortress, 1986, pp. 18-35)

Bultmann, R. Theologie des Neuen Testaments (Tübingen: JCB Mohr, 1977; first published 1953. ET: Theology of the New Testament. Vol 2. London: SCM, 1955)

Bultmann, R. 'Untersuchungen zum Johannesevangelium' ZNW 27 (1928) 113-163, ZNW 29 (1930) 169-192

Burge, G.M. The Anointed Community. The Holy Spirit in the Johannine Tradition (Grand Rapids: Eerdmans, 1987)

Burney, C.F. The Aramaic Origin of the Fourth Gospel (Oxford: Clarendon, 1922)

Burrows, F.W. 'Did John the Baptist call Jesus "Lamb of God"?' ExpT 85 (1974) 245-249

Busse, U. 'Offene Fragen zu Johannes 10' NTS 33 (1987) 516-531

Byrne, B. 'The Faith of the Beloved Disciple and the Community in John 20' JSNT 23 (1985) 83-97

Cadman, W.H. The Open Heaven (Oxford: Blackwell, 1969)

Caird, G. B. 'The Glory of God in the Fourth Gospel' NTS 15 (1968/1969) 265-277

Carson, D.A. 'Some Current Source Criticism of the Fourth Gospel' JBL 97 (1978) 411-429

Carson, D.A. 'The Function of the Paraclete in John 16:7-11' JBL 98 (1979) 547-566

Carson, D.A. 'Historical tradition in the Fourth Gospel' JSNT 23 (1985) 73-81
Carson, D.A. 'Recent Literature on the Fourth Gospel' Themelios 9 (1983) 8-18
Childs, B. The New Testament as Canon. An Introduction (Philadelphia: Fortress, 1984)
Chilton, B.D. 'John xiii 34 and Targum Isaiah lii 13' NovT 22 (1980) 176-178
Clark, D.K. 'Sign and Wisdom in John' CBQ 45 (1983) 201-209
Collins, R.F. 'John's Gospel. A Passion Narrative?' BibToday 24 (1986) 181-186
Colwell, E.C. 'A definite rule for the use of the article in the Greek New Testament' JBL 52 (1933) 12-31
Coppens, J. 'Le Fils de l'Homme dans l'Évangile johannique' EphThLov LII (1976) 28-81
Corell, A. Consummatum Est. Eschatology and Church in the Gospel of John (London: SPCK, 1970)
Cranfield, C.E.B. 'Jn 1:14. "Became"' ExpT 93 (1982) 215
Cullmann, O. Die Christologie des Neuen Testaments (4th imp., Tübingen: JCB Mohr, 1966)
Cullmann, O. Early Christian Worship (SBT 1.10, London: SCM, 1953)
Cullmann, O. The Johannine Circle (London: SCM, 1976)
Cullmann, O. Salvation as History (London: SCM, 1967)
Culpepper, R.A. The Anatomy of the Fourth Gospel (Philadelphia: Fortress, 1983)
Culpepper, R.A. 'The Gospel of John and the Jews' RevEx 84 (1987) 273-288
Culpepper, R.A. The Johannine School: An Evaluation of the Johannine-school Hypothesis based on an Investigation of the Nature of Ancient Schools (SBLDS 26, Missoula: Scholars, 1975)
Culpepper, R.A. 'The Pivot of John's Prologue' NTS 27 (1980) 1-31
Dahl, N.A. 'The Johannine Church and History'. In: The Interpretation of John. Edited by J. Ashton (Issues in Religion and Theology 9, London/Philadelphia: SPCK/Fortress, 1986) pp. 122-140.
Dahms, J.V. 'John's Use of monogenēs reconsidered' NTS 29 (1983) 222-232
Dauer, A. Johannes und Lukas (FzB 50, Würzburg: Echter, 1984)
Dauer, A. Die Passionsgeschichte im Johannesevangelium (StANT 30, München: Kösel, 1972)
Davey, J.E. The Jesus of St John (London: Lutterworth, 1958)
Le Deaut, R. La nuit pascal (AnBib 22, Rome: BibInst, 1963)
Delebecque, E. Évangile de Jean. Texte Traduit et Annoté (Paris: Gabalda, 1987)
Delebecque, E. 'Jésus contemporain d'Abraham selon Jean 8,57' RB 93 (1986) 85-92
Demke, C. 'Der sogenannte Logos Hymnus im johanneischen Prolog' ZNW 58 (1967) 45-58
Derrett, J.D.M. Law in the New Testament (London: DLT, 1970)
Dewailly, L.M. '"D'où est tu?" (Jean 19,9)' RB 92 (1985) 481-496
Dietzfelbinger, C 'Paraklet und theologischer Anspruch im Johannesevangelium' ZThK 82 (1985) 389-408
Dodd, C.H. Historical Tradition in the Fourth Gospel (Cambridge: CUP, 1965)
Dodd, C.H. The Interpretation of the Fourth Gospel (Cambridge: CUP, 1953)
Duke, P.D. Irony in the Fourth Gospel (Atlanta: Knox, 1985)
Dunn, J.D.G. Christology in the Making (London: SCM, 1980)
Dunn, J.D.G. 'Let John be John - A Gospel for its Time'. In: Das Evangelium und die Evangelien. Edited by P. Stuhlmacher (WUNT 28, Tübingen: JCB Mohr, 1983) pp. 309-339

Dunn, J.D.G. 'The Washing of the Disciples' Feet' ZNW 61 (1970) 246-252
Dupont, J. Essais sur la Christologie de Saint Jean (Bruges: Saint-Andre, 1951)
Edwards, R. 'Charin anti charitos (John 1.16). Grace and the Law in the Johannine Prologue' JSNT 32 (1988) 3-15
Ellis, P.F. The Genius of John. A Compositional Critical Commentary on the Fourth Gospel (Collegeville: Liturgical, 1984)
Eltester, W. 'Der Logos und sein Prophet' In: Apophoreta. Festschrift für E. Haenchen (BZNW 30, Berlin: de Gruyter, 1964) pp. 109-134
Emerton, J.A. 'Melchizedek and the Gods. Fresh Evidence for the Jewish Background of John X. 34-36' JTS 17 (1966) 399-401
Emerton, J.A. 'Some New Testament Notes, I: The Interpretation of Psalm 82 in John 10' JTS 11 (1960) 329-332
Evans, C.A. 'On the Prologue and the Trimorphic Protenoia' NTS 27 (1981) 395-401
Evans, C.A. 'On the Quotation Formula in the Fourth Gospel' BZ 26 (1982) 79-83
Evans, C.A. 'The Voice from Heaven. A Note on John 12:28' CBQ 43 (1981) 405-408
Evans, C.F. 'The Passion of John'. In: Explorations in Theology 2 (London: SCM 1977) pp. 50-68
Fennema, D.A. 'John 1.18: "God the only Son"' NTS 31 (1985) 124-135
Fischer, G. Die himmlischen Wohnungen (EurHochschulschr. XXIII, 38, Frankfurt: Lang, 1975)
Fischer, K.M. 'Der johanneische Christus und der gnostische Erlöser' In: Gnosis und Neues Testament. Edited by K.W. Tröger (Berlin: EvVerlagsanstalt, 1973) 245-266
Forestell, J.T. The Word of the Cross (AnBib 57, Rome: BibInst, 1974)
Fortna, R. 'Christology in the Fourth Gospel: Rédaction-Critical Perspectives' NTS 21 (1975) 489-504
Fortna, R.T. The Gospel of Signs. A Reconstruction of the Narrative underlying the Fourth Gospel (SNTSMS 11, Cambridge: CUP, 1970)
Fossum, J.E. 'Jewish-Christian Christology and Jewish Mysticism' VigChr 37 (1983) 260-287
Franck, E. Revelation Taught. The Paraclete in the Gospel of John (Coniectanea Biblica NT Ser 14, Lund: Gleerup, 1985)
Freed, E.D. 'Egō Eimi in Joh 1:20 and 4:25' CBQ 41 (1979) 288-91
Freed, E.D. Old Testament Quotations in the Gospel of John (SupplNovT XI, Leiden: Brill, 1965)
Freed, E.D. 'The Son of Man in the Fourth Gospel' JBL 86 (1967) 402-409
Freed, E.D. 'Theological Prelude to the Prologue of John's Gospel' SJT 32 (1979) 257-269
Freed, E.D. 'Who or what was before Abraham in Jn 8:58? 'JSNT 17 (1983) 52-59
Freed, E.D and Hunt, R.B. 'Fortna's Signs Source in John' JBL 94 (1975) 563-579
Füglister, N. Die Heilsbedeutung des Pascha (StANT 8, München: Kösel, 1963)
Fuller, R.H. 'Christmas, Epiphany, and the Johannine Prologue' In: Spirit and Light. Edited by M. L'Engle and W. Green (New York: Seabury, 1976) pp. 63-73
Fuller, R.H. 'The Theology of Jesus or Christology? An Evaluation of the Recent Discussion.' Sem 30 (1986) 105-116.
Geiger, G 'Aufruf zu Rückkehrenden (Jn 6,31)' Bibl 65 (1984) 449-464
Giblin, C.H. 'Confrontation in John 18,1-27' Bibl 65 (1984) 210-232

Giblin, C.H. 'John's Narration of the Hearing Before Pilate' Bibl 67 (1986) 221-
239
Giblin, C.H. 'The Miraculous Crossing of the Sea (Joh 6.16-20)' NTS 29 (1983)
96-103
Giblin, C.H. 'Suggestion, Negative Response, and Positive Action in St John's
Portrayal of Jesus' NTS 26 (1980) 197-211
Giblin, C.H. 'Two complementary literary structures in John 1:1-18' JBL 104
(1985) 87-103
Glasson, T.F. Moses and the Fourth Gospel (SBT 1.40, London: SCM, 1963)
Gnilka, J. 'Zur Christologie des Johannesevangeliums' In: Christologische
Schwerpunkte. Edited by W. Kasper (Düsseldorf: Patmos, 1980) pp. 92-107
Grässer, E. 'Die antijüdische Polemik im Johannesevangelium' In: Text und
Situation. Gesammelte Aufsätze zum Neuen Testament (Gütersloh: Mohn,
1973) pp. 50-69
Grigsby, B.H. 'The Cross as an Expiatory Sacrifice in the Fourth Gospel' JSNT 15
(1982) 51-80
Grigsby, B.H. '"If any man thirsts.."(Joh 7:37-39' Bibl 67 (1986) 100-108
Grigsby, B.H. 'Washing in the Pool of Siloam. A Thematic Anticipation of the
Johannine Cross' NovT 27 (1985) 227-235
Grundmann, W. 'Matth. xi. 27 und die johanneischen "Der Vater - Der Sohn"
Stellen' NTS 12 (1965/66) 42-49
Grundmann, W. Zeugnis und Gestalt des Johannes-Evangeliums (Stuttgart: 1961)
Guilding, A. The Fourth Gospel and Jewish Worship (Oxford: OUP, 1960)
Haacker, K. Die Stiftung des Heils. Untersuchungen zur Struktur der
johanneischen Theologie (ArbzTh 47, Stuttgart: Calwer, 1972)
Haenchen, E. 'Das Johannesevangelium und Sein Kommentar'. In: Die Bibel und
Wir (Tübingen: JCB Mohr, 1968) pp. 208-234
Haenchen, E. Johannesevangelium. Ein Kommentar. Edited by U. Busse
(Tübingen: JCB Mohr, 1980; ET: John. 2 vols, Philadelphia: Fortress, 1984)
Haenchen, E. 'Aus der Literatur zum Johannesevangelium. 1929-1956' ThR NF
23 (1955) 296-335
Haenchen, E. '"Der Vater, der mich gesandt hat"'. In: Gott und Mensch
(Tübingen: JCB Mohr, 1965) pp. 68-78
Hahn, F. Art 'christos' EWNT III, 1147-1165
Hahn, F, Art. 'huios' EWNT III 912-937
Hahn, F, 'Beobachtungen zu Joh 1:18,34' In: Studies in New Testament Language
and Text. In Honour of G.D. Kilpatrick. Edited by J.K. Elliott (Leiden: Brill,
1976) pp. 239-245
Hahn, F. '"Das Heil kommt von den Juden" Erwägungen zu Joh 4,22b' In: Wort
und Wirklichkeit. Festschrift für E.L.Rapp, Band I (Weisenheim, 1976) pp.
67-84
Hahn, F. 'Die Hirtenrede in Joh. 10' In: Theologia Crucis - Signum Crucis.
Festschrift für E. Dinkler. Edited by C. Andresen and G. Klein (Tübingen:
JCB Mohr, 1979) pp. 185-200
Hahn, F. 'Die Jüngerberufung. Joh 1,35-51' In: Neues Testament und Kirche.
Festschrift für R. Schnackenburg. Edited by J. Gnilka (Freiburg: Herder,
1974) pp. 172-190
Hahn, F. 'Die Juden im Johannesevangelium' In: Kontinuität und Einheit. Für
Franz Mussner (Freiburg, 1981) pp. 430-438.

Hahn, F. 'Der Prozess Jesu im Johannesevangelium'. In: EKK Vorarbeitsheft 2 (Neukirchen/Zürich: Neukirchener/Benziger, 1970) pp. 23-96.

Hahn, F. 'Sehen und Glauben im Johannesevangelium'. In: Neues Testament und Geschichte. Festschrift für O. Cullmann. Edited by H. Baltensweiler and B. Reicke (Zürich/Tübingen: JCB Mohr/TheolVerlag, 1972) pp. 125-141.

Hahn, F. 'Das Verständnis des Opfers im Neuen Testament' In: Das Opfer Jesu Christi und seine Gegenwart in der Kirche. Edited by K. Lehmann and E. Schlink (Freiburg/Göttingen: Herder/V & R, 1983) pp. 51-91.

Hahn, F. 'Die Worte vom lebendigen Wasser im Johannesevangelium'. In: God's Christ and His People. Studies in Honor of N.A.Dahl. Edited by J. Jervell and W. Meeks (Oslo: Universitetsforlaget, 1977) pp. 51-70

Hamerton-Kelly, R.G. Pre-existence, Wisdom and the Son of Man (SNTSMS 21, Cambridge: CUP, 1973)

Hanson, A.T. 'John's Citation of Ps LXXXII' NTS 11 (1965) 158-162

Harner, J.B. The 'I am' of the Fourth Gospel (Philadelphia: Fortress, 1970)

Harner, P.B. 'Qualitative anarthrous predicate nouns. Mark 15:39 and John 1:1' JBL 92 (1973) 75-87

Hartin, P.J. 'A Community in Crisis. The Christology of the johannine Community' Neotest 19 (1985) 37-49

van Hartingsveld, L. Die Eschatologie des Johannesevangeliums (Assen: Van Gorcum, 1962)

Harvey, A.E. Jesus and the Constraints of History (Philadelphia: Westminster, 1982)

Harvey, A.E. Jesus on Trial: A Study in the Fourth Gospel (Atlanta: Knox, 1976)

Hayward, C.T.R. 'The Holy Name of the God of Moses and the Prologue of the Fourth Gospel' NTS 25 (1978) 16-23

Heekerens, H.-P. Die Zeichen-Quelle der johanneischen Redaktion. Ein Beitrag zur Entstehungsgeschichte des vierten Evangeliums (SBS 113, Stuttgart: KBW, 1984)

Hegermann, H. Arts. 'doxa' and 'doxazō' in: EWNT I 832-841, 842-843

Hegermann, H. '"Er kam in sein Eigentum"'. In: Der Ruf Jesu und die Antwort der Gemeinde. Festschrift für J. Jeremias (Göttingen: V & R, 1970) pp. 112-131

Heil, J.P. Jesus Walking on the Sea (AnBib 87, Rome: BibInst, 1981)

Heise, J. Bleiben. Menein in den Johanneischen Schriften (HUTh 8, Tübingen: JCB Mohr, 1967)

Hengel, M. 'The Interpretation of the Wine Miracle at Cana: John 2:1-11' In: The Glory of Christ in the New Testament. Studies in Christology. In Memory of G.B. Caird. Edited by L.D. Hurst and N.T. Wright (Oxford: Clarendon, 1987) pp. 83-112

Hengel, M. The Johannine Question (London: SCM; Philadelphia: TPI, 1989)

Higgins, A.B.J. Jesus and the Son of Man (London: 1964)

Hofbeck, S. Semeion. Der Begriff des 'Zeichens' im Johannesevangelium unter Berücksichtigung seiner Vorgeschichte (2nd edn., Münsterschwarzach: Turme Verlag, 1970)

Hofius, O. 'Struktur und Gedankengang des Logos Hymnus' ZNW 78 (1987) 1-25

Hofrichter, P. Im Anfang war der Johannesprolog (BU 17, Regensburg: Pustet, 1986)

Hofrichter, P. 'Egeneto Anthrōpos. Texte und Zusätze im Johannesprolog' ZNW 70 (1979) 214-237

Hofrichter, P. 'Gnosis und Johannesevangelium' BibKirche 41 (1986) 15-21

282   Bibliography

Hofrichter, P. Nicht aus Blut sondern monogen aus Gott geboren (FzB 31, Würzburg: Echter, 1978)

Holladay, C.R. 'New Testament Christology: A Consideration of Dunn's Christology in the Making' Sem 30 (1984) 65-82

Holtzmann, H.J. Lehrbuch der neutestamentlichen Theologie II (2nd edn., Tübingen: JCB Mohr, 1911)

Hooker, M.D. 'The Johannine Prologue and the Messianic Secret' NTS 21 (1974) 40-58

Horbury, W. 'The Benediction of the Minim and Early Jewish-Christian Controversy' JTS 33 (1982) 19-61

Hoskyns, E.C. and Davey, F.N. (ed.) The Fourth Gospel (London: Faber and Faber, 1967)

Ibuki, Y. Die Wahrheit im Johannesevangelium (BBB 39, Bonn: Hanstein, 1972)

Isaacs, M.E. 'The Prophetic Spirit in the Fourth Gospel' Heythrop 24 (1983) 391-407

Jeremias, J. Art. 'amnos' TDNT 1, 338-341

Jeremias, J. Art. 'pais theou' TDNT 5, 654-717

Jervell, J. Jesus in the Gospel of John (Minneapolis: Augsburg, 1984)

Johnston, G. 'Ecce Homo. Irony in the Christology of the Fourth Evangelist' In: The Glory of Christ in the New Testament, Studies in Christology. In Memory of G.B. Caird. Edited by L.D. Hurst and N.T. Wright (Oxford: Clarendon, 1987) pp. 125-138.

Johnston, G. The Spirit Paraclete in the Gospel of John (SNTSMS 12, Cambridge: CUP, 1970)

de Jonge, M. Jesus: Stranger from Heaven and Son of God (SBLMS X, Missoula: Scholars, 1977)

Juel, D. 'Incarnation and Redemption. A Response to Reginald H. Fuller' Sem 30 (1984) 117-121

Kaefer, J.P. 'Les discours d'adieu en Jean 13:31 - 17:26' NovT 26 (1984) 253-282

Käsemann, E. Jesu Letzter Wille nach Johannes 17 (3rd edn., Tübingen: J.C.B. Mohr, 1971; ET of 1st edn., 1966: The Testament of Jesus. London: SCM, 1968)

Käsemann, E. 'The Structure and Purpose of the Prologue to John's Gospel' In: New Testament Questions of Today (London: SCM, 1969) pp. 138-167

Kaufman, S.A. 'On Methodology in the Study of the Targums and their Chronology' JSNT 23 (1985) 117-124

Kee, H.C. 'Christology and Ecclesiology: Titles of Christ and Models of Community' Sem 30 (1984) 171-192

Kee, H.C. Miracles in the Early Christian World (New Haven: Yale, 1983)

Kieffer, R. 'L'Espace et le Temps dans l'Évangile de Jean' NTS 31 (1985) 393-409

Klaiber, W. 'Die Aufgabe einer theologischen Interpretation des vierten Evangeliums' ZThK 82 (1985) 300-324

Klauck, H.J. 'Gemeinde ohne Amt? Erfahrungen mit der Kirche in den johanneischen Schriften' BZ 29 (1985) 193-220

Klos, H. Die Sakramente im Johannesevangelium (SBS 46, Stuttgart: KBW, 1970)

Kossen, H.B. 'Who were the Greeks of John 12,20?' In: Studies in John. Presented to J.N. Sevenster (SuppNovTest XXI, Leiden: Brill, 1970) pp. 97-110

Kremer, J. 'Jesu Verheissung des Geistes. Zur Verankerung von Joh 16,13 im Leben Jesu' In: Die Kirche des Anfangs. Für H. Schürmann. Edited by R.

Schnackenburg, J. Ernst and J. Wanke (Freiburg: Herder, 1978) pp. 247-276

Kremer, J. Lazarus. Die Geschichte einer Auferstehung (Stuttgart: KBW, 1985)

Kremer, J. Die Osterevangelien: Geschichten um Gechichte (Stuttgart: KBW, 1981)

de Kruijf, T.C. '"The Glory of the Only Son" (John I 14).' In: Studies in John. Presented to J.N. Sevenster (SuppNovTest XXI, Leiden: Brill, 1970) pp. 111-123

Kruse, H. 'Jesu Seefahrten und die Stellung von Joh 6' NTS 30 (1984) 508-530

Kügler, J. 'Das Johannesevangelium und seine Gemeinde. Kein Thema für Science Fiction' BN 23 (1984) 48-62

Kühl, J. Die Sendung Jesu und der Kirche nach dem Johannesevangelium (St Augustin: Steyler, 1967)

Kundsin, K. 'Charakter und Ursprung der johanneischen Reden' Acta Universitatis Latviensis Teologijas Fakultatis Serija 1,4 (1939) 185-301

Kysar, R. 'Community and Gospel. Vectors in Fourth Gospel Criticism' Interp 31 (1977) 355-366

Kysar, R. The Fourth Evangelist and His Gospel (Minneapolis: Augsburg, 1975)

Kysar, R. 'The Fourth Gospel. A Report on Recent Research'. In: ANRW II 25, 3 (Berlin: de Gruyter, 1985) pp. 2389-2480

Kysar, R. John's Story of Jesus (Philadelphia: Fortress, 1984)

Lagrange, M.-J. Évangile selon saint Jean (Études Bibliques, Paris: Gabalda, 1964)

Lamarche, P. 'The Prologue of John' In: The Interpretation of John. Edited by J. Ashton (London/Philadelphia: SPCK/Fortress, 1986) pp. 36-52

Langbrandtner, W. Weltferner Gott oder Gott der Liebe (BET 6, Frankfurt: Lang, 1977)

Lattke, M. Einheit im Wort (StANT 41, München: Kösel, 1975)

Leidig, E. Jesu Gespräch mit der Samaritanerin (TheolDiss XV, Basel, 1979)

Leistner, R. Antijudäismus im Johannesevangelum? (Theologie und Wirklichkeit 3. Frankfurt: Lang, 1974)

Léon-Dufour, X. '"Père, fais-moi passer sain et sauf à travers cette heure" (Jean 12,27)' In: Neues Testament und Geschichte. Festschrift für O. Cullmann. Edited by H. Baltensweiler and B. Reicke (Tübingen: JCB Mohr, 1972) pp. 157-166

Léon-Dufour, X. 'Towards a Symbolic Reading of the Fourth Gospel' NTS 27 (1981) 439-456

Leroy, H. Rätsel und Missverständnis (BBB 32, Bonn: Hanstein, 1968)

Lieu, J.M. 'Gnosticism in the Gospel of John' ExpT 90 (1979) 233-237

Lieu, J.M. The Second and Third Epistles of John (Edinburgh: Clark, 1986)

Lindars, B. Behind the Fourth Gospel (London: SPCK, 1971)

Lindars, B. 'Discourse and Tradition. The Use of the Sayings of Jesus in the Discourses' JSNT 13 (1981) 83-101

Lindars, B. The Gospel of John (London: Oliphants, 1972)

Lindars, B. Jesus Son of Man (London: SPCK, 1983)

Lindars, B. 'John and the Synoptic Gospels. A Test Case' NTS 27 (1981) 287-294

Lindars, B. New Testament Apologetic (London: SCM, 1961)

Lindars, B. 'The Passion in the Fourth Gospel'. In: God's Christ and His People. Studies in Honor of N.A.Dahl. Edited by J. Jervell and W. Meeks (Oslo: Universitetsforlaget, 1977) pp. 71-86

Lindars, B. 'Slave and Son in Joh 8:31-36' In: The New Testament Age, Essays in

Honor of B.Reicke. Vol II. Edited by W.C. Weinrich (Mercer: Macon, 1984) pp. 271-286

Lindars, B. 'The Son of Man in the Johannine Christology' In: Christ and the Spirit. In Honour of C.F.D.Moule. Edited by B. Lindars and S.S.Smalley (London: SCM, 1973) pp. 43-60

Lindars, B. 'Traditions behind the Fourth Gospel'. In: L'Évangile de Jean. Sources, Rédaction, Théologie. Edited by M. de Jonge (BibEphThLov XLIV, Leuven: Gombleux, 1977) pp. 107-124

Lindars, B. 'Word and Sacrament in the Fourth Gospel' SJT 29 (1976) 49-63

Lindemann, A. 'Gemeinde und Welt im Johannesevangelium'. In: Kirche. Festschrift für G. Bornkamm. Edited by D. Lührmann and G. Strecker (Tübingen: JCB Mohr, 1980) pp. 131-161

Loader, W.R.G. 'The Apocalyptic Model of Sonship' JBL 97 (1978) 525-554

Loader, W.R.G. 'The Central Structure of Johannine Christology' NTS 30 (1984) 188-216

Loader, W.R.G. 'The Feasts of the Jews and the Sabbath Controversy (John 5:1-47)' in: The Years of John. Edited by H. McGinlay (Melbourne/Sydney: Joint Board of Christian Education/ Desbooks, 1985) pp. 18-27

Loader, W.R.G. The Johannine Epistles (London: Epworth, 1992)

Loader, W.R.G. 'John 1:50-51 and the "Greater Things" of Johannine Christology' in: Anfänge der Christologie. Für Ferdinand Hahn. Edited by C. Breytenbach and H. Paulsen (Göttingen: V & R, 1991) pp. 255-274

Loader, W.R.G. Sohn und Hoherpriester. Eine traditionsgeschichtliche Untersuchung zur Christologie des Hebräerbriefes (WMANT 53, Neukirchen: Neukirchener, 1981)

Loader, W.R.G. Review of M. Hengel, The Johannine Question, in Kings Theological Review XIII (1990) 50-52

Lohse, E. 'Miracles in the Fourth Gospel' In: What about the New Testament? In Honour of C. Evans. Edited by M.D. Hooker and C.J. Hickling (London: SCM, 1975) pp. 64-75

Lona, H.E. Abraham in Johannes 8 (EurHochschulschr XXIII, 65, Frankfurt: Lang, 1976)

Lona, H.E. 'Glaube und Sprache des Glaubens im Johannesevangelium' BZ 28 (1984) 168-185

Lorenzen, T 'Der Lieblingsjünger im Johannesevangelium (SBS 55, Stuttgart: KBW, 1971)

Lowe, M. 'Who were the IOUDAIOI?' NovT 18 (1976) 101-130

Lüdemann, G. Art. 'hypsoō' In: EWNT III 981f.

Lütgert, W. Die Johanneische Christologie (2nd edn. Gütersloh: Bertelsmann, 1916)

McArthur, H.K. 'Christological Perspectives in the Predicates of the Johannine Egw Eimi Sayings' In: Christological Perspectives. in Honor of H.K. McArthur. Edited by R.F. Berkley and S.A. Edwards (New York: Pilgrim, 1982) pp. 74-94.

McGehee, M. 'A less theological reading of John 20:17' Bibl 67 (1986) 299-307

McGinlay, H. (ed) The Year of John. Melbourne/Sydney: Joint Board of Christian Education/ Desbooks, 1985

McNamara, M. 'The Ascension and Exaltation of Christ in the Fourth Gospel' Script 19 (1967) 65-73

McNamara, M. The New Testament and the Palestinian Targum to the Pentateuch

(AnBib 27, Rome: BibInst, 1966)
MacRae, G.W. 'The Ego Proclamations in Gnostic Sources' in: The Trial of Jesus.
    In Honour of C.F.D.Moule. Edited by E. Bammel (SBT 2.13, London: SCM,
    1970) pp. 122-134
Maddox, R.L. 'The Function of the Son of Man in the Gospel of John' In:
    Reconciliation and Hope. Festschrift for L. Morris. Edited by R. Banks
    (Exeter: Paternoster, 1974) pp. 184-204
Mahoney, R. Two Disciples at the Tomb (Theologie und Wirklichkeit 6,
    Frankfurt: Lang, 1974)
Malatesta, E. Interiority and Covenant (AnBib 69, Rome: BibInst, 1978)
Manns, F. 'Exégèse Rabbinique et Exégèse Johannique' RB 92 (1985) 525-538
Martyn, J.L. 'Glimpses into the History of the Johannine Community'. In: The
    Gospel of John in Christian History (New York: Paulist, 1978) pp. 90-121.
Martyn, J.L. The Gospel of John in Christian History (New York: Paulist, 1978)
Martyn, J.L. History and Theology in the Fourth Gospel (2nd edn., Nashville:
    Abingdon, 1979)
Martyn, J.L. 'Source Criticism and Religionsgeschichte in the Fourth Gospel' In:
    The Interpretation of John. Edited by J. Ashton (London/Philadelphia:
    SPCK/Fortress, 1986) pp. 99-121
Mastin, B.A. 'A Neglected Feature of the Christology of the Fourth Gospel' NTS
    22 (1975) 32-51
Meagher, J.C 'John 1:14 and the New Temple' JBL 88 (1969) 57-68
Mealand, D. 'The Christology of the Fourth Gospel' SJT 31 (1978) 449-467
Meeks, W. 'The Divine Agent in the Fourth Gospel'. In: Aspects of Religious
    Propaganda in Judaism and Early Christianity. Edited by E. Schüssler
    Fiorenza (Notre Dame: Univ of Notre Dame Press, 1976) pp. 43-67
Meeks, W. 'The Man from Heaven in Johannine Sectarianism' JBL 91 (1972) 44-
    72
Meeks, W. The Prophet-King (NovTSuppl XIV, Leiden: Brill, 1967)
Mees, M. 'Erhöhung und Verherrlichung Jesu im Johannesevangelium nach dem
    Zeugnis neutestamentlicher Papyri' BZ 18 (1974) 32-44
Mees, M. Die Heilung des Kranken vom Bethesdateich' NTS 32 (1986) 596-608
Mees, M. Jesu Selbstzeugnis nach Joh 5,19-30 in frühchristlicher Sicht'
    EphThLov 62 (1986) 147-158
Mees, M. Joh 1,12.13 nach frühchristlicher Überliefering' BZ 29 (1985) 107-115
Mees, M. 'Lectio Brevior im Johannesevangelium und ihre Beziehung zum
    Urtext' BZ 12 (1968) 111-119.
Michel, O. 'Der aufsteigende und herabsteigende Gesandte' In: The New
    Testament Age, Essays in Honor of B.Reicke. Vol II. Edited by W.C.
    Weinrich (Mercer: Macon, 1984) pp. 335-361
Miller, E.L. 'The Christology of John 8,25' TZ 36 (1980) 257-265
Miller, E.L. 'The Logic of the Logos Hymn' NTS 29 (1983) 552-561
Minear, P.S. 'Diversity and Unity: A Johannine Case Study' In: Die Mitte des
    Neuen Testaments. Festschrift für E. Schweizer. Edited by U. Luz and H.
    Weder (Göttingen: V & R, 1983) pp. 162-175
Minear, P.S. John. The Martyr's Gospel (New York: Pilgrim, 1985)
Minear, P.S. '"We don't know where..." John 20:2' Interp 30 (1976) 125-129
Miranda, J.P. Die Sendung Jesu im vierten Evangelium (SBS 87, Stuttgart, 1977)
Miranda, J.P. 'Der Vater, der mich gesandt hat' (EurHochschulschr XXIII, 7, 2nd
    edn., Frankfurt: Lang, 1976)

Mlakuzhyil, G. The Christocentric Literary Structure of the Fourth Gospel (AnBib 117, Rome: BibInst, 1987)

Moloney, F.J. 'From Cana to Cana (John 2:1 - 4:54) and the Fourth Evangelist's Concept of Correct (and Incorrect) Faith.' In: Studia Biblica 1978. II Papers on the Gospels. Sixth International Congress on Biblical Studies. Edited by. E.A. Livingstone (JSNTS 2, Sheffield: JSOT, 1978) pp. 184-213

Moloney, F.J. 'The Johannine Son of God' BTB 6 (1976) 175-189

Moloney, F.J. The Johannine Son of Man (Bibl di Scienze Religiose 14, 2nd edn., Rome: Las, 1978)

Moloney, F.J. 'John 1:18: "in the bosom of" or turned towards?' ABR 31 (1983) 63-71

Moloney, F.J. 'The Structure and Message of John 15.1 - 16.13' ABR 35 (1987) 35-49

Moloney, F.J. 'When is John talking about the Sacraments?' ABR 30 (1982) 10-33

Moody, D. 'God's only Son: The translation of John 3:16 in the Revised Standard Version' JBL 72 (1953) 213-214

Morchen, R. 'Weggehen (Joh 12,36b)' BZ 28 (1984) 240-242

Morgan-Wynn, J.E. 'The Cross and the Revelation of Jesus as *egō eimi* in the Fourth Gospel' In: Studia Biblica 1978. II Papers on the Gospels. Sixth International Congress on Biblical Studies. Edited by. E.A. Livingstone (JSNTS 2, Sheffield: JSOT, 1978) pp. 219-226

Morris, L. The Gospel according to John (Grand Rapids: Eerdmans, 1971)

Moule, C.F.D. An Idiom-Book of New Testament Greek (Cambridge: CUP, 1960)

Moule, C.F.D. 'A Neglected Factor in the Interpretation of Johannine Eschatology.' In: Studies in John. Presented to J.N. Sevenster (SupplNovTest XXIV Leiden: Brill, 1970) pp. 155-160,

Mowvley, H. 'John 1:14-18 in the Light of Exodus 33:7 - 34:35' ExpT 95 (1984) 135-137

Müller, T.E. Das Heilsgeschehen im Johannesevangelium (Zürich: Gotthelf, n.d.; Diss. Bern, 1961)

Müller, U.B. 'Die Bedeutung des Kreuzestodes im Johannesevangelium' KuD 21 (1975) 49-71

Müller, U.B. Christologie in der Johanneischen Gemeinde (SBS 77, Stuttgart: KBW, 1975)

Müller, U.B. 'Die Parakletenvorstellung im Johannesevangelium' ZThK 71 (1974) 31-77

Mussner, F. 'Die johanneischen Parakletsspruche und die apostolische Tradition'. In: Praesentia Salutis (Düsseldorf: Patmos, 1967) pp. 146-158

Mussner, J. Die johanneische Sehweise (QD 28, Freiburg: Herder, 1965)

Mussner, F. '"Kultische" Aspekte im Johanneischen Christusbild'. In: Praesentia Salutis (Düsseldorf: Patmos, 1967) pp. 133-145

Neyrey, J.H. 'Jacob Traditions and the Interpretation of John 4:10-26' CBQ 41 (1979) 419-437

Neyrey, J.H. 'John III - A Debate over Johannine Epistemology and Christology' NovT 23 (1981) 115-127

Neugebauer, F. Die Entstehung des Johannesevangeliums (AzTh I 36, Stuttgart: Calwer, 1968)

Nicholson, G. Death as Departure. The Johannine Descent-Ascent Schema (SBLDS 63, Chico: Scholars, 1982)

Nicol, G.G. 'Jesus' Washing his Disciples' Feet. A Model for Johannine

Christology?' ExpT 91 (1979) 20f

Nicol, W. The Semeia in the Fourth Gospel (SupplNovTest XXXII, Leiden: Brill, 1972)

Noack, B. Zur Johanneischen Tradition (Copenhagen: Rosenzilde, 1954)

O'Day, G.R. 'Narrative Mode and Theological Claim: A Study in the Fourth Gospel' JBL 105 (1986) 657-668

O'Day, G.R. Revelation in the Fourth Gospel (Philadelphia: Fortress, 1986)

O'Grady, J.F. 'The Human Jesus in the Fourth Gospel' BTB 14 (1984) 63-66

O'Grady, J.F. 'Recent Development in Johannine Study' BTB 12 (1982) 54-58

O'Rourke, J.J. 'Asides in the Gospel of John' NovT 24 (1979) 210-219

Odeberg, H. The Fourth Gospel (Amsterdam: Gruener, 1968; reprint of edn. of Uppsala, 1929)

Olsson, B. Structure and Meaning in the Fourth Gospel (Coniectanea Biblica: NT Series 6, Lund: Gleerup, 1974)

Onuki, T. Gemeinde und Welt im Johannesevangelium (WMANT 56, Neukirchen: Neukirchener, 1984)

Osborn, E. 'Negative and Positive Theology in John' ABR 31 (1983) 72-80;

Osborne, G.R. 'Christology and New Testament Hermeneutics: A Survey of the Discussion' Sem 30 (1984) 49-62

von den Osten-Sacken, P. 'Leistung und Grenze der johanneischen Kreuzestheologie' EvT 36 (1976) 154-176

Pagels, E.H. The Johannine Gospel in Gnostic Exegesis. Heracleon's Commentary on John (SBLMS 17, Nashville: Abingdon, 1973)

Painter, J. 'Christ and the Church in John 1,45-51'. In: L'Évangile de Jean. Sources, Rédaction, Théologie. Edited by M. de Jonge (BibEphThLov XLIV Leuven: Gombleux, 1977) pp. 359-362

Painter, J, 'Christology and the Farewell Discourses' ABR 31 (1983) 45-62

Painter, J. 'Christology and the History of the Johannine Community in the Prologue of the Fourth Gospel' NTS 30 (1984) 460-473

Painter, J. 'The Church and Israel in the Fourth Gospel: A Response' NTS 25 (1978) 103-122

Painter, J. 'Eschatological Faith in the Gospel of John' In: Reconciliation and Hope. Festschrift for L. Morris. Edited by R.Banks (Exeter: Paternoster, 1974) pp. 36-52

Painter, J. 'The Farewell Discourses and the History of Johannine Christianity' NTS 27 (1981) 525-543

Painter, J. 'John 9 and the Interpretation of the Fourth Gospel' JSNT 28 (1986) 31-61

Painter, J. John: Witness and Theologian (3rd edn., Melbourne: Beacon Hill, 1986)

Painter J. 'The "Opponents" in 1 John' NTS 32 (1986) 31-47

Painter, J. 'Text and Context in John 5' ABR 35 (1987) 28-34

Pamment, M. 'Eschatology and the Fourth Gospel' JSNT 15 (82) 81-85

Pamment, M. 'Focus on the Fourth Gospel' ExpT 97 (1985) 71-75

Pamment, M. 'The Meaning of Doxa in the Fourth Gospel' ZNW 74 (1983) 12-16

Pamment, M. 'The Son of Man in the Fourth Gospel' JTS 36 (1985) 58-66

Pamment, M. 'Is there convincing evidence of Samaritan influence on the Fourth Gospel?' ZNW 73 (1982) 221-230

Pancaro, S. The Law in the Fourth Gospel (NovTSupp XLII, Leiden: Brill, 1975)

Perkins, P. Resurrection. New Testament Witness and Contemporary Reflection (New York: Doubleday, 1984)

Pokorný, 'Der irdische Jesus im Johannesevangelium' NTS 30 (1984) 217-228
Pollard, T.E. Johannine Christology and the Early Church (SNTSMS 13, Cambridge: CUP, 1970)
Pollard, T.E. 'The Father-Son and Son-Believer Relationships according to St John'. In: L'Évangile de Jean. Sources, Rédaction, Théologie. Edited by M. de Jonge (BibEphThLov XLIV Leuven: Gombleux, 1977) pp. 363-369
Porsch, F. Pneuma und Wort (FrankTheolStud 16, Frankfurt: Knecht, 1974)
de la Potterie, I. 'L'emploi dynamique de eis dans S. Jean et ses incidences théologiques' Bibl 43 (1962) 366-387
de la Potterie, I, 'Genèse de la Foi Pascal d'après Jn 20' NTS 30 (1984) 26-49
de la Potterie, I. 'Jésus roi et juge d'après Jn 19,13' Bibl 41 (1960) 217-247
de la Potterie, I. 'La notion de "commencement" dans les écrits johanniques' In: Die Kirche des Anfangs. Für H. Schürmann. Edited by R. Schnackenburg, J. Ernst and J. Wanke (Freiburg: Herder, 1978) pp. 379-404
de la Potterie, I. 'Parole et Esprit dans S. Jean'. In: L'Évangile de Jean. Sources, Rédaction, Théologie. Edited by M. de Jonge (BibEphThLov XLIV Leuven: Gombleux, 1977) pp. 177-201
de la Potterie, I. 'Structure du Prologue de Saint Jean' NTS 30 (1984) 354-381
de la Potterie, I. La Vérité dans Saint Jean (AnBib 73/74, 2 vols, Rome: BibInst, 1977)
Preiss, T. Life in Christ (SBT 1.13, London: SCM, 1954)
Pryor, J.W. 'Of the Virgin Birth or the Birth of Christians? The Text of John 1:13 Once More' NovT 27 (1985) 296-318
Radermakers, J. Mission et Apostolat en Jean' In: Studia Evangelica II (Berlin: de Gruyter, 1964) pp. 100-121
du Rand, J.A. 'The characterization of Jesus as depicted in the narrative of the fourth gospel' Neotestamentica 19 (1985) 18-36
Reim, G. 'Jesus as God in the Fourth Gospel' NTS 30 (1984) 158-160
Reim, G. 'John iv.44 - Crux or Clue?' NTS 22 (1976) 476-480
Reim, G. 'Zur Lokalisierung der johanneischen Gemeinde' BZ 32 (1988) 72-86
Reim, G. Studien zum alttestamentlichen Hintergrund des Johannesevangeliums (SNTSMS 22, Cambridge: CUP, 1974)
Reim, G. 'Targum und Johannesevangelium' BZ 27 (1983) 1-13
Rengstorf, K.H. Art. 'apostellō' TDNT I 398-447.
Rensberg, D. 'The Politics of John: the Trial of Jesus in the Fourth Gospel' JBL 103 (1984) 395-411
Ricca, P. Die Eschatologie des Vierten Evangeliums (Zürich: Gotthelf, 1966)
Richard, E. 'Expressions of Double Meaning and their Function in the Gospel of John' NTS 31 (1985) 96-112
Richter, G. Die Fusswaschung im Johannesevangelium (BU 1, Regensburg: Pustet, 1967)
Richter, G. Studien zum Johannesevangelium (BU 13, Regensburg: Pustet, 1977)
Riedl, J. Das Heilswerk nach Johannes (Freiburger ThStud 93. Freiburg: Herder, 1973)
Riedl, J. '"Wenn Ihr den Menschensohn erhöht habt, werdet Ihr erkennen" (Joh 8,28)'. In: Jesus und der Menschensohn. Für Anton Vögtle. Edited by R. Pesch and R. Schnackenburg (Freiburg: Herder, 1975) pp. 355-370
Riesenfeld, H. 'The Gospel Tradition and its Beginnings' In: The Gospels Reconsidered. A Selection of Papers read to the International Congress on the Four Gospels, 1957 (Oxford: Blackwell, 1969) 131-153

Rissi, M. 'Der Aufbau des vierten Evangeliums' NTS 29 (1983) 48-54

Ritt, H. Das Gebet zum Vater (FzB 36, Würzburg: Echter, 1979)

Robinson, J.A.T. 'The Fourth Gospel and the Church's Doctrine of the Trinity' In: Twelve More New Testament Studies (London: SCM, 1984)

Robinson, J.A.T. The Human Face of Jesus (London: SCM, 1973)

Robinson, J.A.T. The Priority of John (London: SCM, 1985)

Robinson, J.A.T. The Redating of the New Testament (London: SCM, 1976)

Robinson, J.A.T. Twelve More New Testament Studies (London: SCM, 1984)

Robinson, J.A.T. 'The Use of the Fourth Gospel for Christology Today' In: Christ and Spirit in the New Testament. In Honour of C.F.D. Moule. Edited by B. Lindars and S.S.Smalley (Cambridge: CUP, 1973) pp. 61-78

Robinson, J.M. 'the Johannine Trajectory' In: Trajectories through Early Christianity (Philadelphia: Fortress, 1971) 232-268

Roloff, J. 'Der johanneischen "Lieblingsjünger" und "der Lehrer der Gerechtigkeit"' NTS 15 (1968/1969) 129-151

Rowland, C.C. 'John 1.51. Jewish Apocalyptic and Targumic Tradition' NTS 30 (1984) 498-507

Ruckstuhl, E. 'Abstieg und Erhöhung des johanneischen Menschensohnes'. In: Jesus und der Menschensohn. Für Anton Vögtle. Edited by R. Pesch and R. Schnackenburg (Freiburg: Herder, 1975) pp. 314-341.

Ruckstuhl, E. 'Die Johanneische Menschensohnforschung, 1957-1969.' In: Theologische Berichte I (Zürich: Benzinger, 1972) pp. 171-284

Ruckstuhl, E. 'Johannine Language and Style'. In: L'Evangile de Jean. Sources, Rédaction, Théologie. Edited by M. de Jonge (BibEphThLov XLIV Leuven: Gombleux, 1977) pp. 125-147

Ruckstuhl, E. 'Der Jünger den Jesus liebte' BibKirche 40 (1985) 77-83

Ruckstuhl, E. 'Kritische Arbeit am Johannesprolog' In: The New Testament Age, Essays in Honor of B.Reicke. Vol II. Edited by W.C. Weinrich (Mercer: Macon, 1984) pp. 443-454

Ruckstuhl, E. Die literarische Einheit des Johannesevangeliums (Studia fribourgensia, NF 3, Freiburg in der Schweiz: Paulus, 1951)

Sanday, W. The Criticism of the Fourth Gospel (Oxford: Clarendon, 1914)

Sanders, J.N. and Mastin, B.A. A Commentary on the Gospel according to St. John (Black's NT Comm, London: Black, 1968)

de Satge, J, 'The Human Integrity of St John's Jesus' In: Studia Biblica 1978. II. Papers on the Gospels. Sixth International Congress on Biblical Studies. Edited by E.A. Livingstone (Sheffield: JSOT, 1980) pp. 75-78

Schenke, H.M. Review of L. Schottroff, Der Glaubende und die feindliche Welt. TLZ 97 (1972) 751-755

Schenke, L. 'Die formale und gedankliche Struktur von Joh 6,26-58' BZ 24 (1980) 21-41

Schenke, L. 'Die literarische Vorgeschichte von Joh 6,26-58' BZ 29 (1985) 68-89

Schillebeeckx, E. Christ. The Christian Experience in the Modern World (London: SCM, 1980)

Schlier, H. 'Zur Christologie des Johannesevangeliums' In: Das Ende der Zeit. Exegetische Aufsätze und Vorträge III (Freiburg: Herder, 1971) pp. 85-101

Schmithals, W. 'Der Prolog des Johannesevangeliums' ZNW 70 (1979) 16-43

Schnackenburg, R. 'Die ecce-homo-Szene und der Menschensohn' In: Jesus und der Menschensohn. Für A. Vögtle. Edited by R. Pesch and R. Schnackenburg (Freiburg: Herder, 19759 pp. 371-386

Schnackenburg, R. 'Ist der Gedanke des Sühnetodes Jesu der einzige Zugang zum
    Verständnis unserer Erlösung durch Jesus Christus?' In: Der Tod Jesu.
    Deutungen im Neuen Testament. Edited by K. Kertlege (QD 74, Herder:
    Freiburg, 1978) 205-230
Schnackenburg, R. Das Johannesevangelium. I. Teil. Einleitung und Kommentar
    zu Kap. 1-4 (HThK IV. 1, 5th edn., Freiburg: Herder, 1981); II. Teil.
    Kommentar zu Kap. 5-12 (HThK IV. 2, 2nd edn., Freiburg: Herder, 1977);
    III. Teil. Kommentar zu Kap. 13-21 (HThK IV. 3, 4th edn., Freiburg: Herder,
    1982); IV. Teil. Ergänzende Auslegungen und Exkurse (HThK IV. 4,
    Freiburg: Herder, 1984) ET (Vols 1-3): The Gospel according to John. 3 vols
    (London: Burns & Oates, 1968/1980/1982)
Schnackenburg, R. 'Johannesevangelium als hermeneutische Frage' NTS 13
    (1967) 197-210
Schnackenburg, R. 'Logos-Hymnus und johanneischer Prolog' BZ 1 (1957) 69-
    109
Schnackenburg, R. 'Die Messiasfrage im Johannesevangelium' In:
    Neutestamentliche Aufsatze: Festschrift für J. Schmid. Edited by J. Blinzler,
    O. Kuss and F. Mussner (Regensburg: Pustet, 1963) pp. 240-264
Schnackenburg, R. 'Der Menschensohn im Johannesevangelium' NTS 11
    (1964/65) 123-137
Schnackenburg, R. 'Die "situationsgelösten" Redestücke in Johannes 3' ZNW 49
    (1958) 88-99
Schnackenburg, R. '"Und das Wort ist Fleisch geworden"', Internationale
    Katholische Zeitschrift/Communio 8 (1979) 1-9
Schneiders, S. The Johannine resurrection Narrative. An Exegetical and
    Theological Study of John 20 as a Synthesis of Johannine Spirituality (Rome:
    GregUniv, 1975)
Schnelle, U. Antidoketische Christologie im Johannesevangelium. Eine
    Untersuchung zur Stellung des vierten Evangeliums in der johanneischen
    Schule (Göttingen: V & R, 1987)
Schnider, F. and Stenger, W. Johannes und die Synoptiker (München: Kösel,
    1971)
Schoonenberg, P. 'A Sapiential Reading of John's Prologue' TheolDig 33 (1986)
    403-421
Schottroff, L. Der Glaubende und die feindliche Welt (WMANT 37, Neukirchen:
    Neukirchener, 1970)
Schramm, T.L. The Use of IOUDAIOS in the Fourth Gospel (Diss Amsterdam,
    1971)
Schulz, S. Das Evangelium nach Johannes (NTD 4, Göttingen: V & R, 1972)
Schulz, S. Komposition und Herkunft der Johanneischen Reden (BWANT 81,
    Stuttgart: Kohlhammer, 1960)
Schulz, S. Untersuchungen zur Menschensohn-Christologie im
    Johannesevangelium (Göttingen: V & R, 1957)
Schürmann, H. 'Joh 6,51c - ein Schlüssel zur grossen johanneischen Brotrede' BZ
    2 (1959) 244-262
Schweizer, E. Ego Eimi (FRLANT 56, 2nd edn., Göttingen: V & R, 1965)
Schweizer, E. Jesus Christus im vielfältigen Zeugnis des Neuen Testaments
    (Hamburg: Siebenstern, 1968)
Schweizer, E. 'Jesus der Zeuge Gottes.' In: Studies in John. Presented to J.N.
    Sevenster (SupplNovTest XXIV, Leiden: Brill, 1970) pp. 161-166

Schweizer, E. 'Das johanneische Zeugnis vom Herrenmahl' EvTh 12 (1952/1953) 341-363

Schweizer, E. 'Der Kirchenbegriff im Evangelium und in den Briefen des Johannes'. In: Studia Evangelica I (TU 73, Berlin: de Gruyter, 1959) pp. 363-381

Scott, E.F. The Fourth Gospel. Its Purpose and Theology (Edinburgh: Clark, 1908)

Scroggs, R. Christology in Paul and John (Philadelphia: Fortress, 1988)

Segal, A.F. 'Heavenly Ascension in Hellenistic Judaism, Early Christianity and their Environment' In: ANRW 23.2 (1980) 1333-1394

Segal, A.F. 'Pre-Existence and Incarnation: A Response to Dunn and Holladay' Sem 30 (1984) 83-95

Segal, A.F. Two Powers in Heaven. Early Rabbinic Reports about Christianity and Gnosticism (Leiden: Brill, 1977)

Segovia, F.F. Love Relationships in the Johannine Tradition (SBLDS 58, Chico: Scholars, 1982)

Segovia, F.F. 'John 13:1-30. The Footwashing in the Johannine Tradition' ZNW 73 (1982) 31-51

Segovia, F.F. 'John 15:18-16. A First Addition to the Original Farewell Discourse?' CBQ 45 (1983) 210-230

Segovia, F.F. 'The Love and Hatred of Jesus and Johannine Sectarianism' CBQ 43 (81) 258-272

Segovia, F.F. 'The Structure, Tendenz and Sitz im Leben of John 13:31 - 14:31' JBL 104 (1985) 471-493

Segovia, F.F. 'The Theology and Provenance of John 15:1-18' JBL 101 (1982) 115-128

Seynaeve, J. 'Les verbes *apostellō* et *pempō* dans le vocablaire théologique de Saint Jean' In: L'Évangile de Jean. Sources, Rédaction, Théologie. Edited by M. de Jonge (BibEphThLov XLIV, Leuven: Gombleux, 1977) pp. 385-389.

Sidebottom, E.M. The Christ of the Fourth Gospel (London: SPCK, 1961)

Smalley, S.S. 'Johannes 1,51 und die Einleitung zum vierten Evangelium.' In: Jesus und der Menschensohn. Für Anton Vögtle. Edited by R. Pesch and R. Schnackenburg (Freiburg: Herder, 1975) pp. 300-313

Smalley, S.S. 'The Johannine Son of Man Sayings' NTS 15 (1969) 278-301

Smalley, S.S. John: Evangelist and Interpreter (Exeter: Paternoster, 1978)

Smalley, S.S. 'Keeping up with Recent Studies, XII: St. John's Gospel' ExpT 97 (1986) 102-108

Smalley, S.S. 'Salvation Proclaimed VIII: John 1:29-34' ExpT 93 (1982) 324-329

Smith, D.M. 'Johannine Christianity: Some Reflections on its Character and Delineation' NTS 21 (1975) 225-248

Smith, D.M. 'The Setting and Shape of a Johannine Narrative Source' JBL 95 (1976) 231-241

Smith, M. 'Ascent to the heavens and the Beginning of Christianity' Eranos Jahrbuch 50 (1981) 403-430

Sproston, W.E. '"Is not this Jesus, the son of Joseph?" (John 6:42). Johannine Christology as a Challenge to Faith' JSNT 24 (1985) 77-97

Stevens, G.B. The Theology of the New Testament (Edinburgh: Clark, 1889)

Strachan, R.H. The Fourth Gospel (London: SCM, 3rd. edn., 1941)

Strathmann, H. Das Evangelium nach Johannes (NTD 4, 10th edn., Göttingen: V & R, 1963)

Strecker, G. 'Die Anfänge der johanneischen Schule' NTS 32 (1986) 31-47

Suggit, J. 'John 19:5. "Behold the Man"' ExpT 94 (1983) 333-334
Talbert, C.H. 'The Myth of the Descending and Ascending Redeemer in
    Mediterranean Antiquity' NTS 22 (1976) 418-439
Taylor, M.J. (ed.) A Companion to John. Readings in Johannine Theology (New
    York: Alba House, 1977)
Teeple, H.M. The Mosaic Eschatological Prophet (SBLMS 10, Philadelphia:
    Fortress, 1957)
Temple, S. The Core of the Fourth Gospel (London: OUP, 1975)
Theobald, M. Im Anfang war das Wort. Textlinguistische Studie zum
    Johannesprolog (SBS 106, Stuttgart: KBW, 1983)
Thüsing, W. Die Erhöhung und Verherrlichung Jesu im Johannesevangelium
    (NTAbh 21, 3rd edn., Münster: Aschendorff, 1979)
Thyen, H. '"...denn wir lieben die Brüder" (1 Joh 3,14)'. In: Rechtfertigung.
    Festschrift für E. Käsemann. Edited by G. Friedrich and others (Tübingen:
    JCB Mohr, 1976) pp. 527-542.
Thyen, H. 'Entwicklungen innerhalb der johanneischen Theologie und Kirche im
    Spiegel von Joh 21 und der Lieblingsjüngertexte des Evangeliums'. In:
    L'Évangile de Jean. Sources, Rédaction, Théologie. Edited by M. de Jonge
    (BibEphThLov XLIV, Leuven: Gombleux, 1977) pp. 259-299
Thyen, H. '"Das Heil kommt von den Juden"'. In: Kirche. Festschrift für G.
    Bornkamm. Edited by D. Lührmann and G. Strecker (Tübingen: JCB Mohr,
    1980) pp. 163-184
Thyen, H. 'Johannes 13 und die "Kirchliche Redaktion" des vierten Evangeliums'
    In: Tradition und Glaube. Festschrift für K.G. Kuhn. Edited by G. Jeremias
    and others (Göttingen: V & R, 1971) pp. 343-356
Thyen, H. 'Aus der Literatur zum Johannesevangelium' ThR 39 (1974) 1-69, 222-
    252, 289-330; 42 (1977) 211-270; 43 (1978) 328-359; 44 (1979) 97-134
Thyen. H. '"Niemand hat grössere Liebe als die, dass er sein Leben für seine
    Freunde hingibt" (Joh 15,13).' In: Theologia Crucis - Signum Crucis.
    Festschrift für E. Dinkler. Edited by C. Andresen and G. Klein (Tübingen:
    JCB Mohr, 1979) pp. 467-481
Trites, A.A. The New Testament Concept of Witness (SNTSMS 31, Cambridge:
    CUP, 1977)
Trudinger, L.P. 'The Israelite in whom there is no guile' EQ 54 (1982) 117-120
Tsuchido, T. 'Tradition and Redaction in John 12.1-43' NTS 30 (1984) 609-618
Untergassmair, F. Im Namen Jesu (FzB 13, Stuttgart: KBW, 1973)
Vellanickel, M. The Divine Sonship of Christians in the Johannine Writings
    (AnBib 72, Rome: BibInst, 1977)
Vermes, G. Scripture and Tradition in Judaism (Leiden: Brill, 1961)
von Wahlde, U.C. 'The Johannine "Jews": a Critical Survey' NTS 28 (1982) 33-60
von Wahlde, U.C. 'Literary Structure and Theological Argument in the Discourses
    with the Jews in the Fourth Gospel' JBL 103 (1984) 375-384
von Wahlde, U.C. 'The Terms for Religious Authorities in the Fourth Gospel: A
    Key to Literary Strata?' JBL 98 (1979) 231-253
von Wahlde, U.C. 'Wiederaufnahme as a mark of Rédaction in John 6,51-58'
    Biblica 64 (1983) 542-549
von Wahlde, U.C. 'The Witnesses of Jesus in John 5:31-40 and Belief in the
    Fourth Gospel' CBQ 43 (1981) 385-404
Watson, F. 'Is John's Christology Adoptionist?' In: The Glory of Christ in the
    New Testament. Studies in Christology. In Honour of G.B. Caird. Edited by

L.D. Hurst and N.T. Wright (Oxford: Clarendon, 1987) pp. 113-124

Watson, N. 'Risen Christ and Spirit Paraclete in the Fourth Gospel' ABR 31 (1983) 81-89

Wead, D.W. The Literary Devices in John's Gospel (Basel: Reinhardt, 1970)

Weder, H. 'Die Menschwerdung Gottes' ZThK 82 (1985) 325-360

Weiss, B. Lehrbuch der Biblischen Theologie des Neuen Testaments (5th edn., Berlin, 1888)

Wengst, K. Bedrängte Gemeinde und verherrlichter Christus (BthSt 5, Neukirchen: Neukirchener, 1981)

Wengst, K. Christologische Formeln und Lieder des Urchristentums (Gütersloh: Mohn, 1972)

Westcott, B.F. The Gospel according to John (London: Clarke, 1958)

Wetter, G.P. Der Sohn Gottes (FRLANT 26, Göttingen: V & R, 1916)

Whitacre, R.A. Johannine Polemic (SBLDS 67, Chico: Scholars, 1982)

Wiefel, W. 'Die Scheidung von Gemeinde und Welt im Johannesevangelium auf dem Hintergrund der Trennung von Kirche und Synagoge' ThZ 35 (1979) 213-227

Wilckens, U. 'Der eucharistische Abschnitt der johanneischen Rede vom Lebensbrot (Joh 6,51c-58)' In: Neues Testament und Kirche. Festschrift für R. Schnackenburg. Edited by J. Gnilka (Freiburg: Herder, 1974) pp. 220-248

Wilckens, U. 'Der Paraklet und die Kirche'. In: Kirche. Festschrift für G. Bornkamm. Edited by D. Lührmann and G. Strecker (Tübingen: JCB Mohr, 1980) pp. 185-203

Wilkens, W. Die Entstehungsgeschichte des vierten Evangeliums (Zollikon: EvVerlag, 1958)

Wilkens, W. Zeichen und Werke (AbhThANT 55, Zürich: Zwingli, 1969)

Williams, J,T. 'Cultic Elements in the Fourth Gospel' In: Studia Biblica 1978. II. Papers on the Gospels. Sixth International Congress on Biblical Studies. Edited by E.A. Livingstone (Sheffield: JSOT, 1980) pp. 339-350

Wilson, R. M. 'Nag Hammadi and the New Testament' NTS 28 (1982) 289-302

Witkamp, L.T. 'The Use of Traditions in John 5:1-18' JSNT 25 (1985) 19-47

Wojciechowski, M. 'Le don de l'Esprit Saint dans Jean 20.22 selon Tg. Gn. 2.7' NTS 33 (1987) 289-292

Woll, D.B. Johannine Christianity in Conflict (SBLDS 60, Chico: Scholars, 1981)

Woll, D.B. 'The Preparation of "the Way": The First Farewell Discourses in the Gospel of John' JBL 99 (1980) 225-239

Wrede, W. Charakter und Tendenz des Johannesevangeliums (Sammlung gemeinverständlicher Vorträge und Schriften aus dem Gebiet der Theologie und Religionsgeschichte 37, 2nd edn., Tübingen: JCB Mohr, 1933; 1st edn. 1901)

Zeller, D. 'Der Ostermorgen im vierten Evangelium'. In: Auferstehung Jesu und Auferstehung der Christen. Edited by H. Oberlinner (QD 105, Freiburg: Herder, 1986) pp. 145-161

Zimmermann, H. 'Das absolute egō eimi als neutestamentliche Offenbarungsformel' BZ 4 (1960) 54-69, 266-76

Zimmermann, H. 'Christushymnus und johanneischer Prolog' In: Neues Testament und Kirche. Festschrift für R. Schnackenburg. Edited by J. Gnilka (Freiburg: Herder, 1974) pp. 249-265

Index of Selected Passages

INDEX OF MODERN AUTHORS

BEITRÄGE ZUR BIBLISCHEN EXEGESE UND THEOLOGIE

Herausgegeben von Jürgen Becker und Henning Graf Reventlow.